FUTU

FASTFORWARD

The Zionist Anglo-American Empire Meltdown

By Matthias Chang

First American Edition – 2006
American Free Press
Washington, D.C. 20003

FUTURE
FASTFORWARD
The Zionist Anglo-American Empire Meltdown

Originally published in Malaysia by Thinker's Library Pte Ltd

This first-ever American edition is published by:

American Free Press
645 Pennsylvania Avenue SE, #100
Washington, DC 20003
1-888-699-6397
americanfreepress.net

To contact the author:

Matthias Chang
No. 6, Jalan Kampar, Suite 10.01,
10th Floor, Plaza Permata,
50400 Kuala Lumpur, Malaysia
Email: Matthias@skzcchambers.com

WARNING

The Enemies of Islam and
Christianity will Pay their Agents
—Hypocrites in the Guise of Believers—
to denounce the
Truth and Evidence
Revealed in this Book

Read the Entire book—not just
Excerpts or Reviews by
the Zionist-Controlled Media

Check every Source
Annotated in this Book

Then, and only then, Decide
to Believe or Not to Believe
the Zionist Agenda

Unite! Unite! Unite!
For Total Victory

DEDICATION

To the memory of the
Untold Innocents—the Youngest of
Martyrs to the Zionist Agenda—those
Heroic Palestinian Children,
Mercilessly Butchered
by Ariel Sharon

Table of Contents

Acknowledgements

This has been a lonely journey, a *via dolorosa*[1] even, as I could not confide in any one the vow I had made to publish this book, for fear that I would not be able to do so. But the pictures of the children of Palestine and Iraq, and their cries for justice and truth, kept me going, even when there were times when I wanted to stop writing. I thank them all for their inspiration and guidance. They spoke to me as they saw it—the oppression, the injustice, and the calculated genocide—when I was with them in 2003, just before the Iraq war started.

And I am also writing as I saw it, as I still see it,—the oppression and the injustice—and I trust that I have done justice to the cause of the brave Palestinians and the heroic people of Iraq. A day will surely come when the world will bow in shame for their betrayal of the Palestinians, and for the debt it owes them for their untold sacrifices in their struggle to vanquish the Zionist Anglo-American war cabal. Their courageous resistance against overwhelming odds is yet another source of inspiration.

To my family for being there these past seven weeks, your understanding is appreciated more than you know. I love you guys. The first draft was written soon after the invasion of Iraq by the United States. It was completed within six weeks or so. But my political engagements were such that I could not see it through. It collected dust on my shelf. In January, 2005, a horrible picture of Palestinians being massacred stunned me from my slumber, and this time, I told myself that I will not stop till I have finished. Little did I know that it amounted to almost writing a new book as so much has happened since March, 2003. The task was daunting but after nearly seven weeks of 5 a.m. wake-up calls, two hours of feverish typing, then to my law office and other responsibilities, and resumption at midnight, I am glad it is over, thanks to my Acer laptop which has never failed me.

A special thanks to Christopher for the cover design concept and the daily encouragement. You are very fortunate for you have your freedom.

Whenever I look at you, I am reminded of the thousands of young Palestinians denied their freedom. This spurs me on. But you are more than a reminder. Jacqueline and Michelle likewise remind me of those heroines who gladly gave their lives for their cause so that their brothers and sisters might live. All of you brought me back to earth—to reality—whenever flights of fancy distracted me.

To my dear and trusted friend and colleague, Michael Collins Piper, for making the publication possible in the USA. You have been a source of inspiration and your courage in the face of adversity is exemplary and long may you continue. And to everyone at *American Free Press* for your faith and hard work in making this American edition a reality. You are an incredible team. Special thanks to production manager Paul Angel for his efforts.

To Tatsun Hoi and Alvin Toh for the artwork to the cover design and for working under a pressure cooker schedule. A big thank you. And to Mustafa Zubair, for the nice touches in making the book "a better read."

Finally, to Tun Dr. Mahathir Mohamad, a great patriot who almost single-handedly defied the odds and defeated the Zionist international financiers during the 1997 financial crisis, so that Malaysia remains independent. In a way, this is also my "thank you" for his sacrifices in that incredible battle.

The views expressed in this book are entirely mine and do not in any way represent those of the organizations, institutions or governments that I may be acquainted with. Any reference to any individual or organization, directly or indirectly, is merely for the historical record.

Finally I seek your indulgence and understanding for any error that might have occurred during the printing process. Any error, if duly notified, shall be rectified in subsequent editions.

Matthias
22 February 2005
Kuala Lumpur

ENDNOTE:

[1] The Via Dolorosa (Latin for "Painful Path") is believed to be the route taken by Jesus Christ through Jerusalem to Cavalry. Figuratively, *via dolorosa* describes a distressing or painful journey or process, which this certainly was for me.

Introduction

Since the collapse of the Soviet Empire, the United States has been depicted as the unchallenged sole superpower. The U.S. boasts of having the world's largest war machine. Her defense budget accounts for about fifty percent of world's military expenditure, post Iraq War. Natalie J Goldring, executive director of the program on global security and disarmament at the University of Maryland commented that the $417 billion for the Department of Defense in 2005 was merely a down payment on the year's military spending.[1] According to Frida Berrigan, a senior research associate at the World Policy Institute's Arms Trade Resource Centre, the U.S. will spend about $1.5 billion a day or $11,000 a second on defense in 2005.[2] To spend such sums for war preparations and making war is mind boggling when millions are surviving on less than $2 a day.

The United States is a country nurtured in war. The United States government is also a "serial war criminal" (if I may be allowed to coin this description) as it has continuously for the last sixty years, violated the Nuremberg Principles, the 1949 Geneva Conventions relating to the protection of civilian prisoners of war, the wounded and sick, and the amended Nuremberg Principles as formulated by the International Law Commission 1950, proscribing war crimes and crimes against humanity. The wanton killing of civilians is dismissed as inevitable, portrayed merely as "collateral damage" by the American mass media.

More importantly, the present power elites have betrayed the principles enunciated by American Founding Fathers enshrined in the Declaration of Independence, 1776 and the United States Constitution. They have discarded the wisdom of the leaders of the American Revolution. John Quincy Adams in 1821 counselled: *"When ever the standard of freedom and independence has been or shall be unfurled, there will her heart, her benedictions*

1

and her prayers be. <u>But she goes not abroad, in search of mon-</u> *<u>sters to destroy. She is the well wisher to the freedom and inde-</u>* *<u>pendence of all. She is the champion and vindicator only of her</u>* *<u>own. She well knows that by once enlisting under other ban-</u>* *<u>ners than her own, were they even the banners of foreign inde-</u>* *<u>pendence, she would involve herself, beyond the power of</u>* *<u>extrication, in all the wars of interest and intrigue, of individual</u>* *<u>avarice, envy, and ambition, which assumes the colors and</u>* *<u>usurp the standard of freedom...</u> She might become the dicta-* *tress of the world; she would no longer be the ruler of her own* *spirit. Glory is not dominion, but liberty. Her march is the march* *of the mind. She has a spear and a shield: but the motto upon* *her shield is Freedom, Independence, Peace. This has been her* *Declaration: this has been, as far as her necessary intercourse* *with the rest of mankind would permit, her practice."*[3] (Emphasis added)

A trip down memory lane to the recent past will suffice to fully appreciate the United States power elites' insatiable appetite for war and needless destruction and how they have flouted John Quincy Adam's injunction. Since 1940, the United States has been at war, in one form or another, from CIA sponsored interventions in South America in support of dictatorial regimes to major engagements in Asia and Africa. On the evening of 13th February 1945, the defenseless German city of Dresden, one of the greatest cultural centers in Europe was reduced to rubble and flames by saturation bombings with "fire bombs" by British and American air force. An estimated one third of the city's inhabitants were massacred, the figures ranging from 300,000 to half a million. These civilians have to pay for the crimes of Adolf Hitler. In August of 1945, the United States dropped atomic bombs on the cities of Hiroshima and Nagasaki killing an estimated 150,000 and injuring approximately another 130,000. By 1950, another 230,000 died from injuries and radiation. Earlier, fire bomb raids on Tokyo killed 140,000 and injured a million more.[4] This was truly victor's justice.

On 7th September 1945, General Douglas MacArthur, proclaimed that the forces under his command *"will today occupy the territory of Korea south of 38th degrees north latitude."* Thus began the Korean War of 1945-1953. In the period 1958-1965, the United States was complicit in undermining and eventually over-throwing the administration of President Sukarno. Documents at the George Washington University's National Security Archive reveal that information sent by the U.S. Embassy on November 1965 to General Suharto enabled the Indonesian army to massacre 50 to 100 PKI members every night in East and Central Java. An air-gram from the US Embassy to Washington on 15th April 1966 admitted that, *"We frankly do not know whether the real figure for the PKI killed is closer to 100,000 or 1,000,000."*[5]

During the Vietnam War, it has been estimated that more than 3 million Vietnamese were killed, with 300,000 missing in action and presumed dead. The United States lost nearly 59,000 while her allies lost some 6,000. The South Vietnamese army accounted for 225,000 dead. The rational for this insane war was that the United States national security would be endangered by communist domination in Southeast Asia – *the Domino Theory,* once Vietnam falls to the com-munists, the rest of Southeast Asia would follow. S.E.A.T.O. (South-East Asia Treaty Organization)[6] was established to counter the per-ceived threat, and the women of the member states were prostitut-ed, as the costs of membership, to satisfy the sexual lust of depraved and deprived soldiers on "R.R." (Rest & Recreation) after their tours in Vietnam. Drugs were freely available, brought in by G.I. Joes and the youths of our societies are still suffering from this consequence today.

In the war in Afghanistan, the United States air force was drop-ping the huge GBU-28 bombs, commonly referred to as "bunker buster bombs" to obliterate the likes of Osama Bin Laden and his cahoots! GBU-28s (guided bomb units) are 5,000 lb laser guided bombs armed with BLU-113 warheads. These warheads are the most advanced and powerful "earth penetrating warheads" ever cre-ated, and the B61-11 is its nuclear version. UNICEF spokesman Eric Larlcke stated, *"As many as 100,000 more children will die in Afghanistan this winter unless food reaches them in sufficient quantities in the next six weeks."*[7] Recently, In Iraq, we witnessed the immense firepower of the American military in Rumsfeld's "Shock and Awe" campaign which resulted in the "quick victory". In a recent report published by the Lancet, it has been estimated that at least 100,000 civilians have died as a result of the war. With a stockpile of over 10,000 nuclear warheads, the United States is also the number one nuclear superpower.

However, I do not share the view of those political pundits who accepts uncritically that the United States at the present point in time is at the height of its power, unrivaled in military and economic strength. I cannot but recall the dictum of Mao Tse-Tung, *"All the reputedly powerful reactionaries are merely paper tigers. The reason is that they are divorced from the people. Look! Was not Hitler a paper tiger? Was Hitler not overthrown? U.S. Imperialism has not yet been overthrown and it has the atomic bomb. I believe it also will be overthrown. It, too, is a paper tiger."*

You *don't* have to be a commie to come to that conclusion. A very insightful article by Andre Gunder Frank refers to the dollar as *"Uncle Sam's Paper Tiger Dollar."*[8] Despising the United States strategically as a paper tiger does not mean that we can dismiss its awesome military strength tactically. In dealing with the present reactionary U.S. administration, it is crucial that we adopt the correct strategic perspective. For the record, my beef is not with the American people, a nation which I have utmost respect. The heroic resistance war against the Zionist Anglo-American Empire in Iraq has demonstrated conclusively, as in the case of the Vietnam War that the Empire war machine is not invincible, notwithstanding its overwhelming fire-power. The raw pictures of injuries suffered by the U.S. armed forces are more gruesome than those from the Vietnam War. If not for advancement in medical science in the treatment of battle injuries, much more would have died from the injuries. With over 1,500 dead and counting, close to 25,000 injured (maybe more) and thousands more (some estimate over 30,000) suffering severe mental illness, defeat is a foregone conclusion. Just as the Tet Offensive was the critical turning point in the Vietnam War, the Battle for Fallujah has tipped the scale in favor of the anti-occupation forces in Iraq. To conclude otherwise is to wear blinkers and deny the harsh reality.

I can anticipate that many will object to the reference that the

United States administration is reactionary. But I take comfort that Noam Chomsky, who according to the New York Times is *"arguably the most important intellectual alive"*, refers to the elements in the Reagan-Bush 1 and Bush II administration as being reactionary and that recent polls indicated that 80% of the respondents in Europe regarded the U.S. as the greatest threat to world peace and that many people in the world increasingly think that President Bush is a greater threat to world peace than President Saddam Hussein, when he was in power.[9]

We must have no illusions as to the predatory nature of the Zionist Anglo-American Empire. It is in its death throes and as such will do everything in its power to prolong its survival. Robert Higgs of the Independent Institute in his essay, "Benefits and Costs of the US Government's War Making" warned that, *"In matters of war making, as elsewhere in their wielding of power, governments act in the interest of their own leaders, with as many concessions as necessary to retain the support of the coalition of special-interest groups that keeps them in power. Libertarians, of all people, understand that, in Randolph Bourne's now-hackneyed phrase, 'war is the health of the state.' This claim is not some wild-eyed ideological pronouncement; it is as well-established as any historical regularity can be...."*

The state of the Zionist Anglo-American empire has degenerated to such an extent that it warranted Higgs to comment that, *"Congress has become so pusillanimous that it provides no check whatever on the president's war making. In 'authorizing' the president to attack Iraq or not, entirely as he pleased, Congress not only abrogated its clear constitutional duty, but it did so with grotesquely cavalier disregard for the gravity of the matter at stake. It did not even bother to debate the issue, but simply handed over its power to the executive and returned to the workaday plundering that is its only remaining raison d'etre. The president and his chief underlings keep telling is that 'we are at war,' but it's just a turn of phrase for public relations purposes, inasmuch as the constitutional requirement of a congressional declaration of war has gone unfulfilled. It provokes no great public outcry, however, so conditioned have the peo-*

ple become to this form of executive usurpation."

Higgs's conclusion on the present state of affairs is both coura-geous, scathing and frightening: *"Because national-security mat-ters lie outside the immediate experience of the great bulk of the citizens, the government can get away with waste, fraud, brutality, and idiocy far more easily in foreign affairs than it can when prescribing student exams, building houses for the poor people, or relieving grandma's aches and pains. The history of U.S. foreign and defense policy in the past sixty years is an unrelieved tale of mendacity, corruption, and criminal blunder-ing. If the government can't fix the potholes in Washington D.C., it certainly can't build a viable liberal democratic state in Iraq. No one of sound mind could have supposed that it would even try, much less that it would succeed. This adventure, like so much else that the government undertakes, is a gigantic hoax, and all too much of it verges on racketeering of the sort described by the legendary U.S. Marine General Smedley Butler."*[10]

The purpose of this book is to explain and show why the Zionist Anglo-American Empire is in rapid decline and the inevitable violent and destructive consequences arising thereof. If we can analyze and project the likely future scenarios, we can also make the necessary preparations and take such precautionary measures to mitigate the horrors that will follow from such a meltdown.

There are five propositions that I would like to put before you, namely:

1. The rapid and irreversible decline of the Zionist Anglo-American Empire;

2. The inevitable nuclear wars;

3. Why Israel is the linchpin to the coming nuclear wars;

4. The end of empire capitalism; and

5. By the middle of the 21st century, national borders will be re-aligned. The 21st century world map will be quite different from what we are accustomed to.

We have already witnessed a major re-alignment following the collapse of the Soviet empire, as evident in the countries constituting the "New Europe" and Central Asia. It follows that the world and her borders will not be the same after the demise of the Zionist Anglo-American Empire. The 21st century will be the most violent century in the history of mankind. *The hidden enemy will not go away quietly, that's for sure.*

But I am also confident that patriotic Americans will rise to the occasion to claim back the America that gave them the Declaration of Independence and the Constitution, beacons in man's quests for freedom and the pursuit of happiness. The true patriots have made too many sacrifices to stand pat and allow the *Zionist-Neo Conservative cancer* to overwhelm the body politic. I hold the firm belief that a consequence of the demise of the empire will be a New America, faithful to its constitution and founding principles, with a new vision and mission for a better world, one that is at peace with itself and with the community of nations.

This is not a soothsayer's book, as I am not a speculator or crystal ball gazer. The evidence in support of my five propositions are in the public domain, some have yet to see the full light of the day, but already accepted as fact by the Imperial elites of the Anglo-American shadow governments in the dark corridors of their inner sanctum.

As an attorney and political analyst for 29 years, I cannot afford the luxury of submitting for your consideration speculative theories or propositions unsubstantiated by corroborated evidence. Such an exercise serves no purpose, and at most a frivolous intellectual masturbation. Let me assure you that I have no inclination to indulge in such an activity. I intend to submit detail and irrefutable evidence in support of my five propositions. Unfortunately the issues have been distorted by the establishment mass media and wrong conclusions have been drawn. The fog of war has wrought further confusion to the debate. But I am confident that once you have reviewed the evidence contained in this book, you would arrive at the same conclusions as I did.

Thus far, the majority of the views expressed and evidence presented on the issues taken up in this book are from the elite of the Zionist Anglo-American Empire and Europe. And although some enlightened U.S. elites have written and spoken out against their own fascist evil empire, they have shied away from confronting the five issues that is being presented in this book. And notwithstanding that a substantial part of the European establishment has opposed the Iraq war and some of the policies of the Zionist Anglo-American Empire, one cannot but be suspicious of their aspirations for the Euro and the re-colonialization of their former colonies. We must be particularly vigilant with regard to the United Kingdom's imperial ambitions emerging from the skirts of the Anglo-American Empire. If I may borrow a local expression that aptly describes such a threat: ***"A cobra in your trouser pocket."***

One additional point – recently, Donald Rumsfeld the United States Defense Secretary was quoted as saying, in response to a query from a soldier whether he was aware that scrap heaps in Iraq were cannibalized by soldiers for "hillbilly armor" that was then bolted on to their trucks, ***"you go to war with the army you have, not the army you might want or wish to have at a later time."***[11] This doesn't say very much about the often touted superiority and effectiveness of the U.S. war machine. If there is one quote that settles the issue that the U.S. war machine is indeed a paper tiger, this must be it!

How long the U.S. military will put up with the follies of the Zionist Anglo-American power elites, only God knows. When the red line has been crossed, I bet your bottom dollar, that those who have sworn to uphold the code of honor will set things right, but my only fear is that it may be too late.

Critics miss the point when they criticize Rumsfeld for being callous and insensitive to the plight of the soldiers exposed to the devastating fire fights with the Iraqi anti-occupation and resistance forces. There were two messages in that frank and brutal admission. Firstly, to the soldiers, Rumsfeld is saying that given the time constraints of the war agenda, even if he had to arm the soldiers with muskets, and send them to war and to certain death, he would have done so. He had no choice. Secondly, to the segment of the power elite who still did not get the full picture and the doubting Thomas, he is saying in the plainest of language, that you cannot have a war economy, without a war. "It's the economics, stupid!" And not forgetting the problem of peak oil and the coming resource wars.

For those who still hold to the view that President Bush is a moron and the joker in the pack, I would humbly invite them to have a major rethink. He has been re-elected for a second term which cannot be said of his father. This is no mean feat. I can appreciate your question, why would the elites of the Zionist Anglo-American shadow government want Bush and not Kerry or Howard Dean?

Simple! I am reminded of the famous Nixon quip about Pinochet, *"He's a bastard, but he's our bastard."* The Zionist Anglo-American shadow government needed a bastard. President Bush is their bastard who can be trusted to do the dirty work of launching illegal wars, even at the expense of the goodwill and support of major allies and world opinion.[12] When the national security and strategic interests of the United States were threatened externally, the U.S. had Pinochet, the Shah of Iran, Nguyen Van Thieu and the likes of Park Chung Hee and Papa Doc Duvalier to be the bastards to do the dirty work of putting down resistance to U.S. hegemony. Now that the United States is about to implode because of antagonistic economic contradictions within the Empire and the inherent destructive nature of Empire Capitalism, the shadow government needed a point man who is mean and vicious enough to wield the hatchet. Even though Kerry was a war veteran and a decorated war hero (purple hearts etc), and vowed to do a better job in kicking Iraqi butts in the recent 2004 election campaign, he was just not dirty, mean and vicious enough. He had a track record of being an anti-war protester on his return from Vietnam. The shadow government cannot afford the risk of having a commander-in-chief to wage ruthless wars at home and abroad that has an anti-war track record. Kerry did not qualify to be their bastard!

There is a poster in the old Wild West, "Wanted – Dead or Alive." This is an invitation for bounty hunters to hunt down the enemy. President Bush is the perfect fit for the job. But should we be surprise by this choice of the Commander-in-Chief and President?

The history of the United States is replete with such Presidents. Let me give you a quick run down on the various past Presidents and how they have been perceived by their *peers*:

Robert Taft on Harry Truman: *"It defies all common sense to send that roughneck ward politician back to the White House."* President Truman dropped the atomic bomb on Hiroshima and Nagasaki.

Harry Truman on Nixon: *"He is a no-good lying bastard. He can lie out of both sides of his mouth at the same time, and if he ever caught himself telling the truth, he'd lie just to keep his hand in."* President Nixon authorized the illegal war in Cambodia and ordered the "carpet bombing" of Hanoi and Haiphong and other war crimes in Vietnam.

Robert Kennedy on Lyndon Johnson: *"He tells so many lies that he convinces himself after a while that he's telling the truth. He just doesn't recognize truth or falsehood."* On being President, escalated the war in Vietnam and was complicit in allowing Israel to have the nuclear bomb.[13]

Henry Kissinger on Carter: *"His administration has managed the extraordinary feat of having, at one and the same time, the worst relations with our allies, the worst relations with our adversaries, and the most serious upheavals in the developing world since the end of the Second World War."* President Carter gave the directive for secret aid to the Mujahideens to oppose the Soviets in 1979 that gave birth to the Talibans and the Jihadists, the fore-runners of Al Qaeda and the bogus War on Terrorism.[14]

The United States must reap what it has sowed in the past sixty years.

A good many evidence presented in this book cannot be found in the main stream mass media for obvious reasons. Since when would CNN, Fox News, The Weekly Standard etc, be the messengers of bad news? I hope this modest effort will spur the reader to indulge in his/her own research. Let me assure you that it is indeed a very satisfying journey. The rewards are enormous, knowing that you no longer have your head buried in the sand or slam dunked by the Zionist Anglo-American establishment mass media into a memory hole where fairy tales reside.

ENDNOTES:

1. Cited in "military Spending Nears $1 trillion" by Thalif Deen, www.atimes.com, 23rd Aug.2004.

2. Ibid.

3. John Quincy Adams's speech on July 4, 1821, in celebration of American Independence Day to the U.S. House of Representatives. Source, The Future of Freedom Foundation, www.fff.org.

4. "United States War Crimes" by Lenora Foerstal & Brian Wilson, www.globalresearch.ca/ , 26th Jan.2002

5. Ibid. See also George Washington University's National Security Archive, 27th July 2001 at www.Narchives.org

6. An Alliance organized (1954) under the S'East Asia Collective Defense Treaty by Australia, France, Gt. Britain, New Zealand Pakistan, Philippines, Thailand and the U.S. It was disbanded in 1977.

7. The Times of India, 16th October 2001 – "100,000 Afghan Children Could Die This Winter."

8. "Geopolitical Catch 22: Uncle Sam's Paper Tiger" http://globalresearch.ca/articles/ FRA501B.html

9. Noam Chomsky, *Hegemony or Survival* at page 41 and 109, (2003 Penguin Books) citing Washington Post Weekly, 3rd March 2003 and Newsweek, 24th March 2003.

10. Robert Higgs is Senior Fellow in Political economy at the Independent Institute, author of *Against Leviathan* and *Crisis and Leviathan,* and editor of the scholarly journal *The Independent Review* – www.independent.org

11. Deborrah Orr, "Donald Rumsfeld and the Myths of the War", The Independent, 21st December 2004.

12. There are always the hypocrites who have nothing better to do than to criticize the language used here, but let me remind them, that I am merely echoing the sentiments of the American power elites. If Truman can call Nixon a lying bastard, let us not be a wimp in confronting reality. But if you wish to bury your head in the sand, please stop reading and throw the book away.

13. See Michael Collins Piper, *Final Judgment,* 6th Ed. American Free Press

14. The quotations can be found at www.historymatters.gmu.edu/text/puzzle.14ans.html. For President Carter's directive, see Zbigniew Brzezinski interview with Le Nouvel Observateur.

Part 1

Mighty Empire or Paper Tiger?

"There is a reason for the vulnerability of empires. To maintain one against opposition requires war — steady, unrelenting, unending war. And war is ruinous — from a legal, moral and economic point of view. It can ruin losers, such as Napoleonic France, or Imperial Germany in 1918. And it can ruin the victors, as did the British and the Soviets in the twentieth century."

— Professor James K. Galbraith

"The United States is facing the prospect of a major defeat in Iraq that is likely to constitute a serious setback in the ongoing campaign to expand the American Empire. Behind the pervasive war propaganda as evidenced in the 'victorious' attack on Fallujah lies the reality of a U.S. war machine that is fighting a futile battle against growing guerrilla forces, with little chance for a stable political situation to the conflict that could possibly meet U.S. imperial objectives."

**— Editors, Monthly Review
January, 2005**

1

The Financial Mess

The United States is in a financial mess. Forget about the exuberance still reflected in the Dow Jones Index. Don't waste your time reading and analyzing the employment figures. At the present state of play, it is almost irrelevant. If you are a seasoned poker player or a regular gambler at one of those 5-star casinos in Las Vegas, knowing the odds is second nature and explanations are superfluous. For the rest (other than the elites), it is time for the wake-up call.

Read carefully the following headlines, comments and analysis from the financial insiders and then tell me if I am wrong.

1) "SENATE OKs $800 BILLION DEBT LIMIT HIKE"

Associated Press Writer Alan Fram wrote: *"Congress is ready to send President Bush an $800 billion debt limit increase, a testament to the massive federal deficits that have marked his administration. With no alternative but an unprecedented federal deficit, the House planned to vote Thursday to boost the debt ceiling from its current $7.38 trillion, following Senate passage Wednesday. The government reached the cap last month, paying its bill since with cash from the civil service retirement account, which it plans to repay.[1]"*

Did you get that? The U.S. government had looted the civil service retirement account! The report continues:

"'We are nearing the end of our rope, and it is crucial that Congress act,' said Treasury Department spokesman Rob Nichols. The Republican-led Senate approved the debt limit by 54-44, with only two Democrats and one Republican switching sides. The debate prompted Senator John Kerry, D-Mass., to

make his first speech in the Senate since his defeat in the Nov.2 presidential election. 'The United States is operating a borrow-and-spend government, continuously stretched by demands for more tax cuts and more spending,' he said. 'And when they don't have the money to pay for their choices, they must put the tab on the national credit card and send the bill to our kids.'

"Not a single Republican spoke during the debate on the debt limit bill, reflecting how politically uncomfortable the measure is for them. That discomfort was highlighted when they refused to bring the bill to a vote before the elections. <u>Completion of the debt limit measure would raise the government's borrowing limit to $8.18 trillion. That is $2.23 trillion higher than when Bush became president in 2001 and more than eight times the debt President Reagan faced when he took office in 1981.</u> Democrats noted that the $5.6 trillion in surpluses that were projected for the next ten years when Bush took office in 2001 has been transformed into $2.3 trillion in deficits now estimated for the coming decade. This is the third time since he entered the White House that Bush has gotten Congress to boost the borrowing limit." (Emphasis added)

2) "ELITE BANKERS NOW PULLING PLUG ON U.S. ECONOMY & CURRENCY"
By former Senator Tim Ferguson — The Ferguson Report

"I have warned for a long time that the Federal Reserve is planning to destroy the U.S. economy by printing the U.S. dollar in exponentially riskier quantities until it blows off the charts and crashes, and by easing credit rates until the average individual and corporate debt loads are so enormous that the resulting massive distortions in the economy suddenly bring on an economic heart attack, leaving no possibility of a short or even medium term recovery. That day is here!

"There is nothing more important in your life right now than the exceedingly dire economic crisis unfolding as I write, and the state of your soul! In other words, if your spiritual house is not in order, the building financial collapse will be so horrible that you will not be able to emotionally or mentally endure it, and I am addressing the healthy and strong here."

When was the last time you had your medical check-up?

Read on.

"This collapse will knock you out cold, flat on your back, with violence, and most of mankind will never get back up. While the elite are sending signals to their friends that the switch has been thrown, that final preparations for safety are now in order, they are not saying how bad it will be. That is why I began this site. Because I could not find anyone, even doom-sayers, who spelled out clearly what is at stake here. I believe that even the elite, such as Sir Templeton, does not fully understand the implications of this crash — <u>that this is the end of America as we know it.</u>" (Emphasis added)

You would have thought that a senator would be considered part of the "elite" but he is not even in the loop. I suppose there are "elites" and elites, such that even Sir Templeton is not part of the inner sanctum. So is the "Empire Economic Meltdown" a fantasy or a reality? Read on.

"That great criminal enterprise — the Federal Reserve — has accomplished step 1, trashing and ending the dollar system, culminating a multi-year, massive, insane inflation of money supply and credit. The Illuminati corporations such as Freddie Mae, Fannie Mae, Farmer Mac, FHA, GM, Ford, and GE (which are actually banks), worked hand-in-hand with the Bank Cartel on this sickening, twisted game, switching from pumping credit cards and cars…. to a last ditch horrendous push into mortgage lending. This insane lending will destroy the lending institutions themselves, as Ford and GE are well aware, but the elite do not care, as after this collapse, there will be only one corporation in the world, and they are all pulling together to put everyone as deep into debt as possible, to assure that no American state or corporation or region will survive when the debt mountain suffocates all life. That is why so many CEOs are bailing out with insane profits from questionable practices which would normally ruin their career for life, as they raped their corporations (the latest is Grasso of the New York Stock Exchange); but they know the game is over, and it is now or never — this is their last chance to make millions and move on to an island, for insiders are able to see that the economy is literally going to hell, and it will not climb out of hell in their lifetimes."

17

Some of you might not know who former Senator Tim Ferguson is, especially if you are foreign to American politics. Some might even consider him a maverick and his views and conclusions perhaps exaggerated. I can appreciate your reluctance at this point to come to grips with reality. But what follows will be the knockout blows.

3) RED ALERT — FINANCIAL CRISIS

Rodrigo de Rato, Managing Director of the International Monetary Fund sounded the alarm bells when he said: *"We believe such a large imbalance of growing indebtedness by the United States is a risk not only for the United States economy, but for the world economy."*

Laurence Kotlikoff, Economics Chairman, Boston University put the matter in its proper perspective when he said: *"To give you an idea how big the problem is, you'd have to have an immediate and permanent 78% hike in the Federal Income Tax [to close the $51 trillion fiscal gap].... The country's absolutely broke, and both Bush and Kerry are irresponsible in not addressing this problem. This administration and previous administrations have set us up for a major financial crisis on the order of what Argentina experienced a couple of years ago."* (Emphasis added)

Richard Russell, Editor-Publisher, Dow Theory Letters, observed: *"Due to our never-ending deficits, what we're seeing is a massive transfer of assets from the U.S. to creditors, probably the greatest transfer of assets in history. Over time this is going to mean a lowered standard of living for my kids and your kids, and if it happens quickly it will also mean a lowered standard of living for you and me. When you build up gigantic debts, somebody has to pay for those debts. The great American debt-sponsored party is slowly coming to an end."* (Emphasis added)

Martin Wolfe, Associate Editor and Chief Economics Commentator of the Financial Times gave a chilling forecast: *"The U.S. is now on the comfortable path to ruin. It is being driven along a road of ever rising deficits and debt, both external and fiscal that risk destroying the country's credit and the global role of its currency."*

The direction in which the U.S. is heading is assuredly down and out. Richard Arvedlund, Founder, Cypress Capital Management pessimistically pointed out: *"...the direction of the dollar is down. The dollar is declining because of our loose money policy, our terrible fiscal deficit and our current account deficit, all of which are heading the wrong way."*

He is corroborated by Bob McTeer, President of Reserve Bank of Dallas: *"Over time there is only one direction for the dollar to go — lower."* And Jagdeesh Gokhale, Senior Fellow, Cato Institute & research publisher for the Federal Reserve Bank of Cleveland who was equally grim in his assessment: *"The long-term picture is pretty bad."* Paul Volker, the former Chairman, Federal Reserve Board has been quoted as saying: *"... we have a 75% chance of a crisis within 5 years."*

How precarious is the situation is best summed up by Bill Gross, Chief Financial Officer of Pimco, the world's largest bond fund manager when he warned: *"Too much debt, geopolitical risks and several bubbles have created a very unstable environment which can turn any minute. With all this consumer debt, business debt, government debt, smaller movements in interest rates have a magnified effect. A small movement can tip the boat.*[2]*"* The ensuing financial storm and devastation will dwarf even the recent Tsunami in Asia.

The United States is like the stuntman walking on the tight rope over the Niagara Falls. One small slip and he plunges.

Take another perspective, from the outsider's view. Foreign creditors put up 90% of the approximately $2 billion a day that is required to ensure that the U.S. does not go into a default. These creditors hold an estimated $11 trillion or 43% of U.S. privately held national debt, a substantial increase from the 30% since President Bush came to office in 2001. Foreign creditors, the majority of which are central banks, are caught in a dilemma. Either they stand pat and watch the value of their reserves fall drastically or move out of the dollar regime into Euros or a basket of currencies.[3] Harvard University President, Lawrence Summers has dubbed this the *"balance of financial terror.*[4]*"*

In addition to the above woes, the U.S. economy is also undermined by the Banking Derivatives Scam. The double whammy of the debt crisis and the derivatives meltdown will assuredly bankrupt the mighty United States and shatter the dreams of the Zionist Anglo-American Empire.

4) GAMBLING ON DERIVATIVES — FINANCIAL TSUNAMI

Warren Buffet, the world's greatest stock market investor, known as the 'Sage of Omaha', in his Chairman's Letter in the Berkshire Hathaway 2002 Annual Report said: *"We view them as time bombs both for the parties that deal in them and the economic system. In our view derivatives are financial weapons of mass destruction, carrying dangers that while now latent, are potentially lethal."* (Emphasis added)

As far back as 1990, Sir Julian Hodge in a memo dated November of that year to senior executives of the Julian Hodge Bank said: *"In no circumstances enter the derivatives trading market without first agreeing it in writing with me.... At some time in the future, it could bring the world's financial system to its knee.*[5]*"*

We need only to recall the fear and panic caused by the collapse of the hedge fund LCTM whose principal shareholders were Prof. Robert C. Merton of Harvard University and Prof. Myron S. Scholes, who shared the Nobel Prize in Economics for groundbreaking research in determining the value of derivatives. The Federal Reserve had to intervene and rescue the fund at a cost of $3.5 billion as it was feared that its collapse would cause a meltdown of the world's financial system.

The OCC Bank Derivatives Report for the 3rd quarter of 2004 reported that the notional value of derivatives held by U.S. banks rose to a record US $84.2 trillion, from $81 trillion in the 2nd quarter. This is mind-boggling! The report stated that derivatives volumes continued to be dominated by interest-rate contracts, which grew $2.4 trillion during the quarter to $73 trillion or 87% of the total derivatives volumes. Foreign exchange contracts rose $163 billion during the same period to $7.9 trillion or 9% of the total. The remaining 4% was made up of equity, commodity and credit derivatives. The banks total risk exposure through these financial instruments rose to $804 billion, up from the previous quarter of $752 billion.

It should be noted that as at December 31, 2003, the top 25 U.S. commercial banks and trust companies accounted for 95.5% of total derivatives traded. They are as follows:

1)	JPMorgan Chase	$	36.8 trillion
2)	Bank of America NA	$	14.8 trillion
3)	Citibank	$	11.1 trillion
4)	Wachovia Bank National Assn	$	2.3 trillion
5)	HSBC Bank USA	$	1.3 trillion
6)	Bank One National Assn	$	1.2 trillion
7)	Bank of New York	$	561 billion
8)	Wells Fargo Bank	$	557 billion
9)	Fleet National Bank	$	443 billion
10)	State Street Bank & Trust Co	$	369 billion
11)	National City Bank	$	252 billion
12)	National City Bank of In	$	133 billion
13)	Keybank National Assn	$	91 billion
14)	Mellon Bank National Assn	$	88 billion
15)	Standard Federal Bank NA$	$	78 billion
16)	Suntrust Bank	$	77 billion
17)	La Salle Bank National Assn	$	70 billion
18)	PNC Bank National Assn	$	48 billion
19)	Deutsche Bank TR Co Americas	$	46 billion
20)	US Bank National Assn	$	43 billion
21)	Merrill Lynch Bank USA	$	35 billion
22)	Capital One Bank	$	28 billion
23)	Northern Trust Co	$	26 billion
24)	Irwin Union Bank & Trust Co	$	19 billion
25)	Union Bank of California NA	$	19 billion *

All figures have been rounded up to nearest billion.

What is of concern is that the three top banks have exposures far in excess of their assets. The statistics in the QCC report is alarming. In the case of JPMorgan Chase, while exposure is $36 trillion, assets are only $628 billion which works out to approximately $58 of derivatives per dollar of asset. Credit exposure to Risk Based Capital Ratio is approximately 844%. Bank of America's exposure is $14.8 trillion while assets are $617 billion, the ratio being approximately $24 of derivatives per dollar of asset. Credit exposure to Risk Based Capital Ratio is approximately 221%. And in the case of Citibank, exposure $11.1 trillion while assets are $582 billion, the ratio being approximately $19 of derivatives per dollar of asset. Credit exposure to Risk Based Capital Ratio is approximately 96%.

In the course of my research, I came across a brilliant article by Adam Hamilton of Zeal Research who wrote two ground-breaking essays on JPMorgan Chase's derivatives vulnerabilities. He has painted a frightening scenario. Based on 2001 figures, he pointed out that JPMorgan Chase (JPM) shareholders own roughly $43 billion (actual figure: $42.735 billion). This small equity capital balance is supporting a crushing inverted derivatives pyramid of $30,434 billion or **$30.4 trillion** of notional value derivatives. This works out to a leverage of derivatives to equity of 712 times![6] If LTCM with Nobel Prize economists working for them can collapse, why can't JPM fold under when its exposure is so disproportionate to its asset base?

By any measure these figures are alarming, and should any of the top three banks get into a gridlock, the entire U.S. and world's banking system would collapse. **The derivatives time bomb has already started ticking and the question is not if, but when it will explode! The Financial Tsunami is coming!**

5) OTHER CRITICAL INDICATORS

What I have presented thus far is the big picture. But there are many other indicators that support and corroborate this big picture. These small pictures taken together are not pretty either. The first grim picture that will literally hit you in your stomach is U.S. ports lined with containers and bulk cargo ships bringing massive amount of food. From being an exporter, the U.S. will be a net importer of food as early as 2005. The U.S. had an agriculture trade surplus of $13.6 billion in 2001 and is projected to be in negative territory in 2005. The problem will be aggravated further, once WTO forces the U.S. to reduce trade barriers. That alone will ensure a huge import of beef and other foodstuffs. And despite the low dollar, U.S. food exports for 2005 will be $6.3 billion less than 2004. Brazil has already overtaken the US in the exports of soy products and is fast becoming a major food exporter.[7]

On September 23, 2004, the US-China Economic & Security Review Commission, a congressional appointed panel convened to review the impact of China on U.S. Industries. It was not a happy picture. China had impacted the U.S. industries and manufacturers across the board. In a special report for BusinessWeek,[8] Pete Engardio and Dexter Roberts wrote that the three scariest words in U.S. industry are: "The China Price". What this means is that China's costs are 30% to 50% less than U.S. producers. And in the worst case, it can mean below the cost of materials. In the result, 2.7 million jobs evaporated since 2000 and America's deficit with China continue to grow at an enormous pace, and will pass $150 billion in 2004. The report further states that while U.S. companies are no longer investing in much new capacity at home, and the ranks of U.S. engineers are thinning, China, in contrast is emerging as the most competitive manufacturing platform ever. The issue is not just price alone. According to Janet E. Fox, vice-president for international procurement for J.C. Penny Co, *"The reason practically all home furnishings are now made in China factories is that they simply are better suppliers. American manufacturers are not even in the same game."* (Emphasis added)

And according to the U.S. Conference Board, the productivity of private industry in China has grown at an incredible 17% annually for five years. The writers of the report concluded not too optimistically: *"...unless it can deal with the industrial challenge, it will suffer a loss of economic power and influence. Can America afford the China price? It's the question U.S. workers, execs, and policymakers urgently need to ask."*

If this is the problem with China, what will be the scenario when India and Vietnam follow the path of China?

I can understand the anxiety of Leonard Burman, Co-director of Tax Policy of the Urban Institute when he said: *"I got four children and it really disturbs me. I just think it's irresponsible what we are doing to them.*[9]*"* If we are worried about our children, what about those who are retiring?

The International Monetary Fund is of the view that an immediate and permanent 60% increase in Federal Income Tax is needed to address promised future benefits. But this is not going to happen during President Bush's watch. In despair, Pat Buchanan said: *"On this issue of Social Security, we got coming up in 2008 the first 77 million baby boomers hit early retirement... for the next 20 years after that, the major contributors to Social Security and Medicare become major consumers. The real deficit then will come out of the water like a volcano. And there is no way it seems to me that we are ever going to have a balanced budget again, given the forces in Washington and this perfect storm that's ahead.*[10]*"*

6) BACK TO THE BIG PICTURE

The sad part about this financial mess is that the majority of the average Americans are not aware of the impending catastrophe, and even if they are somewhat conscious of the issues, they have not fully grasped the implications. It is not easy to explain such economic issues and I was at wits' end trying to find an analogy to explain the situation. Fortunately, I came across an article by Pedro Nicolaci da Costa[11] that sums up nicely the problem confronting the average American. The writer interviewed Paul Krugman, the Princeton economics professor and what the professor said needs to be made known to every American who cares about his country and what needs to be done to save it. And this is what the good professor said:

"If you go back and you look at the sources of the blow-up of Argentina debt during the 1990s, one little-appreciated thing is that social security privatization was an important source of that expansion of debt.[12] So if you ask the question do we look like Argentina, the answer is a whole lot more than anyone is quite willing to admit at this point. We have become a banana republic. The break can come either from the Reserve Bank of China deciding it has enough dollars, thank you, or from private investors saying, 'I'm going to take a speculative bet on the dollar plunge,' which then ends up being self-fulfilling prophecy. Both scenarios are pretty unnerving." (Emphasis added)

It is not every day that you get a blue chip economist making such stark admissions that America has become a banana republic.

Obviously not everyone subscribes to the above scenario. One such economist is James K. Galbraith who, in an interview with editors of Tompaine.com, took the view that the U.S. had not reached the stage of apocalypse.[13] However, I am of the view that the difference of opinion (if any) is really one of timing — when rather than if. Professor Galbraith explored four scenarios and gave an explanation for his conclusions:

(1) Run On The Dollar

"What could up-end the apple cart? An unstoppable panic is probably not yet the largest risk. There are too many dollars in the theatre of the world economy, too few exits and only a few elephantine players. The latter would soon be dis-

couraged from selling by the soaring price of the available alternative assets, and the run would fizzle out. Thus the dollar crisis will probably wait until a political crisis — say, someday with China — sets it off."

It is clear that the somewhat optimistic assessment is premised on the assumption that China, in the short- or middle-term, would not rock the boat, and only a major confrontation in the ***distant*** future will be the trigger. But, President Bush, however, has declared that China is one of the countries targeted for nuclear war.

(2) Rising Long Term Interest Rates

"Some fear rising long term interest rates — and a recession — simply on account of the sliding dollar and price inflation. But this also won't necessarily happen. For an inflation premium to be built into the long term interest rates there needs to be higher expected inflation on a continuing basis. Notwithstanding the cheap psychology of 'rational expectations,' beloved of economists, actual inflation can rise for a long time before expectations. And the inflation adjustments, coming (let us say) primarily through a rising dollar oil price, could come and go rather quickly. It need not get built into a spiral of wages and prices. So far, despite the substantial dollar decline that has already occurred, long term interest rates have hardly budged. They have generally risen no more, and in some cases less, than the short-term rates, Greenspan started pushing up last spring."

What if the dollar drops another 20% – 30% in value and the oil price hits $80 or more per barrel? The learned professor has yet to address these issues.

(3) A Change in European Policy — Towards High Growth

"A Change in European policy — towards a high growth, full employment Keynesianism — could bring a shift in the world balance of economic power. Such a shift would create profits in Europe (where there presently are few) attracting capital. It would open up a European current account deficit, where there is presently a surplus. Soon the euro would not be a scarce currency any longer, and the reduction of the dollar's reserve status could truly get underway. Unfortunately for

Europeans, European policymakers don't see — and won't see — this opportunity. Frankly, they are too reactionary and too stupid. That's a tragedy for Europe, though in some ways its undeserved good luck for the United States."

Is this guy for real? He is telling the Europeans how to bring down the dollar and take over from the U.S. as the next money-printing machine, if the Euro is to, one day, replace the dollar as the premier reserve currency! But it seems to me that if the Europeans have not embarked on this path, it may be that they do not want to end up eventually like the U.S. — a banana republic!

(4) Alan Greenspan Raising Interest Rates

"And the fourth possibility is that Alan Greenspan could change his mind, raise interest rates and inflict on us all a monumental 'defense of the dollar.' Morgan's Roach worries about this with some good reason; I've worried about it too. While sharply rising interest rates could cure both inflation and the weak dollar — as they did in the early 1980s — <u>the resulting slump would be even more disastrous than it was then, because debt levels are higher now than they were.</u> Just as the slump then destroyed Latin America and Africa, a new one could bring China, Japan, India and others into worldwide recession. There would be no easy way out." (Emphasis added)

The professor offered some prescriptions, but for the purpose of this exercise, I would highlight just one, as it is addressed to Americans, since after all, their government is the cause for all this mess. This is his message:

"America must [also] change. <u>Specifically, we must turn away from our present over-reliance on armed forces and private bankers, far away from the fantasy of self serving dominance</u> for which, the markets are clearly telling us, the world will not agree to pay. We need an industrial strategy based on technological leadership, collective security, and smart use of the world's resources. The financial counterpart must be a new source of liquidity for many developing countries, permitting them to step up imports, and correspondingly our exports and employment. This will properly require a new network of regional regulatory agents, empowered to enforce capital control and to take responsibility for successful development strategies among their members." (Emphasis added)

I couldn't agree more. The enlightened professor is saying in no uncertain terms, that the U.S. cannot rely on a war economy and the avarice of Wall Street bankers and hedge fund managers to put things right. Since 1997, Malaysia, under the leadership of the then Prime Minister Tun Dr. Mahathir Mohamad, has been saying that the international community's economic policy should be one that ***"prosper thy neighbor, and not beggar thy neighbor."*** Thank you, sir, for your resounding endorsement for capital controls, which was one of the instruments with which Malaysia overcame the 1997 Asian financial crisis, and for which Malaysia was unfairly labeled "a pariah" and its Prime Minister "a dud". But fortunately, it has come to pass that Malaysia was correct and her people barely suffered the ill effects of the crisis.

However, there is a caveat. The above prescription is a long-term solution. Unfortunately, the U.S. Empire may not have the luxury of time on its side. And that is why I find it strange that the scholarly professor in his conclusion, indicated no sense of urgency, and even if there was a tinge of anxiety, it was dressed up in academic sophistry. Judge as you please, this:

"The point is not that any of this would be easy. Nor can it be done in the lifetime of this administration or of the political dominance that Bush now seeks to achieve. The point is, rather, that there is no viable alternative, so far as I know. Absent a fully articulated strategy, the attempt to pretend otherwise with a few slogans is an economic and also a political dead end. Two steps are required. The first is thought, and the second, when the opportunity arises will be action. The scope of action cannot be small, for the problem exceeds six hundred billion dollars every year. But only dealing with it, over time, can we hope to gain full employment without witnessing, sooner or later, the final run on the dollar."

This is why I believe that there will be **blood on the streets, and it will be very ugly.** No hint whatsoever to the ordinary folks as to how to prepare for the worst of times. Hope is held out that over time, things will work out alright. It is worth repeating here what the former Senator Tim Ferguson has to say about the deceit of the elites and how their spokesmen (spin doctors) mislead and lull the average American in believing that there is a better tomorrow, when they have already packed their bags, hidden their stolen millions and gone off to their secured islands.

"The collapse will knock you out cold, flat on your back, with violence, and most mankind will never get back up. <u>While the elite are sending signals to their friends that the switch has been thrown, that final preparations for safety are now in order, they are not saying how bad it will be</u>…. They know that the game is over, and it is now or never — this is their last chance to make millions <u>and move to an island,</u> for insiders are able to see that the economy is literally going to hell, <u>and it will not climb out of hell in their lifetimes.</u>" (Emphasis added)

There is at least one point of convergence between the former senator and the sagacious professor. The solution is in the long term, and how long that will be only God knows! And that is why I am saying that when the shit hits the ceiling fan, all hell will break loose. No average American, having discovered that they have been conned and robbed, and the rich and famous are nestling with some young Dixie chicks in some faraway islands, will stand pat. They are going to be mean, vicious and they will want blood. What they will do will shame the bounty hunters of the Wild West. Just imagine the kind of riots that took place in Los Angeles decades ago spreading all over the United States. This time round it will not be just the blacks. Latinos and good white folks, even from the Bible belt will be on a rampage. And you can bet your bottom dollar on that!

While we may take issue with the professor's lack of urgency, we cannot find fault with his analysis as to how and why the Zionist Anglo-American Empire came to the present state of affairs. Read this:

"The current jitters are no surprise; the few Keynesians left in the economics profession have long thought them overdue… We have, over many years, worn down our trade position in the world economy, from overpowering supremacy 60 years ago, to the point where high employment in the United States gener-ates current account deficits well over half a trillion dollars per year. We have become dependent for our living standards on the willingness of the rest of the world to accept our assets — stocks, bonds and cash — in return for real goods and servic-es, the product of hard labor by people much poorer than our-selves in return for chits that require no effort to produce."

Yet President Bush is making enemies all over the place, threatening to let go nuclear bombs, even on China who is presently picking up all these useless chits (I.O.U.s), pissing on the Arabs and provoking the Muslims. Can you believe that? I am getting ahead of myself. Let's continue with his analysis:

"For decades, the Western World tolerated the 'exorbitant privilege' of a dollar reserve economy because the United States was the indispensable power, providing reliable security against communism and insurrection without intolerable violence and oppression, thus conditions under which many countries on this side of the Iron Curtain grew and prospered. Those rationales evaporated 15 years ago, and the 'Global War on Terror' is not a persuasive replacement. Thus, what was once a grudging bargain with the world's stabilizing hegemonic country is now widely seen as a lingering subsidy for a predator state."

In my Introduction, I drew your attention that we must not have any illusions as to the predatory nature of the US Empire. Some of you might have considered my allusion as mere left-wing diatribe. But what we have here is one of the most respected economists of the Zionist Anglo-American establishment saying that Uncle Sam is a predator. Have I got your attention now? Read on. Explaining what would happen if there was a run on the greenback, the professor said:

"And once a rush gets going, jacking up interest rates won't stop it either. Small interest hikes do normally affect exchange rates, but only when no player has the kind of extreme market weight now enjoyed by China and Japan. When they do, reactions are unpredictable, if not perverse. The Fed's moves earlier this year could well have been aimed, mainly, at deterring the Japanese and Chinese from dumping. Think of them as a petty bribe — a percent or so on a few trillion dollars. Or you might call it a reaction to blackmail, deemed expedient in view of the election. But the election is now past, and that game is up.

"Now we hear rumors of Russia trading dollars for euro, of India diversifying its reserves, of China contemplating the same. The reaction on Wall Street has been a trifle unnerved. In comments relayed furiously across the internet, Morgan Stanley economist Steven Roach apparently told clients to gird

for an 'economic Armageddon.' The dike, once solid, starts to crack; none can say just where or when it will break. But the little Dutch boy, Alan Greenspan, went to Frankfurt a few days back and plainly stated that he did not have enough fingers."

But watching CNN, ABC and CNBC, you would believe that all is well in Alice's Wonderland. Hold on a minute. There is more bad news. What the distinguished professor is saying about President Bush and his friends is really scary and I want you to read this and tell your neighbors. In essence, he is saying that President Bush is **playing the ultimate poker game, and is challenging the foreign creditors to make him and his cronies, especially those in the oil business, bankrupts and the United States a banana republic.** If the erudite professor's reading of the situation is correct, then President Bush is the most irresponsible leader the world has ever seen. It is also reckless leadership. Read on:

"The most stunning aspect of these events has been the insouciance of the Bush administration. Neither the President, nor the Secretary of the Treasury John Snow, nor any one else has troubled even to emit the usual platitudes about the greenback — not, at least with the slightest conviction. It's almost as if they've figured out. <u>It's almost as if they realize the awful truth. Which is that the dollar's decline is mainly good for his friends, and bad mainly for those about whom they couldn't care less.</u> (Emphasis added)

"Yet that is the truth. The dollar's decline immediately boosts the stock market, for a simple reason. Multinationals have earnings in the United States and in Europe. When the dollar falls, US earnings stay the same but the European earnings go up when measured in dollars. Oil prices will stay up — at least enough to prevent the price in euro from falling. This too helps the US oil company profits, measured in dollars. Meanwhile China will keep its renminbi tied to the dollar, and prices of Chinese imports won't rise much, so Wal-Mart isn't badly hurt. The American consumer will get hit, but mainly on the oil price rather than on the rest of the consumption basket. Many will grumble, but few will recognize the political roots of their problem.

"Since the US owes its debts in dollars, the financial blow will fall first on China and Japan, in the form of depreciation of

their holdings. Tough luck. Latin America countries will get hit on their exports, but helped on their debt service. Those (like Mexico) who export almost exclusively to the US will get squeezed; others (like Argentina) who market to Europe but pay interest in dollars will be hurt less. An unequivocal loser is Europe, which has been hoping for an export led fix to their own, largely self-inflicted, mass unemployment. The Europeans can forget about that.

"If Bush insouciance works, the dollar could decline smoothly for a while and then, simply, stop declining. US exports might recover somewhat, helping manufacturing, though there's no chance exports and imports will balance. But even so, the dollar system could stay intact, so long as China and Japan remain willing to add new dollars to their depreciated hoard. Given that their interest lie in maintaining export activity and the job it creates, they may very well make that choice. Large-scale dollar purchases by the European Central Bank are also a remote possibility (the option has been mentioned on the periphery of the ECB). The problems would return later on, but meanwhile, such action would prove that God really does look after children, small dogs and the United States."

Have we really come to this? Relying on God to set things right. It is clear that President Bush's reckless play hinges on one critical assumption — China and Japan will stand pat and do nothing. But as the professor pointed out candidly, even if China stands pat, the problem **would return** later on. This is indeed a short-term play, but highly reckless. In any high-stakes 5-card game, no gambler would call a bluff with absolutely nothing in hand. But why would President Bush play this reckless hand?

Because President Bush doesn't give two hoots for you and me, and he has already made plans for his island getaway. This gambit is also a psychological ploy as illustrated by the cliché: *"If you owe the bank a million, you have a problem, but if you owe the bank a billion, the bank has a problem."* By this reckoning, China and Japan are the bankers and America's debts are their problems. If you are the average American, would you risk your future and your children's future on your President making a reckless bet? Joseph Stiglitz, in an open letter to the American public, with nine other American Nobel Prize winners in economics, said this about President Bush: *"President Bush and his administration*

31

have embarked on a reckless and extreme course that endangers the long-term economic health of our nation.[14]*"*

I am going to reveal to you one other insider information. It may mean nothing to you. But when this group of people dump the dollar in a big way, it means trouble, big trouble.

You may be surprised to know that the world's financial system is awash with cocaine and heroin money (and monies from whatever illicit drugs that you can think of). The drug business is a $500 billion a year business, and growing. I am being conservative here. Where do you think the money is stashed? Not in a shoe box, that's for sure. It is in the system. So when the mafia bosses (not your Italians in New York but the mean Russians and those in the breakaway Muslim Central Republics), the Columbian and Afghan drug cartels and the international arms dealers see their hard-earned money depreciate by some 20% – 30% or more, they are not going to stand pat. They are going to do something about it. Drug kingpins and others who indulge in funny businesses like big denomination notes, big amounts in small packages, less to carry and easier to move. The euros have 200 and 500 denominations, whereas the most common and easily available greenback is the $100 bill. So now, if you are a drug kingpin and you are counting your money in Columbia, Hong Kong or some corner in Afghanistan and the scenario is as painted above, what would be your next move?

Think about it.

Their girlfriends and mistresses are already complaining that they are not getting as much diamonds and fur coats from their pocket money. Next thing you know, grandma is going to get mad as well.

Let me share something with you now. What could really up-end the apple cart is not any of the four scenarios painted by the optimistic professor. It is something more frightening and I will share this with you later. **When the hidden enemy opens his hands and deals the last card, be prepared for the meltdown. It will be ugly. They would want blood on the streets to further their hidden agenda.**

ENDNOTES:

1. Alan Fram, "Senate OKs $800 billion Debt Limit Hike" Guardian Unlimited, 18th November, 2004.

2. The quotations can be found @ www.margotbworldnews.com

3. Arnaud de Borschgrave, "Our Disappearing Dollar", 18th December, 2004, Pittsburgh Tribune Review

4. Jim Landers, "Weak Dollar May Threaten Balance", 19th December, 2004, the Dallas Morning News

5. Quoted in the Western Mail, Tuesday 28th February, 1995

6. Adam Hamilton, "JPM Derivatives Monster Grows", www.ZealLLC.com

7. James Ridgeway, "Homeland Insecurity", The Village Voice, 30th December, 2004

8. Businessweek Online, 6th December, 2004: "The China Price".

9. Pedro Nicolaci da Costa, "Krugman: Economic Crisis a Question of When, Not If", Reuters, 22nd November 2004 @ www.reuters.com

10. Ibid.

11. Ibid.

12. In 2001, Argentina defaulted on an estimated $100 billion debt, the largest in modern economic history.

13. "Apocalypse Not Yet" Tompaine.com interview with James K Galbraith, Lloyd M Bentsen Jr. Chair in government/business relations at the Lyndon B Johnson School of Public Affairs, The University of Texas at Austin and senior scholar at the Levy Economics Institute.

14. Joseph Stiglitz, "Bush is Dead Wrong", the Guardian 6th October, 2004.

2

Lies, Deceptions, Frauds and Criminal Conspiracies

The average American may not know that the Declaration of Independence of the United States in 1776 has inspired a generation of liberation fighters, pre- and post-Second World War. It may also come as a surprise to Americans that it inspired Ho Chi Minh sufficiently, to have it referenced in the Declaration of Independence of the then Democratic Republic of Vietnam on September 2, 1945. I would like to quote the relevant parts of the Declaration read by Ho Chi Minh on that historic day:

"'All men are created equal. They are endowed by their creator with certain inalienable rights, among these are Life, Liberty, and the pursuit of Happiness.'

"This immortal statement was made in the Declaration of Independence of the United States of America in 1776. In a broader sense, this means: All the peoples on earth are equal from birth, all the peoples have a right to live, to be happy and free.

"The Declaration of the French Revolution made in 1791 on the Rights of Man and the Citizen also states: 'All men are born free and with equal rights, and must always remain free and have equal rights.' Those are undeniable truths.

"After the Japanese had surrendered to the Allies, our whole people rose to regain our national sovereignty and to found the Democratic Republic of Vietnam.

"The truth is that we have wrested our independence from the Japanese and not the from French.

"The French have fled, the Japanese have capitulated, and Emperor Bao Dai has abdicated. Our people have broken the chains which for nearly a century have fettered them and have won independence for the Fatherland. Our people at the same time have overthrown the monarchic regime that has reigned supreme for dozens of centuries. In its place has been established the present Democratic Republic.

"For these reasons, we, members of the Provisional Government, representing the whole Vietnamese people, declare that from now on we break off all relations of a colonial character with France; we repeal all the international obligations that France has so far subscribed to on behalf of Vietnam and we abolish all the special rights the French have unlawfully acquired in our Fatherland.

"The whole Vietnamese people, animated by a common purpose, are determined to fight to the bitter end against any attempt by the French colonialists to re-conquer their country.

"We are convinced that the Allied nations which at Tehran and San Francisco have acknowledged the principles of self-determination and equality of nations will not refuse to acknowledge the independence of Vietnam.

"A people who have courageously opposed French domination for more than eighty years, a people who have fought side by side with the Allies against the fascists during these last years, such a people must be free and independent.

"For these reasons, we, members of the Provisional Government of the Democratic Republic of Vietnam, solemnly declare to the world that Vietnam has the right to be a free and independent country and, in fact, it is so already. The entire Vietnamese people are determined to mobilize all their physical and mental strength, to sacrifice their lives and property in order to safeguard their independence and liberty."

One would have thought that if there is one nation that would appreciate these lofty sentiments, it must be the United States. America was in the eyes of Ho Chi Minh and his peasant soldiers, an ally in the Second World War. The Tehran and San Francisco principles of self-determination gave hope to all oppressed people under the yoke of colonialism. Peoples across Asia made huge sacrifices to enable the Allied Powers to defeat fascism. But their legitimate hopes for freedom and independence were dashed by empire ambitions of the ruling Zionist Anglo-American Power Elite, spurred on by other European neocolonialists.

This is essentially the history of post-Second World War, how the propaganda lie, the need to resist the Soviet Union and the communist hordes, legitimized the US barbaric interventions in support of brutal fascist regimes in Latin America, Africa and many parts of Asia. The Iron Curtain was the fiction of Sir Winston Churchill, but this psychological barrier crippled the minds of a generation. The best of our generation were pitted against each other in struggles orchestrated by the CIA and British intelligences. Till today, within the corridors of power of former colonies, there are civil service Mandarins who are still carrying the baggage left over by "Mother England," fifth columns for the Zionist Anglo-American Power Elites.

The Zionist Anglo-American Power Elites are still at it, meddling all over the world, lying to the American people, and putting fear into them. The last time, it was the Soviet communists. Today, the enemy is the Muslim fanatics. And they are already conditioning our minds that the enemy of the future will be the yellow hordes from China. What they failed to do with opium in suppressing the proud and resilient Chinese people during the 19th and 20th centuries, they will endeavor to do with the most heinous chemical, biological and space-based environmental weapons, the next time round. I offer no apologies for being unable to see conflict in international relations in plain simple terms as a contest between capitalism versus communism, good versus evil. Ideologies are mere camouflage for more mundane objectives — **war profits.** And there cannot be wars unless there are two opposing sides. History has shown that **war profiteers provoke wars and then fund both sides,** and regardless which side wins, their bounty is assured. For starters, just ask the Bush Dynasty how they got their billions. In case you forgot, grandfather Prescott Bush financed Hitler. **The real enemy remains hidden, the Zionist Anglo-American war profiteers and banking houses.**

I would like to invite you once again to ponder on what Professor James K. Galbraith has to say on this:

"For decades, the Western World tolerated the 'exorbitant

privilege' of a dollar reserve economy because the United States was the indispensable power, providing reliable security against communism and insurrection without intolerable violence or oppression, thus conditions under which many countries on this side of the Iron Curtain grew and prospered. Those rationales evaporated 15 years ago, and the 'Global War on Terror' is not a persuasive replacement.[1] "

Since there are no more commies to fight, the Zionist Anglo-American Power Elites have to create new enemies — the Osama bin Laden and the Jihadists. So now we have the "War on Terror". When a government repeatedly lies to its people for profits and power, and systematically erodes the constitutional rights of the people, it is a reflection that its very core is evil and morally bankrupt. And this is another key indicator of the impending demise of the Zionist Anglo-American Empire. And one of the consequences arising from such a state of affairs has been adequately spelt out in the Declaration of Independence of July 4, 1776, and I quote:

"We hold these truths to be self-evident, that all men are created equal, that they are endowed by their Creator with certain unalienable Rights, that among these are Life, Liberty, and the pursuit of Happiness. That to secure these rights, Governments are instituted among Men, deriving their just powers from the consent of the governed. <u>That whenever any Form of Government becomes destructive of these ends, it is the Right of the People to alter or to abolish it, and to institute new Government, having its foundation on such principles and organizing its powers in such form, as to them shall seem most likely to effect their Safety and Happiness.</u> Prudence, indeed, will dictate that Governments long established should not be changed for light and transient causes; and accordingly all experience hath shown that mankind are more disposed to suffer, while evils are sufferable, than to right themselves by abolishing the forms to which they are accustomed. <u>But when a long train of abuses and usurpations pursuing invariably the same Object evinces a design to reduce them under absolute Despotism, it is their right, it is their duty, to throw off such Government, and to provide new Guards for their future security. Such has been the patient suffrance of these Colonies; and such is now the necessity which constrains them to alter their</u>

former Systems of Government. The history of the present King of Great Britain is a history of repeated injuries and usurpations, all having in direct Object the establishment of an absolute Tyranny over these States." (Emphasis added)

Substitute the King of Great Britain with past Presidents of the United States in the last sixty years, and the consequences of blowback are inevitable. However, thus far, political pundits have written about the blowback from the "colonies". The blowback from within America is yet to come, but it will come. Of this I will address later.

What is the long train of abuses and usurpations committed by the Zionist Anglo-American establishment and the U.S. administrations in the last sixty years? To these we shall now turn our attention.

I shall start with President Bush, the neocons, and the poodle Blair.

On May 28, 2003, Paul Wolfowitz, the Deputy Secretary of Defense in his usual candor made the shocking admission that the invasion was based on one overriding concern:

*"For **bureaucratic reasons,** we settled on one issue, weapons of mass destruction, because it was the one reason everyone could agree on.*[2]*"* (Emphasis added)

This was the best propaganda tool for war, for the invasion of Iraq. This has been conveniently overlooked. Instead, a whole new industry has grown churning out all sorts of spin regarding intelligence failures. Every one seems to have forgotten this brutal admission. Obviously, something must be done to soothe their conscience (if any).

Take another brutal admission: The White House Press Conference on January 31, 2003, with President Bush and Prime Minister Blair.

Adam Boulton, Sky News (London): *"One question for you both. Do you believe that there is a link between Saddam Hussein, a direct link, and the men who attacked on September 11?"*

The President: *"I can't make that claim."*

The Prime Minister: *"That answers your question."*

In a February, 2001, meeting with Egypt's foreign minister in Cairo, Secretary of State, Colin Powell defended the efficacy of UN sanctions in containing Saddam Hussein's WMD ambitions:

"Frankly, they have worked. He has not developed any significant capability with respect to weapons of mass destruction. He is unable to project conventional power against his neighbors.[3]*"*

Yet surveys showed that the majority of Americans believed that Saddam Hussein had ties with Al Qaeda and was responsible for September 11, and that Iraq had weapons of mass destruction. In August, 2002, an ABC News/Washington Post poll found that 79% of Americans felt that Iraq posed a threat to the United States. A December, 2002, Los Angeles Times poll showed that 90% of Americans thought Saddam Hussein was developing WMDs. And a September, 2003, Washington Post poll found that 69% of Americans believed Saddam was personally involved in the September 11 attacks.[4]

Yet the establishment mass media chose to ignore the above-mentioned frank and unambiguous admissions. Instead, they confused the issue by giving extensive coverage to the lies and deceptions and failed to highlight the inherent contradictions of the press statements by the President and the neocons until after the invasion and when the war got real messy. Here are some samples:

President George W. Bush, Speech to UN General Assembly, September 12, 2002: *"Right now, Iraq is expanding and improving facilities that were used for the production of biological weapons."*

Donald Rumsfeld, Testimony to Congress, September 19, 2002: *"No terrorist state poses a greater or more immediate threat to the security of our people and the stability of the world than the regime of Saddam Hussein in Iraq."*

White House Spokesman, Ari Fleischer, Press Briefing, January 9, 2003: *"We know for a fact that there are weapons there."*

President George W. Bush, State of the Union Address, January 28, 2003: *"Our intelligence officials estimate that Saddam Hussein had the materials to produce as much as 500 tons of sarin, mustard, and VX nerve agents. The British gov-*

ernment has learned that Saddam Hussein recently sought significant quantities of uranium from Africa."

Colin Powell, Statement to UN Security Council, February 5, 2003: *"We know that Saddam Hussein is determined to keep his weapons of mass destruction, is determined to make more... He is so determined that he has made repeated attempts to acquire high-specification aluminum tubes from 11 different countries even after inspection resumed. We also have intelligence from multiple sources that Iraq is attempting to acquire magnets and high speed balancing machine to enrich uranium."*

White House Spokesman Scott McClellan, Press Briefing, February 10, 2003: *"This is about an imminent threat."*

Vice-President, Dick Cheney, NBC Meet the Press, March16, 2003: *"We believe [Hussein] has, in fact, reconstituted nuclear weapons."*

President George W. Bush, Address to U.S., March 19, 2003: *"The people of the United States and our friends and allies will not live at the mercy of an outlaw regime that threatens the peace with weapons of mass murder."*

Gen. Tommy Franks, Press Conference, March 22, 2003: *"There is no doubt that the regime of Saddam Hussein possesses weapons of mass destruction. And as this operation continues, those weapons will be identified, found, along with the people who have produced them and who guard them."*

Defense Policy Board Member, Kenneth Adelman, quoted in The Washington Post, March 23, 2003: *"I have no doubt we're going to find big stores of weapons of mass destruction."*

Donald Rumsfeld, ABC Interview, March 30, 2003: *"We know where they are. They are in the area around Tikrit and Baghdad and east, west, south and north somewhat."*

Colin Powell's remarks to reporters, May 4, 2003: *"I'm absolutely sure that there are weapons of mass destruction there and the evidence will be forthcoming. We're just getting it just now."*

After the rape and plunder and slaughter of thousands, and still not having found anything, President Bush and his chorus sang a different tune. Read these snippets:

Donald Rumsfeld, Fox News Interview, May 4, 2003: *"We never believed that we'd just tumble over weapons of mass destruction in that country."*

President George W. Bush, remarks to reporters, May 6, 2003: *"I'm not surprised if we began to uncover the weapons program of Saddam Hussein — because he had a weapons program."*

It should be noted that President has shifted his stance. The certainty is not actual weapons of mass destruction, but **programs for WMD**.

Condoleezza Rice, Reuters Interview, May 12, 2003: *"U.S. officials never expected that 'we were going to open garages and find' weapons of mass destruction."*

Donald Rumsfeld, Senate Appropriations Sub-Committee on Defense Hearing, May 14, 2003: *"I don't believe anyone that I know in the administration ever said that Iraq had nuclear weapons."*

Lt. Gen. James Conway, 1st Marine Expeditionary Force, Press Interview, May 30, 2003: *"It was a surprise to me then — it remains a surprise to me now — that we have not uncovered weapons, as you say, in some of the forward dispersal sites. Believe me, it's not for the lack of trying. We've been to virtually every ammunition supply point between the Kuwait border and Baghdad, but they are simply not there."*

White House Spokesman, Scott McClellan, Press Briefing, January 31, 2004: *"I think some in the media have chosen to use the word 'imminent.' Those were not words we used. We used 'grave and gathering' threat.*[5]*"*

So far, we have examined the lies and deceptions of the U.S. regime. The position of poodle Blair and the British regime is no different. A few quotes will suffice:

Jack Straw, Foreign Secretary, April 2, 2003: *"Saddam's removal is necessary to eradicate the threat from his weapons of mass destruction."*

41

Tony Blair, March 18, 2003: *"We are asked to accept Saddam decided to destroy those weapons. I say that such a claim is palpably absurd."*

Tony Blair, April 28, 2003: *"Before people crow about the absence of weapons of mass destruction, I suggest they wait a bit."*

One may very well ask, why such a massive campaign of lies, deceptions and disinformation? The answer is that people don't want wars and having their husbands, brothers, sisters and boyfriends killed or maimed for life. But they can be persuaded to go to war. The method is simple as explained by Hitler's Luftwaffe chief, Hermann Goering at the time of the Nuremberg War Crimes trials:

"People don't want war. But they can always be brought to the bidding of the leaders. That is easy. All you have to do is tell them they are being attacked and denounce the pacifists for lack of patriotism and exposing the country to danger."

The neocons' campaign to deceive the American people to support the illegal war, has raised the propaganda bar to a whole new level, far more lethal and sophisticated that what the Nazis ever conceived during the Second World War. Without a doubt, Karl Rove is a genius in this department. To get away with so much spin and hype, in spite of the unprecedented access of the American people to the mass media, is unparalleled in modern psychological warfare. There were over ten million worldwide who protested against the invasion, and the European press were highly critical of the war. Yet, the polls showed that the average American believed the Bush regime's propaganda machine. It was an incredible display of totalitarian control of information and the mass media. Even in his wildest imagination, Stalin would not have been able to conjure such total propaganda control.

Let me endeavor to put the issue in perspective. Dato Seri Dr. Mahathir Mohamad, the then Prime Minister of Malaysia[6] was one of the most vocal opponents of the invasion of Iraq, yet *prior* to the invasion, the local mass media failed to *adequately* expose the lies, deceptions and frauds of the Bush regime. They were uncritically downloading the propaganda stories from the major news services, even the headlines. The same can be said of the mass media in most countries of Asia, Africa and Latin America. My critics and supporters of the local mass media may take offense and disagree. But how else can we explain the almost total news blackout of the deliberations at the Security Council, wherein Hans Blix[7] and Mohammed Elbaradei[8] systematically debunked every lie and deception churned out by Colin Powell.

There were no headlines or lead stories of any substance that cried out:

"The Nuclear weapons program is defunct."

"There is no indication of resumed nuclear activities or prohibited activities."

"There is no indication that Iraq is attempting to import enriched uranium."

There is no indication that Iraq is attempting to import tubes for uranium enrichment."

"There is no indication to date that Iraq imported magnets per se in centrifuge developments."

With regard to chemical and biological weapons, Han Blix was equally emphatic in exposing the Bush/Blair lies and even commented that the then ongoing inspections had "few difficulties." This is what Han Blix said:

"Iraq had been forthcoming."

"Inspections are moving forward."

"They have made important progress."

"No evidence so far has been found for mobile biological weapons units."

"No underground facilities were found for chemical and biological weapons (so far).[9]"

However, the most telling exposure of Bush/Blair lies must be the testimony of Elbaradei regarding U.S., British and Israeli intelligences on the alleged purchase of uranium from Niger, the "yellow cake" story. And I quote:

"Iraq has provided a comprehensive explanation of its relation with Niger. The IA was able to review correspondence from the government of Niger and compare full format contents

and signature of that correspondence with those of the alleged procurement related documentation. Based on thorough analysis the IA has concluded, with concurrence of outside experts, that these documents which formed the basis for the reports of recent uranium transactions between Iraq and Niger are, in fact, not authentic.[10] "

There can only be one conclusion, and one conclusion only. The U.S. and British governments lied and provided false documents, to wit forgeries, to the UN to justify their illegal war plans and the brutal invasion of Iraq. This is a war crime by any legal interpretation. While a war crime tribunal has been constituted against Milosevic for alleged war crimes, there are no indictments against Bush and Blair on uncontroverted evidence duly recorded in the proceedings of the UN Security Council. The mass media of the member countries of NAM (Nonaligned Movement) and the OIC (Organization of Islamic Conference) should hang their heads in shame for failing, till to date, to launch a worldwide media counter-offensive, and to call for war crime indictments against President Bush, Prime Minister Blair, Prime Minister Howard and the neocons. Such is the hypocrisy and political impotence!

There is one more issue we need to nail down and debunk — the issue of intelligence failures. This is horseshit, bullshit and whatever else you may want to call it. The intelligence prior to the invasion, specifically prior to the publication of the October, 2002 National Intelligence Estimate (NIE), was spot on and corroborated in all material particular with the findings of the UN inspectors.[11] A study by the renowned Carnegie Endowment of International Peace entitled "WMD in Iraq, Evidence and Implications" has settled the issue once and for all.[12]

In summary, the said study analyzed the (i) intelligence prior to the publication of the October, 2002 NIE; (ii) the October, 2002 NIE; (iii) the findings of the UN weapons inspectors in March, 2003; and (iv) the findings of the Iraq Survey Group compiled after the March, 2003 invasion. The study concluded that the most accurate was that of the findings of the UN weapons inspectors, followed by the intelligence gathered before publication of the CIA's October, 2002 NIE. The Iraq Survey Group has since confirmed the findings of the UN weapons inspectors. The October, 2002 NIE prepared by the CIA was deemed consistently inaccurate and/or misleading.

The issue therefore **is not intelligence failure**. What the Bush regime and the CIA did was to present a falsified document, by way of the October, 2002 National Intelligence Estimate. The National Intelligence Estimate is considered by Congress and the American people to be the most thorough, accurate and detailed intelligence given to a President. Few would challenge its integrity and that is how the scam was played out. It was a confidence trick par excellence. The Bush regime even tricked its own lapdogs, the most pathetic being David Kay, the head of the Iraq Survey Group, a seasoned CIA operative, who was spying for the U.S. while as a member of the UN inspection team in Iraq that was withdrawn by the UN in 1998. While working as an inspector, he passed bombing target intelligence to the Clinton administration. Clinton unleashed a bombing campaign against Iraq to divert attention from the Monica Lewinsky sex scandal. It is indeed sweet justice that this rabid warmonger had to admit that he was conned by his boss and the neocons. In shame, he declared:

"We were almost all wrong and I certainly include myself here." There is deceit in this contrition. No one that mattered got it wrong. Not the UN weapons inspectors or the intelligence officials whose findings were made prior to the October, 2002 NIE. David Kay was played like a fiddle and it must have been mind-shattering for him to realize that he was part of the con. He told the Senate Armed forces Committee on January 28, 2004, *"It turns out that we were all wrong, probably in my judgement, and that is most disturbing."* He had access to all the accurate intelligence, but chose to ignore them as he was hell bent to go to war, as any war-monger properly primed by his master would. This is a critical weak link in the U.S. Empire's armor, but more of this later.

The lies, deceptions and disinformation would not have been effective had the mass media not been complicit in hyping the propaganda for war. At present, six corporations are in control of the major U.S. mass media. Rupert Murdoch's News Corporation manipulates Fox, HarperCollins, New York Post, DirecTV and 34 other TV stations; Time-Warner controls AOL, CNN, Warner Bros., Time and over 100 magazines; Disney pulls the strings at ABC, Disney Channel, ESPN, 10 TV and 29 radio stations; Viacom controls CBS, MTV, Nickelodeon, Paramount Pictures, Simon & Schuster and 185 radio stations; General Electric sits on NBC, CNBC, MSNBC, Telemundo, Bravo and 13 TV stations; and Bertelsmann controls Random House and 80 magazines. One company that is closely connected to the Bush regime and unashamedly acts as its mouthpiece is Clear Channel Communications. With 1,200 radio stations, 36 television stations nationwide and 776,000 advertising displays in 66 countries, it is a media power by any reckoning. During the war, the company sponsored several prowar rallies.[13]

A survey conducted by Steve Rendall and Tara Broughel during the first three weeks of the war revealed that the sources for the major evening news shows (ABC, CBS, NBC, CNN, FOX and PBS) were predominantly prowar, from the military, and a majority of former and current government employees. Antiwar sources constituted 10%, academia, think tanks and NGOs made up 4% and government officials who were antiwar numbered 4 as compared to 840 prowar officials.[14] What was truly astounding was the attitude of some of the leading journalists concerning the lies and deceptions perpetrated by Bush's regime. Thomas Friedman of the New York Times comes to mind. He wrote:

"As far as I'm concerned, we do not need to find any weapons of mass destruction to justify this war. Mr. Bush doesn't owe the world any explanations for missing chemical weapons (even if it turns out that the White House hyped this issue). It is clear that in ending Saddam's tyranny, a huge human engine for mass destruction has been broken.[15]"

And we are told that the press is free and honest. Paul Wardman, however, sums up well the state of affairs:

"The unfortunate truth is this: George W. Bush is a fraud.[16]"

This is a damning indictment, but appropriate in the circumstances. He has lied blatantly about Iraq and Saddam Hussein and continues to lie about the health of the economy. However, President Bush is not unique in deceiving his fellow countrymen. He is merely following the footsteps of his predecessors. To them shall we now turn our attention. A few examples will suffice.

When the Vietnam War started, I was still in school and I could not comprehend how patrol boats of a backward country would want to attack a modern destroyer of the U.S. Navy. August 4, 1964 was the day I began in earnest to study about wars and international relations and not before long began to understand the deviousness of big powers in the conduct of their foreign affairs.

It was that fateful day, August 4, 1964, that President Johnson announced on television that he had just ordered U.S. forces to bomb North Vietnam. In retrospect, the rhetoric for war was no different from that of the present Bush regime: the same eagerness to display the military might of the United States and the need to demonstrate that *"you don't mess with the U.S. Empire"*. The justification for war was that, ***"the aggression by terror against the peaceful villagers of South Vietnam has now been joined by open aggression on the high seas against the United States of America... Repeated acts of violence against the armed forces of the United States must be met not only with alert defense, but positive reply. That reply is being given to you as I speak tonight."*** President Johnson assured the American people that, ***"we will seek no wider war."***

The incident alluded to by President Johnson was subsequently referred to as the "Gulf of Tonkin Incident." In fact there were two incidents at the Gulf of Tonkin and it was the second that triggered Johnson's announcement. The first incident took place on August 2, 1964. Unknown to the commander of the destroyer Maddox, who had entered the Gulf on July 31, South Vietnamese Commandos had attacked two North Vietnamese islands a day earlier. Further raids were conducted on August 1, and August 2. The North Vietnamese retaliated and as Maddox was in the vicinity, confronted the destroyer. The brief engagement resulted in one North Vietnamese patrol boat destroyed while the remainder retreated. On August 3, further raids were conducted against North Vietnam's coastline. Intercepts allegedly received by the National Security Agency indicated that the North Vietnamese would mount retaliation operations in the gulf. But there was no attack. Reports of a torpedo attack on the destroyer Maddox were mistaken. The false reports started a chain of events that led to the announcement on August 4, 1964.[17] The second unprovoked Gulf of Tonkin incident was merely a pretext for war.

Stepping back in time for a moment will enable us to have a proper perspective. The Vietnamese people under the leadership of

Ho Chi Minh wanted freedom and independence. Following the 1954 Geneva Conference, they were looking forward to the nationwide elections in 1956 that was stipulated by all the parties to the Geneva Conference. The consensus was that Ho Chi Minh would win by a landslide, as much as 80% of the vote.[18] The United States had other plans for Vietnam and Indo-China as a whole, as was detailed in the National Security Council document, entitled "Reviewing the U.S. policy in the Far East".

The U.S. wanted to intervene in Vietnam and it was a matter of time before they committed their forces. SEATO (Southeast Asia Treaty Organization) was established in anticipation of such an intervention. When Johnson took over the presidency, there was already a substantial presence of military personnel in support of the Diem regime, sent in by President Kennedy. He had already decided to go to war notwithstanding intense debates on the issue. President Johnson explained why he had to go to war thus:

"You see, I was as sure as any man could be that once we showed how weak we were, Moscow and Peking would move in a flash to exploit our weakness. They might move independently or they might move together. But move they would — whether through nuclear blackmail, subversion, with regular armed forces or in some other manner. As nearly as anyone can be certain of anything, I knew they couldn't resist the opportunity to expand their control over the vacuum of power we would leave behind us. And so would begin World War III.[19]"

History has proven President Johnson wrong. There was no power vacuum. Communism did not spread to the rest of Southeast Asia. Vietnam, Laos and Cambodia are thriving independent states, but at horrendous costs. Senator Wayne Morse (D-OR) rightly predicted that, *"history will record that we have made a great mistake in subverting and circumventing the Constitution of the United States by giving the president war making powers in the absence of a declaration of war. What is wrong with letting the Constitution operate as written by our constitutional fathers? Why should we give arbitrary discretion to mere men who happen to hold office at a given time, when the American people and their lives are at the mercy of those mere men?[20]"*

It is telling that the brave senator who defended the Constitution was rejected by the electorate when he sought re-election to the senate. And those who subverted the Constitution, President Johnson and his war cabinet suffered not, but sacrificed 59,000 of the best Americans ever to serve their country. They went to war obediently and to certain death, without ever knowing the reasons for the misadventure and worst, not knowing whether their sacrifice made any difference.

In the 80s, the United States Constitution was subverted again, and, as in the 60s, allegedly for the high ideal of combating communism in Latin America. I refer to the Iran-Contra scandal.

In the early 1980s, President Reagan was confronted with two major dilemmas: (1) How to provide financial support to Nicaraguan exiles, known as Contras, to subvert and overthrow the socialist Sandinista government; and (2) how to obtain the release of American hostages held in Beirut by Islamic militants. The problem was compounded by the fact that Congress had passed the Boland Amendment Act which made it illegal for the CIA and all sectors of the government to aid the Contras or to provoke a war between Nicaragua and Honduras. To circumvent the legal obstacles, the Reagan administration conducted two secret operations. The Iran operations involved efforts in 1985 and 1986 to obtain the release of hostages through the sale of U.S. weapons to Iran (despite an embargo on such sales), who agreed to negotiate the release of the hostages. A total of more than 2,000 missiles and spare parts were sold to Iran. What was most interesting was that Israel, reviled by Iran and most Muslims, acted as the go-between in the arms sale. The Contra operations from 1984 to 1986 were essentially a funding exercise. What finally transpired was that the two operations merged: funds generated from the sale of weapons to Iran were diverted to finance the Contras.

The secret operations were exposed when on October 1986, a U.S. cargo plane was shot down and the sole survivor, one Eugene Hasenfus on being captured, revealed to the Sandinista army that he was in the employ of the CIA. A month after the plane was shot down the illegal arms sale was exposed by a Lebanese magazine. The scandal rocked the very foundations of the establishment. However, the resulting investigations by the Tower Commission was a whitewash, even though the report placed "ultimate responsibility" on the White House, the Commission essentially blamed a "cabal of zealots" who had "undermined the powers of Congress as a co-equal branch and subverted the Constitution." A minority report by the 8 Republicans on the 28-member committee was more generous. They found only errors of judgement, "no constitutional crisis, no systematic disrespect for the rule of law, no grand conspiracy and no administration-wide dishonesty or cover up."

Eleven defendants were convicted of various crimes. Two were overturned on appeal (North and Poindexter) because they were granted immunity by the Tower Commission. One case was dismissed. On December 24, 1992, President Bush pardoned Casper Weinberger, Duane R. Clarridge, Clair E. George, Elliot Abrams, Alan D. Fiers, Jr. and Robert C. McFarlane.

The Final Report[21] of Independent Counsel, Lawrence Walsh concluded that the President's most senior advisers and the Cabinet members participated in the strategy to make National Security staff members McFarlane, Poindexter and North the scapegoats whose sacrifice would protect the Reagan administration in its final two years. The report further concluded that the governmental problems presented by Iran-Contra are not those of rogue operators, but rather those of the Executive Branch to evade congressional oversight. The report also pointed out that congressional oversight alone cannot correct the deficiencies that result when an Attorney-General abandons the law-enforcement responsibilities of that office and undertakes, instead, to protect the President.

In retrospect, no one could paint a better picture of what transpired during those Reagan years than the remark made by then White House chief of staff Donald Regan to the New York Times on August 25, 1988:

"We do many things at the federal level that would be considered dishonest and illegal if done in the private sector."

ENDNOTES:

1. Prof. James K. Galbraith's interview with Tompaine, 6th Dec., 2004 @ www.tompaine.com

2. Quoted by Garland Favorito, "One Nation Betrayed" @ www.blackforestpress.com. Vanity Fair interview with Paul Wolfowitz on 28th May, 2003.

3. A transcript can be found @ http://www.msnbc.com/news/971717.asp

4. Graydon Carter, *What We've Lost*, pg. 31, citing the polls (2004, Little Brown Books).

5. Quotes compiled by Jackson Thoreau @ http://globalresearch.ca/articles/THO402A.html

6. He has been, upon retirement, conferred the Highest Award by the King of Malaysia and is now respectfully addressed Tun Dr. Mahathir Mohamad.

7. He was the then UN Chief Inspector for Chemical and Biological weapons.

8. He was, and still remains so at press time, the Chief UN Nuclear Weapons Inspector.

9. All quotes taken from "Our Nation Betrayed: The Iraq WMD Intelligence Deception" by Garland Favorito @ www.blackforest.com/cat_law_politics.htm

10. Ibid. See also *The Five Biggest Lies Bush Told us About Iraq*, (2003 Akashic Books)

11. The N.I.E. of October, 2002 made several false statements and conclusions, in spite of dissents from other intelligence agencies.

12. See http://www.ceip.org/files/Publications/IraqReport3.asp. See also www.AlterNet.org

13. Amy Goodman, *Exception to the Rulers*, (2004 Hyperion Books)

14. Ibid. See also Extra, May/June 2003, "Amplifying Officials, Squelching Dissent."

15. Thomas L. Friedman, "The Meaning of a Skull", New York Times, April 27, 2003

16. Paul Wardman, *Fraud: The Strategy Behind The Bush Lies And Why The Media Didn't Tell You*, (2004 Sourcebooks Inc)

17. Commander Herrick of Maddox did in fact send a report calling for a review of the situation, "Review of action makes many reported contacts and torpedoes fired appear doubtful. Freak weather effects on radar, and overeager sonar men may have accounted for many reports. No actual visual sightings by Maddox. Suggest complete evaluation before any further action taken." Quoted in *Presidential Decisions — Gulf of Tonkin Attacks*, Vol. 1, cited by Eric Altermann in *When Presidents Lie*, (2004 Penguin Books).

18. This was the estimation of President Eisenhower, *Mandate for Change, 1953-56: The white House Years*, (1963, Doubleday)

19. Eric Altermann, citing Doris Kearns, *Lyndon Johnson and the American Dream* (1976 Harper & Rowe)

20. Ibid., citing Congressional Records, 88th Congress, 1st Sess., August 7, 1964

21. For summary of report, see www.webcom/pinknoiz/covert/icsummary.html

3

In Search of Monsters to Destroy

In declaring the War on Terror, President Bush promised the American people that he will smoke the terrorists out from the caves in Afghanistan and punish the rogue states that gave shelter to the terrorists. He further promised that he will put a stop to the proliferation of nuclear weapons and prevent rogue states from passing weapons of mass destruction to terrorists. He had grand plans to reshape the Middle East, bringing democracy and enlightenment. He targeted three countries as comprising the Axis of Evil: Iran, Syria and North Korea. The agenda was regime change. He warned his nation that the war on terror would be exacting and long-drawn, and probably with no end in sight. The War on Terror was likened to the Crusades. Acting the part of a War President, he threw the challenge, *"Bring them on."* He promised to subjugate the rogue states, forgetting that the U.S. is the biggest rogue state of all.

What William Faulkner said about the past is most poignant. *"The Past is never dead. It isn't even past.*[1]*"* Let us recap:

1. The United States is the first country to have nuclear bombs;

2. The United States is the first country to unleash the nuclear bombs;

3. The United States is the first country to proliferate nuclear weapons, sharing nuclear weapons technology with Britain;

4. The United States is the largest arms supplier in the world;

5. The United States sold arms to Iran as exposed in the Iran-Contra scandal; and

6. The United States armed Saddam Hussein with weapons of mass destruction.

And to this sordid episode, let us now turn.

In 1979, The Shah of Iran was overthrown. The United States thus lost a key ally in the Middle East. Ayatollah Khomeini became an immediate threat to U.S. oil interests in the region. There was also the fear that Khomeini's brand of Islam would spread quickly to the other Gulf States and destabilize the entire region. Saddam Hussein was therefore armed to confront the threat, and so, on September 22, 1980, Iraq launched an invasion of Iran. In the ensuing eight years of war, chemical and biological weapons were used by both sides, resulting in the loss of at least a million lives.

It is interesting to note that in 1982, President Reagan removed Iraq from the State Department's list of countries supporting terrorism, and on December 19-20, 1983, Donald Rumsfeld was dispatched to Baghdad with a handwritten offer for the resumption of diplomatic relations which was severed during the six-day Arab-Israeli War of 1967. How can we forget the smug Rumsfeld shaking hands with Saddam Hussein? This scandal of U.S. arming Iraq was dubbed "Iraqgate" which prompted the right-wing columnist William Safire to lament on December 7, 1992 in the New York Times, *"Iraqgate is uniquely horrendous: a scandal about the systematic abuse of power by misguided leaders of three democratic nations [U.S., Britain and Italy] to secretly finance the arms build up of a dictator."*

Sam Gejdenson, Chairperson of a Congressional subcommittee investigating U.S. exports to Iraq disclosed that the U.S. government approved over 700 licenses for the export of $1.5 billion worth of biological agents and high-tech dual use equipment. A subsequent senate report also revealed that biological and chemical agents, including bacillus anthracis (anthrax) and clostridium botulinum (botulism) were also exported to Iraq. It was also disclosed that exports included precursors to chemical warfare agents, blueprints for chemical and biological facilities and other related equipment. Companies like Hewlett Packard, Unisys, Data General, Honeywell, etc., supplied sophisticated and specialized computers, lasers and testing equipment.

Recent headlines and leading articles in U.S. major mass media exposed the hypocrisy of the U.S. government. Now, cast your eyes on these:

"Officers Say U.S. Aided Iraq in War Despite Use of Gas[2]"

"A covert American program during the Reagan administra-

tion provided Iraq with critical battle planning assistance at a time when American intelligence agencies knew that Iraq commanders would employ chemical weapons in waging the decisive battle of the Iran-Iraq War, according to senior military officers with direct knowledge of the program.

"Those officers, most of whom agreed to speak on the condition that they not be identified, spoke in response to a reporter's question about the nature of gas warfare on both sides of the conflict between Iran and Iraq from 1981 to 1988. Iraq's use of gas in that conflict is repeatedly cited by President Bush and, this week, by his national security adviser, Condoleezza Rice, as justification for regime change in Iraq."

"A Tortured Relationship[3]"

"Indeed, even as President Bush castigates Saddam's regime as a 'grave and gathering danger,' it's important to remember that the United States helped arm Iraq with the very weapons that administration officials are now citing as justification for Saddam's forcible removal from power."

"Following Iraq's Bio-weapons Trail[4]"

"An eight-year-old Senate report confirms that disease-producing and poisonous materials were exported, under U.S. government licenses, to Iraq from 1985 to 1988 during the Iran-Iraq War. Furthermore, the report adds, the American-exported materials were identical to microorganisms destroyed by United Nations inspectors after the Gulf War."

"Iraq Got Germs for Weapons Program from U.S. in 80s[5]"

"The Iraqi bio-weapons program that President Bush wants to eradicate got its start with help from Uncle Sam two decades ago, according to government records that are getting a new scrutiny in light of discussion of war against Iraq.

"The Centers for Disease Control and Prevention sent samples directly to several Iraqi sites that UN weapons inspectors determined were part of Saddam Hussein's biological weapons program, CDC and congressional records from the early 1990s show. Iraq had ordered samples, saying it needed them for legitimate research.

"The CDC and a biological samples company, the American Type Culture Collection, sent strains of all the germs Iraq used to make weapons, including anthrax, the bacteria that make botulinum toxin and the germs that cause gas gangrene, the records show. Iraq also got samples of other deadly pathogens, including the West Nile virus. The transfer came in the 1980s, when the United States backed Iraq in its war against Iran."

"Iraq Used Many Suppliers for Nuke Program[6]"

"Dozens of suppliers, most in Europe, the United States and Japan, provided the components and know-how Saddam Hussein needed to build an atomic bomb, according to Iraq's 1996 accounting of its nuclear program."

Iraq's report says the equipment was either sold or made by more than 30 German companies, 10 American companies, 11 British companies and a handful of Swiss, Japanese, Italian, French, Swedish and Brazilian firms. It says more than 30 countries supplied its nuclear program.

But is Saddam Hussein such a villain as President Bush, poodle Blair and the neocons make him out to be? There is in fact a more sinister villain than Saddam Hussein. For over 50 years, the world, in particular the Third World, was led to believe that this "War Hero" was a man of high morals. The bust of the man has been placed in the Oval Office, as he is an inspiration to President Bush. This sinister chameleon is none other than Winston Churchill, the geopolitical neighborhood bully.

In 1917, following the defeat of the Ottoman Empire, the Middle East was carved out and shared between Britain and France. The British occupied what is now known as Iraq and established a colonial government. The Iraqi people resisted the colonial occupation and revolted. The British could not accept such insolence from *"uncivilized"* tribes, and retaliated by using poison gas against them. The historical records bear witness to this barbaric cruelty.

Departmental Minutes – Churchill, May 12, 1919 War Office[7]

"I do not understand this squeamishness about the use of gas. We have definitely adopted the position at the Peace Conference of arguing in favor of the retention of gas as a per-

manent method of warfare. It is sheer affectation to lacerate a man with the poisonous fragment of a bursting shell and to boggle at making his eyes water by means of lachrymatory gas.

"I am strongly in favor of using poisoned gas against uncivilized tribes. The moral effect should be so good that the loss of life should be reduced to a minimum. It is not necessary to use only the most deadly gasses. Gasses can be used which cause great inconvenience and would spread a lively terror and yet would leave no serious permanent effects on most of those affected."

In the book, ***Iraq: From Sumer to Sudan***,[8] Geoff Simons gave a vivid account of the barbaric manner by which the British massacred the Iraqis and the Kurds. Here are some passages, specifically excerpted for your reading benefit:

"Churchill remained unimpressed by such considerations, arguing that the use of gas, a 'scientific experiment,' should not be prevented 'by the prejudice of those who do not think clearly'. In the event, gas was used against Iraqi rebels with excellent moral effect.

"Wing Commander Sir Arthur Harris (later Bomber Harris, head of wartime Bomber Command) was happy to emphasize that 'Arabs and Kurds now know what real bombing means in casualties and damage. Within forty-five minutes a full size village can be practically wiped out and a third of its inhabitants killed or injured.' It was an easy matter to bomb and machine-gun the tribe's people, because they had no means of defense or retaliation. Iraq and Kurdistan were also useful laboratories for new weapons; devices specifically developed by the Air Ministry for use against tribal villages. The ministry drew up a list of possible weapons, some of them the forerunners of napalm and air-to-ground missiles: Phosphorus bombs, war rockets, metal crowsfeet [to maim livestock], man-killing shrapnel, liquid fire, delay-action bombs. Many of these weapons were first used in Kurdistan."

Winston Churchill's Secret Poison Gas Memo[9]

This secret memo was addressed to General Ismay for C.O.S

Committee, dated July 6, 1944.

"1. I want you to think very seriously over this question of poison gas. I would not use it unless it could be shown either that (a) it was life or death for us, or (b) that it would shorten the war by a year.

"2. It is absurd to consider morality on this topic when everybody used it in the last war without a word of complaint from the moralists or the church. On the other hand, in the last war bombing of open cities was regarded as forbidden. Now everybody does it as a matter of course. It is simply a question of fashion changing as she does between long and short skirts for women.

"3. I want a cold-blooded calculation made as to how it would pay us to use poison gas, by which I mean principally mustered. We will want to gain more ground in Normandy so as not to be cooped up in a small area. We could probably deliver 20 tons to their 1 and for the sake of the 1 they would bring their bomber aircraft into the area against our superiority, thus paying a heavy toll.

"4. Why have the Germans not used it? Not certainly out of moral scruples or affection for us. They have not used it because it does not pay them. The greatest temptation ever offered to them was the beaches of Normandy. This they could have drenched with gas greatly to the hindrance of the troops. That they thought about it is certain and that they have prepared against our use is also certain. But the only reason that they have not used it against us is that they fear the retaliation. What is to their detriment is to our advantage.

"5. Omitted.[10]

"6. ... I should be prepared to do anything that would hit the enemy in a murderous place. I may certainly have to ask you to support me in using poison gas. We could drench the cities of the Ruhr and many other cities in Germany in such a way that most of the population would be requiring constant medical attention. We could stop all work at the flying bomb starting point. I do not see why we should have disadvantages of being the gentleman while they have all the advantages of being the cad. There are

times when this may be so but not now...."

By any stretch of imagination, can we, the people of the Third World accept and believe that the Imperial powers of the past and the present Zionist Anglo-American Empire in their noble misadventures to **"search and destroy monsters"** have our interests at heart, when the majority of those killed are innocent civilians?

Niall Ferguson, historian and author[11] was rather pathetic in his attempt to justify the excesses of the British Empire when he wrote:

"It spread and enforce the rule of law over vast areas. Though it fought many small wars, the Empire maintained global peace unmatched before or since. In the twentieth century too it more than justified its own existence, for the alternatives to British rule represented by the Germans and Japanese Empires were clearly far worse. And without its Empire, it is inconceivable that Britain could have withstood them."

Ferguson seems to have a warped memory and a perverse sense as to how Japan and Germany were defeated in the Second World War. The Russians, at the cost of sixty million people, were primarily responsible for the defeat of the German army. The Battle of Stalingrad was the turning point and not D-Day, on Normandy Beach as has been touted by colonial historians. In the case of Malaya, the British force, more than twice the size of the Japanese army capitulated without much of a fight and surrendered in Singapore, prompting Churchill to declare that it was the most humiliating defeat in the history of the Empire. The Malayan People's Anti-Japanese Army bore the brunt of the resistance and took the fight to the Japanese. And when the Japanese surrendered, the British were no where to be seen. It was only through subterfuge and bribery of sorts that they got to re-colonize Malaya.

Now, let us examine the record of the Zionist Anglo-American Power Elites' quest to seek and destroy monsters for global peace. If Geoff Simons' description of the massacre of the Kurds is anything to go by, then the track record of the Zionist Anglo-American Empire is one of **State Terrorism,** plain and simple. This was achieved through direct and indirect rule, but more often through the latter by the financing and military support of fascist dictators and oligarchies.

The rationale for promoting and sustaining right-wing or fascist dictatorships in furtherance of empire objectives was propounded in

1922 by Elihu Root.[12] The former U.S. Secretary of State justified such support for dictatorships because the populace of the victim country was incapable of democratic rule.[13] Such is the white man's burden as Rudyard Kipling described it when appealing to the U.S. to discharge its imperial responsibilities. It is obvious that the U.S. at the further urging of Elihu Root did respond to that call. However, we should have no illusions that the practice was adopted throughout U.S. history. What Elihu Root did was merely to formalize the practice into a doctrine and gave it an added legitimacy — and it has been applied ever since.

There is a myth about Wilsonian idealism that it concerned itself with the noble virtue of *"redeeming the world by giving it peace and justice.[14]"* President Wilson in fact invaded no less than four countries: Mexico, Haiti, Cuba and the Dominican Republic on behalf of American interests. Between the period of the Spanish American War and the Great Depression, the U.S. dispatched troops to Latin America 32 times and before that, intervened on 103 occasions.

The policy made economic sense, as it was much cheaper than organizing invasions or wars of conquest. Central to the success of the policy was generous support — economic, military and diplomatic — for the local tyrants and their death squads. Presently, in so far as Iraq is concerned, President Bush seems to have departed from the Root Doctrine and opted for invasion, which events have shown to have been rather costly.

Post-Second World War, the Root Doctrine was transformed into the Truman Doctrine. Though the features remained the same, propaganda purports change from civilizing the primitives and conferring imperial prosperity to that of maintaining the free world and preventing it from falling into the clutches of communism. The support of the fascist military Junta in Greece was grounded on the fear that should it fall, then the communist infection would spread to the Middle East, Africa and even Europe. When the U.S. intervened in Vietnam, the theory was relabeled the "Domino Theory." **Once again the Zionist Anglo-American war machine remained hidden.**

Let us now examine briefly the United States' *Legacy of State Terrorism*.

1. Nicaragua: The U.S. involvement in this country started in 1912 when U.S. Marines were sent by President Coolidge in support of the fascist dictatorship of President Adolfo Diaz. The U.S. established the National Guard under the command of Anastacio Somoza who eventually became the President of the moribund state. Every U.S. administration without exception supported the regime until the Somoza regime was overthrown in 1979.[15] During the reign of the Somozas, Nicaragua was used as a launching pad for U.S. military interventions in the neighboring countries of Guatemala in 1954 and Cuba in 1961.

When the Sandinistas seized power, the U.S. carried out subversive operations to destabilize the new administration, leading to the Iran-Contra scandal. What was interesting was that the Sandinistas administration on April 9, 1984 sought the assistance of the International Court of Justice to determine whether the U.S. had violated international law and the several treaties entered into between the two countries. The Court handed down two decisions, one in 1984, when the U.S. was directed to *"respect the sovereignty and political independence of Nicaragua and to cease action affecting Nicaraguan ports, in particular the laying of mines,*[16]*"* and in 1986, where it held that the U.S. contravened international law in arming and financing the Contras, in laying mines in the territorial waters of Nicaragua and other illegal acts and directed that the U.S. pay damages to Nicaragua. But the U.S. refused to abide by the court decisions and has never paid any compensation to that country.

When the matter was brought to the Security Council, the U.S. exercised her veto powers to nullify the resolution calling for her compliance. On November 3, 1986, when the issue came before the General Assembly, 94 countries voted in favor, 47 abstained and three opposed, namely, the U.S. herself, and two of her cronies: El Salvador and Israel. And *now* the U.S. has the audacity to lecture other countries to respect international law.

In Chapter Two, I drew your attention to the Iran-Contra scandal. Go to any bookshop or library and, with little effort, you will be able to find books on that scandal. What is harder to find are books, articles in prestigious journals or news reports relating to the landmark decision of the International Court of Justice in **Nicaragua vs United States of America (1986) ICJ Reports.**[17]

The attention was diverted to the Iran-Contra scandal, and although it exposed the corruption of the Reagan administration and the subversion of the U.S. Congress, the far more important issue of the aforesaid case was slam-dunked into the memory hole, and for a good reason. The timing of the exposure of the Iran-Contras scandal cannot be coincidental, as the judgment was handed down in June 27, 1986. The case is of historic importance, **as the United States is the first nation post Second World War to have been adjudged of having contravened International Law by conducting an illegal war against Nicaragua.**[18]

Isn't it incredible that a poor country, which had been portrayed by the U.S. propaganda machine as a pariah, took the battle with the United States to the International Court of Justice? One would have thought that the U.S., which boasts of having some of the most prestigious law schools in the world and internationally renowned law professors and attorneys, would have trounced the Sandinista government and teach them a lesson or two in international law. But instead, the U.S. government has the audacity to submit that the Court has no jurisdiction, and when the Court ruled otherwise, refused to take any further part in the proceedings. I would urge every American and, for that matter, every citizen of the world to read the entire judgement.

But for the purpose of this book, I shall only highlight the most salient part of the judgement. The Court ruled as follows:

a) By **eleven votes to four** decides that in adjudicating the dispute brought before it by the Application filed by the Republic of Nicaragua on April 9, 1984, the Court is required to apply the "multi treaty reservation" contained in proviso *(c)* in the declaration of acceptance of jurisdiction made under article 36, paragraph 2, of the Statute of the Court by the Government of the United States of America deposited on August 26, 1946.

b) By **twelve votes to three** rejects the justification of collective self-defense maintained by the United States of America in connection with the military and paramilitary activities in and against Nicaragua, the subject of this case.

c) By **twelve votes to three** decides that the United States of America, by training, arming, equipping, financing and supplying the contra forces or otherwise encouraging, supporting and aiding military and paramilitary activities in and against Nicaragua, has acted, against the Republic of Nicaragua, in breach of its obligation under customary international law not to intervene in the affairs of another state.

d) By **twelve votes to three** decides that the United States of America by certain attacks on Nicaragua territory in 1983-1984, namely attacks on Puerto Sandino on September 13 and October 14, 1983; an attack on Corinto on October 10, 1983; an attack on Potosi Naval Base on January 4/5, 1984; an attack on San Juan del Sur on March 7, 1984; attacks on patrol boats at Puerto Sandino on March 28 and 30, 1984; an attack on San Juan del Norte on April 9, 1984; and further by those acts of intervention referred to in subparagraph (3) hereof which involve the use of force, has acted, against the Republic of Nicaragua, in breach of its obligations under customary international law not to use force against another state.

e) By **twelve votes to three** decides that the United States of America by directing or authorizing over Rights of Nicaraguan territory, and by the acts imputable to the United States referred to in subparagraph (4) hereof, has acted, against the Republic of Nicaragua, in breach of its obligation under customary international law not to violate the sovereignty of another state.

f) By **twelve votes to three** decides that, by laying mines in the internal or territorial waters of the Republic of Nicaragua during the first months of 1984, the United States of America has acted, against the Republic of Nicaragua, in breach of its obligations under customary international law not to use force against another state, not to intervene in its affairs, not to violate its sovereignty and not to interrupt peaceful maritime commerce.

g) By **fourteen votes to one** decides that the United States of America, by failing to make known the existence and location of the mines laid by it, referred to in subparagraph (6) hereof, has acted in breach of its obligations under customary international law in this respect.

h) By **fourteen votes to one** that the form and amount of such reparation, failing an agreement between the Parties, will be settled by the Court, and reserves for this purpose the subsequent procedure in this case.

i) **Unanimously** recalls to both Parties their obligation to seek a solution to their disputes by peaceful means in accordance with international law.

From the aforesaid salient points of the judgment, it is clear that Nicaragua has exposed the hypocrisy of the United States as a champion for international law. And further, by her action in referring the dispute to the ICJ, Nicaragua has in fact upheld her obligation to resolve disputes by peaceful means. I am proud to say that my lecturer in international law, Mr. Ian Brownlie, Q.C., F.B.A., Chichele Professor of Public International Law at the University of Oxford while I was studying at the Inns of Court School of Law[19] was the lead counsel for the Republic of Nicaragua.

I shall now turn to some critical facts and admissions by the U.S. Government in which the ICJ took cognizance.

On October 19, 1983, nine days after the attack on Corinto, a question was put to President Reagan at a press conference. The Court was supplied a copy of the transcript, which read as follows:

Question: "Mr. President, regarding the recent attacks on a Nicaraguan oil depot, is it proper for the C.I.A. to be involved in planning such attacks and supplying equipment for air raids? And do the American people have a right to be informed about any C.I.A. role?"

The President: "I think covert actions have been a part of government and a part of government's responsibilities for as long as there has been a government. I'm not going to comment on what, if any, connection such activities might have had with what has been going on with some of the specific operations down there. But I do believe in the right of a country when it believes that its interests are best served to practice covert activity and then, while your people may have a right to know, you can't let your people know without letting the wrong people know, those that are in opposition to what you're doing."

The decision of the ICJ has shown just how wrong President Reagan was in thinking that he could act as a bully.

2. <u>El Salvador:</u> In 1932, there was a peasant revolt following the collapse of the economy when food prices skyrocketed, and the main export, coffee, suffered a drastic fall in prices. The rebellion was brutally put down. It was estimated that at least 30,000 peasants were killed by security forces under the dictatorship of General Martinez. Initially, the U.S. did not recognize the regime but ultimately established diplomatic relations in 1934. In justifying the massacre, the State Department labeled the peasants revolt as a communist insurgency. In the 80s, U.S. aid was channeled into the reorganization of the El Salvador's security system and paved the way for the establishment of death squads.[20] The repression was so harsh that over 75,000 were massacred and a quarter of the population was displaced. When a ceasefire was established in 1992, the United Nations established a Truth Commission to investigate into the horrors that took place in the past decades and to facilitate reconciliation. It is not within the scope of this book to analyze in detail the Report of the Truth Commission[21], but suffice to say that the military Junta was responsible for the death squads. The assassination of Archbishop Oscar Anulfo Romero was an example of the work of the death squads. When over 100,000 people gathered for his funeral, the security forces fired upon the mourners and killed at least forty. The report also exposed the torture, rape and murder of three American nuns and one lay missionary and the cover-up by the authorities. Yet, we have Jeanne Kirkpatrick who offered her opinion that the El Salvador government was not complicit to the murders. She conjectured:

"I don't think the government was responsible. The nuns were just not nuns; the nuns were political activists. We ought to be a little clear-cut about this than we usually are. They were political activists on behalf of the Frente and somebody who is using violence to oppose the Frente killed them.[22]"

The then Secretary of State, Alexander Haig was even more ludicrous when he said:

"I would like to suggest to you that some of the investigations would lead one to believe that perhaps the vehicle that the nuns were riding in had tried to run a roadblock or may have accidentally been perceived to have been doing so, and there may have been an exchange of fire.[23]"

To the above ridiculous suggestions, the American member of the Truth Commission, Professor Buergenthal denied having received any evidence in support of the said allegations and said, *"No. The statement is outrageous.[24]"*

And those nuns were Americans!

3. Guatemala In 1954, the C.I.A. engineered the overthrow of the democratically elected government of Jacobo Arbenz in part because of the allegation of an American company, the United Fruit Company, that its extensive agricultural holdings would be expropriated by the government. Thereupon, the C.I.A. ensured over 40 years of military dictatorship and the brutal suppression of the people of Guatemala. Government-sponsored death squads killed lawyers, school teachers, journalists, priest, nuns, trade union leaders, politicians and students. The UN-sponsored Historical Clarification Commission reported that the government exterminated over 200,000 people, mostly Mayans. During the dictatorship of General Efraín Ríos Montt, thousands of Indians were slaughtered on mere suspicions of aiding anti-government forces. Entire villages were destroyed. Yet President Reagan congratulated the war criminal for his dedication to democracy![25]

If anyone wants to know about a personal account of the nightmare that was Guatemala, they need only read the story of the torture and rape of Sister Diana Ortiz.[26] She was gang-raped and tortured repeatedly and suffered more than 100 cigarette burns all over her body. After the torture, she was thrown into an open pit filled with the bodies of men, women and children. Some were dead, and some were alive. The whole pit was swarming with rats. Sister Ortiz recounts her ordeal somewhat in the following words:[27]

"The memories of what I experienced that November day haunt me even now. I can smell the decomposing bodies, disposed of in an open pit. I can see the blood gushing out of the woman's body as I thrust the small machete into her. For you see, I was handed a machete. Thinking it would be used against me, and at that point in my torture wanting to die, I did not resist. But my torturers put their hands on to the handle, on top of mine. And I had no choice. I was forced to use it against another human being. What I remember is blood gushing — spurting like a water fountain — and my screams lost in the cries of the woman. In spite of the memories of the humiliation, I stand with the people of Guatemala. I demand the right to heal and to know the truth. I demand the right to a resurrection."

In the preface to her courageous book, Sister Ortiz had no hesitation in accusing her own country as follows:

"The U.S. government funded, trained, and equipped the Guatemalan death squads — my torturers themselves. The United States was the Guatemalan army's partner in a covert war against a small opposition force — a war the United Nations would later declare as genocidal."

On July 30, 2000 she was conferred by Pope John Paul II, the Teacher of Peace Award.

I believe that I need not go on to illustrate other misadventures of the empire in seeking out monsters. If the story of Sister Diana Ortiz does not shock you and open your eyes to the barbaric legacy of the empire, nothing will.

The good American people must realize that no one and no nation is above the law. Additionally, American patriots must acquaint themselves with their own laws, without which they would be misled by the power elites' propaganda machinery, and once again allow their government to commit war crimes. Ignorance of the law is no defense to a criminal charge.

I would like to conclude this Chapter by reminding the good American people that Article VI, clause 2, of the Constitution of the United States[28] provides that international treaties have the same status as Federal laws. The provision reads:

"This Constitution, and the Laws of the United States which shall be made in Pursuance thereof; and all Treaties made, under the Authority of the United States shall be the Supreme Law of the Land; and the Judges in every State shall be bound thereby, any Thing in the Constitution or Laws of any State to the Contrary notwithstanding."

The above provision clearly states all treaties entered into by the United States shall be the *"Supreme Law of the Land"*. Back in 1928, President Coolidge signed into law the Kellogg-Briand Pact of Paris which was ratified by the Senate. It was named after the U.S. Secretary of State Frank B. Kellogg and the French statesman, Aristide Briand. This treaty outlawed the launching of wars of aggression, following the devastation and horrors of the First World War.

The significance of the treaty was explained in the Nuremberg judgement:

"The question is, what was the legal effect of this pact? The nations who signed the pact or adhered to it unconditionally condemned recourse to war for the future as an instrument of policy, and expressly renounced it. After the signing of the pact, any nation resorting to war as an instrument of national policy breaks the pact. In the opinion of the Tribunal, the solemn renunciation

of war as an instrument of national policy necessarily involves the proposition that such a war is illegal in international law; and that those who plan and wage such a war, with its inevitable and terrible consequences, are committing a crime in so doing.

"The charges in the indictment that the defendants planned and waged aggressive wars are charges of the utmost gravity. War is essentially an evil thing. Its consequences are not confined to the belligerent states alone, but affect the whole world. To initiate a war of aggression, therefore, is not only an international crime; it is the supreme international crime differing only from the other war crimes in that it contains within itself the accumulated evil of the whole."

To avoid further wars of aggression after the Second World War, the Charter of the United Nations, by Article 2, clause 4, reiterated the aforesaid principles stating that *"All members shall refrain in their international relations from the threat or use of force against the territorial integrity or political independence of any state."* And by Article 39, the Charter further provides that it is the Security Council, and not any individual nation, that would *"determine the existence of any threat to the peace, breach of the peace, or act of aggression... and decide what measures to be taken."*

It is clear from these provisions and from the judgement of the ICJ in the case of Nicaragua that the United States has committed, over the last sixty years, the supreme international crime: **waging wars of aggression.** The invasion of Iraq is but another recent example. The United States is indeed a **serial war criminal**.

ENDNOTES:

1. William Faulkner, *Requiem for a Nun*, Act, Scene III.
2. Patrick Tyler, August 18, 2002 New York Times.
3. Chris Bury, September 18, 2002 ABC.
4. Robert Novak, September 26, 2002.
5. Matt Kelly, October 1, 2002, Associated Press
6. December 17, 2002, Associated Press. All the above quotes were cited in Jacob G. Hornberger, "Reagan's WMD Connection to Saddam Hussein", www.fff.org
7. From Companion Vol. 4, Part 1 of the official biography Winston Churchill by Martin Gilbert (London: Heinemann, 1976) Source: http://globalresearch.ca/articles/ CHU407A.html
8. *Iraq: From Sumer to Sudan*, (1994, London: St. Martin's Press).
9. Source: photographic copy of original page memo in Guenther W. Gellermann, *Der Krieg, der nicht stattfand*, Bernard & Greafe Verlag, 1986, pgs. 249-251. Visit: www.globalresearch.ca/articles/CHU407A.html
10. There are all together 7 paragraphs, and I have omitted paragraphs 5 and 7 due to constraints of space. The omission has not diluted the force of the memo in any way.
11. Niall Ferguson, *Empire: How Britain Made The Modern World*, (2004 Penguin Books)
12. I am much indebted to Frederick H Gareau, *State Terrorism and the United States*, (2004, Clarity Press, Inc.) for his brilliant analysis of the Root Doctrine and its application in Latin America, Africa and Asia. This is one book you should have at all times with you.
13. Niall Ferguson seems to agree with this rationale. He explains and justifies the British argument for postponing the transfer of democracy to the colonies was that they were not ready for it.
14. Arthur Schlesinger Jr., "Foreign Policy and the American Character" in the *Cycles of American History* (1986, Houghton Mifflin).
15. In actual fact, the regime was eased out by the U.S. as the rebellion by the Sandinistas was spreading throughout the country. A moderate regime was installed in its place but this proved futile.
16. Everyone's United Nations, U.N., New York, 1986.
17. See www.icj-cij.org/icjwww/cases
18. It does not follow that the various other wars of aggression by the U.S. were not illegal. It is just that Nicaragua, unlike Vietnam, etc., chose to request the ICJ for a determination of the legality of U.S. military actions in Nicaragua.
19. The Inns of Court School of Law, London.
20. For a detailed account of the history of U.S. involvement in El Salvador and Latin America, see Michael McClintok, *The American Connection: Vol.II, State Terror and Popular Resistance In Guatemala* (1985, Zed Books) and *Instruments of State Craft: U.S. Guerrilla Warfare, Counter-Insurgency and Counter-terrorism, 1940-1990* (1992, Pantheon Books). See also Frederick Gareau's *State Terrorism*.
21. For those who are interested, see *From Madness to Hope: the Twelve Year War in El Salvador. Report of the Commission on the Truth for El Salvador*, (1993 United Nations)
22. Lawyers Committee for International Human Rights, *A Report on the Investigation into the Killings of four American Church women in El Salvador* (1981 Appendix 1-4)
23. Frederick Gareau, *State Terrorism*, pg 39.
24. Ibid.
25. Walter LaFeber, *Inevitable Revolutions: the United States in Central America, 2nd Ed.* (1993, W.W. Norton)
26. Sister Diana Ortiz, *The Blindfold Eyes* (2002, Orbis Books)
27. Frederick Gareau, *State Terrorism*, pg 24.
28. More commonly known as the "Supremacy Clause."

4

Crimes Most Foul

The nomination of Alberto Gonzales as the Attorney General has raised quite a storm during the confirmation hearings of the Senate Judicial Committee. No one has questioned how an administration lightweight like Gonzales had the audacity to advice President Bush to ignore the Geneva Conventions and to permit the use of torture on prisoners of war in Afghanistan and in Iraq. While rank and file soldiers are being hauled up before military courts to answer criminal charges, the masterminds have all escaped censure.

The Bush regime's adoption of torture as a policy is but a reflection of the fascist culture that prevails in the United States. The policy is being promoted by a large segment of the establishment. The man who gave respectability to the use of torture is none other than Alan Dershowitz, Harvard University law professor, who finally removed his mask as a civil libertarian and exposed his Zionist core. For the Zionists to use this card and reveal their strategic sleeper or mole is indicative that they were either supremely confident of the outcome in Iraq or that they were desperate, bearing in mind that the war against Saddam was only launched in 2003. This was a classic exercise in preparing public opinion for extreme measures and to instill fear. I believe that the Zionist Anglo-American establishment was hell-bent to go down that slippery road. After all, like Churchill, they were only dealing with "uncivilized tribes."

On November 8, 2001, in a commentary in the Los Angeles Times entitled, *"Is There a Torturous Road to Justice"*, Dershowitz proposed that torture be legalized. And his spurious reasoning was that since the use of torture will in any event be inevitable, let the end justify the means. This is what he wrote:

"I have no doubt that if an actual ticking-bomb situation were to arise, our law enforcement authorities would torture. The real debate is whether such torture should take place outside our legal system or within it. The answer to this seems clear: If we are to have torture, it should be authorized by law."

At the present moment, international as well as most domestic (or municipal) laws prohibit torture, and hence its use is both unlawful and criminal; and the fact that it has been used before — and will be used again — does not in any way inverse its illegality. But notwithstanding, Dershowitz's proposal, however, suggests that: torture should be legalized be it though morally vile and reprehensible; and be it though that confessions extracted therefrom would be of questionable evidential value, and their legal admissibility highly suspect.

To further buttress his argument he went on:

"Democracy requires accountability and transparency, especially when extraordinary steps are taken. Most important, it requires compliance with the rule of law. And such compliance is impossible when an extraordinary technique, such as torture, operates outside the law."

How then is this dilemma to be resolved? The Zionist professor offered this solution:

"Judges should have to issue a 'torture warrant' in each case. Thus we would not be winking an eye of quiet approval at torture while publicly condemning it."

It follows from this, that the evidence obtained under such legalized torture would in fact be admissible, but this hypothesis is evidently dubious as there is no guarantee that legalized torture would do away with unauthorized torture in the new scheme of things. And in a befuddled acknowledgement detrimental to his own lines of argumentation, Dershowitz admitted:

"We know from experience that law enforcement personnel who are given authority to torture will expand its use."

Supposing we have this situation where the enforcement personnel are issued a 'torture warrant' and they proceed to torture the suspect in accordance with the method of torture permissible in that warrant. Now, let's say that the method of torture warranted was the insertion of sterile needles beneath fingernails to cause intense pain, but he is seen as stubbornly refusing to respond to the torture as **they had hoped that he would**. So, the enforcement officers, mayhap in zeal, in desperation, or in vexation break his fingers. The suspect thereupon confesses to the charge against him, rather in surrender to the excruciating agony than otherwise, while his interrogators congratulate themselves on the success **that they had hoped for**.

From just this simple scenario, we can adduce at least two broad categories of difficulties.

First: Who shall see to it that the torture inflicted is in total compliance of the warrant issued? Will an impartial judge be appointed, or an equitable moderator on hand, to witness the interrogations and to ensure that the interrogatee suffers no injustice at the hands of his interrogators?

Second: Who shall decide upon the forms of torture and their degrees of severity: the forms which produce genuine results, not specious ones; and the intensity of the torture that remains within the humanely barbarous threshold without crossing over to the inhumanly barbaric? Would there be an initiation of an international committee (perhaps, under the aegis of the UN) to study, implement and monitor the forms, degrees and results of an 'Approved Standards of Torture'?

Be that as it may, but such convoluted arguments are in no danger of extinction. In fact, it was these serpentine meanderings of pseudo-logic that gave birth to the world's number one hypocrisy: the United States' policy of enforcing non-proliferation of nuclear technology on the one hand, and unashamedly reserving the right to use nuclear weapons to protect its own interests on the other.

However, let's get back to our involute professor. In early January, 2002, he reiterated his 'civilized' proposal when he appeared on "60 Minutes", and I quote:

*"**Every democracy, including our own, has employed torture outside the law. Throughout the years, police officers have tortured murder and rape suspects into confessing – sometimes truthfully, sometimes not truthfully. The 'third degree' is***

all too common, not only on TV shows such as 'NYPD Blue', but in the back rooms of real police station houses. No democracy, other than Israel¹ has ever employed torture within its law....

"In my new book, 'Shouting Fire: Civil Liberties in a Tur-bulent Age,' I offer a controversial proposal designed to stim-ulate debate about this difficult issue. Under my proposal, no torture would be permitted without a torture warrant being issued by a judge. An application for a torture warrant would be based on the absolute need to obtain immediate information in order to save lives coupled with probable cause that the sus-pect had such information and is unwilling to reveal it. The sus-pect would be given immunity from prosecution based on information elicited by the torture.² The warrant would limit the torture to non-lethal means, such as sterile needles being inserted beneath the nails to cause excruciating pain without endangering life.³ It may sound absurd for a distinguished judge to be issuing a warrant to do something so awful, but consider the alternatives: either police torture below the radar screen of accountability, or the judge who issued the warrant would be accountable. Which would be more consistent with democratic values?⁴ "

The ultimate Zionist rationale: a judge who approves torture is better than the police who torture in secret, on the erroneous assumption that all judges are virtuous and incorruptible!

On March 3, 2003 following the capture of Khalid Sheikh Mohamed, the question arose again whether torture should be allowed, if he refused to disclose key intelligence on Al Qaeda. Dershowitz was interviewed by Wolf Blitzer of the CNN.⁵ I shall reproduce a substantial portion of the interview as I believe all law-abiding citizens of America should be exposed to this kind of fascist thinking which has laid the groundwork for the Abu Ghraib Torture scandal. The professor's rationale was given a new twist. This is what he said:

"We have bombed civilian targets during every single one of our wars. We did it in Dresden. We did it in Vietnam, notwith-standing these rules [Geneva Conventions]. So you know, hav-ing laws on the books and breaking them systematically just creates disdain... It's much better to have rules that we can

actually live within. And absolute prohibitions, generally, are not the kind of rules that countries could live within."

Such is the perverse logic of the Harvard law professor. If the U.S. can bomb Vietnamese peasants, Americans ought to be allowed to torture their enemies. A nation under unlawful occupation cannot resist. And if they do, they shall be treated as "non-combatants" and shall therefore be exempted from the protection of the Geneva Conventions. However, the good professor was put to shame when the other guest on the CNN show, Ken Roth, the Executive Director of the Human Rights Watch made the following comments:

"The prohibition on torture is one of the basic absolute prohibitions that exist in international law. It exists in time of peace as well as in time of war. It exists regardless of the severity of a security threat. And the only other comparable prohibition that I can think of is the prohibition of attacking innocent civilians in time of war or through terrorism. If you are going to have a torture warrant, why not create a terrorism warrant. Why not go in and allow terrorists to come forward and make their case for why terrorism should be allowed....

"Yes, that's the ticking-bomb scenario, which everybody loves to put forward as an excuse for torture. Israel tried that. Under the guise of just looking at the narrow exception of where the ticking-bomb is and that you could save poor school children whose bus was about to be exploded some place. They ended up torturing on the theory that — well, it may not be the terrorist, but it's somebody who knows the terrorist or it's somebody who might have information leading to the terrorist. They ended up torturing, say, 90 percent of the Palestinian security detainees they had until finally the Israeli Supreme Court had to say this kind of rare exception isn't working. It's an exception that's destroying the rule. So let us learn a lesson from the Israelis, which is you can't open the door a little bit. If you try, you end up having torture left and right. The other alternative, rather than legitimizing with torture warrants, is to prohibit it and prosecute the offenders. And we have murder on the street every day. We don't ask for murder warrants." (Emphasis added)

It is clear that the Bush regime accepted Dershowitz's arguments. And they didn't just "open the door a little bit"; they gate-crashed the torture chamber! The Gonzales memo[6] and John Yoo's defense of Gonzales is but an echo of the Zionist professor's rationale for torture. It came from the same mould.

But allow me to share this with you: remember, Gonzales and John Yoo are attorneys and they are especially familiar with the penalties relating to war crimes. The Gonzales memo seeks to exempt the entire chain of command from bring prosecuted for war crimes, from the foot soldier to the Commander-in-Chief. This has been admitted by John Yoo[7] when he wrote:

"Gonzales also observed that denying POW status would limit the prosecution of U.S. officials under a Federal law criminalizing a grave breach of the Geneva Conventions."

What the public fails to grasp is that the President of the United States — or for that matter, any head of state — acting on the advice of the legal counsel, or otherwise, has absolutely no constitutional authority to exempt anyone from being prosecuted for war crimes whatsoever.

John Yoo described the situation as, ***"we are in the midst of an unconventional war."*** What he is saying is this: when states go to war, they can bomb cities, kill civilians, conduct special operations to assassinate political leaders, and if they win the bloody war, they need not answer to any war crimes committed; but when an oppressed people under a cruel occupation resort to similar tactics, they are labeled as "terrorists" and, as such, have no rights whatsoever. In essence, he is simply saying that **state terrorism is conventional warfare but wars of liberation are terrorist insurgencies.**

When whole cities are bombed to smithereens, resulting in thousands of civilian casualties, it is "collateral damage". One or two buildings collapse by retaliatory action,[8] and it is "terrorism". The Zionist Anglo-American Empire has slaughtered more people in the last sixty years than any so-called terrorist groups.

Recently, an article by Robert Parry[9] revealed that the Bush regime is considering adopting the brutal practices that were used in Latin America, in particular in El Salvador, appropriately named the

"Salvador Option".[10] Parry wrote:

"...by employing the 'Salvador Option' in Iraq, the U.S. military would crank up the pain, especially in Sunni Muslim areas where resistance to the U.S. occupation of Iraq has been strongest. In effect, Bush would assign other Iraqi ethnic groups the job of leading the 'death squad' campaign against the Sunnis. 'One Pentagon proposal would send Special Forces teams to advise, support and possibly train Iraqi squads, mostly hand-picked Kurdish Perhmerga fighters and Shiite militiamen, to target Sunni insurgents and their sympathizers, even across the border into Syria, according to military insiders familiar with discussions,' Newsweek reported. Newsweek quoted one military source as saying, 'The Sunni population is paying no price for the support it is giving the terrorists... From their point of view, it is cost-free. We have to change that equation....' Many Americans have fantasized about how they would enjoy watching Osama Bin Laden tortured to death for his admitted role in the September 11 attacks. There is also a tough-guy fondness for torture as shown in action entertainment — like Fox Network's '24' — where torture is a common-sense shortcut to get results."

Some of you, on reading this, may be appalled by these developments, especially the revelations about the Abu Ghraib prison tortures. I can still recall the orchestrated chorus that it was only the action of a handful of soldiers, and that it was un-American to indulge in such abuse.

We do have short memories. Let me remind the American people what their leaders have done and condoned these past sixty years. I hope the My Lai massacres still ring a bell. But I will share two more abominable stories with you.

The first story is taken from an article by Doug Ireland in the LA Weekly, entitled **"Teaching Torture".**[11]

"Remember how congressional leaders on both sides of the aisle deplored the torture of prisoners at Abu Ghraib as 'un-American'? Last Thursday, however, the House quietly passed a renewed appropriation that keeps open the U.S.'s most infamous torture-teaching institution, known as the School of the Americas (SOA), where the illegal physical and psychological

75

abuse of prisoners of the kind the world condemned at Abu Ghraib and worse has been routinely taught for years.

"A relic of the Cold War, the SOA was originally set up to train military, police and intelligence officers of U.S. allies south of the border in the fight against insurgencies Washington labeled as 'communists'. In reality, the SOA's graduates have been the shock troops of political repression, propping up a string of dictatorial and repressive regimes favored by the Pentagon.

"The interrogation manuals long used at the SOA were made public in May by the National Security Archive, an independent research group, and posted on its website after they were declassified following the Freedom of Information Act requests by among others, the Baltimore Sun. In releasing the manuals, the NSA noted that they 'describe coercive techniques such as those used to mistreat the detainees at Abu Ghraib'. The Abu Ghraib torture techniques have been field tested by SOA graduates — seven of the U.S. army manuals that were translated into Spanish, used at the SOA's training and distributed to our allies, offered instructions on torture, beatings and assassination. As Dr. Miles Schuman, a physician with the Canadian Centre for Victims of Torture who has documented torture cases and counselled their victims, graphically wrote in May 14, Toronto Globe and Mail under the headline 'Abu Ghraib: The Rule, Not the Exception'."

Alan Dershowitz, please have the decency to apologize for your misleading commentaries and interviews, and resign from your post as a law professor at the Harvard University. The good and innocent American people should not have to bear the burden and suffer the consequences of any blowbacks from your Fascist and Zionist propaganda.

Back to Doug's article, he continues:

"The black hood covering the faces of naked prisoners in Abu Ghraib was known as 'La Capuchi' in Guatemalan and Salvadorean torture chambers. The metal bed frame to which a naked and hooded detainee was bound in a crucifix position in Abu Ghraib was 'La Cama', named for a former Chilean prisoner who survived the U.S.-installed regime of General Augusto

Pinochet. In her case, electrodes were attached to her arms, legs and genitalia, just as they were attached to the Iraqi detainee poised on a box, threatened with electrocution if he fell off. The Iraqi man bound naked on the ground with a leash attached to his neck, held by a smiling young American recruit, reminds me of the son of peasant organizers who recounted his agonizing torture at the hands of the Tonton Macoutes, U.S.- backed dictator John-Claude (Baby Doc) Duvalier's right-hand thugs, in Port-au-Prince in 1984. The very act of photographing those tortured in Abu Ghraib to humiliate and silence parallels the experience of an American missionary, Sister Diana Ortiz, who was tortured and gang-raped repeatedly under supervision of an American in 1989, according to her testimony before the Congressional Human Rights Caucus."

The second story concerns the terror campaign conducted by the U.S. Armed Forces in the Central Highlands in Vietnam, written by Toledo Blade staff writers, Michael D. Sallah and Mitch Weiss, entitled *"Rogue GIs Unleashed Wave of Terror in Central High-lands*[12]*"*. This is a story about an elite U.S. army unit known as Tiger Force and the atrocities that they have committed.

Here are excerpts from that article:

"Though the farmers were not carrying weapons, it didn't matter. No one was safe when the Special Forces arrived on July 28, 1967. No one. With bullets flying, the farmers — slowed by the thick, green plants and muck — dropped one by one to the ground. Within minutes it was over. Four were dead, others wounded. Some survived by lying motionless in the mud. Four soldiers later recalled the assault. 'We knew the farmers were not armed to begin with,' one said, 'but we shot them anyway.'

"For seven months, Tiger Force soldiers moved across the Central Highlands, killing scores of unarmed civilians — in some cases torturing and mutilating them — in a spate of violence never revealed to the American public. They dropped grenades into underground bunkers where women and children were hiding — creating mass graves — and shot unarmed civilians, in some cases as they begged for their lives. They frequently tortured and shot prisoners, severing ears and scalps for souvenirs.

"A review of thousands of classified Army documents, National Archive records, and radio logs reveals a fighting unit that carried out the longest series of atrocities in the Vietnam War — and commanders who looked the other way... No one knows how many unnamed man, women, and children were killed by platoon members 36 years ago. For 4 years, the Army investigated the platoon, finding numerous eye witnesses and substantiating war crimes. But in the end, no one was prosecuted, the case buried in the archives for three decades."

I am sure that just as there are Americans watching Fox Network's "24" and fantasizing torturing Osama Bin Laden, there are also Iraqis and Afghans who would likewise fantasize torturing Professor Dershowitz, turning the screws and inserting sterilized needles beneath his fingernails. I am sure there will be some clerics who will issue a *fatwa*[13] legalizing torture of the likes of the good professor.

Getting rid of people you don't like is also a specialty of the United States. I would like to append below a list of U.S. Government Assassination Plots, taken from the excellent work by William Blum between 1949 and 1991.[14]

1949	Kim Koo, Korean Opposition Leader
1950	CIA/Neo-Nazi hit list of more than 200 political leaders in West Germany in the event of a Soviet invasion; Zhou En Lai, Prime Minister of China; President Sukarno of Indonesia
1951	Kim Il Sung, Premier of North Korea
1952	–
1953	Mohamed Mossadegh, Prime Minister of Iran
1954	–
1955	Jawaharlal Nehru, Prime Minister of India
1956	–
1957	Gamal Abdul Nasser, President of Egypt
1958	–
1959	Norodom Sihanouk, King of Cambodia
1960	Brig Gen. Abdul Karim Kassem, leader of Iraq
1961	Francois "Papa Doc" Duvalier, Haiti; Gen. Trujillo, Dominican Republic

1962	–
1963	Ngo Dinh Diem, President of South Vietnam; Fidel Castro, President of Cuba (several attempts from 60s to 90s)
1964	–
1965	Charles de Gaulle, President of France
1966	–
1967	–
1968	–
1969	–
1970	Gen. Rene Schneider, Commander-in-Chief of Army, Chile; Salvador Allende, President of Chile; Gen. Omar Torrijos, of Panama (also an attempt in 1981)
1971	–
1972	Gen. Manuel Noriega, Panama
1973	–
1974	–
1975	Mobutu Sese Seko, President of Zaire
1976	Michael Manly, Prime Minister of Jamaica
1977	–
1978	–
1979	–
1980	Gaddafi, President of Libya (several times until 1986)
1981	–
1982	Ayatollah Khomeini, leader of Iran
1983	Gen. Ahmed Dlimi, Moroccan Army Commander; Miguel d'Escoto, Foreign Minister of Nicaragua
1984	The nine *comandantes* of the National Directorate of Nicaragua
1985	Sheikh Mohamed Hussein Fadlallah, Lebanese Shiite leader
1986	–
1987	–
1988	–

1989   –

1990   –

1991   Saddam Hussein, President of Iraq.

In 1999, an attempt was made on Slobodan Milosevic, President of Yugoslavia, and in 2003, another attempt was made on Saddam Hussein.

When a nation's moral compass is skewered, that is the surest sign of its impending collapse. When a nation or regime has no sound moral judgments, no respect for the rule of law and compassion for its neighbors, it will first turn its ugliness externally, to plunder and conquer. And when it has exhausted itself and face extinction, it will then turn its sight inwards and oppress its own people.

The PATRIOT Act is already an indication of things to come for the American people. Hopefully, before things turn really ugly, there will be Americans who can recall their Declaration of Independence and respond to the clarion call to overthrow the regime that has made a mockery of their Constitution. It is indeed heartening, for a start, to learn that senior retired generals of the U.S. Armed Forces have written an Open Letter[15] to the Senate Judicial Committee expressing their deep concerns about the nomination of Alberto Gonzales as the next Attorney General. It would be a real shame if the views of the generals are ignored. Their concerns regarding the Geneva Conventions deserve serious consideration. The following excerpt is most pertinent:

"During his tenure as White House Counsel, Mr. Gonzales appears to have played a significant role in shaping U.S. detention and interrogation operations in Afghanistan, Iraq, Guantanamo Bay, and elsewhere. Today, it is clear that these operations have fostered greater animosity toward the United States, undermined our intelligence gathering efforts, and added to the risks facing our troops serving around the world. Before Mr. Gonzales assumes the position of Attorney General, it is critical to understand whether he intends to adhere to the positions he adopted as White House Counsel, or chart a revised course more consistent with fulfilling our nation's complex security interest, and maintaining a military that operates within the rule of law....

80

"Among his past actions that concern us most, Mr. Gonzales wrote to the President on January 25, 2002, advising him that the Geneva Conventions did not apply to the conflict then underway in Afghanistan. More broadly, he wrote that the 'War on Terrorism' presents a 'new paradigm that renders obsolete Geneva's protection.'....

"Perhaps most troubling of all, the White House decision to depart from the Geneva Conventions in Afghanistan went hand in hand with the decision to relax the definition of torture and to alter interrogation doctrine accordingly.... The Army Field Manual was the product of decades of experience — experience that had shown among other things that such interrogation methods produce unreliable results and often impede further intelligence collections. Discounting the Manual's wisdom on this central point shows a disturbing disregard for the decades of hard won knowledge of the professional American military. The United States' commitment to the Geneva Conventions — the Laws of War — flows not only from field experience, but also from the moral principles on which this country was founded, and by which we all continue to be guided. We have learned first hand the value of adhering to the Geneva Conventions and practicing what we preach on the international stage."

The generals who signed the letter are some of the most distinguished military leaders. They are:

General John Shalikashvili (Ret. USA), was the Chairman of the Joint Chiefs of Staff from 1993 till 1997. He was, prior to serving as Chairman, NATO's Supreme Allied Commander for Europe, and was also the Commander-in-Chief of the U.S. European Command.

General Merrill A. McPeak (Ret. USAF) served as the Chief of Staff of the U.S. Air Force. Previously, he served as Commander-in-Chief of the U.S. Pacific Air Forces. He is a command pilot and has flown more than 6,000 hours, principally in fighter aircraft.

General Joseph Hoar (Ret. USMC) was Commander-in-Chief of U.S. Central Command. He was Deputy for Operations for the Marine Corps during the first Gulf War and served as General Norman Schwarzkopf's Chief of Staff at Central Command.

Lieutenant General Claudia J. Kennedy (Ret. USA) was the first and only woman to achieve the rank of a three-star general in the United States Army. She served as Deputy Chief of Staff for Army Intelligence, Commander of the U.S. Army Recruiting Command and as Commander of the 703rd Military Intelligence Brigade in Kunia, Hawaii.

Lieutenant General Robert Gard (Ret. USA) served in the U.S. army and his assignments included combat service in Korea and Vietnam. He is currently President Emeritus of the Monterey Institute for international Studies.

Major General Melvyn Montano (Ret. USAF Nat. Guard) was the Adjutant General in charge of the National Guard in New Mexico from 1994 to 1999. He is the first Hispanic National Guard officer appointed as an Adjutant General in the United States.

Brigadier General David M Brahms (Ret. USMC) served in the Marine Corps from 1963-1988 and was the senior legal adviser for the corps from 1983 until his retirement in 1988.

Brigadier General James Cullen (Ret. USA) is a retired Brigadier General in the US Army Reserve Judge Advocate General's Corps and last served as the Chief Judge (IMA) of the U.S. Army Court of Criminal Appeals.

Brigadier General Evelyn P. Foote (Ret. USA) was Commanding General of Fort Belvoir in 1989. She was recalled to active duty in 1996 to serve as Vice-Chair of the Secretary of the Army's Senior Review Panel on Sexual Harassment.

Rear Admiral John D. Hutson (Ret. USN) served as the Navy's Judge Advocate General from 1997-2000 and now serves as President and Dean of the Franklin Pierce Law Centre in Concord, New Hampshire.

Rear Admiral Don Guter (Ret. USN) served as the Navy's Judge Advocate General from 2000 to 2002 and is now CEO of Vinson Hall Corporation and Executive Director of the Navy Marine Coast Guard Residence Foundation in McLean, Virginia.

Vice Admiral Lee F. Gunn (Ret. USN) served as the Inspector General of the Department of Navy until his retirement in August, 2000. He commanded the USS BARBEY and the destroyer,

Squadron "Thirty-One", a component of the Navy's Anti-Submarine Warfare Destroyer Squadron.

It is interesting to note that the New York Times[16] carried the story that at the urging of the White House, Congressional leaders scrapped a legislative provision that would have imposed new restrictions on the **use of torture by intelligence officers**. Condoleezza Rice, the National Security Adviser, opposed the restrictions on the grounds that, *"it provides legal protection to foreign prisoners to which they are not now entitled under applicable law and policy."*

The United Nations 1985 Convention against Torture, which was ratified by President Clinton in 1994, seems to have escaped everyone's minds, slam-dunked in some dark memory hole. Yet, it is the intelligence services, in particular the CIA, which are most prone to use torture. But as you can see, Condoleezza Rice does not want any restrictions on the CIA, which is in the process of massive reforms. What reforms can there be if, torture culture still prevails?

One would have thought that Congressional leaders would act responsibly, in the light of the Open Letter from the distinguished generals. It cannot be said that members of Congress are ignorant of the laws that prohibit such crimes. But they have all been cowed by the Bush regime's fascist policymakers. But the American people, the last bastion against Fascism in the United States must be told of the war crimes in the starkest terms that have been committed by the Bush regime.

Professor Francis Boyle, Professor of Law, University of Illinois College of Law expressed similar sentiments when in a recent round-table conference on **"Torture and International Human Rights**[17]**"** said:

"We have even more reason to bring this to our people's attention: The Nuremberg Principles were in fact originally the idea of the U.S. Government which then orchestrated the prosecutions in Nuremberg. People need to understand the pedigree and heritage here. These are very grave offenses which the U.S. Government a generation ago prosecuted and executed Nazis for committing. And Japanese war criminals too."

The crimes committed recently in Afghanistan and Iraq cannot be attributed to just a few foot soldiers as asserted by Donald Rumsfeld. According to Professor Boyle, it goes directly up the chain of command under the terms of the U.S. Army Field Manual 27-10, specifically paragraph 501, which makes clear that commanders who have ordered, or knew, or should have known about, war crimes and failed to stop them are themselves guilty of war crimes. For your benefit I shall quote the good professor:

"If you look at the record, it is clear that Gens. Sanchez and Miller ordered war crimes and both should be relieved of command immediately for abuse of prisoners in violation of the Geneva Convention. As for General Abizaid, the overall commander of U.S. forces in Southwest Asia, he admitted in his Senate hearings that he should have known about the war crimes in Abu Ghraib, so basically he's already incriminated himself under the rules of the U.S. Army Field Manual 27-10. In addition, above Abizaid you have Rumsfeld and Wolfowitz. Again, my reading of the public record, including the Taguba and Red Cross reports, is that they either knew, or should have known about, all these war crimes... the widespread and systematic nature of these abuses rise to the level of crimes against humanity, going all the way up through the chain of command. Culpability also extends to Undersecretary of Defense for intelligence General William G. Boykin and Undersecretary Stephen Cambone, who reports directly to Undersecretary of Defense Douglas Feith. And through this line it appears to me that Rumsfeld is culpable, because he was at Abu Ghraib last fall. Indeed, Sy Hersh's New Yorker article on Abu Ghraib claims with good substantiation that he was totally aware and even signed off on the use of techniques which are clearly torture... And President Bush, as Commander-in-Chief would be accountable under Field Manual 27-10 precisely because he is Commander-in-Chief of the U.S. Armed Forces under the Constitution. We know the White House knew this because if you read White House Counsel Alberto Gonzales's memo, he specifically tries to exempt the U.S. from the Geneva Conventions for Guantanamo and Afghanistan. You can see that Gonzales was afraid of Bush and others being held directly accountable... So ultimately what we have here are people at the highest level of the Chain of Command guilty of ordering,

or not preventing torture, which is both an international crime against the Geneva Conventions and the Torture Convention and a domestic crime as well."

Liz Holtzman, the former New York Comptroller and Congresswoman, who served as a member of the House Judicial Committee that drafted the letters of impeachment for President Nixon during Watergate, explains further the implications:

"Once the Geneva Conventions apply, so does the War Crimes Act of 1966, which is not an international statute but rather a U.S. criminal statute. Like bank robbery, murder... committing a war crime is a federal crime prosecutable in U.S. federal courts. This point is clear not just from the language of the War Crimes Act itself, but from White House Counsel Gonzales's January 2002 memo to President Bush. Under the terms of the War Crimes Act 1966, any U.S. national who engages in war crimes is subject to imprisonment, and if death results, the death penalty."

Her forthright and courageous conclusion serves as a wake-up call for all Americans. This is what she said:

"The President was made aware of this by a great number of international lawyers around the world before the invasion, and even if he claimed ignorance, I'm sure he's heard that ignorance of the law is no excuse. Bush and his administration and the U.S. commanders involved are all guilty of this supreme crime. Since the war was unlawful, the many thousands of deaths predictably resulting from it are also crimes, murder in fact, for which Bush and his officials and commanders are guilty in flagrante."

The red line has been crossed. From now on, nothing is off-limits to the Bush regime. And unless the American people start doing something about this, their country will slide down very fast on the slippery road to Fascism, civil war and doom. A bit dramatic you might say, but then, no one thought Germany would end up under Hitler's rule, either!

ENDNOTES:

1. This must certainly be a joke: Israel a democracy! What can be said or done when the injustice served by the conviction of an innocent man, whose confessions elicited under torture, are ultimately proven false? This from your Harvard University law professor! And indeed, Israel must be applauded for legalizing torture!
2. How reassuring for the suspect — he won't be prosecuted!
3. I suppose suspects would be given a thorough medical before the torture so as to preclude the likelihood of a suspect succumbing to shock and death from a heart attack in the course of the torture.
4. See transcripts @ www.sfgate.com/cgi-bin/article
5. See http://edition.cnn.com/2003/LAW/03/03/cnna.Dershowitz
6. "Behind the Torture Memo", John Yoo, January 2, 2005, the San Jose Mercury News. John Yoo was the Deputy Assistant Attorney General in the Office of Legal Counsel of the Justice Department from 2001 to 2003 and is now a law professor at the University of California-Berkeley and a visiting scholar at the American Enterprise Institute.
7. Ibid.
8. I am not saying here that the attack on the Twin Towers is a retaliatory action. The example is merely to highlight the double standards. I am of the view that September 11 is the "New Pearl Harbor." An operation executed by a certain state in collusion with intelligence services. More of this later.
9. "Bush Death Squads", Robert Parry, January 11, 2005 @ www.consortiumnews.com. Robert Parry was responsible for many of the Iran-Contra stories in the 80s for the Associated Press and Newsweek and is the author of *Secrecy & Privilege: Rise of the Bush Dynasty, from Watergate to Iraq.*
10. See the preceding chapter.
11. "Teaching Torture", Doug Ireland, LA Weekly, July 23-29, 2004 @ www.laweekly.com
12. Article published October 19, 2003, (Toledo Blade)
13. *Fatwa*: a ruling on a point of Islamic law given by a recognized authority.
14. William Blum, *Killing Hope* (2003 Zed Books Ltd, London) This is a wholly revised, extended and updated edition of the book originally published as *The C.I.A.: A Forgotten History* (1986 Zed Books)
15. Visit www.truthout.org
16. January 12, 2005, New York Times. Douglas Jehl and David Johnston. The story can also be obtained from www.theledger.com
17. January 9, 2005, reported in www.zmag.org. The participants were Professor Francis Boyle, H. Victor Conde, Michael Mandel, Liz Holtzman and Mark Levine.

5

The Black Economy — Drugs and Money Laundering

In 1987, I came across the book, ***The Underground Empire: Where Crime and Governments Embrace*** by James Mill,[1] which spurred my interest in the black economy of drugs and money laundering and the real powers behind this global menace. From my research, my world view of economics and politics took a dramatic 180-degree turn. While I had a fairly good idea about the drug economy, I was not able at the material time, to put all the pieces of the puzzle together. Even today, I don't pretend to know everything about this evil. And I don't believe that anyone has been able to get to the bottom of the power structure that controls the global trade in drugs, save the Masterminds themselves. But if we want to understand some of the problems that we are now faced with, the financial mess, the War on Terrorism, globalization, international banking, etc., we must come to grips with the drug economy, and how it affects our everyday lives, and in particular, the U.S. economy.

The opening paragraph of Chapter One of James Mill's book ought to put you in the proper perspective for a start, hence I quote:

"The inhabitants of the earth spend more money on illegal drugs than they spend on food. More than they spend on housing, clothes, education, medical care, or any other product or service. The international narcotics industry is the largest growth industry in the world. Its annual revenues exceed half a trillion dollars — three times the value of all United States currency in circulation, more than the gross national products of all but a half dozen of the major industrialized nations. To imagine the immensity of such wealth consider this: A million dol-

lars in gold weigh as much a large man. A half-trillion dollars would weigh more than the entire population of Washington, D.C."

But how pervasive is this menace and what is its power and influence? Once again, author James Mills did not mince his words when he wrote:

"The international narcotics industry is, in fact, not an industry at all, but an empire. Sovereign, proud, expansionist, this Underground Empire, though frequently torn by internal struggle, never fails to present a solid front to the world at large. It has become today as ruthlessly acquisitive and exploitative as any nineteenth-century imperial kingdom, as far reaching as the British Empire, as determinedly cohesive as the States of the American Republic. Aggressive and violent by nature, the Underground Empire maintains its own army, diplomats, intelligence services, banks, merchant fleets and airlines. It seeks to extend its dominance by any means, from clandestine subversion to open warfare. Legitimate nations combat its agents within their borders, but effectively ignore its power internationally. The United States government, while launching cosmetic 'wars' on drugs and crime, has rarely attacked the Empire abroad, has never substantially diminished its international power, and does not today seriously challenge its growing threat to world stability."

This was written in 1986. Nothing has changed today. In fact things have gone from bad to worse. Let me now share something with you — the drug barons and bankers that controlled the drug economy centuries ago are still in control through their descendants and an international network of corporations, foundations, think tanks, banks, educational institutions, the mass media and political parties.

The Chinese, in general, are familiar with the issue of drugs, in particular with opium, and how it destroyed their country. China is the only country that was targeted by the British imperialist policy of using the drug, opium, as a weapon for imperialist control and exploitation. Today, the Zionist Anglo-American Empire is using the same methodology in their quest for world domination. A brief examination of this scourge during the last three centuries will afford us a glimpse into the international operations of these drug barons, the partners of the global political power elites.

It was the Dutch who began trading in opium in the 1600s. They also used opium as a weapon to break the moral resistance of the Indonesians when they colonized Indonesia. And the British were quick to learn from them.

According to the China Year Book for 1916, poppy has been known in China for 12 centuries and its medicinal use for some 9 centuries. But it was not until the 17th century that opium mixed with tobacco for smoking was introduced to China.[2] It was viewed negatively by the Chinese as a weapon of the foreigners. The Emperor issued two edicts, one in 1729 and another in 1796, prohibiting the smoking of opium. The opium came from India. The British East India Company (B.E.I.C.) successfully invaded Bengal and defeated the local ruler in 1757 and Bengal became the centre of the company's opium trade. The B.E.I.C. had an army of 150,000 to enforce its dictates and, when required was further supported by the British Army.

It must be remembered that at the material time, there was roaring trade between China and Britain for tea, giving rise to a trade surplus in favor of China. However, there was nothing which the British could offer to the Chinese Emperor. China had no need for British goods. But there was opium. So began the smuggling of opium into China and the revenue by 1804, was sufficient to cover Britain's cost of importation of tea from China. By 1831, the opium trade was two and a half times greater than the tea trade. One of the largest smugglers was Jardine, Matheson & Co., and the partners William Jardine and James Matheson made a fortune from this illicit trade. On their return to Britain they acquired substantial land holdings. In fact Matheson became the second largest landowner and was made a baron by Queen Victoria.

The Chinese Imperial government was alarmed by this growing menace and an official named Lin Zexu was dispatched to Canton to stop the trade. He was successful in destroying 20,000 chests of opium. An appeal was made to Queen Victoria to stop the trade but to no avail. The destruction of the opium made the British furious. The continued clampdown on opium by the Imperial government gave the British a pretext for war. James Matheson, as the representative of the opium traders, went back to Britain to rally for war. He appealed to the cotton manufacturers for support, enticing them that China ought to be opened for British cotton products, especially cloth. Thus began the First Opium War. The Treaty of Nanking, which was signed by the Chinese at gunpoint in August 1842, brought that war to an end. This was the beginning of what the Chinese would refer to as the "Unequal Treaties". For the British, however, the treaty more than fulfilled their original goals and their prize was Canton and a string of other ports, namely Amoy, Foochow, Ningpo and Shanghai. These "treaty ports" were the principal entry points for the importation of opium. Britain also took over the Island of Hong Kong and received 21 million dollars in compensation. The British also demanded "extraterritoriality"; British citizens were no longer subject to Chinese laws, even if they commit any offenses in China. Britain was also granted "most favored nation" status in her trade with China.

Slightly more than a decade later, the Second Opium War was launched by the British, resulting in five more "treaty ports" being opened up for the opium trade. In 1858, opium was legalized in China. And for the next 100 years or so, China was weighed down by this scourge, becoming a nation of opium addicts! In the absence of national resistance, Britain asserted total control of China's economy and plundered at will. The merchant banks and trading corporations banded together and established the Hong Kong and Shanghai Banking Corp., which became the *de facto* central bank of Hong Kong. The opium traders literally had a field day, controlling the trade and finance!

When the Japanese attacked China and invaded Manchuria, they replicated the British policy and flooded Manchuria with drugs. It was estimated that over a third of the population were addicts by 1944. Millions died from this scourge, but no one paid for this monstrous crime.

Americans may not be aware that Americans were also involved in the opium trade in China. Let's start with the Perkins family. The Perkinses were one of the oldest sailing families in Boston. It was George Perkins who set up the business as a British Empire merchant, in Smyrna, Turkey (now Yzmyr) that gave the family access to Turkish opium. The first shipment arrived in China in 1816. The family quickly made their presence felt in Canton. Ralph Bennett Forbes married T.H. Perkins' sister, Margaret, and their son, Robert Bennett Forbes, became the foreign affairs manager of a merchant by the name of Houqua, who had been appointed to oversee China's foreign relations with the West by the Emperor. Robert's brother, John Murray Forbes, took over the business upon his death.

The Sturgis family is another interesting one. Russell Sturgis married T.H. Perkins' sister, Elizabeth, and joined the firm. His grandson became the chairman of the Barings Bank, the bankers of the British East India Company. The Chinese opium trade was financed almost entirely by the Barings Bank in England. The Perkins' syndicate did their business in China in collaboration with British Empire merchants and officials.[3]

An American firm, Russell & Company, was equally successful, and after the First Opium War, became the third largest opium dealer in the world. This company later merged with the Perkins' operations which dominated the American trade in opium. Russell & Company's partners comprised of some of the wealthiest Americans, namely John Clive Green, banker and railroad investor and trustee for Princeton; A. Abiel Low, shipbuilder, merchant and railroad owner; and merchants Augustine Heard and Joseph Coolidge. Coolidge's son organized the United Fruit Company and his grandson, Archibald C. Coolidge was a co-founder of the Council on Foreign Relations.

In the early part of the 20th century, the opium trade declined as China and India agreed to put a stop to it. However, by the 1930s, there was a surge in the importation of heroin from Japan, and the heroin trade grew immensely. American crime syndicates Arnold Rothestein's Jewish-American and Lucky Luciano's American-Sicilian became involved in the trade of heroin to America and Europe.[4]

I hope at this stage, you are able to see some of the connections between drug smugglers, crime syndicates and banking families in the drug business. Remember these names. I shall now attempt to link these names to the leading political families of America.[5] I shall start with the Cabot family. Like the Perkinses, they were involved in shipping and found their fortune during the war years of 1776-1783. However, the bulk of the family's fortune was acquired later through their alliance with T.H. Perkins in the slave trade. Dr. Samuel Cabot married Eliza Perkins, daughter of T. H. Perkins. Through marriages, the Perkins family had links with the following powerful American families: Lowell, Higginson, Forbes and Sturgis.

Earlier, I had mentioned Robert Bennett Forbes who, in 1840, got involved in the opium trade. That same year, Warren Delano II joined the fray. As you may be aware, he was the maternal grandfather of President Franklin Delano Roosevelt. The young Delano quickly learned the trade and made his fortune. In 1843, Warren Delano returned to America and was introduced to Judge Joseph Lyman's daughter, Catherine Robbins Lyman. After his wedding he returned to China to expand his fortune. In 1846, he returned to America and invested in railroads, properties, copper mines, and other investments. Warren's brother, Frank, married the granddaughter of John Jacob Astor, then the wealthiest man in America. In 1854, Sara Delano was born. Their charmed life was disrupted in 1857 as a result of the failure of the Ohio Life Insurance and Trust Company which was aggravated by excessive speculation in the railroad business. The Warrens were almost bankrupt as a result. In 1860, Warren Delano II returned to China, but this time, he based himself in Hong Kong to resume the lucrative opium trade.

In 1926, Sara Delano became the second wife of James Roosevelt. They had one child, Franklin, who was to become the 32nd President of the United States years later, on the strength of the family's fortune and contacts. I must also mention two other families, the Coolidge family and the link between the Forbes and the Cabot families. From the opium fortune, John Murray Forbes invested in the inventions of Alexander Graham Bell and years later, his son, William H. Forbes, became the president of the company (American Bell Telephone Company). William married the daughter of Ralph Waldo Emerson and their son married Elise Cabot. Joseph Coolidge was the man hired by Jardine Matheson to smuggle opium into China, His son, Thomas Jefferson Coolidge was part of the Boston venture capitalists known as the "Boston Concern" that invested heavily in the railroads. Their securities were managed and marketed by the Barings Bank which, as mentioned earlier, was the chief financier of the opium trade in China. He donated the Jefferson Laboratory to Harvard University.

Another prominent Coolidge was Archibald Coolidge who helped establish the Council on Foreign Relations by merging the American Institute of International Affairs (sister of the British Royal Institute for International Affairs) and the New York Council on Foreign Relations and became the first editor of the magazine, Foreign Affairs.

In the previous few paragraphs, what I had tried to do was to show the links in the Zionist Anglo-American establishment through the drug trade and how these Boston families are interconnected, and in turn linked to the financial house of Barings. It should also be noted that some of the names that have been mentioned and their descendants have been in control of the Harvard University since its founding. Interestingly, some of the families were also connected to the Yale University. William Huntingdon Russell, together with Alphonso Taft, formed the society of Skull and Bones, and whose members include President George W. Bush and his father, President H. W. Bush.

There is therefore a thread that joins the old British and American families who were involved in the opium trade in China to the powerful political families that rule America today. And drugs continue to play an important role in American politics as revealed in the Iran-Contra scandal, among others.

For those who still persist in holding the view that the Iran-Contra scandal was an exception, I shall append below the transcripts of two remarkable interviews given by Lt. Col. (Ret.) James "Bo" Gritz and Professor Alfred W. McCoy respectively.[6]

LT. COL. JAMES "BO" GRITZ

Lt. Col. James "Bo" Gritz is the most decorated Green Beret Commander of the Vietnam era, with sixty-two citations for valour, five Silver Stars, eight Bronze Stars, two Purple Hearts and a presidential citation. If you do not believe him, who else can you trust?

"What I want to tell you very quickly is something that I feel is more heinous than the Bataan death march. Certainly it is of more concern to you as Americans than the Watergate. What I'm talking about is something we found out in Burma — May 1987. We found it from a man named Khun Sa. He is the recognized overlord of heroin in the world. Last year he sent 900 tons of opiates and heroin into the free world. This year it will be 1200 tons.

"On video tape he said to us something that was most astounding: that US government officials have been and are now his biggest customers, and have been for the last twenty

93

years. I wouldn't believe him. We fought a war in Laos and Cambodia even as we fought whatever it was in Vietnam. The point is that there are as many bomb holes in those two countries as there are in Vietnam. Five hundred and fifty plus Americans were lost in Laos. Not one of them ever came home. We heard a President say, 'The war is over, we are out with honor — all of the prisoners are home.' And a few other lies. Now we got rid of the president, but we didn't get rid of the problem. We ran the war in Laos and Cambodia through drugs. The money that would not be appropriated by a liberal Congress was appropriated. And you know who we used for distribution? Santos Trafficante, old friend of the CIA and mobster out of Cuba and Florida. We lost the war!

"Fifty-eight thousand American were killed. Seventy thousand became drug casualties. In the sixties and seventies you saw an infusion of drugs into America like never before. Where do you think the Mafia takes the heroin and opiates that it gets through its arrangement with the US government? It doesn't distribute them in Africa or Europe. This is the big money bag HERE. We are Daddy Warbucks for them. So I submit to you that the CIA has been pressed for solutions. Each time they have gone to the sewer to find it. And you can't smell like a rose when you've been playing in the cesspool. We have been embracing organized crime. Now you've all looked and heard about Ollie North, about the Contras, about nobody knowing anything.

"We have a Constitution that says that the laws will be made by the Congress, enforced by the executive branch, interpreted by the judicial branch. But in reality we have an executive branch that has for more than twenty years operated in what Ollie North called a parallel government. When Congress says no, it makes no difference. They're gonna do it anyway. And it is special intelligence — top secret. Why? Not because the communists don't know about what we are doing. It's to keep it a secret from YOU. You're not capable of making those kinds of decisions — according to those in parallel government. The reason I know... I was there. I've been a product of the parallel government myself."

In another part of the transcript, Lt. Col. Gritz recounts a conversation with General Fred Weiyan during the Vietnam War, when he was about to sign up for the fifth tour. He was then a major and he recalls:

"I was a major and special operations chief. I'll never forget that day. I stood there and heard that man say: 'Bo, you're not going to win the war, and neither am I.' That was the most disillusioning moment of my life. It meant that every man who had ever lost his finger or his life had lost it for nothing. I decided, on the spot, to leave Vietnam. I would not kill another enemy or risk another comrade's life."

Today in Iraq, brave American soldiers are being sacrificed for a war that cannot be won and for a lie as well. And as more body bags come home, more will be disillusioned, just like the brave Lt. Col. "Bo" Gritz. The feature films "Rambo: First Blood Part II", "Uncommon Valour" and "Missing in Action" were based in part upon his real life experiences.

PROFESSOR ALFRED W. McCOY

On being asked how he got to write the book, *The Politics of Heroin: CIA Complicity in the Global Drug Trade*, the professor explained that when he was a graduate student in 1971, studying Southeast Asia history, he came across some reference to the opium trade in Laos and was invited by an editor of Harper & Row to do a background book on the heroin plague that was sweeping the U.S. forces in Vietnam. He found out that one third of the combat forces in Vietnam, a conservative estimate, were heroin addicts. He says:

"I went to Paris and interviewed retired general Maurice Belleux, the former head of the French equivalent of the CIA, an organization called SDECE [Service de Documentation Exterieure et du Contre-Espionage]. In an amazing interview he told me that the French military intelligence had financed all their covert operations from the control of the Indochina drug trade. The French paratroopers fighting with the hill tribes collected the opium and French aircraft would fly the opium down to Saigon and the Sino-Vietnamese mafia that was the instrument of the French intelligence would then distribute the

opium. The central bank accounts, the sharing of the profits, were all controlled by French military intelligence. He concluded the interview by telling me that it was his information that the CIA had taken over the French assets and were pursuing something of the same policy.

"During the 40 years of the Cold War, from the 1940s to this year[7] the CIA pursued a policy that I called radical pragmatism. Their mission was to stop communism and in pursuit of that mission they would ally with anyone and do anything to fight communism.

"During the long years of the Cold War the CIA mounted major covert guerrilla operations along the Soviet-Chinese border. The CIA recruited as allies, people we now call drug lords for their operation against communist China in north-eastern Burma in 1950, then from 1965 to 1975 [during the Vietnam War] their operation in Northern Laos and throughout the decade of the 1980s, the Afghan operation against Soviet forces in Afghanistan.

"If there were any allegations about involvement of their allies in the drug trade, the CIA would use their good offices to quash those allegations. This meant that these drug lords, connected to the CIA, and protected by the CIA, were able to release periodic heroin surges, and in Latin America, periodic cocaine surges. You can trace very precisely during the 40 years of the Cold War, the upsurge in narcotics supply in the United States with covert operations."

This is truly incredible. The CIA operatives have the warped mind of drugging their very own people, innocent Americans, to finance the Cold War. Does the end justify the means? What would be your answer, if your children became junkies? The good professor explains further:

"The Afghan operation: from 1979 to the present, the CIA's largest operation anywhere in the world, was to support the Afghan resistance forces fighting the Soviet occupation in their country. The CIA worked through Pakistan military intelligence and worked with Afghan guerrilla groups who were close to the Pakistan military intelligence... In 1979, Pakistan had no heroin addicts, in 1980 Pakistan had 5,000 heroin addicts, and by May

1985, according to official Pakistan government statistics, Pakistan had 1.2 million heroin addicts, the largest heroin addict population in the world."

So what we have here is an Islamic state with an Islamic government becoming a willing partner for some crumbs (dollar corruption) at the expense of making their people drug addicts! And today, we are hearing from so-called Muslim leaders calling their followers to rally to the call to fight the War on Terrorism, unleashed by the bully George Bush. But the real blowback is yet to come.

Further on in the interview, Professor McCoy explains how the drug monies were laundered:

"There have been three times in the past 15 years in which the CIA's money transfer activities have surfaced. The first came in the late 1970s when the IRS investigated a Nassau Bank called the Castle Bank. It's a very interesting bank. It was set up by a man named Paul Helliwell, a very senior CIA operative who had retired from the agency. He set up this bank and it grew into a Latin American network of banks. It was used by the CIA to launder money...

"As soon as Castle Bank collapsed, a small merchant bank based in Australia, operating offshore between Australia and Southeast Asia, suddenly mushroomed into a global network of banks, acquiring Latin American and European structures that had belonged to Castle Bank. This bank in Australia, called the Nugan-Hand Bank, began very quickly in the late 1970s, to acquire a board of retired U.S. intelligence officials, either CIA or various military intelligence services. The most prominent example, the former Director of Central Intelligence, William Colby, became the Legal Counsel of Nugan-Hand Bank. The bank was founded by Frank Nugan, an insecure and incompetent Australian lawyer, and by Michael John Hand, a man with a high school degree who had gone to Vietnam with the Green Berets. He had served in Laos in the 1960s as a contract CIA operative, fighting with three of the people who became prominent in the CIA's privatized operations, Thomas Clines, Theodore Shackley and Richard Secord, all very big names in the Iran-Contra scandal... In 1980 the bank went belly up and it collapsed, Frank Nugan committed suicide, and then a really amazing event occurred. Thomas Clines, the former CIA

Chief of Station from Laos, a man of great prominence in the Iran-Contra scandal, flew to Sydney, Australia and exfiltrated Michael John Hand, who disappeared in the United States and was never seen since.

"Then we come to BCCI.... There's one large question that nobody is asking about BCCI. It's a Pakistani Bank, it booms during the 1980s, in exactly the same period that Pakistan emerges as the world's largest heroin centre.... In fact the boom in the Pakistan drug trade was financed by BCCI. The inter-relationship between the Afghan resistance and the CIA and the Pakistan drug trade can be seen through the medium of BCCI, the banker to both operations, the resistance and the drug trade."

At the present, it is reported that the illegal drugs rake in an estimated $500 billion to $1 trillion annually. As explained earlier by the professor, this money cannot be hidden in shoes boxes; it must be circulated within the system so that they can be used legitimately. The process of doing this is called money laundering. Al Capone was credited with coining the term, because he used coin operated Laundromats to "wash" the millions he made from all his illegal activities. However, in today's circumstances, money laundering is effected through the international banking system and major banks are involved. Kelly P. O'Meara in an article[8] explains how this is done:

"Money laundering through cooperative banking institutions is a three-step process: placement, layering and integration. The intent is to make sure that the origin and ownership of the money is concealed while maintaining control. Placement, the first step is the most vulnerable. The aim is to take a large amount of cash and move it without a trace into the financial system, retail economy, or a safe haven outside the country.... Layering, the second step in the process, is to dissociate or screen the monies being moved by banking or other financial institution through a series of complex transactions. This usually is accomplished with a series of electronic wire transfers that take only seconds to move in and out of shell accounts in international banks around the world. Integration is the final step, in which the money, now disguised and dissociated from its origin, is moved into the legitimate business and financial system."

Another method is to exploit the loopholes in the securities industry. Money market accounts are not subject to "Cash Transaction Report" (CTR) and have been available since the 1980s. Such accounts can accept cash deposits. A recent scandal concerning money laundering involved the prestigious Bank of New York, America's oldest financial institution. The bank was accused of laundering in excess of $12 billion of funds from the former Soviet Union.

Senator Carl Levin was reported to have said that:*"**Estimates are that $500 million to $1 trillion of international criminal proceeds are moved internationally and deposited into bank accounts annually. It is estimated that half of that money comes into the United States.**[9]"*

A leading expert with the Brookings Institute estimates that *"the flow of corrupt money out of developing (Third World) and transitional (ex-communist) economies into Western coffers at $20 to $40 billion a year and the flow stemming from mispriced trades at $80 billion a year or more.*[10]*"*

Thus, in any evaluation of the U.S. economy, the laundering of illicit money must be factored into account. It is apparent that the U.S. deficit cannot be sustained without this huge inflow of illicit monies. James Petras observed that *"the $500 billion of criminal and dirty money flowing into and through the major U.S. banks far exceeds the net revenues of all IT companies in the U.S., not to speak of their profits. These yearly inflows surpass all the net transfers by the U.S. oil producers, military industries and airplane manufacturers. The biggest U.S. banks, particularly Citibank, derive a high percentage of their banking profits from serving these criminal and dirty money accounts. The big U.S. banks and key institutions sustain U.S. global power via their money laundering and managing of illegally obtained overseas funds.*[11]*"*

Yet, on reading all the major news media, the impression is that the United States, the IMF and other international agencies are in the forefront fighting money laundering. Given the state of the U.S. economy and the role of dirty money, one should only expect more of the same. This seems to be the view of the former private banker, Antonio Geraldi, in his testimony to the Senate Subcommittee predicting significant growth in U.S. bank laundering. Professor James Petras paints a grim picture when he wrote:

"The U.S. Congress has held numerous hearings, provided detailed exposés of the illicit practices of the banks, passed several laws and called for stiffer enforcements by any number of public regulators and private bankers. Yet the biggest banks continue their practices, the sum of dirty money grows exponentially, because <u>both the state and the banks have neither the will nor the interest to put an end to the practices that provide high profits and buttress an otherwise fragile empire.</u>[12] *"* (Emphasis added)

In conclusion, what we have is a corrupt empire, whose global might and reach is sustained by dirty money. The cancer has spread and it is terminal!

ENDNOTES:

1. James Mill, *The Under Ground Empire: Where Crime and Government Embrace*, 1986, (Dell Publishing)
2. Cited by Ellen N. La Motte in "The Opium Monopoly", Schaffer Library for Drug Policy. www.druglibrary.org/schaffer/history
3. "The History of Tea" @ www.geocities.com/Igol27/HistoryTeaUSA.htm
4. R.A. Kris Millegan, "The Boodle boys" @ www.ctrl.org/boodleboys/boodleboys1.html
5. The following discussion is adapted from the excellent work by Linda Minor, "Follow the Yellow Brick Road: From Harvard to Enron". Source: www.newsmakingnews.com. All serious researchers should make an attempt to read all her articles on these issues.
6. "A Nation Betrayed", transcript of Interview given by Col. James "Bo" Gritz. Transcript by Jim Burnes. Source: www.pd.org/topos/perforations/perf2/betrayed interview.html. Interview given by Professor Alfred W. McCoy. Transcript by Paul DeRienzo. Source: www.bearcave.com. Prof. Alfred is professor of Southeast Asian History at the University of Wisconsin, Madison. Educated at Columbia and Yale, and author of *The Politics of Heroin in Southeast Asia* (1972) and *The Politics of Heroin — CIA Complicity in the Global Drug Trade.*
7. The interview was in 1991.
8. Kelly P. O'Meara, "Dirty Dollars", published in Insight on the News. www.insightmag.com
9. Cited by James Petras, "Dirty Money: Foundation of U.S. Growth and Empire". Source: www.fromthewilderness.com. James Petras is Professor of Sociology at Binghamton University, New York.
10. Ibid.
11. Ibid.
12. Ibid.

6

A Requiem for the Empire

In the previous chapter, you were told of the story of the brave Lt. Col. James "Bo" Gritz who, after being betrayed by the political leaders of his country, vowed that he would not kill another enemy or risk another comrade's life. 59,000 of America's best lost their lives for nothing. Bush went AWOL. Today, in Iraq we are witnessing the same senseless killings and devastation that have caused the death of over 100,000 Iraqis, mainly civilian men, women and children — non-combatants — so-called "collateral damage". The American death toll is mounting daily and the wounded have already exceeded 10,000. Death is knocking on America's doors.

I was in Iraq just before the war started on a special mission for my government. The sufferings of the brave Iraqis that I saw, as a result of 12 years of UN sanctions, cannot be expressed with mere words. I was not mentally prepared for the emotional and psychological onslaught on being shown little children suffering from the effects of depleted uranium — deformed babies and children suffering from cancer. It was ugly. I can only describe them as 'Frankenstein Children'. An appalling appellation, I know, but in trying to describe what I saw, it is the best (or worst) that I could think of. As I have said, mere words suffice not.

In the hospitals that I visited, I could not restrain my emotions, and as the tears welled in my eyes, a searing pain ripped through my guts. Why? It was reported that over 500,000 children have died as a result of the sanctions imposed by the United Nations. And on that day, I vowed that I will do everything within my ability to expose the crimes of the Zionist Anglo-American Empire.

Madeleine Albright, the Zionist former U.S. Secretary of State, when asked if the deaths of half a million Iraqi children was a price worth paying for the sanctions, callously replied, *"We think the price is worth it."* And as callously she justified the actions of America: *"...If we have to use force, it is because we are America. We are the indispensable nation. We stand tall. We see further into the future."*

Since 1991, thousands of Iraqis have died from cancer as a result of the radiation epidemic caused by depleted uranium bombs and shells. While Kuwait was allowed and assisted in the clean-up, Iraq was left to face the consequences unaided. Professor Doug Rokke, the U.S. Army Physicist responsible for the clean-up operations in Kuwait had this to say:

"I am like many people in Iraq. I have 5,000 times the recommended radiation in my body. The contamination was right throughout Iraq and Kuwait. With the munitions testing and preparation in Saudi Arabia, uranium contamination covers the entire region. The effect depends on whether a person inhaled it or ingested it by eating or drinking, or if they got it from an open wound. What we are seeing now, respiratory problems, kidney problems, cancers, are the direct result of the use of this highly toxic material. The controversy over whether or not it's the cause is a manufactured one; my own ill-health is a testament to that... There are two urgent issues to be confronted by people in the West, those with a sense of right and wrong: first the decision by the United States and Britain to use a weapon of mass destruction, such as depleted uranium. In the Gulf War, well over 300 tons were fired. An A-10 Warhog attack aircraft fired over 900,000 rounds, each individual round was 300 grams of solid uranium 238. When a tank fired its shells, each round carried over 4,500 grams of solid uranium. These rounds are not coated, they are not tipped; they are solid uranium. Moreover, we have evidence to suggest that they were mixed with plutonium. <u>What happened in the Gulf was a form of nuclear warfare.</u>[1] " (Emphasis added)

Professor Karol Sikora, head of the cancer program of the WHO, exposed the inhuman and cruel campaign to block requested radiotherapy equipment, chemotherapy drugs and analgesics by British and United States advisers to the Sanctions Committee . He commented:

"The saddest thing I saw in Iraq was children dying because there was no chemotherapy and no pain control. It seemed crazy they couldn't have morphine, because for everybody with cancer pain it is the best drug. When I was there, they had a little bottle of aspirin pills to go round 200 patients in pain.[2]"

I do not know if my guides, who also became my dearest friends, are alive or dead. But this, I know. They were saddened by the inevitable war and hoped that the world would see through the lies of the Bush and Blair regimes. They impressed upon me the urgency of getting out before the war started, to tell the world what I saw — a Malaysian witness to the war crimes inflicted by the Zionist Anglo-American war machine. I met several leaders, and interacted with ordinary people. I left Iraq, with the regrets that I was not able to join their ranks to oppose Zionism and Imperial occupation, but I came home with fond memories of a proud nation, a very cultured and learned people who, in spite of their sufferings, ensured that I had every comfort during my stay. It was true friendship.

When I returned to Malaysia, many colleagues and friends expressed the view that the war would be over in weeks, a one-sided affair. They were surprised when I differed with their assessment and made a report that after the 1st Phase of the war, the invasion, the heroic Iraqi people would launch a devastating people's war, similar to that during the Vietnam War, but launched by urban dwellers, not country folk.

In my discussions with some of the leaders, I expressed the view that the Imperialists will apply the policies of divide and rule, and that it was most likely that the Shiite leaders would be seduced by the sophistry and cunning of the British. The Shiites would be assured of British presence, and their involvement would be the guarantee that 1991 would not be repeated again.[3] The Shiites and their leaders would never be able to see through the ploy. All credit must be given to Blair and his spin doctors for the effective execution of this gambit. The Shiites have short memory, for the treachery of the British in 1920 seemed to be forgotten.

Given the cards that were available, the centre of resistance had to be in Baghdad, a more favorable strategic battlefield for urban resistance than Somalia. If you had visited Baghdad and other cities, you would know what I mean. Creativity would be the key to developing all sorts of booby traps that would wear down the foreign foot soldiers. This would then be the **Iraqi equivalent of the U.S. Shock and Awe campaign. No soldier who escaped death with grievous injury would ever be able to overcome the emotional and psychological trauma of shattered limbs and missing body parts. Suicide would be but one option.**

The resistance war would be ugly. The choice was made by President Bush who refused to fight by the rules of the Geneva Conventions. The U.S. and British forces and their mercenaries tortured and massacred with impunity. It was just too bad that the Iraqis refused to remain willing victims, and rose to the challenge and adapted quickly.

The U.S. Army did not plan this war game on that premise. They were told that it would be a tea party. Nor were they trained to face an enemy who would die for **family honor**, a concept completely alien to the American psyche, while Abu Ghraib further hastened the defeat of the occupying forces.

The intelligence I gathered showed that six months' rations were already distributed to the future resistance fighters and support groups. Arms amounting millions were also carefully distributed well before the invasion. Wells were dug in numerous strategic and tactical locations in anticipation of the massive destruction to the infrastructures from aerial bombardment. I detected no signs of hopelessness nor defeat in their eyes. From the strategic military point of view, even though the 12 years of sanctions have crippled the Iraqi's conventional war machine, it hardened the people's resolve and determination for resistance. It was their turn for payback and they were ready and waiting. My sources have since been confirmed by Seymour Hersh in his book, ***The Chain of Command***[4]. Here I quote the relevant passages from the book:

"...Saddam had drawn up plans for a widespread insurgency in 2001, soon after George Bush's election brought into office many of the officials who had directed the 1991 Gulf War. Huge amounts of small arms and other weapons were stockpiled around the country for use by the insurgents....

"One of the most critical dates, according to Sadik,[5] was April 7, 2003 as American troops were moving at will on the out-

skirts of Baghdad and were obviously prepared for rough door-to-door urban warfare. American commanders had feared, and planned for, a drawn-out siege of Baghdad. Instead, the troops, who included members of the Baath Party hierarchy, the Special Republican Guard, the Special Security Organization, and the Mukhabarat, were ordered to return to their homes and initiate the resistance from there... Saddam loyalists had stopped chatting on satellite phones and other devices and simply melted away overnight.

"Sadik further told me that Saddam, in his 2001 directive, had ordered three insurgency divisions to be set up, each to operate underground under the direct control of a handpicked Iraqi official. The divisions were to contain two to four thousands members, organized in small cells of three to four. The first division, Sadik said, commanded by Izzat al-Douri, one of Saddam's deputies, 'was composed of Baathists not publicly known at that time.' Their mission was to operate independently in small cells, while hiding out in well-fortified safe houses. The second division, under the command of Taha Yassin Ramadan, was composed of Baath party members whose assignment was to back up the first division by providing operating instructions via a series of carefully screened dead drops. Ramadan was captured by Kurdish troops in Mosul in August, but his capture, Sadik said, did not lead to an unravelling of the operations because Ramadan, by the very nature of the compartmentalization process, did not know which cell was operating where. The third division was composed of technocrats — 'doctors, lawyers, engineers, administrators,' Sadik said, 'and people who run the country — power plants, the water, the sewage, in the Ministry of Commerce and the Ministry of Finance.' The technocrats also had left Baghdad overnight on April 7th, Sadik said."

There were setbacks, no doubt. But a good military commander, while not able to foresee each and every contingency, can minimize the initial setbacks in the face of an overwhelming force, preserve its strength and, when the time is ready, counter-attack preselected targets with deadly force. Precisely what is happening in Iraq. Tribal justice is now in full swing. The cry of "Allahu Akbar" strengthens the Iraqis' resolve, but send shivers down the spines of the occupying mercenaries and foot soldiers.

105

I am sure the Zionist Anglo-American Empire received the same intelligence I did, but they were too arrogant and too self-assured that their Shock and Awe campaign would, with a single stroke, psychologically demoralize the Iraqi resistance. Even seasoned military commanders were taken in by this made-for-television propaganda.

General Tommy Franks and his staff of generals failed in their duty and betrayed their soldiers in waging this war. They thought that money could buy cogent intelligence. While a few corrupt generals and officials succumbed, the patriots of Iraq remained true to their country. Despite the millions in greenbacks at their disposal, the intelligence services and Special Forces made little headway in strategic intelligence gathering. Even with the capture of President Saddam Hussein, the military situation did not improve, but deteriorated further. In a people's war, intelligence is the critical key to victory; without which, death and defeat is certain!

They failed to learn from the experience of the Vietnam War. The Phoenix program failed. The Tiger Force brutality failed. The tortures failed. The corrupt puppet regime failed. The puppet army failed. The carpet bombing of Hanoi and Haiphong and elsewhere by B-52s and other modern warplanes was the best that the U.S. war machine could deliver. But it could not deliver the knockout blow. The bombings failed. The ultimate battle had to be won on the ground. I visited the Chu Chi tunnels and saw how the Liberation Fighters survived on simple meals of steamed tapioca mixed with salt or sugar and nuts. They dug a maze of tunnels over two hundred kilometers to encircle the enemy, some two to three storeys below ground, with nothing more than simple tools and basic engineering skills. In the day they braved the bombs and planted rice in the fields; in the night, they controlled the battlefields. Many were simple womenfolk; such an army can never be defeated. Period!

Likewise, Rumsfeld's shock and awe campaign was a strategic failure; and Tommy Franks essentially waged a war for U.S. cable televisions, the New York Times, and the likes of Judith Miller. The Washington Post reported[6] that while she was embedded with MET Alpha, her role in the unit's operations became so central that it became known as the "Judith Miller Team." When a bitch of a journalist interferes with ground unit operations, there is only one conclusion — the U.S. army is all screwed-up. And because they went into Iraq on false pretenses, and for the real estate and oil, they lost the battle for the minds and hearts. Since when did a rapist-robber-murderer have consideration for his victims? Now, his brave soldiers are now paying the price for his unqualified arrogance and unmitigated stupidity. Tommy Franks' campaign reminds me of the medical cliché, "the operation *[the invasion]* was successful, but the patient *[the invaders]* died."

I am confident that just as there were brave and honorable soldiers like Lt. Col. James "Bo" Gritz from the Vietnam War who exposed the truth, so will there also be brave American soldiers from the Iraq War who will put the generals to shame; they will kill no more or put their comrades' lives at risk.

I take no joy in seeing another generation of America's best bearing the brunt of the misguided policies of civilian warmongers. But they can stop these senseless killings, before the number of tombstones in Arlington exceeds 59,000 again. The young should ask their elders: ***"Must two generations of the young and brave pay for the crimes and folly of their elders?"***

Dante Zappala, a part-time teacher has just buried his brave brother and is calling on his fellow Americans to end the war and stop this madness. He wrote about his brother in the Los Angeles Times[7]. My heart cries out for him, his brother and his family. This is what he wrote and I hope that good American citizens will respond to his call.

"This week, the White House announced, with little fanfare, that the two-year search for weapons of mass destruction in Iraq had finally ended, and it acknowledged that no such weapons existed there at the time of the U.S. invasion in 2003.

"For many, this may be a story of only passing interest. But for me and my family, it resonates with profound depth.

"My brother was Sgt. Sherwood Baker. He was a member of the Pennsylvania National Guard deployed a year ago with his unit out of Wilkes-Barre. He said goodbye to his wife and his 9 year-old son, boarded a bus and went to Ft Dix, N.J., to be hastily retrained. His seven years of guard training as a forward observer was practically worthless because he would not face combat. All he needed to do was learn how to not die.

"He received a crash course in convoy security, including practice in running over cardboard cut outs of children. We bought him a GPS unit and walkie-talkies because he wasn't supplied with them. In Iraq, Sherwood was assigned to the Iraq Survey Group and joined the search for weapons of mass destruction.

"David Kay, who led the group until January 2004, had already stated that they did not exist. Former United Nations weapons inspector Hans Blix had expressed serious doubts about their presence during prewar inspections. In fact, a cadre of former UN inspectors and U.S. generals have been saying for years that Iraq posed no threat to our country. On April 26, 2004, the Iraq Survey Group, at the behest of the stubborn administration sitting safely in office buildings in Washington, was still on its fruitless but dangerous search. My brother stood atop his Humvee, securing the perimeter in front of a suspect building in Baghdad. But as soldiers entered the building, it exploded; the official cause is still unknown. Sherwood was struck by debris in the back of his head and neck, and he was killed.

"Since that day, my family and I have lived with the grief of losing a loved one. We have struggled to explain his death to his son. We have gazed at the shards of life scattered at our feet, in wonder of its fragility, in perpetual catharsis with God.

"I have moved from the frustration to disappointment to anger. And now I have arrived at a place not of understanding but of hope — blind hope that this will change.

"The Iraq Survey Group's final report, which was filed in October but revealed only on Wednesday, confirmed what we knew all along. And as my mother cried in the kitchen, the nation barely blinked.

"I am left now with a single word seared into my consciousness: accountability. The chance to hold our administration's feet to that flame has passed. But what of our citizenry? We are the ones who truly failed. We shut down our ability to think critically, to listen, to converse and to act. We are to blame.

"Even with every prewar assumption having been proved

false, today more than 130,000 U.S. soldiers are trying to stay alive in a foreign desert with no clear mission at hand.

"At home, the sidelines are overcrowded with patriots. These Americans cower from the fight they instigated in Iraq. In a time of war and record budget deficits, many are loath to even pay their taxes. In the end, however, it is not their family members who are at risk, and they do not sit up at night pleading with fate to spare them.

"Change is vital. We must remind ourselves that the war with Iraq was not a mistake but rather a flagrant abuse of power by our leaders — and a case of shameful negligence by the rest of us for letting it happen. The consequence is more than a quagmire. The consequence is the death of our national treasure — our soldiers.

"We are all accountable. We all share the responsibility of what has been destroyed in our name. Let us begin to right the wrongs we have done to our country by accepting that responsibility."

This letter has given me tremendous hope that patriotic Americans will reclaim their country from the clutches of the Zionist Anglo-American Power Elites. Those of us who share this grief must likewise play a part. Citizens of the member countries of the Nonaligned Movement (NAM), the Organization of Islamic Conference (OIC), and other peace loving countries cannot, simply because of trade with the United States, turn a blind eye to the horrors of this war. Today, they are Palestinians and Iraqis. Tomorrow, it may very well be your own father, brother or sister who would be sacrificed and your memories seared by some retrieved body parts. I pray that you be spared from having to write a similar letter.

There is a choice to be made. And the time is now!

Malaysia holds the Chairs of NAM and OIC. The Palestinians and Iraqis, and many more in the third world are looking to us for leadership and support. And should we fail, expect not a response to our cry for help when our turn should come.

Stop advertising and promoting Malaysia as a "Moderate Muslim Country." It is irrelevant to the 500,000 Iraqi children who have died, and are dying by the thousands in the present 2nd Gulf

War. When men and women are tortured, raped and humiliated, it is justice that they want, not cheap talk. It is no consolation to the Palestinians massacred in Jenin, Nablus and in other centers of resistance by the Fascist Ariel Sharon and the Zionist war machine, funded by the United States. The call for unity of the Muslim *Ummah*[8] rings hollow, when we prostrate ourselves before the Zionist Anglo-American Empire for some economic crumbs. The role of leadership is not given to many. We have been given this role at a time which many have considered as one of the most perilous in history. There is a time for words, and there is a time for action. When an American part-time teacher who lost a brother can see so clearly the road that needs to be travelled, why are we still so blinkered? We must exercise leadership to stop this madness.

Squander it and the price shall be heavy!

Malaysia be forewarned!

ENDNOTES:

1. For a more detailed discussion on this issue read *Behind the War On Terror: Western Secret Strategy and the Struggle for Iraq* by Nafeez Mosaddeq Ahmed (2003, Clairview Books) pgs 157–164.
2. Ibid.
3. After the 1st Gulf War, the U.S. instigated the Shiites to rebel against Saddam Hussein, but when Saddam retaliated, President Bush discontinued the support.
4. Seymour Hersh, *Chain of Command: The Road from 9-11 to Abu Ghraib*, (2004 Allen Lane)
5. Sadik was an Iraqi Air Force Brigadier General.
6. Cited by Amy Goodman in *The Exception to the Rulers*, (2004, Hyperion Books, New York)
7. Dante Zappala, "It's Official: My Brother Died in Vain", January 14, 2005, Los Angeles Times.
8. *Ummah*: In Arabic, literally "people" or "community"; in the Islamic context it refers to the entire Muslim community as a whole.

Part 2

Unravelling the Hidden Agenda

"Obstacle or no obstacle, it is certain that the Temple will be rebuilt. Prophesy demands it. With the Jewish Nation reborn in the land of Palestine, ancient Jerusalem once again under total Jewish control for the first time in 2600 years... It is a time of electrifying excitement."

— Hal Lindsey

"We shall have a world government whether or not we like it. The only question is whether world government will be achieved by conquest or consent."

— James P. Warburg

7

The Zionist Anglo-American Shadow Government: The Three-way Tango — Part I

It is almost surreal, when discussing with political pundits the present international situation, the focus is always on the third part of this triumvirate — the United States. While some focus is placed on Israel and the Likud Party and the Jewish influence on the U.S., Britain is invariably considered as a spent power. In this part of my book, I intend to adduce evidence that the British Zionists play a hidden role on the geopolitical stage, hence my reference to the Zionist Anglo-American Empire in the six chapters of Part I of this book. To put it crudely, the U.S. Zionists form the muscle, the Israeli Zionists comprise the spin doctors, and the British Zionists[1] incorporate the brains and finances. To avoid any misunderstanding, British Zionists are not confined to any geographical location, and their tentacles reach out far and wide through their incestuous financial relationships with banking empires in the United States and Europe. No doubt, this is an oversimplification, but the purpose here is to enable the reader to focus on the three major strands of the Zionist Anglo-American web. And it goes without saying that the activities of each strand overlaps.

When Britain had her Empire, she ruled directly — and Britannia did rule the waves. When she overstretched herself and knew that she would have to give up her colonies, she had already laid plans, well before handing over power, for indirect rule through the financial octopus, the city of London, and the sustained indoctrination via her educational establishments and overseas linkages. Britain learned well from the experience of the American War of Independence. Since that time, the United States has been, and continues to be, the indispensable muscle behind the British Zionists' imperial ambitions. The history of the United States' involvement in the First and Second World Wars bears testimony to this fact. Believe me, the British Zionists are still the experts in the Imperial Chess game.

Anyone who considers otherwise should read Carroll Quigley's *Tragedy & Hope: A History of the World in Our Time*, *The Anglo-American Establishment: From Rhodes to Cliveden* and *The Evolution of Civilizations*. From being a Pharaoh at the height of her powers, she adapted skillfully to become the High Priest for those who are more suited to play the temporary role of Emperor, post-Second World War. I have always been amazed by the craftiness and skills of the British Zionists' imperial diplomats and the intricate geopolitical web that they have spun. And only a fool will say that they are no longer in control of world affairs. For starters, let's examine briefly, what Professor Carroll Quigley has written:[2]

"It is not easy for an outsider to write the history of a secret group of this kind, but... it should be done, for this group is as I shall show, one of the most important historical facts of the twentieth century... In this group were the persons who must command the admiration and affection of all who know of them. On the other hand, in this group were persons whose lives have been a disaster to our way of life. Unfortunately... the influence of the latter kind has been stronger.

"The Rhodes scholarships, established by the terms of Cecil Rhodes's seventh will, are known to everyone. What is not so widely known is that Rhodes in five previous wills left his fortune to form a secret society, <u>which was to devote itself to the preservation and expansion of the British Empire.</u> And what does not seem to be known to anyone is that <u>this secret society was created by Rhodes and his principal trustee, Lord Milner, and continues to exist to this day.</u> To be sure, this secret society is not a childish thing like the Ku Klux Klan, and it does not have any secret robes, secret handshakes, or secret passwords. It does not need any of these, since its members know each other intimately. It probably has no oaths of secrecy nor any formal procedure of initiation. It does, however, exist and holds secret meetings, over which the senior member present presides. At various times since 1891, these meetings have been presided by Rhodes, Lord Milner, Lord Selborne, Sir Patrick Duncan, Field

Marshal Jan Smuts, Lord Lothian, and Lord Brand. They have been held in all British Dominions, starting in South Africa about 1903; in various places in London, chiefly 175 Piccadilly; at various colleges at Oxford, chiefly All Souls; and at many English country houses such as Tring Park, Blickling Hall, Cliveden, and others." (Emphasis added)

So powerful and secretive was this society that it was unknown even to historians of British History at the material time. The society wielded its power through various means but one of the chief methods was propaganda. The group plotted the Jameson Raid of 1895; caused the Boer War of 1899-1902; established the Union of South Africa in 1906-1910; established the British Empire periodical, *The Round Table*; exercised a powerful influence in the colleges of All Souls and Balliol at Oxford; controlled *The Times* for more than 50 years; promoted the concept and name, *The Commonwealth of Nations*; was the chief influence in Lloyd George's war administration in 1917-1919 and dominated the delegation to the Peace Conference of 1919; played a major and critical role in the formation of the League of Nations; founded the Royal Institute of International Affairs in 1919 and still controls it; was one of the chief influences on British policy toward Ireland, Palestine, and India in the period 1917–1945.[3]

The next quotation is most revealing of the mindset of Professor Carroll Quigley and he is not the only American exception. And sooner, we the victims of colonialism understand this mindset, the better prepared we would be for the coming *Final Phase* of the Zionist Anglo-American imperial onslaught. This is the key to the understanding of the *"Special Relationship"* between the United States and Britain.

"In general, I agree with the goals and aims of the Milner Group.[4] I feel that the British way of life and the British Commonwealth of Nations are among the great achievements of all history. I feel that the destruction of either of them would be a terrible disaster for mankind. I feel that the withdrawal of Ireland, of Burma, of India, or of Palestine from the Commonwealth is regrettable and attributable to the fact that the persons in control of these areas failed to absorb the British way of life while they were parts of the Commonwealth. I suppose, in the long view, my attitude would not be far different from that of the members of the Milner Group."

115

To be fair to Professor Quigley, he did express the view that while he agreed with the goals of the group, it did not mean that he agreed with or condoned the methods adopted to achieve those ends. At the end of his book, the professor was rather pessimistic and felt that the *"the great idealistic adventure which began with Toynbee and Milner in 1875 had slowly ground its way to a finish of bitterness and ashes."* He could not foresee that the Council on Foreign Relations in conjunction with the Royal Institute of International Affairs would continue to implement the grand imperial design. To this story we shall return later.

Long before Carroll Quigley, Andrew Carnegie had expressed similar sentiments:

"Time may dispel many pleasing illusions and destroy many noble dreams but it will never shake my belief that the wound caused by the wholly unlooked for and <u>undesired separation of the Mother from her child is not to bleed forever</u>. Let men say what they will, therefore I say, that surely as the sun in the heavens once shone upon Britain and America united, so surely is it one morning to rise, shine upon, and <u>greet again the United States, the British American Union</u>.[5]" (Emphasis added)

There you have it in the most unambiguous language ever spoken by one of the most powerful representatives of the American financial establishment: the sun will shine upon the *"British American Union."* The Zionist Anglo-American shadow government have always strived to preserve the British American Union, notwithstanding the American Revolution and the Declaration of Independence. The British American Union is now more appropriately referred to as the Zionist Anglo-American Establishment.

You may very well ask, "Is there a modern American servant and spokesman for the Zionist Anglo-American Establishment?"

There is, and he is none other than the war criminal[6], Henry Kissinger. In his speech to the Royal Institute of International Affairs on May 10, 1982, on the occasion of the Bicentenary of the Office of the Foreign Secretary, entitled **"Reflections on a Partnership: British and American Attitudes to Post War Foreign Policy"** he spoke like a true Brit.

THE NATURE OF THE SPECIAL RELATIONSHIP[7]

"In the immediate postwar period we were held together by strategic circumstances which imposed the same necessities, whatever the different philosophical premises. American resources and organization and technological genius, and British experience and understanding of the European balance of power, were both needed to resist the sudden threat from the Soviet Union. The Marshall Plan and the North Atlantic Treaty, while formally American initiatives, were inconceivable without British advice and British efforts to organize a rapid and effective European response. Ernest Bevin, as Professor Howard pointed out in the first lecture, was the indispensable architect of the European response, as well as the staunch helmsman of Britain's journey from power to influence."

Henry Kissinger also took the opportunity to explain how Britain cleverly changed from the Pharaoh to that of the High Priest:

"To the outside world it may have seemed that Britain clung far too long to the illusion of Empire; in her relations with Washington, she proved that an old country was beyond self-deception on fundamentals. Bevin, the unlikely originator of this revolution in British diplomacy, shrewdly calculated that Britain was not powerful enough to influence American policy by conventional methods of pressure or balancing of risks. But by discreet advice, the wisdom of experience, and the presupposition of common aims, she would make herself indispensable, so that American leaders no longer thought of consultations with London as a special favor but as an inherent component of our own decision-making. The wartime habit of intimate, informal collaboration thus became a permanent practice, obviously because it was valuable to both sides."

Henry Kissinger gave examples how this close collaboration was translated into practical results to the resentment and consternation of third parties.

"Our post war diplomatic history is littered with Anglo-American 'arrangements' and 'understandings,' sometimes on crucial issues, never put into formal documents. The stationing of B-29 atomic bombers in Britain in 1948 was agreed between political and service leaders but not committed to writing... The

British were so matter-of-factly helpful that they became a participant in internal American deliberations, to a degree probably never before practiced between sovereign nations. In my period of office, the British played a seminal part in certain American bilateral negotiations with the Soviet Union — indeed they helped draft the key document. In my White House incarnation then, I kept the British Foreign Office better informed and more closely engaged than I did the American State Department ...."

ON FOREIGN POLICY

"Fortunately, Britain had a decisive influence over America's rude awakening to maturity in the years following [the Second World War]. In the 1940s and 1950s our two countries responded together to the geopolitical challenge of the Soviet Union and took the lead in creating the structures of Western cooperation for the postwar era which brought a generation of security and prosperity.

"One of Britain's contributions to the Western Alliance has been to supply a needed global perspective: the Knowledge from centuries of experience in Europe, that peace requires some clear-eyed notion of equilibrium and a willingness to maintain it; the insight, from centuries of world leadership, that Europe's security cannot be isolated from the broader context of the global balance; the awareness from heroic exertions in this century, that those who cherish the values of Western civilization must be willing to defend them. In the Falkland crisis, Britain is reminding us all that certain basic principles such as honor, justice, and patriotism remain valid and must be sustained by more than words."

This is indeed a remarkable speech and puts to rest the blinkered argument, commonly held by Arabs and others that Britain is a spent force. Remember this is Henry Kissinger speaking! It is precisely her centuries of experience, wisdom, and cunning that she is as dangerous and effective a player on the global chessboard today, as when she wielded direct Imperial power. The present military engagement by the British troops in Iraq bears testimony to this cunning. While the U.S. Army bears the brunt of the insurgency, the British Army enjoys a relationship of accommodation with the Shiites in Southern Iraq, on the sinister and devious ploy that they are there to guarantee the Shiites' future political power and to forestall any potential American betrayal.[8] Ayatollah Sistani, the Supreme Shiite cleric, has been obviously suckered into gratefully respecting and accepting the advice of the British Mandarins at White Hall, when he sojourned in London, allegedly for medical treatment. The Muqtadr al-Sadr militia's revolt in Najaf which was creating a problem previously was resolved on his return from Britain in late 2004, following the deal made in London. No doubt the revolt was the bargaining chip of Sistani, but the game was played according to the British Imperial rules.

It is remarkable what the Brits can do with the game of cricket. They really know how to spin the ball. Full marks again to British Imperial diplomacy for this diplomatic coup! They still have a hang for it, notwithstanding that they were last in Iraq way back in the 1920s. They now have access to oil on the cheap, but the difference this time round is that she now has two eager imperial bouncers, the United States and Israel, to protect her turf in the Middle East. One word sums up their imperial strategy for the 21st century — brilliant! The Arabs, unfortunately, have still not got it. And do you know why? Years of indoctrination in elite British institutions and cultural brainwashing have made them intellectually dependent and incapable of escaping from the neocolonial mental gridlock.

Let us now return to the strategic role played by the Royal Institute of International Affairs in preserving and perpetuating British Zionists' imperial influence on the United States (with the help of people like Kissinger) and her former colonies. Recall what Professor Carroll Quigley said about the importance of changing the mindset:

"The second important propaganda effort of the Milner Group in the period after 1909 was the Round Table. This was part of the effort by the circle of the Milner Group to accomplish for the whole Empire what they had done for South Africa."

And surely, propaganda is best achieved through educational establishments, like Universities and think tanks and the mass media, in particular, the print media. The British also realized that it is not possible to keep 430 million people in subjection forever,[9] but hope that, with their propaganda through education, the subjects would be induced to appreciate and cherish British ideals. Lionel Curtis explained:

"A large quarterly like the Round Table[10] is not intended so much for the average reader, as for those who write for the aver-

age reader. It is meant to be a storehouse of information of all kinds upon which publicists can draw.[11]*"*

The average reader has not the foggiest notion on propaganda, so I shall share something here with the still uninitiated. Mr. H.V. Hodson was one of the editors of the *Round Table* and soon after the outbreak of the Second World War, he left the editorship and joined the Ministry of Information (which was then controlled by the Milner Group) as the Director of the Empire Division. After the war he went to the *Sunday Times* as assistant editor.

The British had learned from the American Revolution, in particular, the danger of trying to rule the Empire from London and not to tax without representation as that would lead to certain disruption and turmoil. Britain also came to the realization that the British people do not have the means for the defense of the empire, and at the same time to impose control over its far-flung subjects. The solution was indirect rule and a system of control through indoctrination, so that her subjects would no longer agitate and rebel but would instead cherish and defend her ideals. In this her success is unparalleled in the history of empires.

At this stage, and to prepare the reader for the following discussions, I would like to point out that in three of his wills, Cecil Rhodes appointed Lord Rothschild as a trustee and in one, as his sole trustee.

According to Professor Carroll Quigley, the Royal Institute of International Affairs (RIIA)[12] is nothing but the Milner Group "writ large". It was founded by the Group, has been consistently controlled by the Group, and to this day is still the Milner Group in its widest aspect. It is the legitimate child of the Round Table organization, just as the latter was the legitimate child of the "Closer Union" movement organized in South Africa in 1907. All three of these organizations were formed by a small group of persons; all three received their financial backing from Sir Abe Bailey; and all three used the same methods for working out and propagating their ideas, i.e., the so-called Round Table method of discussion groups, plus a journal. This similarity is not an accident. The new organization was intended to be a wider aspect of the Milner Group, the plan being to influence the leaders of thought through the Round Table and to influence a larger audience through the RIIA.

The real founder of the RIIA was Lionel Curtis and this was

acknowledged in the annual report of the Institute for 1942-1943 where it was stated that: *"**When the institute was founded through the inspiration of Mr. Lionel Curtis during the Peace Conference of Paris in 1919, those associated with him in laying the foundations were a group of comparatively young men and women.**"*

The institute was organized at the Hotel Majestic on May 30, 1919, at a conference attended by British and American experts, hosted by Baron Edmond de Rothschild. The former were essentially the Milner Group, while the latter was a group from *The Inquiry* (the forerunner to the Council on Foreign Relations) and was dominated by associates of J.P. Morgan and Company. This is not surprising as the Milner Group had very close ties with J.P. Morgan and the Carnegie Trust, and merely reflects the interlocking network of international capitalism, or as I prefer, Empire Capitalism. In 1923, the RIIA established its home at No 10, St. James Square, more commonly referred to as Chatham House, and which name is now associated with the institute itself.

The list of the institute's benefactors is most impressive — Carnegie United Kingdom Trustees, the Bank of England, J.D. Rockefeller, the Anglo-Iranian Oil Company, Barclays Bank, Baring Brothers, the British American Tobacco Company, the British South Africa Company, Central Mining and Investment Corporation, Erlangers Ltd., the Ford Motor Company, Hambros' Bank, Imperial Chemical Industries, Lazard Brothers, Lever Brothers, Lloyd's, Lloyds's Bank, the Mercantile and General Insurance Company, the Midland Bank, Reuters, Rothschild and Sons, Stern Brothers, Vickers Armstrong, the Westminster Bank, and Whitehall Securities Corporation.

Now you can see why Henry Kissinger was so eager to sing the praises of the RIIA at the Bicentenary of the Office of Foreign Secretary.

Chatham House has through the years established close working relations with similar organizations. The most important being the Council on Foreign Relations (CFR) in the United States which was regarded as a branch of the RIIA. The close associates and employees of J.P. Morgan and Company controlled the CFR.

How powerful and influential is the RIIA? To answer the question, it is best to let Carroll Quigley say in his own words:

"The extent of that influence is obvious… The Milner Group controls the Institute. Once that is established, the picture changes. The influence of Chatham House appears in its true perspective, not as the influence of an autonomous body but as merely one of many instruments in the arsenal of another power. When the influence which the institute wields is combined with the controlled by the Milner Group in other fields — in education, in administration, in newspaper and periodicals — a really terrifying picture begins to emerge…. The picture is terrifying because such power, whatever the goals at which it may be directed, is too much to be entrusted safely to any group… No country that values its safety should allow what the Milner Group accomplished in Britain — that is, that a small number of men should be able to wield such power in administration and politics, should be given almost complete control over the publications of documents relating to their actions, should be able to exercise such influence over the avenues of information that create public opinion, and should be able to monopolize so completely the writing and teaching of the history of their own period."

And if we look closely at the members of the CFR and what they are doing, a similarly terrifying picture emerges. The ensuing chapter shall examine the CFR in detail.

ENDNOTES:

1. I am not referring to the "elected" British government, but the real power behind the government.
2. All quotes taken from *The Anglo-American Establishment*, (1981, Books In Focus Inc), unless otherwise stated.
3. Ibid. See page 5 of Introduction.
4. The secret society has been known at various times as Milner's Kindergarten, the Round Table, the Rhodes Crowd, the Times Crowd, the All Souls Group, and the Cliveden Set. Carroll Quigley prefers to call the secret society the Milner's Group.
5. Andrew Carnegie, *Triumphant Democracy*, 1893.
6. In Christopher Hitchen's *The Trial of Henry Kissinger*, (2001, Verso), the author gave precise and irrefutable evidence of the various war crimes committed by Henry Kissinger when he was the National Security Adviser to President Nixon and as Secretary of State.
7. Excerpts from the speech.
8. In 1991, President Bush Sr. instigated the Shiites to rebel against Saddam. But when Saddam retaliated brutally to the revolt, the U.S. withdrew their support of the Shiites.
9. This was the approximate number of people under British Rule at the material time.
10. The Round Table is the journal for the Milner's Group, also known as the Round Table Group.
11. Carroll Quigley, *The Anglo-American Establishment*
12. Ibid. page 182

8

The Zionist Anglo-American Shadow Government: The Three-way Tango — Part II

The stated goal of the CFR is a **New World Order under a World Government.** To the average American or, for that matter, the average citizen of the world, this is quackery and a conspiracy theory, notwithstanding that this stated goal was not kept a secret. On February 17, 1950, James P. Warburg, a CFR member, (banker and a member of President FDR's Brain Trust) told the Senate Foreign Relations Committee:

"We shall have a world government whether or not we like it. The only question is whether world government will be achieved by conquest or consent.[1]*"*

That same year, a Chicago Tribune editorial commented:

"The members of the Council are persons of much more than average influence in the community. They have used the prestige that their wealth, their social position, and their education have given them to lead their country towards bankruptcy and military debacle. They should look at their hands. There is blood on them — the dried blood of the last war and the fresh blood of the present one.[2]*"*

Phyllis Schlafly and Rear Admiral Chester Ward, a member of the CFR for 16 years, in their book, ***Kissinger on the Couch***, wrote:

"[The CFR's] purpose of promoting disarmament and submergence of U.S. sovereignty and national independence into an all-powerful one-world government is the only objective

revealed to about 95 percent of 1,551 members (1975 figures). There are two other ulterior purposes that CFR influence is being used to promote; but it is improbable that they are known to more than 75 members, or that these purposes ever have been identified in writing.[3]"

Let us examine its membership.

1) FORMER PRESIDENTS OF THE UNITED STATES

William J. Clinton	George H. W. Bush
Jimmy Carter	Gerald Ford
Richard Nixon	Dwight Eisenhower
Herbert Hoover	

2) FORMER SECRETARIES OF STATE

Madeleine Albright	William Richardson
Warren Christopher	Lawrence Eagleburger
James Baker III	George Schultz
Alexander Haig	Edmund Muskie
Cyrus Vance	Henry Kissinger
William Rogers	Dean Rusk
Christian Herter	John Foster Dulles
Dean Acheson	George Marshall
E.R. Stettinius	Cordell Hull
Henry Stimson	Frank Kellog

3) FORMER SECRETARIES OF DEFENSE

William Cohen	William Perry
Les Aspin	Dick Cheney
Frank Carlucci	Casper Weinberger
Harold Brown	Donald Rumsfeld
James Schlesinger	Elliot Richardson
Melvin Laird	Robert McNamara
George Marshall	James Forrestal

4) FORMER CHAIRMEN, JOINT CHIEFS OF STAFF

John Shalikashvilli	Colin Powell
William Crowe	John Vessy
David Jones	Maxwell Taylor
Lyman Lemnitzer	

5)   FORMER DIRECTORS OF THE CIA

George Tenet	John Deutch
James Woolsey	Robert Gates
William Webster	William Casey
Stanfield Turner	George H. W. Bush
William Colby	James Schlesinger
Richard Helms	John McCone
Allen Dulles	Walter Bedell Smith

I have only listed the members who have attained the Presidency, State Secretaryship, Defense Secretaryship, and the Directorship of the CIA. But its members are also in all the key Departments of the Treasury, the FBI, the Commerce Department, etc. It is not possible to list out the entire membership in this book, but I believe that the members stated above is sufficient to illustrate the power of the CFR. It should also be noted that usually, the key members of the CFR are also members of two other organizations that have similar objectives and who work in tandem with the CFR, namely, the Bilderberg and the Trilateral Commission. The three acting together may be regarded as the *World Wide Web of the Power Elites*. The following quotes ought to put any reader in the proper perspective as to the threat posed by this triumvirate.

"Fifty men have run America, and that's a high figure.[4]"

"The case for government by elites is irrefutable.[5]"

"The Trilateral Commission is intended to be the vehicle for multinational consolidation of the commercial and banking interests by seizing control of the political government of the United States. The Trilateral Commission represents skillful, coordinated effort to seize control and consolidate the four centers of power political, monetary, intellectual and ecclesiastical. What the Trilateral Commission intends is to create a worldwide economic power superior to the political governments of the nation states involved. As managers and creators of the system, they will rule the future.[6]"

Some of the major newspapers that have been controlled or influenced by the CFR are: the New York Times; the Washington Post; the Wall Street Journal; the Boston Globe; the Baltimore Sun; the Chicago Sun-Times; the L.A. Times; the Associated Press; the United Press

International; and Reuters News Services.

With regard to magazines, the following comes to mind: Time; Fortune; Money; People; Entertainment Weekly; Sports Illustrated; Newsweek; Business Week; U.S. News & World Report; the National Review; Reader's Digest; the Atlantic Monthly; Forbes; Look; and Harper's Magazine.

Acknowledgment of their key roles in supporting the elites' agenda was given by David Rockefeller, founder of the Trilateral Commission, in an address to a meeting of the Trilateral Commission, in June, 1991:

"We are grateful to the Washington Post, The New York Times, Time Magazine and other great publications whose directors have attended our meetings and respected their promises of discretion for almost forty years. It would have been impossible for us to develop our plan for the world if we had been subject to the bright lights of publicity during those years. But the work is now much more sophisticated and prepared to march towards a world government. The supranational sovereignty of an intellectual elite and world bankers is surely preferable to the national auto-determination practiced in past centuries."

Companies that have been under their control or influence are: Morgan Stanley; Kuhn-Loeb; Lehman Bros.; Chase Manhattan Bank; J.P. Morgan & Co.; First National City Bank; Brown Brothers; Harriman & Co.; Bank of New York; Citicorp; Chemical Bank; Bankers Trust of New York; Manufacturers Hanover; Morgan Guaranty; Equitable Life; New York Life; Metropolitan Life; Mutual of New York; Exxon; Mobil; Atlantic-Richfield; Texaco; IBM; AT & T; General Electric; ITT; DuPont; General Motors; Ford; Chrysler; R.H. Macy; Allied Stores; and many more.[7]

Let's turn our attention to the Zionists' role as the ultimate spin doctors. Now, if you were to tell your neighbor that the mass media are chiefly instruments of propaganda, what would his response be? In most cases, you will be given a look that would conclusively reveal that he thought that you were nuts. And if you went around saying publicly that the Zionists control the mass media, you would be labeled "anti-semitic" at once. Read on and be prepared for some sweeping admissions by the Zionists themselves.

The Encyclopaedia Judaica[8] states: ***"Since the early years of motion pictures, Jews have played a major role in the development of the industry and have been prominent in all its branches... Thus all the large Hollywood companies with the exception of United Artists (a distributing company established by Hollywood actors who feared that the big producers would restrict their artistic freedom) were founded and controlled by Jews. In addition, the first bank to finance the film industry was the Jewish owned Kuhn, Loeb and Co., in 1919."*** (Emphasis added)

The Judaica's article on the control of television and radio is likewise, illuminating.

"In the U.S. Jews have played a major role in the development of television and radio as they have in other entertainment industries. They have been well represented in all executive and technical aspects of the industry, as well as among performers. Jews held key positions in the emergence and shaping of the three major U.S. networks. David Sarnoff started the first U.S. radio chain, the National Broadcasting Company (NBC) in 1926 as a service of the Radio Corporation of America (RCA). He became president of RCA in 1930. When he retired in 1970, he was succeeded by his son Robert, who had earlier served as president of NBC. Comparable in influence and competitive to NBC is the Columbia Broadcasting System (CBS) which was founded under the presidency of William S. Paley two years after NBC was organized. Both NBC and CBS pioneered in the production of television — black and white and later colour. The third major network, the American Broadcasting Company (ABC), was an outgrowth of the NBC network. It was bought out by United Paramount Theatre, and Leonard H. Goldenson became its president. Apart from the heads of the major networks, many Jews worked at all levels in the organizations as well as in the smaller networks, educational services, local stations, etc."

What is the situation as at 2004?

The largest media conglomerate is without doubt, Time Warner, previously known as AOL-Time Warner, when AOL bought Time Warner for US$160 billion in 2000. Although Gerald Levine (a Jew)[9] was ousted as the CEO, Jewish influence remains. That influence is exercised through Time Inc. by Jodi Khan and Meg Siesfeld (both Jews) under the executive editor Ned Desmond, and they all report to the editor-in-chief, Norman Pearlstine (a Jew). Time Warner's subsidiary, HBO is America's largest pay-TV cable network and boasts of having 26 million subscribers. It also controls the production of feature films through Warner Bros. Studios, Castle Rock Entertainment and New Line Cinema. The publishing division controls over 50 magazines that include Time, Sports Illustrated and People. Up till 2004, it also controlled Warner Music, which had 50 labels. Warner Music was purchased by billionaire Edgar Bronfman, Junior (a Jew).

Following as a close second is the Walt Disney Company controlled by Michael Eisner (a Jew). It controls Walt Disney Television, Touchstone Television, Buena Vista Television and cable networks with more than 100 million subscribers. Feature film companies under its control are Walt Disney Motion Pictures, Hollywood Pictures, Touchstone Pictures, Caravan Pictures and Miramax Films managed by the Weinstein Brothers (Jews). In 1995, Eisner purchased Capital Cities/ABC Inc. which owns the ABC television network. This network has over 200 affiliated TV stations, 2,900 radio stations and produces over 7,000 radio programs. The sports network, ESPN is headed by George W. Bodenheimer (a Jew). And like Time Warner, it is into heavy publishing, controlling Walt Disney Company Book Publishing, Hyperion Books and Miramax Books which publishes books and magazines in over 50 languages and a readership of hundreds of millions.

Ranking third is Viacom, headed by Sumner Redstone (a Jew). The company produces and distributes TV programs for the three major networks and owns 39 television stations. It's wholly-owned CBS television network controls a substantial network of radio stations. Feature films are produced by Paramount Pictures. Viacom also has a publishing division and owns Simon & Schuster, Scribner, The Free Press, Fireside, and Archway Paperbacks. Viacom is the world's largest provider of cable programming via Showtime, MTV, Nickelodeon, Black Entertainment Television and other networks.

NBC Universal ranks fourth and was at one time owned by Edgar Bronfman, Jr. of the Seagram Company, the famous liquor company. His father Edgar Bronfman, Sr. is the President of the World Jewish Congress. And even though the Bronfman family sold Seagram to Vivendi in 2000, Edgar Bronfman, Jr. continues to play a critical role in the merged company. Ron Meyer (a Jew) is the President and Chief Operating Officer of Universal Studios, Stacey Snider (a Jew) is Chairman of Universal Pictures and Jeff Zucker (a Jew) is the President of NBC Universal Television Group.

The right-wing Fox Television network is owned by Rupert Murdoch's News Corporation. And although Rupert Murdoch is an Australian, he is an ardent supporter of Zionism and Israel. It can be said that Fox News was the official mouthpiece for President George Bush for the invasion of Iraq. The key man in Murdoch's organization is Peter Chernin (a Jew) who is the President and Chief Operating Officer. He is ably supported by Gail Berman who heads Fox Entertainment, Jane Friedman, CEO of HarperCollins and Thomas Rothman who heads Fox Film Entertainment. The most virulent right-wing newspaper, the Weekly Standard, headed by the neoconservative William Kristol is published by the News Corporation.

The control of the print media by the Jews is equally impressive. A good starting point is the Newhouse media empire which owns 31 daily newspapers and several major magazines, which includes the New Yorker, Vogue, Wired, Glamour, and Vanity Fair. Newhouse uses underhanded tactics, such as slashing down advertising rates, to bankrupt its competitors and to acquire them.

The three leading newspapers in the United States are owned and controlled by the Jews. The New York Times was originally owned by Henry J. Raymond and George Jones. It was acquired by Adolph Ochs (a Jew) and today the newspaper is run by his great-great-grandson Arthur Sulzberger, Jr. This family also owns several other newspapers, including the Boston Globe, and several TV and radio stations. They also publish the International Herald Tribune, touted to be the most widely distributed English language daily in the world.

The equally prestigious Washington Post is also owned and controlled by the Jews. In 1933, it was purchased by Eugene Meyer and was for a long time run by his daughter, Katherine Meyer Graham. She has since been succeeded by her son, Donald Graham. The magazine Newsweek is published by the Washington Post company with an estimated circulation of over 3 million.

The Wall Street Journal is controlled by Peter R. Kann (a Jew), who is the Chairman and CEO of Dow Jones. Dow Jones & Company publishes several other key newspapers and the reputable financial weekly, Barron's.

What I have just detailed is merely an outline of the Zionists' total control of the mass media. But still, there may be some who would yet find it difficult to believe this fact, as the United States has been ceaselessly touted as the world champion of press freedom, and Human Rights Activists have been incessantly advertising the 'genuine press freedom' of the West and denouncing the mass media of third world countries as government-controlled mouthpieces.

If so, it is time for another wake-up call.

For the establishment to induce public cooperation with its program, it has always been expedient to manipulate the information industry that is very much responsible for what the people think of the current affairs. A prime mover in this process was J.P. Morgan.[10]

In 1917, Congressman Oscar Callaway inserted the following statement in the Congressional Record:[11]

"In March 1915, the J.P. Morgan interests, the steel, shipbuilding and power interests, and their subsidiary organizations, got together 12 men high up in the newspaper world and employed them to select the most influential newspapers in the United States and sufficient number of them to control generally the policy of the daily press of the United States. These 12 men worked the problem out by selecting 179 newspapers, and then began, by an elimination process, to retain only those necessary for the purpose of controlling the general policy of the daily press throughout the country. They found that it was only necessary to purchase the control of 25 of the greatest newspapers. The 25 papers were agreed upon; emissaries were sent to purchase the policy, national and international, of these papers; an agreement was reached; the policy of the papers were bought, to be paid for by the month; an editor was furnished for each paper to properly supervise and edit information regarding the question of preparedness, militarism, financial policies, and other things of national and international nature considered vital to the interests of the purchasers. This policy also included the suppression of everything in opposition to the wishes of the interest served."

Soon after World War II, the suppression of the press came into play again, which drew a comment from the eminent historian Charles Beard, former president of the American Historical Association:[12]

"The Rockefeller Foundation and the Council on Foreign Relations... intend to prevent, if they can, a repetition of what they call in the vernacular 'the debunking journalistic campaign following World War I.' Translated into precise English, this means that the foundation and the council do not want journalists or any other persons to examine too closely and criticize too freely the official propaganda and official statements relative to 'our basic aims and activities' during World War II. In short, they hope that, among other things, the policies and measures of Franklin D. Roosevelt will escape in coming years the critical analysis, evaluation and exposition that befell the policies and measures of President Woodrow Wilson and the Entente Allies after World War I."

In 1953, Harry E. Barnes explained how the censorship process worked:[13]

"The methods followed by the various groups interested in blacking out the truth about world affairs since 1932 are numerous and ingenious, but, aside from subterranean persecution of individuals, they fall mainly into the following patterns or categories: (1) excluding scholars suspected of revisionist views from access to public documents which are freely opened to 'court historians' and other apologists for the foreign policy of President Roosevelt; (2) intimidating publishers of books and periodicals, so that even those who might wish to publish books and articles setting forth the revisionist point of view do not dare to do so; (3) ignoring or obscuring published material which embodies revisionist facts and arguments; and (4) smearing revisionist authors and their books.

"...The book clubs and the main sales outlets for books are controlled by powerful pressure groups which are opposed to truth on such matters. These outlets not only refuse to market critical books in this field but also threaten to boycott other books by those publishers who defy the blackout ultimatum."

What happened back in the 1950s is still in operation today. The late journalist Gary Webb, who broke the story of the CIA's involvement in drug trafficking in *The Dark Alliance*, has this to say about the free press:

"Do we have free press today? Sure we do. It's free to report all the sex scandals it wants, all the stock market news we can handle, every new health fad that comes down the pike, and every celebrity marriage or divorce that happens. But when it comes to the real down and dirty stuff — stories like Tailwind, the October Surprise, the El Mozote massacre, corporate corruption, or CIA involvement in drug trafficking — that's where we begin to see the limits of our freedom. In today's media environment, sadly, such stories are not even open for discussion.[14]*"*

George Monbiot in a recent article[15] was scathing in his criticism of the U.S. media. He penned:

"The role of the media corporation in the U.S. is similar to that of oppressive state regimes elsewhere: they decide what the public will and won't be allowed to hear, and either punish or recruit the social deviants who insist on telling a different story. The journalists they employ do what almost all journalists working under repressive regimes do: they internalize the demands of the censor, and understand, before anyone has told them, what is permissible and what is not. So, when they are faced with a choice between a fable which helps the Republicans, and a reality which hurts them, they choose the fable. As their fantasies accumulate, the story they tell about the world veers further and further from reality. Anyone who tries to bring the people back down to earth is denounced as a traitor and a fantasist. And anyone who seeks to become president must first learn to live in fairyland."

In the preceding paragraphs, I have tried to show how the media is controlled by powerful forces, and in particular the Zionist Power Elites. It is never easy to come face to face with the stark reality. It is disorientating. But we must take the bull by the horns and confront it head on, for it was propaganda that hoodwinked so many Americans to support the illegal invasion of Iraq. But for those who still refuse to come to grips with what is happening, I would suggest that you recall and re-examine every major statement by President Bush, Dick Cheney, Donald Rumsfeld, Condoleezza Rice, Collin Powell, Paul Wolfowitz and the other neoconservatives prior to the invasion and how these statements were embellished in the major newspapers as well as the TV and radio networks.

Next, carefully read the following summary of the ***Israeli Communications Priorities 2003,*** prepared for the Wexner Foundation, and then ask yourself to what extent have you been influenced by the strategies contained in that document and how those strategies are reflected in the mass media.

The document is essentially a propaganda road map for the Zionists to exploit the political ramifications of 9-11 and the invasion of Iraq to their advantage. Thus far, the Zionists have achieved all the objectives mapped out. It is an incredible accomplishment given the time constraints. Once again, it illustrates the total dedication and commitment of the Zionist Agenda.

Here is the summary; my comments are in bold.

Wexner Analysis: Israeli Communications Priorities

Overview

The world has changed. The words, themes and messages on behalf of Israel must include and embrace the new reality of a Post-Saddam world. In the past, we have URGED A LOWER PROFILE for Israel out of fear that the American people would blame Israel for what was happening in the rest of the Middle East. Now is the time to link America's success in dealing with terrorism and dictators from a position of strength to Israel's ongoing efforts to eradicate terrorism on and within its borders. In the current political environment, you have little to lose and lots to gain by aligning with America. With all the anti-Americanism across the globe and all the protest and demonstrations, we are looking for allies that share our commitment to security and an end to terrorism and are prepared to say so. Israel is just such an ally.

Perceptions of Israel and the Israeli-Palestinian conflict are being almost entirely colored and often overshadowed by the continuing action in Iraq. Partisan differences still exist (the political left remains your problem) and complaints about Israeli heavy-handedness still exist. Advocates of Israel have about two weeks to get their message in order before world attention turns to the so-called "road map" and how best to "solve" the Israeli-Palestinian conflict. Developing that message is the purpose of this memo.

Author's Note: This is not a policy document. This document is strictly a communications manual. As with every memo we provide, we have

133

used the same scientific methodology to isolate specific words, phrases, themes and messages that will resonate with at least 70% of the American audience. There will certainly be some people, particularly those on the political left, who will oppose whatever words you use, but the language that follows will help you secure support from a large majority of Americans. These recommendations are based on two "dial test" sessions in Chicago and Los Angeles conducted during the first ten days of the Iraqi war for the Wexner Foundation.

Essential Conclusions

This document is rather long because it is impossible to communicate all that is needed in simple one-sentence sound-bites. Yes, we have provided those on pages that follow, but we have taken the space to explain why the language is so important and the context in which it needs to be used. If you only read two pages, these are the key conclusions:

1) <u>Iraq colors all. Saddam is our best defense, even if he is dead</u>

> The American worldview is entirely dominated by developments in Iraq. This is a unique opportunity for Israelis to deliver a message of support and unity at a time of great international anxiety and opposition from some of our European "allies." For a year — A SOLID YEAR — you should be invoking the name of Saddam Hussein and how Israel was always behind America's efforts to rid the world of this ruthless dictator and liberate their people. Saddam will remain a powerful symbol of terror to Americans for a long time to come. A pro-Israeli expression of solidarity with the American people in their successful effort to remove Saddam will be appreciated.

Comments: The Zionists have achieved 100% success. 60% of Americans still believe that Saddam is connected to 9-11 and has WMD. The Arabs and Muslims are being negatively perceived by the Americans.

2) <u>Stick to your message but don't say it the same way twice</u>

> We have seen this in the past but never so starkly as today. Americans are paying very close attention to international developments and are particularly sensitive to any kind of apparent

dogma or canned presentation. If they hear you repeating the exact words over and over again, they will come to distrust your message. If your speakers can't find different ways to express similar principles, keep them off the air.

Comments: Again total success. Every right-wing spokesman has played it just right, the latest example being the President's inaugural speech. The agenda was same, but the presentation was not.

3) It DOES NOT HELP when you compliment President Bush. When you want to identify with and align yourself with America, just say it. Don't use Bush as a synonym for the United States

Even with the destruction of the Hussein regime and all the positive reactions from the Iraqi people, there remains about 20% of America that opposes the Iraq War, and they are overwhelmingly Democrats. That leaves about half the Democrats who support the war even if they don't support George Bush. You antagonize the latter half unnecessarily every time you compliment the President. Don't do it.

Comments: Although I do not agree with the statistics, the 2004 elections have proven this strategy as the right one.

4) Conveying sensitivity and a sense of value is a must

Most of the best performing sound bites mention children, families and democratic values. Don't just say that Israel is morally aligned with the U.S. Show it in your language. The children component is particularly important. It is essential that you talk about *"the day, not long from now, when Palestinian children and Israeli children will play side-by-side as their parents watch approvingly."*

Comments: That says it all. Peace initiatives are just so much hogwash. The Zionists have no real intention to have a lasting peace with the Palestinians. What is important is getting the correct image. So the Palestinians are terrorists and Sharon, a man of peace. Again 100% success.

5) <u>SECURITY sells</u>

Security has become the key fundamental principle for all Americans. Security is the context by which you should explain Israel's need for loan guarantees and military aid, as well as why Israel just can't give up land. The settlements are our Achilles heel, and the best response (which is still quite weak) is the need for security that this buffer creates.

Comments: This has always been the classic Israeli hard sell and they have always succeeded. The provocation against Iran is another example of this strategy.

6) <u>The Language in this document will work, but it will work best when it is accompanied with passion and compassion</u>

Too many supporters of Israel speak out of anger or shout when faced with opposition. Listeners are more likely to accept your arguments if they like how you express them. They will bless these words but they will truly accept them if and only if they accept you.

Comments: True PR tactics. Form is as important as content. This is the greatest failure of the Muslims, in their inability to convey the true message of Islam.

7) <u>Find yourself a good female spokesperson</u>

In all our testing, women are found to be more credible than men. And if the woman has children, that's even better.

Comments: Is it any wonder that Judith Miller of the New York Times can get away with murder?

8) <u>Link Iraqi Liberation with the plight of the Palestinian people</u>

It is likely that the most effective argument you have right now are those that link the right of the Iraqi people to live in freedom with the right of the Palestinian people to be governed by those who truly represent them. If you express your concern for the plight of the Palestinian people and how it is unfair, unjust and immoral that they be forced to accept leaders who steal and kill in their name, you will be building credibility for your support of the average Palestinian while undermining the credibility of their leadership.

Comments: It cannot be said that this strategy has worked. But it explains why Sharon refuses to deal with Arafat.

9) Of course rhetorical questions work, don't they?

Ask a question to which there is only one answer is hard to lose. It is essential that your communication be laced with rhetorical questions, which is how Jews talk anyway.

Comments: Cannot fault this tactic. This tactic is a fundamental principle in the art of cross-examination by attorneys and is very effective.

10) Mahmoud Abbas is still a question mark. Leave him that way

You stand much more to lose by attacking him now. But similarly, he is not worthy of praise. Talk about your hopes for the future, but lay out the principles you expect him to uphold: an end to violence, recognition of Israel, reform of his own government etc.

Comments: Spot on. Israel is playing Abbas like a fiddle and Abbas is a willing puppet. But this will not work in the long term. Ultimately Abbas will be rejected by his people.

Such is the deviousness of the Israelis and their Zionist masters. But credit must be given to this brilliant propaganda strategy and the success that it has given to the Zionists and Israel.

Notwithstanding this public document, it is indeed pathetic to see the inability of the Arabs and the Muslims to launch effective counter-information offensives to overcome the widespread Zionist misinformation. Al Qaeda and the Jihadists have now replaced the former Soviet Empire as the enemy of the so-called free world.

For the Americans, I hope this is a wake-up call, but I guess not. It is only too apparent that Americans still continue to believe the Zionist-controlled mass media. 59,000 dead Americans in Vietnam have not brought home the lessons of the fascist Zionist propaganda. The youths of the United States today are being brainwashed likewise into becoming canon fodder for the Zionist Anglo-American Empire's ambitions to control the world's fast depleting resources, particularly oil.

Empire Capitalism can only be sustained through wars of aggressions, and that is why, every two decades or so, a new war needs to be unleashed to usher in a new cycle of growth and economic expansion. The dead will be forgotten when a new consumer boom replaces the hardships of preceding years. If, as according to Madeleine Albright, 500,000 dead Iraqi children were worth the price for containing Saddam Hussein, what are a few thousand dead Americans, if the endgame is total control of the Middle East oil supplies?

ENDNOTES:

1. David Allen Rivera, *The New World Order Exposed*, (2004, Thinkers Library)
2. Ibid., pg. 179
3. Phyllis Schlafly and Chester Ward, Kissinger on the Couch, (1975, New York, Arlington House Publishers)
4. Joseph Kennedy, July 26, 1936, quoted in the New York Times.
5. Senator William Fulbright, Former Chairman of the U.S. Senate Foreign Relations Committee, stated at a 1963 symposium entitled, "The Elite and the Electorate — Is Government by the People Possible?"
6. U.S. Senator Barry Goldwater, *With No Apologies,* (1979, Morrow)
7. David Allen Rivera, *The New World Order Exposed*, pg. 187
8. Encyclopaedia Judaica, pgs. 446 and 449
9. The reference to Jew hereinafter merely follows the connotation given by Encyclopaedia Judaica
10. James Perloff, *The Shadows of Power*, (1988 Western Island), pg. 178
11. Ibid., citing Congressional Record, February 19, 1917, Volume 54, pgs. 2947–48
12. Ibid., pg. 179, citing Charles Beard, "Who's to Write the History of the War?", Saturday Evening Post, October 4, 1947, pg. 172
13. Ibid., pg. 180, citing Harry E. Barnes, ed., "Perpetual War for Perpetual Peace", Saturday Evening Post (1953) pgs. 15–16 and 18
14. Gary Webb, "The Mighty Wurlitzer Plays On", from *Into the Buzzsaw*, ed. Kristina Borjesson, (2002 Prometheus Books)
15. George Monbiot, "A Televisual Fairyland", January 18, 2005, The Guardian

9

Case Studies in Zionist Deceptions

Americans are generally unaware of the lie that led America into the First World War. On April 2, 1917, President Woodrow Wilson addressed both chambers of Congress and urged them to declare war on Germany. The justification for going to war was a lie — that a German submarine had sunk S.S. Sussex in the English Channel in violation of international law and that U.S. citizens on board the ship were killed. In the ensuing war, the United States suffered over 115,000 killed in action, and over 200,000 were either injured or maimed for life. The S.S. Sussex had not been destroyed and there were, in fact, no American casualties.

What made President Wilson commit such a dastardly act?

By October 1916, Britain was on the verge of defeat. Germany had made an offer for peace with Britain, but this was rejected. Why did Britain, on the verge of defeat, reject the peace offer?

A bargain was made between the British War Cabinet and the British Zionists, known as the London Agreement, in which the Zionists promised that in exchange for Britain's support for a Jewish State in Palestine, they would conspire to compel the United States to enter the war as an ally of Britain. The Prime Minister of Britain at the material time was Lloyd George, a Zionist, who dispatched a trusted representative, one Mr. Josiah Wedgewood to the United States to put into effect the London Agreement.

In the United States, Mr. Wedgewood's critical assignment was assisted by Col. Edward Mandel House who arranged a meeting with U.S. Zionists on December 25, 1916, at the old Hotel Savoy. Mr. Wedgewood conveyed to the Zionists, gathered at the meeting, Britain's undertaking to turn over Palestine upon the defeat of

Germany. Assured by this assurance, the Zionists of the United States railroaded the U.S. to declare war on Germany. Justice Louis Dembitz Brandeis, a Zionist who was appointed to the U.S. Supreme Court by President Wilson wrote the opinion to the President that the alleged sinking of S.S. Sussex and the loss of American lives justified the declaration of war.

In his book, **Makers of War**[1], the Member of Parliament Mr. Francis Neilson wrote:

"In America, Woodrow Wilson, desperate to find a pretext to enter the war, found it at last in the 'sinking' of the Sussex in mid-channel. Someone invented a yarn that American lives had been lost. With this excuse he went to Congress for a declaration of war. Afterwards, the Navy found that the Sussex had not been sunk and that no lives had been lost."

The Zionist bargain is corroborated by the letter of November 2, 1917, from Lord Balfour to Lord Rothschild, commonly known as the **Balfour Declaration**, which is reproduced below:

"Dear Lord Rothschild,

"I have much pleasure in conveying to you on behalf of His Majesty's Government the following declaration of sympathy with Jewish Zionist aspirations, which has been submitted and approved by the Cabinet.

"His Majesty's Government view with favor the establishment in Palestine of a national home for the Jewish people and will use their best endeavors to facilitate the achievement of this object, it being clearly understood that nothing shall be done which may prejudice the civil and religious rights of existing non-Jewish communities in Palestine or the rights and political status enjoyed by Jews in any other country.

"I should be grateful if you would bring this Declaration to the Knowledge of the Zionist Federation.

"Yours sincerely,

"Arthur James Balfour"

Such is the arrogance of the British government and the power of the British Zionists in extracting this Declaration as, at the material time, Palestine was still under the jurisdiction and control of Turkey. Thus we have a situation whereby one country (Britain) promises to a Zionist organization (not even a country) that they could have a piece of real estate, then under the jurisdiction of another country (Turkey), and make that their country. The present turmoil in the Middle East is the direct result of this Zionist deceit and deception.

A similar deception was perpetrated during the Second World War. A debate raged across the country on whether the U.S. should intervene. The majority of Americans were against intervention, but President Roosevelt felt otherwise, although in public speeches he pledged, *"I have said this before, but I shall say it again and again and again: Your boys are not going to be sent into any foreign wars.*[2]*"* But although he was for intervention, he did not have any valid reason to enter the war. Like President Wilson, during the First World War, President Roosevelt needed a pretext; and Britain was in dire straits and needed the U.S. to intervene on her behalf once again.

In the ground-breaking book, ***Desperate Deceptions: British Covert Operations in the United States***,[3] Thomas Mahl reveals how British Intelligence contributed to Roosevelt's success in overcoming domestic opposition to the war. In 1940, a millionaire businessman by the name of William Stephenson, code-named Intrepid, was dispatched to the United States to head the British Security Coordination (BSC) housed at the 38th floor of the International Building of the Rockefeller Centre. The activities of the BSC were described graphically by Ernest Cunco, who served as the liaison between the BSC and the White House:

"It ran espionage agents, tampered with the mails, tapped telephones, smuggled propaganda into the country, disrupted public gatherings, covertly subsidized newspapers, radios, and organizations, perpetrated forgeries, violated the Alien Registration Act, shanghaied sailors numerous times, and possibly murdered one or more persons in the country."

Manipulation of opinion polls was one of the methods used to swing public opinion, and the Gallup Poll was effectively infiltrated by British agents. David Ogilvy wrote:

"I could not have a better boss than Dr. Gallup. His confidence in me was such that I do not recall his ever reading any of my reports I write in his name."

In 1940–1941, a series of polls were rigged to show pro-British sentiments among leading organizations, sentiments for intervention, and antagonistic opposition to the isolationist movement.

The author also revealed how the British Intelligence aided Roosevelt's re-election, by rigging the Republican Party's nomination of Wendell Willkie, an unknown lawyer for J.P. Morgan as the GOP's presidential nominee, who was pro-British and a supporter for intervention and marginalizing Robert Taft who was firmly against intervention. Thus, the American electorate was not given a real choice, as both contenders were for intervention, and as President Roosevelt was the incumbent, he had a decided advantage. The British efforts were aided by the Rockefeller-Morgan financial interests.

The recent 2004 presidential elections seem like a repeat performance as Kerry was picked to marginalize Howard Dean, the anti-war candidate. Kerry, like Willkie, was for intervention. Kerry repeatedly affirmed that he would do a better job kicking Iraqi butts and would, in fact, escalate the conflict by pouring more troops into Iraq. Thus once again, the American electorate were denied a real choice. But this was exactly what the Zionists wanted, a devious warmonger in the person of George W. Bush. Again, there was a secret campaign orchestrated by Britain and the U.S. to lie to the American people. The same propaganda method was used.

Leading public figures of the press and news media were recruited or persuaded by the BSC, to sway public opinion in favor of intervention, the most notable being George Backer, publisher of the New York Post; Helen Ogden Reid of the New York Herald Tribune; Paul Patterson, publisher of the Baltimore Sun; A.H. Sulzberger of the New York Times; Walter Lippman and Marshall Field of the Chicago Sun; and Henry Luce, publisher of the Time, Life and Fortune magazines.

So what's new?

Notwithstanding the fact that it was the attack on Pearl Harbor that gave President Roosevelt the pretext to declare war, the concerted campaign by the British Zionists and their counterparts in the

United States laid the groundwork for a more hostile public opinion against Germany. To appreciate the extent of the deceit of President Roosevelt, I need only quote Robert Sherwood, the president's biographer who said:

"If the isolationists had known the full extent of the secret alliance between the United States and Britain, their demands for the President's impeachment would have rumbled like thunder through the land.[4] *"*

This secret alliance resulted in Roosevelt sending, without congressional approval, fifty destroyers to Britain, hundreds of millions of ammunition rounds. Roosevelt also ordered U.S. ships to sail directly into the war zone to provoke German attacks on the ships, and dropped depth charges on German U-boats. Germany did not respond to this provocation, knowing full well that America's intervention would lead to her defeat as in the First World War.[5]

Similar provocations were directed at Japan, as evidenced in the diary of Henry Stimson, Secretary of the War Department. He wrote:

"We face the delicate question of the diplomatic fencing to be done so as to be sure Japan is put into the wrong and makes the first bad move – overt move…. The question was how we should manoeuvre them [the Japanese] into the position of firing the first shot.[6] *"*

The answer was a trade embargo against Japan. Additionally, Japanese assets were frozen in the United States and the Panama Canal was closed to Japanese shipping. The final provocation was made eleven days before the attack on Pearl Harbor when President Roosevelt sent an ultimatum to the Japanese that unless they withdrew from China, trade would not resume. The rest is history.

In *Infamy: Pearl Harbor and Its Aftermath*, John Toland reveals that America knew in advance the plans by the Japanese to attack Pearl Harbor, but the intelligence was withheld from the Commanders in Hawaii, Admiral Kimmel and General Walter C. Short, who were made patsies by a commission headed by Supreme Court Justice Owen Roberts. But a subsequent Court Martial mandated by Congress in 1944, overturned the Commission's findings. However, President Roosevelt suppressed the findings of the Court Martial on the grounds of national security in wartime.

143

In the First World War, the Zionists orchestrated the U.S. intervention to defeat Germany in exchange for Britain's aid and agreement in establishing a Zionist state in Palestine. The objective could not be achieved due to various geopolitical considerations. But the Zionists held on to the promise made by Britain. In the Second World War, the defeat of Germany was crucial to the Zionists' plans. Once again, the British Zionists orchestrated the U.S. intervention to defeat Germany. And in 1948, they were duly rewarded with the prize they had yearned for so long — the State of Israel.

Since that time, Israel has harbored her imperial ambition to be the **Overlord of the Middle East**, from the Nile to the Euphrates.

The occupation of Iraq has to a large extent helped Israel fulfill that ambition. To this our attention will be directed at in the next two Chapters. Like Pearl Harbor, which enabled President Roosevelt to wage war in Europe, the invasion of Iraq could not have been possible without 9-11. In fact, 9-11 has been referred to as the "New Pearl Harbor". Perhaps, in years to come, there might be a book entitled *Infamy: 9-11 and its Aftermath* by a truth seeker to expose the lies and deceits of 9-11 and how it was used as a pretext for the open-ended War on Terror and the coming nuclear wars.[7]

ENDNOTES:

1. Francis Neilson, *Makers of War*, (1950, Flanders Hall Publishers)
2. Cited by James Perloff in *Shadows of Power*. Source: *The Public Papers and Addresses of Franklin D. Roosevelt*, Samuel I. Rosenman, comp., (1941, New York, Macmillan).
3. Thomas E. Mahl, *Desperate Deceptions: British Covert Operations in the United States, 1939-1944*, (1998, Brassy's, Washington D.C.)
4. William Stevenson, *A Man Called Intrepid*, (1976, New York, Harcourt Brace Jovanovich)
5. James Perloff, ibid., p. 66
6. Ibid., p. 67
7. Although there have been several books on 9-11, no one as yet has dug up conclusive evidence admissible in a court of law of the Bush regime's complicity in the said attacks. The two leading books on this issue are *The New Pearl Harbor* by David Ray Griffin (2004, Olive Branch Press) and the pioneering work of Ahmed Nafeez Mosaddeq, *The War on Freedom: How and Why America was Attacked on September 11, 2001*, (2002, Calif., Tree of Life Publications)

10

The Zionist Thread

There is a thread that runs through the preceding chapters — the thread of Zionism. In this chapter, I shall endeavor to show that the ultimate beneficiary of all the intrigues, conspiracies and deceptions of the past sixty years up to the present moment is the Zionists and their dream of building the Third Temple at Jerusalem, the keystone in the Zionist Empire edifice. It is in this diabolical quest of the Zionists that will bring about nuclear wars in the near future. This would be detailed in Part III. But first things first.

To put you, in the proper state of mind and to prepare you for the initial emotional and psychological disorientation that will follow from the realization of the inevitable nuclear wars provoked by Zionist Israel in the next few years, I have extracted key statements from Zionist leaders and their collaborators in Britain and the United States for your perusal. I offer no commentaries as the statements are plainly understood. The principal source for the quotations are from *Expulsion of the Palestinians: The Concept of 'Transfer' in Zionist Political Thought, 1882-1948* and *Imperial Israel and the Palestinians: The Politics of Expansion* both by Nur Masalha, without which the first part of this chapter could not have been written. I believe that upon reading these quotations, you will come to the same conclusion as myself, that Zionism is evil.

1) Zionist Rationale for the Creation of the Zionist State of Israel

"A land without a people for a people without a land.

"If Lord Shaftesbury was literally inexact in describing Palestine as a country without a people, he was essentially correct, for there is no Arab people living in intimate fusion with the country, utilizing its

145

resources and stamping it with a characteristic impress: there is at best an Arab encampment.¹"

"If we wish to give a country to a people without a country, it is utter foolishness to allow it to be a country of two peoples. This can only cause trouble. The Jews will suffer and so will their neighbors. One of the two: a different place must be found either for the Jews or for their neighbors.²" — **Israel Zangwill**

"In its initial stage, Zionism was conceived by its pioneers as a movement wholly depending on mechanical factors: there is a country which happens to be called Palestine, a country without a people and on the other hand, there exist the Jewish people, and it has no country. What else is necessary, then, than to fit the gem into the ring, to unite this people with this country? The owners of the country [the Turks] must therefore, be persuaded and convinced that this marriage is advantageous not only for the Jewish people and for the country, but also for themselves.³"

"The British told us that there are some hundred thousand Negroes [Kushim] and for those there is no value.⁴"

"By a Jewish national home, I mean the creation of such conditions that as a country is developed, we can pour in a considerable number of immigrants and finally establish such a society in Palestine that Palestine shall be as Jewish as England is English, or America, American.⁵" — **Chaim Weizmann**

"Let us not be too familiar with the Arab fellahin lest our children adopt their ways and learn from their ugly deeds. Let all those who are loyal to the Torah avoid ugliness and that which resembles it and keep their distance from the fellahin and their base attributes.⁶" — **Moshe Smilansky**

"When we occupy the land, we shall bring immediate benefits to the state that received us. We must expropriate gently the private property on the estates assigned to us. We shall try to spirit the penniless population across the border by procuring employment for it in the transit countries, while denying it any employment in our country. The property owners will come over to our side. Both the process of expropriation and the removal of the poor must be carried out discreetly and circumspectly. Let the owners of immovable property believe that they are cheating us, selling us something far more than they are worth. But we are not going to sell them anything back.⁷" — **Theodore Herzl**

"There is a fundamental and decisive difference between the situation of the Arabs as a nation and that of the Jews as a nation. Palestine is not needed by the Arabs from the national point of view. They are bound to other countries. There in Syria, in Iraq, in the Arabian Peninsula lies the homeland of the Arab peoples.[8]"

On whether Palestinians can be deprived of their rights:

"There is no answer to this question nor can there be, and we are not obliged to provide it because we are not responsible for the fact that a particular individual man was born in a certain place, and not several kilometers away from there.[9]"   **— Moshe Beilinson**

2) The Modus Operandi: Expulsion and Genocide

"We must be prepared either to drive out by sword the Arab tribes in possession as our fathers did or to grapple with the problem of a large alien population, mostly Mohammedans and accustomed for centuries to despise us.[10]"   **— Israel Zangwill**

"He [Baron Edmond James de Rothschild] advised me to carry on in similar activities, but it is better, he said, not to transfer the Arabs to Syria and Trans-Jordan as these are parts of the land of Israel, but to Mesopotamia [Iraq]. He added that in these cases he would be ready to send Arabs, at his expense, new agricultural machines, and agricultural advisers.[11]"   **— Shabtai Levi**

"There is no chance of an understanding with the Arabs unless we first reach an understanding with the English, by which we will become a preponderant force in Palestine. What can drive the Arabs to a mutual understanding with us? Facts… only after we manage to establish a great Jewish fact in this country. Only then will the precondition for discussion be met.[12]"

"This is only a stage in the realization of Zionism and it should prepare the ground for our expansion throughout the whole country through Jewish-Arab agreement. The state, however, must enforce order and security and it will do this not by moralizing and preaching 'sermons on the mount' but by machine guns, which we will need.[13]"

— David Ben-Gurion

"Zionist colonization, even the most restricted, must either be terminated or carried out in defiance of the will of the native population. This colonization can, therefore, continue and develop only under the protection of a force independent of the local population — an iron will which the native population cannot break through. This is, in toto, our policy towards the Arabs. To formulate it any other way would be hypocrisy.

"In this sense, there is no meaningful difference between our 'militarists' and our 'vegetarians.' One prefers an iron wall of Jewish bayonets, the other proposes an iron wall of British bayonets, the third proposes an agreement with Baghdad, and appears to be satisfied with Baghdad bayonets — a strange and somewhat risky taste — but we shall applaud, day and night, the iron wall.[14]"

"If you wish to colonize a land in which people are already living, you must provide a garrison for the land, or find a benefactor who will maintain the garrison on your behalf. Zionism is a colonizing adventure and, therefore, it stands or falls on the question of armed forces.[15]"

"We Jews, thank God, have nothing to do with the East... The Islamic soul must be broomed out of Eretz Yisrael.[16]"

— **Vladimir Jabotinsky**

"We must continually raise the demand that our land be returned to our possession ... if there are other inhabitants there, they must be transferred to some other places. We must take over the land. We have a greater and nobler ideal than preserving several hundred thousands of Arab fellahin.[17]"

— **Menahem Ussishkin**

"Zionist mainstream thought had always regarded a Jewish State from the Mediterranean to the Jordan River as its ultimate goal. The vision of 'Greater Israel' as Zionism's ultimate objective did not end with the 1948 war. The politicians of the right, primarily from the revisionist Herut Party, led by Menachem Begin, continued throughout 1949 and the early and mid-1950s to clamor publicly for conquest of the West Bank.[18]"

— **Benny Morris**

"He does not give great weight to the formal peace with the Arab states. Dayan believes that the first battle in the process of the establishment of Israel as an independent state has not yet been completed because we have not yet determined whether the special character of today's state is final. The state must decide if our existing borders satisfy us and will remain as they are in the future. During the 1948 war, a

view prevailed that if we moved eastwards towards the Jordan River we would have to face the British. General Dayan is not sure that this view was well founded and he believes that our time is still open to changes.[19]"

— Meeting of Ministers of Israel, July 7–23, 1950

"Its motives in embarking on this military venture included the consolidation of its alliance (and nuclear cooperation) with France, territorial expansion, the overthrow of the Egyptian President Gamal Abdel Nasser and the destruction of the radical regime; and the establishment of a new political order in the Middle East.[20]"

— Motti Golani

"Ben-Gurion had always seen the Jewish State as part of the West, not as part of the region: a Middle East without Western Colonialism would be too dangerous for Israel; Israel should and could be turned into an American strategic asset in the region.[21]"

— Avi Schlaim

"Jordan had no right to exist and should be divided: Trans-Jordan to be annexed to Iraq which would have to be committed to absorbing and settling Arabs refugees in it; the territories west of the Jordan River will be annexed to Israel, as an autonomous region. Lebanon will have to get rid of some of its Muslim regions to assure stability based on the Christian part. Britain will hold sway over Iraq (including Trans-Jordan) and over the Southern Arabian Peninsula. France — over Lebanon, perhaps even Syria, with close ties to Israel. The Suez Canal will have international status and the Red Sea Straits of Elat — under Israel control.[22]"

"We have not abandoned your dream and we have not forgotten your lesson. We have returned to the mountain, to the cradle of our people, to the inheritance of our Patriarchs, the land of the Judges and the fortress of the Kingdom of the House of David. We have returned to Hebron and Schem [Nablus], to Bethlehem and Anatot, to Jericho and the fords of the Jordan at Adam Ha'ir.[23]"

— Moshe Dayan

"Mass transfer would only be possible as an agreed solution in the framework of a peace agreement, or in the opposite case, that is a solution implemented in the midst of war.[24]"

— Haim Yahiel

"If we want to prevent mutual and continuous bloodshed, there is only one solution — the transfer of the Arab population of the land of

Israel to Arab states. True. This is a little painful (who know this like us the Jews), but it is inevitable and preferable than cumulative poisoning which undermines the whole body. There is no doubt that this solution will come sooner or later. The question is only whether it will be by peaceful ways through regional planning and international assistance or, God forbid, as a result of bloody events.

"The state of Israel has to show political courage at an opportune moment, and to announce that according to experiences in other places and similar situations there is no other solution but population transfer. The problem of Arab minority in the Land of Israel remains without a solution because the minority has not been transferred to Arab states.

"We should also not be deterred from repeating time and again in the ears of the world nations that Jordan (or the combination of Jordan and Syria) actually constitutes a Palestinian homeland and only in it will the Arabs of the Land of Israel have self-determination. This should be the central Israeli demand in any negotiations with Arab countries.[25]*"*

"The government of Israel must set up, as early as possible, a special information department, which would conduct a worthy information/propaganda campaign — with the assistance of experts on the mentality of the Arab leaders and the interests of Arab states, on the one hand, and the political, strategic and economic interests of European states, and especially of the two superpowers, on the other.[26]*"*

— Dr. Dov Yosefi

"Had it not been for Deir Yasin, half a million Arabs would be living in the State of Israel. The State of Israel would not have existed. We must not disregard this, with full awareness of the responsibility involved. All wars are cruel. There is no way out of that. This country will either be Eretz Yisrael with an absolute Jewish majority and a small Arab minority, or an Eretz Ishmael, and Jewish emigration will began again, if we do not expel the Arabs one way or another and the men of spirit should tell how to do that.[27]*"*

"Anyway the refugees are displaced. If the refugees reside in Balata or Dehayshe [two refugee camps on the West Bank] or any other camp, let us suppose that there are not many among us who would agree to its return to Jaffa or Acre. Kibbutz Ma'abarot would not return,

God forbid, the lands to the Arabs who had lived there before and are now in Sabra and Chatila. And our notables at the University in Ramat Aviv [Tel Aviv University] which is situated on the site of Shaykh Muannis village would not, in their goodness, and much humanitarianism, give up the university and return it to the refugees in Sabra and Chatila.[28]*"*

— **Yisrael Eldad**

"It was not as though there was a Palestinian people in Palestine considering itself as a Palestinian people and we came and threw them out and took their country away from them. They did not exist.[29]*"*

"They had a state in Jordan anyway.[30]*"*   — **Golda Meir**

"Hundreds of thousands of Arabs are residing in the liberated territory. The inclusion of this hostile population within the boundaries of the state of Israel is considered as a time-bomb in the heart of the state. Leaving them in these territories endangers the state and its national Jewish character. The only solution is to organize their emigration and settlement in Arab countries abundant in land and water such as Syria and Iraq.[31]*"*   — **Tzvi Shiloah**

"We don't use the word annexation. You annex foreign land, not your own country.[32]*"*   — **Menachem Begin**

"Public opinion in the West is being exposed to loud clamors in support of the Palestinian cause. Arab propaganda is calling for a homeland, as they put it, for the homeless Palestinians. It is important to understand the 'Jordan is Palestine' aspect and that the conflict is not, and never was, between Israel and a stateless people. Once this is understood, the emotional dimension that evokes problems of conscience in some minds will be removed. If it is perceived in this light, you have on one hand a Palestinian-Jordan Arab state, and Israel on the other, then the problem is reduced to its true and manageable proportions.[33]*"*

"We think that Judea, Samaria and Gaza are an inseparable part of the State of Israel, and we will fight to put that thought into practice.[34]*"*

"This is it. This is the goal: it should not be bitten or fragmented. This is an a priori principle; it is beyond argument. You should not ask why; this is the be-all and end-all. Why this land is ours requires no explanation. From as far back as the pre-state days, I have not been able to abide by such words. Is there any other nation in the world that argues about its

*Motherland, its size and its dimensions, about territories, territorial com-
promises, or anything similar? What may be forgiven when it comes
from people in the Diaspora cannot be forgiven in this land, from the
people ruling it.*35"

— Yitzhak Shamir

3) The Zionist Master Plan for Israel

*"The right of the Jewish people to Eretz Yisrael is eternal and indis-
putable, and linked to our right to security and peace. The State of Israel
has a right and a claim to sovereignty over Judea, Samaria and the
Gaza Strip. In time, Israel will invoke this claim and strive to realize it.
Any plan involving the handover of parts of Western Eretz Yisrael to foreign rule, as proposed by the Labor Alignment, denies our right to this
country.*36"   **— Likud Party's Manifesto**

*"The Arabs of Palestine are not a nation. There is no 'Palestine
Arab nation'.*

*"They were and have remained a fragment of the large Arab peo-
ple. They lack the inner desire, the spiritual cement and the concentrated passion of a nation.*37"   **— Samuel Katz**

*"One hundred years of Zionism prove that as long as too many
Arabs exist in the Western land of Israel, that is Palestine, the future of
Israel will be in danger.*38"   **— Lev-Ami**

*"Begin and Sharon share the same dream: Sharon is the dream's
hatchet man. The dream is to annihilate the PLO, douse any vestiges of
Palestinian nationalism, crush PLO allies and collaborators in the West
Bank and eventually force the Palestinians there into Jordan and cripple, if not end, the Palestinian nationalist movement. That, for Sharon
and Begin, was the ultimate purpose of the Lebanese war.*39"

— Amos Perlmutter

*"With a fragmented and dispersed PLO, Israeli leaders foresaw the
Palestinian population in the West Bank and Gaza – deprived of outside
moral support – coming to accept permanent Israeli control there, in a
situation in which much of the Palestinian population could be induced
(or gradually coerced) to migrate across the Jordan River into Jordan.
The Israeli invasion of Lebanon was designed to break any final resistance to total Israeli control and to pave the way for making life so diffi-*

cult for those who valued their freedom and political self-expression that they would eventually leave for Jordan.[40]"

— Harold Saunders, U.S. Assistant Secretary of State

"There are also people in official posts who are prepared to create a situation which would force most of the population of the territories to leave their homes and to wander off to Jordan. The policy of collective punishment is not new. We saw it in its full glory in the days when Moshe Dayan served as 'Emperor of the Territories.' But the difference between the policy pursued then and the one carried out under the Likud government is that now it is done with the clear purpose of making the inhabitants' life unbearable [and making them want to leave]. The curfew in Hebron, which lasted over two weeks, was not the end of the story. The daily harassment of the inhabitants and the cutting of all elementary services — such as the disconnection of all the telephones in the town, even those in doctors' clinics — all of these are designed to deter... and not to punish them... but to make life unbearable so that the inhabitants will either rise up and be expelled by the instruments that have been prepared for this [as revealed by General Yariv] or they will prefer to leave voluntarily.[41]"   **— Ammon Kapeliouk**

"Israel should have exploited the repression of the demonstrations in China, when world attention focussed on that country, to carry out mass expulsion amongst Arabs of the territories. Regrettably, there was not support for this policy, which I put forward then and still recommend.[42]"   **— Benjamin Netanyahu**

"There is no possibility that Jordan will exist in its present shape and structure in the long term, and the policy of Israel, whether in war or in peace, must be to bring about the dissolution of Jordan under the present regime [and the consequent] termination of the problem of the occupied territories densely populated with Arabs west of the River Jordan, whether in war or under conditions of peace; emigration from the territories, and economic demographic freeze in them... we have to be active in order to encourage this change speedily, in the nearest time... It is no longer possible to live in this country in the present situation without separating the two peoples, the Arabs [including Arab citizens of Israel] to Jordan and the Jews to the territories west of the Jordan River. The Palestinian Arabs can only have security and existence in Jordan.[43]"

"There, all the events which are only our wish on the Western front, that is, Egypt are happening before our eyes today. The total disintegra-

*tion of Lebanon into five regional localized governments as the prece-
dent for the entire Arab world... the dissolution of Syria, and later Iraq,
into districts of ethnic and religious minorities, following the example of
Lebanon, is Israel's main long-range objective on the Eastern front...
Syria will disintegrate into several states along the lines of its ethnic and
sectarian structure. As a result, there will be a Shi'ite Alawi state, the district of Aleppo will be a Sunni state, and the district of Damascus another state which is hostile to the Northern one. The Druze — even those
of the Golan — should form a state on Houran and in Northern Jordan...
oil rich but very divided and internally strive-ridden land of Iraq is certainly a candidate to fit Israel's goals. Every kind of inter-Arab confrontation will help us to prevail in the short run and will hasten the
achievement of the supreme goal, namely breaking up Iraq into elements like Syria and Lebanon. There will be three states or more, round
the three major cities, Basra, Baghdad and Mosul, while Shi'ites in the
south will separate from Sunni north, which is mostly Kurdish. The entire
Arabian Peninsula is a natural candidate for dissolution.*[44]"

— Oded Yinon

*"Anyone who searches the Code of Maimonides, which is the pillar of
the Halacha in the Jewish world, [and searches for] the concept 'you
shall not murder' or the concept 'Holy Blood' with regard to the killing of
a non-Jew will search in vain, because he will not find it... It follows from
the words of Maimonides that a Jew who kills a non-Jew... is exempt
from the prohibition 'you shall not murder.' And so Maimonides writes in
the Halachas of murder: 'An Israelite who kills a resident alien is not
sentenced to death' in a court of law.*[45]"

— Rabbi Yisrael Ariel

*"The Arabs are a cancer in the heart of the nation; they are grow-
ing at a frightening pace, six in the belly of one woman.*[46]"

*"The Arabs of Israel are a stark desecration of God's name. Their
non-reconciliation to Jewish sovereignty over the land of Israel is a
rejection of the sovereignty of the God of Israel and of his Kingdom.
Their removal from the country is more than a political affair. It is a religious matter, a religious duty, a commandment to wipe out the desecration of God's name. Instead of worrying about the reactions of the
Gentiles if we do act to remove them, we should tremble at the thought
of God's anger if we do not act. Tragedy will befall on us if we do not
remove the Arabs from the country. Since redemption can come imme-*

*diately and in its full glory, if we do that which God commands... Let us
hasten the redemption.*[47]*"*

— **Rabbi Meir Kahane**

From these quotations, it is easy to understand the imperial ambitions of the Zionists of *Eretz Yisrael*[48] and their British and American counterparts. That has been long in the planning, but for our purpose, it is sufficient to analyze their evil schemes in the last three decades. However, before proceeding further, we need to make a clarification with regard to the true nature of Zionism.

I must point out that not all Jews are Zionists. In fact, there are many Jews who oppose Zionism and the State of Israel. There is therefore a need to clarify some very basic issues concerning Zionism.

On October 5, 2003, the Washington Post published an Open Letter from the Torah True Jews Inc., to President Bush, the contents of which would come as a surprise to many non-Jews. Zionist propaganda, for too long have confused the non-Jews with regard to the State of Israel, Judaism and the Jewish people in general. The authors of this Open Letter have sought to clarify the issues and have succeeded admirably in debunking various Zionist myths and propaganda. I therefore feel justified in reproducing the entire letter here. The words in bold in the body of the letter is to show my own emphasis.

TORAH TRUE JEWS INC.

September 21, 2003[49]

Dear Honorable President George W. Bush:

I am writing to you because of your deep and abiding interest in the suffering of the peoples of the Middle East and your desire to finally bring an end to all the bloodshed and violence there. We pray for peace and brotherhood.

However, I would like to respectfully bring to your attention that although you are aware that there are many Jews who support the State of Israel, what you may not have heard about is that there is a silent majority of Jews opposed to Zionism who remain ignored by the media, and who remain steadfast in loyalty to the teachings of our rabbis that the **ideology of Zionism is in utter opposition to our religion**. For more information there are a number of websites on the internet that discuss this subject, e.g., www.jewsagainstzionism.com, which we know you will find most interesting as it includes historical documents and photographs relating to the long-time opposition of revered rabbis to Zionism.

Ever since the destruction of the Holy Temple in Jerusalem and the exile of the Jewish People some two thousand years ago, **we have been enjoined to be scrupulously loyal to the countries we reside in, and never seek to undertake to establish independent sovereignty in the Holy Land or anywhere throughout the world.** One of the great Biblical prophets, Jeremiah, in Chapter 29 of his book proclaimed G-d's[50] message to all the exiled; verse seven reads, *"seek out the welfare of the city to which I have exiled you and pray for it to the Almighty, for through its welfare will you have welfare."* This has been the cornerstone of Jewish morality throughout our history to this day.

The Zionist movement rejects all of the fundamental principles of our Torah and rabbis. **Jews do not need a state of their own. The very establishment of a "Jewish" state is a grave violation of Jewish tradition and law**.

Therefore they don't represent the Jewish people in any way whatsoever. They have no right to speak in the name of the Jewish people. Therefore, their words, declarations and actions are not in any way representative of the Jewish people. We deplore acts and policies of violence carried out by those who — misusing the name of Israel — have substituted the ideal of nationalism for the teachings of the Holy Torah.

Therefore, Mr. President, it is of the utmost urgency that the State of Israel should not be referred to as a Jewish State, but as the Zionist State. **The foundation of its existence is not Judaism, but the Zionist ideology**. We are extremely concerned that referring to it as a "Jewish" State endangers the welfare of Jews worldwide by linking Jews and Judaism to the terrible actions of the Zionist State. The Zionist State with its supporters worldwide seeks to take all measures possible, including provoking hatred of Jews through Israeli policies, in order to convince Jews to move from their native countries to the State of Israel!!! **Indeed, hatred of Jews is the very lifeblood and oxygen of**

the Zionist movement and their state, which stand in total opposition to Judaism.

We also feel great pain about the misplaced sympathy of Christian
evangelicals for Zionism. **If they knew the truth about Zionism they
would not support the Zionist movement**.

Throughout history when persecution resulted in expulsions, there
were always other nations who opened their doors to the Jews, and
were blessed by G-d for doing so. We believe that our country would
even welcome those Jews who would wish to leave the State of Israel,
and bring great blessings onto the United States.

Your good intentions and kind consideration in relation to Jews is
greatly appreciated, but we strongly believe that G-d's blessings upon
the United States would grow if there is greater understanding and different policies in relation to this issue of the difference between Judaism
and Zionism.

We await the days when all the world will recognize the sovereignty of the Creator, and the words of the prophet Isaiah will yet be fulfilled:
*"And they will beat their swords into plowshares and their spears into
pruning hooks. No nation will lift its sword against any other, not will they
learn warfare anymore."*

The Silent Majority of American Jewry

Contrast the above letter with the arrogance of Ariel Sharon when
he chastised Shimon Peres, as reported on October 3, 2001, by IAP
News when the latter warned him that his policies might "turn the U.S.
against us," Sharon replied:

*"Every time we do something, you tell me Americans will do
this and will do that. I want to tell you something very clear: Don't
worry about American pressure on Israel; we, the Jewish People,
control America. And the Americans know it."*

On the website www.jewsagainstzionism.com there is an article
which warrants repeated reading by all who oppose Zionism, for like the
above Open Letter to the president, it sets out to debunk various myths
about Israel. The article is categorical in stating that, and I quote:

- A Jew is one who remains faithful to the laws of the Jewish religion, that is, the Holy Torah and its commandments.

- The Jewish people became a people before they had their own land, and continued to exist and continued to exist as a people also after they went into exile. From that time, **we are prohibited by the Torah** with a very grave prohibition to establish a Jewish independent sovereignty in the Holy Land or elsewhere throughout the world. Rather we are obligated to be loyal to the nations under whose protection we dwell. (Emphasis as in the original)

- This situation has existed close to 2000 years when the Jewish people were dispersed throughout all corners of the world. During this time, the Jews always remained faithful to the country in which they lived.

- From ancient times, the relations between the Jewish and Islamic peoples have always been those of peace and brotherhood, and friendship always reigned between them. The proof of this is the fact that for centuries, in all Arab lands, hundreds of thousands of Jews lived in honor and amidst mutual esteem.

- Jews throughout all generations yearned to grace the sacred soil of the Holy land and to live there. However, their sole purpose was to fulfill the commandments dependent upon the land and to absorb its holiness. Never, G-d forbid, did they have any nationalist or sovereign intent whatsoever which, as mentioned above, is forbidden to us. Indeed, also here in the Holy Land, our fathers lived in neighborly harmony with the Palestinian residents of the land, helping one another, to mutual benefit.

- Until about two hundred years ago, the vast majority of Jews observed the Torah and the commandments in entirety. Jewry's leaders were Torah scholars, who directed the people according to the Torah. They were loyal citizens in the host nations where they dwelled and to the local laws. They prayed for the welfare of their respective governments. To our sorrow, at that time a small number of Jews slowly left their observance of the Torah and its commandments. Together with this, they began to deride the spiritual leadership of their people. This assimilation was the basis upon which, one hundred years ago, the ideology of Zionism was born. **Its founders**

were assimilated Jews who had abandoned the Torah.
(Emphasis added)

I have further to add regarding the assimilated Jews in a later part of this chapter.

- Immediately at the founding of the Zionist movement, masses of Jews under **the leadership of their Rabbis,** launched a heavy battle against Zionism…. The Zionist incited the nations of the world, demanding political sovereignty over the Holy Land while remaining oblivious to the resentment this would arouse in the Palestinian Arabs, the land's veteran inhabitants. As stated, the leaders of Orthodox Jewry vehemently opposed the movement with all force. (Emphasis as in original)

- The Zionists refused to heed the voice of the Rabbis and Torah authority. They persisted in their ways until they succeeded in influencing the British government to issue the Balfour Declaration concerning the "establishment of a national home for the Jews in the land of Israel." To our great sorrow, **from that point on began the deterioration of the good relations between the Jews and the Arab inhabitants** of the land. This occurred because the Arab people understood that the Zionist wished to seize rulership from them. In addition, the Arab people had suspicions as if the Jewish people wished to seize control of the Temple Mount and other similar sites. Matters worsened as a result. (Emphasis as in original)

- The Jewish leadership of that time saw it as proper to clarify before the leaders that the **Torah-true Jews had no desire whatsoever for sovereignty,** and that our desire was to continue to live in peace with the Arabs, as we had always done. The leader of the G-d fearing Jewish community at that time, **Rabbi Yoseph Chaim Zonnenfeld** of blessed memory, organized a delegation in July of 24' which **visited King Hussein** and his sons Faisal King of Iraq and the Amir Abdullah in order to lucidly present to them the position of the G-d fearing Jewish community. The Jewish delegation clarified unequivocally that Torah Jewry is totally opposed to Zionist sovereignty over the Holy Land. It is worth noting that the delegation was received with great honor. They were even assured that all Arab lands were **completely open to Jews,** however, on the condition that the Jews do not demand political rights. This condition also applied to the Holy Land. One of the members of the Jewish delegation, **Professor Yisroel Yaakov De Haan,** paid with his life for his participation. (Emphasis as in original)

- Torah Jews protest at every opportunity against the Zionist rule over the Holy Land, and the Zionist rebellion against the neighboring nations. Torah Jewry has condemned the Zionist oppression of the Palestinians, the land's veteran inhabitants who have been driven from their homes and properties. The Zionists' barbaric and violent deeds are absolutely antithetical to the essence of the Jewish people.

- Torah Jewry has never ever recognized the Zionist state. Since the Zionist succeeding in establishing their state, Torah Jewry has continuously announced to the world that the Zionists do not represent the Jewish people, and **that the name "Israel" that they use is a forgery.** For as has been stated above, it is forbidden to us from the Torah to rebel against the nations, and all sovereignty by us is prohibited. Rather, we await the days when all the world will recognize the sovereignty of the Creator, and the words of the Prophet Isaiah will yet be fulfilled: "And they will beat their swords into plowshares and their spears into pruning hooks. No nation will lift its sword against another, nor will they learn warfare anymore." (Emphasis added)

- Anti-Zionist Orthodox Jews have refrained to this day from taking any funds from the Zionist regime, whether for their educational institutions, synagogues or other benefits. Obviously, **we do not participate in the Zionist elections,** whether for the "Knesset" or for the municipality. We do not serve in the army, and we even avoid speaking in the Hebrew language that the Zionist invented. (Incidentally, this is not the holy and true Hebrew language in which the Bible is written.) All this is done because Torah Jewry does not recognize the Zionist regime, which is against the Torah and against humanity. (Emphasis as in the original)

- Lately, the question has once again arisen concerning the Temple Mount and sovereignty over it. Thus, we wish to state unequivocally: a) In our time, it is a severe Torah prohibition for any Jew to set foot on any part of the Temple Mount area; b) the Jewish people has no claim whatsoever to sovereignty over this holy site, which is under Islamic authority, nor over any other holy site.

- The Zionists have no right to any sovereignty over even one inch of the Holy Land. They do not represent the Jewish people in anyway whatsoever. They have no right to speak in the name of the Jewish people. This is because the Zionists' seizing of power over the Holy Land is antithetical to Jewish law, and also because the Zionists do not behave like Jews at all, rather, they desecrate the sanctity of the land.

- We once again clarify that it is our desire to live in peace with our Arab and Palestinian neighbors, as we did before the Zionist Revolution, and as Jews all over the world till today live, accepting the yoke of rulership of their host nation, with compete loyalty. Our sole desire is to serve G-d and to fulfill His commandments with a perfect heart and to delight in the radiance of the sanctity of the land.

It is crucial to note that the Torah-true Jews have pointed out that the founders of Zionism, ***"were assimilated Jews who had abandoned the Torah."*** This has escaped the attention of many people and hence the present confusion about the Jewish people. We are indeed fortunate that two prominent Jews, namely Alfred M. Lilienthal[51] and Benjamin Freedman[52] have exposed this insidious deception of the assimilated Jews.

Alfred Lilienthal in his pioneering work, ***What Price Israel***[53] exploded the Jewish racial myth. I seek your indulgence in my quoting at length the profound exposition by Mr. Lilienthal. It is crucial that we should all have a proper understanding of this issue, as it has caused so much confusion, animosity, misunderstanding and the wars that have ravaged the Middle East. I quote:

"There is no reputable anthropologist who will not agree that Jewish racialism is as much poppycock as Aryan racialism. As far back as December 1938, the American Anthropological Association, at its annual Conference in New York, condemned Aryanism as a fallacy and stated that both, 'Aryan' and 'Semitic' were linguistic terms without any racial significance... there is no Jewish or Semitic race.

"Anthropological science divides mankind into three recog-

nized races: Negro, Mongolian or Oriental[54] and Caucasian or white (although some authorities refer to a fourth race — the Australoids[55]). The terms Aryan and Semite have no anthropological connotation. 'Aryan' refers to a group of Indo-European languages, including Russian, English, German, French, Persian, and the language spoken by the Hindus of Northern India. The principal Semitic languages, closely related to the Hamitic languages of ancient Egypt (the Coptic and the Berber tongues), are Hebrew, Syrian, Abyssinian, and Arabic. The ancient Assyrians, Phoenicians, and Babylonians also spoke Semitic languages. The Semitic-speaking peoples are members of the Caucasian race. The word 'Semite' originally designated a descendent of Shem, one of the sons of Noah, and has been applied to certain ancient (no longer existing) people as well as to Arabs and Jews. Incorrect semantic usage has given a racial meaning to a linguistic term, and a further malapropism has included in that meaning all followers of the Judaist faith, most of whom do not understand ancient or Modern Hebrew. And surely, knowledge of Yiddish could not make a person a Semite.

"Twelve tribes started in Canaan about thirty-five centuries ago; and not only that ten of them disappeared — more than half of the members of the remaining two tribes never returned from the 'exile' in Babylon. How then, can anybody claim to descend directly from that relatively small community who inhabited the Holy Land at the time of Abraham's Covenant with God? The Jewish racial myth flows from the fact that the words Hebrew, Israelite, Jew, Judaism, and the Jewish people have been used synonymously to suggest a historic continuity. But this is a misuse. These words refer to different groups of people having varying ways of life in different periods of history. Hebrew is a term correctly applied to the period from the Beginning of Biblical history to the settling in Canaan. Israelite refers correctly to the members of the twelve tribes of Israel.

"The descriptive name Judaism was never heard by the Hebrews or Israelites; it appears only with Christianity. Flavius Josephus was one of the first to use the name in his recital of the war with the Romans to connote a totality of beliefs, moral commandments, religious practices, and ceremonial institutions of Galilee which he believed superior to rival Hellenism. When the *word Judaism was born, there was no longer a Hebrew-Israelite state. The people who embraced the creed of Judaism were already a mixture of many races and strains; and this diversification was rapidly growing."*

Benjamin H. Freedman who was an insider at the highest levels of Jewish organizations and was acquainted with Bernard Baruch, Samuel Untermeyer, President Woodrow Wilson, President Roosevelt, Joseph Kennedy and President Kennedy explained in the article "Facts are Facts" how the confusion was further compounded by the English translation of the Bible in the 18th century. As in the case of Alfred Lilienthal's exposition, it is necessary to quote at length Mr Freedman's research into this area. His approach is unique and extraordinarily clever — **that Jesus was not a Jew, and could not have been a Jew!** In his exposition, he goes straight for the jocular, and I quote:

"Without any fear of contradiction based upon fact that the most competent and best qualified authorities all agree that Jesus Christ was not a so-called or self-styled 'Jew'. They now confirm that during His lifetime Jesus was known as a 'Judean' by his contemporaries and not as a 'Jew', and Jesus referred to himself as a 'Judean' and not as a 'Jew'. Contemporary theologians of Jesus whose competence to pass upon this subject cannot be challenged by anyone today also referred to Jesus during his lifetime here on earth as a 'Judean' and not a 'Jew'.

"Inscribed upon the cross when Jesus was crucified were the Latin words 'Iesus Nazarenus Rex Iudaeorum'. Pontius Pilate was the author of that infamous inscription. Latin was Pontius Pilate's mother tongue. No one questions the fact that Pontius Pilate was well able to accurately express his own ideas in his own mother tongue. The authorities competent to pass upon the correct translation into English of the Latin 'Iesus Nazarenus Rex Iudaeorum' agree that it is 'Jesus the Nazarene Ruler of the Judeans'. There is no disagreement upon that by them.

"During his lifetime here on earth Jesus was not regarded by Pontius Pilate or by the Judeans among whom he dwelt as 'King of the Jews'. The inscription on the Cross upon which Jesus was crucified has been incorrectly translated into the English language only since the 18th century.

163

"At the time of the Crucifixion of Jesus, Pontius Pilate was the administrator in Judea for the Roman Empire. At that time in history the area of the Roman Empire included a part of the Middle East. As far as he was concerned officially or personally the inhabitants of Judea were 'Judeans' to Pontius Pilate and so-called 'Jews' as they have been styled since the 18th century. In the time of Pontius Pilate in history there was no religious, racial or national group in Judea known as 'Jews' nor had there been any group so identified anywhere else in the world prior that time.

"... the Latin word 'rex' means 'ruler, leader' in English. During the lifetime of Jesus in Judea the Latin word 'rex' meant only that to Judeans familiar with the Latin language. With the invasion of the British Isle by the Anglo-Saxons, the English language substituted the Anglo-Saxon 'king' for the Latin equivalent 'rex' used before the Anglo-Saxon invasion. The adoption of 'king' for 'rex' at this late date in British history did not retroactively alter the meaning of the Latin 'rex' to the Judeans in the time of Jesus. The Latin 'rex' to them then meant only 'ruler, leader' as it still means in Latin. Anglo-Saxon 'king' was spelled differently when first used but at all times meant the same as 'rex' in Latin, 'leader' of a tribe.

"In Latin in the lifetime of Jesus the name of the political subdivision in the Middle East known in modern history as Palestine was 'Iudaea'. The English for the Latin 'Iudaea' is 'Judea'. English 'Judean' is the adjective for the noun 'Judea'. The ancient native population... was then called 'Iudaeus' in Latin and 'Judean' in English.

"... in Latin the Genitive Plural of 'Iudaeus' is 'Iudaeorum'. The English translation of the Genitive Plural of 'Iudaeorum' is 'of the Judeans'. It is utterly impossible to give any other English translation to 'Iudaeorum' other than 'of the Judeans'. Qualified and competent theologians and historians regard as incredible any other translation into English of 'Iesus Nazarenus Rex Iudaeorum' than 'Jesus the Nazarene Ruler of the Judeans'.

"There is no factual foundation in history or theology today for the implications, inferences and innuendos that the Greek 'Ioudaios', the Latin 'Iudaeus' or the English 'Judean' ever possessed a valid religious connotation. In these three languages these three words have only indicated a strictly topographical or geographic connotation. In their correct sense these three words

164

in their respective languages were used to identify the members of the indigenous native population of the geographic area known as Judea in the lifetime of Jesus. There was not a form of religious worship practiced in Judea or elsewhere in the known world which bore a name even remotely resembling the name of the political subdivision of the Roman Empire, i.e. 'Judaism' from 'Judea'. No cult or sect existed by such a name.

"It is an incontestable fact that the word 'Jew' did not come into existence until the year 1775. Prior to 1775 the word 'Jew' did not exist in any language. The word 'Jew' was introduced into the English language for the first time in the 18th century when Sheridan used it in his play 'The Rivals', II, (i): 'She shall have a skin like a mummy, and the beard of a Jew.' Shakespeare never used the word 'Jew' in any of his works, the common general belief to the contrary notwithstanding. In his 'Merchant of Venice' (III, (i) 61), Shakespeare wrote as follows: 'what is the reason? I am an Iewe, hath not an Iewe eyes?'

"Jesus is referred as a so-called 'Jew' for the first time in the New Testament in the 18th century... in the revised 18th century editions in the English language of the 14th century first translations of the New Testament into English."

It is interesting to note that through the centuries, from the 4th to the 18th centuries, the words "Gyu", "Giu", "Iu", "Iuu", "Ieuu", "Ieuy", "Iwe", "Iewe", "Ieue", "Iue", and "Iew" was finally transformed in the 18th century to "Jew". The best known 18th century revisions of the New Testament in English are the Douai-Reims Version (also spelt Douay-Rheims) and the Authorized Version (or the King James Version). The Reims translation of the New Testament into English was first printed in 1582, but the word 'Jew' did not appear in it. The Authorized Version of the New Testament was begun in 1604 and first published in 1611. The word 'Jew' did not appear in it either. The word 'Jew' appeared in both these well-known editions in the 18th century revised versions for the first times. To put this issue beyond all argument, we need only to quote what Rabbi Adolph Moses said in his classic, **Yahvism, and Other Discourses**, published in 1903:

"Among the innumerable misfortune which have befallen... the most fatal in its consequences is the name Judaism. Worse still, the Jews themselves, who have gradually come to call their religion Judaism... Yet neither in Biblical nor post-Biblical, neither

in Talmudic, nor in much later times, is the term Judaism ever heard... The Bible speaks of the religion as 'Torath Yahve', the instruction, or the moral law revealed by Yahve... In other places as 'Yirath Yahve', the fear and reverence of Yahve. These and other appellations continued for many ages to stand for the religion... To distinguish it from Christianity and Islam, the Jewish philosophers sometimes designate it as the faith or belief of the Jews. It was Flavius Josephus, writing for the instruction of Greeks and Romans who coined the term Judaism, in order to pit it against Hellenism... Hence the term Judaism coined by Josephus remained absolutely unknown to them. It was only in comparatively recent times, after the Jews became familiar with modern Christian literature, that they began their religion as Judaism."

The eminent Rabbi Louis Finkelstein, the head of the Jewish Theological Seminary of America, often referred to as "The Vatican of Judaism", in his Foreword to the First Edition of his classic, *The Pharisees, The Sociological Background of Their Faith*[56] stated:

"The Pharisees constituted a religious Order of singular influence in the history of civilization...

"Judaism: Pharisaism became Talmudism, Talmudism became Medieval Rabbinism, and Medieval Rabbinism became Modern Rabbinism. But throughout these changes of name, inevitable adaptation of custom, and adjustment of Law, the spirit of the ancient Pharisee survives today."

In summary, Judaism is the modern name for Pharisaism.

It is therefore a myth manufactured by the Zionists that the Judeans at the time of Jesus were "Jews"; that Jesus himself was a "Jew". There was no religion at the time of Jesus called Judaism; it was Pharisaism, and Jesus did neither profess to nor practice this religion. In fact, Jesus denounced Pharisaism and the Pharisees as can be read from the Holy Bible. And the Pharisees, who practiced Pharisaism, were never called "Jews". And so, we now know that, as explained by Rabbi Finkelstein, Judaism is merely the modern name for Pharisaism, the practices of the Pharisees in Judea that was denounced by Jesus Christ!

Dr. Eugene Pittard, Professor of Anthropology at the University of Geneva categorically states: *"There is no more a Christian race than a Musulman race, and neither is there such a thing as a Jewish race.*[57] *"* This statement is supported in a 1952 study of the United Nations Educational, Scientific and Cultural Organization, *What is Race?*[58] Two Columbia University anthropologists in their Book, *Races of Mankind*, wrote:[59]

"Jews are people who acknowledge the Jewish religion. They are of all races, even Negro and Mongolian. European Jews are of many different biological types..."

It is this distinction and difference that is crucial to the understanding the present polemics in the Middle East. The problem started with the assimilated Jews, the Khazars.

The Khazars were a Turkic people from Central Asia. They were a warring people and subsequently settled in what is now Southern Russia. At the height of their influence, the Khazar Empire covered the geographic areas of northern Caucasus, eastern Ukraine, the Crimea, western Kazakhstan and north-western Uzbekistan. Their influence also extended to what is now Hungary and Romania. The Jewish Encyclopaedia refers to the Khazars as having "a well constituted and tolerant government, a flourishing trade and a well disciplined army."

Sometime, during the 7th century, King Bulan adopted Judaism to replace pagan worship and the people of Khazaria converted en masse and invited Rabbis to establish synagogues and Jewish schools. When the kingdom collapsed after the invasion of the Russians, the Khazars scattered throughout Eastern Europe and Russia. These "Jews" are therefore not the progeny of Judah, nor of any the twelve tribes of Israel. They were converts. Today they are referred to as "Ashkenazim Jews", and Chaim Weizmann, the President of Israel, and many Zionist leaders come from this Khazar lineage. That the Khazars are the lineal ancestors of Eastern European Jewry is a historical fact acknowledged by Jewish historians and religious textbooks as well.[60]

Since the conquest of the Khazars by the Russians and the disappearance of their Kingdom, the language of the Khazars became known as Yiddish. It is the modern name for the language of the Khazars, derived mainly from a mediaeval German dialect with some words from Hebrew and Aramaic, but mostly from the Slavonic and Baltic languages. Yiddish is written in Hebrew script, but that fact does not make Yiddish Hebrew, anymore than Jawi[61] Arabic. Benjamin

Freedman explained thus:

"The Yiddish Language is the cultural common denominator for all the so-called or self-styled 'Jews' in or from Eastern Europe. Yiddish serves them like the English language serves the population of the 48 states of the United States.[62]*"*

They identified themselves as Yiddish, rather than as Russian, Polish, Lithuanian, Romanian, and Hungarian or by the nation of which they were citizens. 90% of the world's so-called or self-styled Jews living in 42 countries of the world are either emigrants from Eastern Europe, or the children of such emigrants.

Today, the majority of the so-called Jews are from Eastern Europe and are the descendants of the Khazars. They have absolutely no historical link to the Holy Land whatsoever. And it is these descendants of the Khazars that constitute the force behind Zionism in the forefront claiming the so-called Biblical right to the Holy Land and beyond. But then, Zionism is neither Judaism nor Pharisaism.

Alfred Lilienthal in his Foreword to **The Zionist Connection II: What Price Peace?** asks two very pertinent questions:

1) *"Why has organized Jewry, invariably an unequivocal exponent of the separation of Church and State, condoned their union in an Israeli state demanding the allegiance of everyone everywhere who considers himself a Jew, whether he be an observant practitioner or not?"*

2) *"What validity is there to the insistence of a persistent minority that anti-Zionism is the equivalent of anti-Semitism?"*

In a very frank and brutal admission of the state of affairs then prevailing (which has not changed one iota), Mr Lilienthal gave the answer:

"It was the serious confusion between religion and nationalism that led directly to the 1948 establishment of the Zionist State of Israel in the heart of the Arab world, causing disastrous consequences for all concerned, including Americans whose government had played a major role in that nation-making. The resultant up-rooting of Palestinian Arabs, whose numbers today have swollen to more than 1.6 million, many exiled for thirty years to refugee camps living on a UN dole of seven cents a day, brought down on the U.S. the enmity of an Arab-Muslim world, eroding a

measureless reservoir of goodwill stemming from educational and eleemosynary institutions America helped found. The creation of Israel, likewise, led to the penetration of the area for the first time by the Soviet Union, endangered the security interests of the U.S., and thrust the burden of a premature energy crisis into every American home.

"However much the essence of Judaism may have remained as distinct as ever from Zionism, the nationalist shadow has so overtaken the religious substance that virtually all Jews have, in practice, become Israelists, if not Zionists. Many who mistrust the Zionist connotation can still have their cake and eat it, through Israelism.

"While the vast majority of Jews in the Diaspora (the aggregate of Jews living outside of Palestine) do not believe in Zionist Ideology, out of what is mistaken for religious duty they have given fullest support, bordering on worship, to Israel. Such worship of collective human power is just about as old as Pharaonic Egypt... The prevalence of this worship of collective human power is a calamity. It is a bad religion because it is the worship of a false God. It is a form of idolatry which has led its adherents to commit innumerable crimes and follies. Unhappily, the prevalence of this idolatrous religion is one of the tragic facts of contemporary human life."

Zionism is therefore a racist, fascist, political ideology, hiding beneath the skirts of Judaism. If you think, this is an unfair statement, consider Albert Einstein's letter[63] to the New York Times whose warning about fascist Israel is as relevant in 1948 as it is today. I quote the relevant parts:

To the Editors of *The New York Times*:

Among the most disturbing political phenomena of our times is the emergence in the newly created State of Israel of the "Freedom Party" (Tnuat Heherut), a political party closely akin in its organization, methods, political philosophy and social appeal to the Nazi and Fascist parties. It was formed out of the membership and following of the former Irgun Zvai Leumi, a terrorist, right wing, chauvinist organization in Palestine. The current visit of Menachem Begin, leader of the party, to the United States is obviously calculated to give the impression of

American support for his party in the coming Israeli elections, and to cement political ties with conservative Zionist elements in the United States. Several Americans of national repute have lent their names to welcome his visit. It is inconceivable that those who oppose fascism throughout the world, if correctly informed as to Mr. Begin's political record and perspectives, could add their names and support to the movement he represents....

It is in its actions that the terrorist party betrays its real character; from its past actions we can judge what it may be expected to do in the future.

A shocking example was their behavior in the Arab village of Deir Yassin. This village, off the main roads and surrounded by Jewish lands, had taken no part in the war, and had even fought off Arab bands who wanted to use the village, which was not a military objective in the fighting, killed most of its inhabitants, 240 men, women and children and kept a few of them alive to parade as captives through the streets of Jerusalem... The terrorists far from being ashamed of their act, were proud of this massacre, publicizes it widely and invited all the foreign correspondents present in the country to view the heaped corpses and the general havoc at Deir Yassin. The Deir Yassin incident exemplifies the character and actions of the Freedom Party....

The discrepancies between the bold claims now being made by Begin and his party, and their record of past performance in Palestine bear the imprint of no ordinary political party. This is the unmistakable stamp of a fascist party for whom terrorism (against Jews, Arabs, and British alike), and misrepresentations are means, and a "Leader State" is the goal.

In the light of the foregoing considerations, it is imperative that the truth about Mr. Begin and his movement be made known in this country. It is all the more tragic that the top leadership of American Zionism has refused to campaign against Begin's efforts, or even to expose to its own constituents the dangers to Israel from support to Begin.

The undersigned therefore take this means of publicly presenting a few salient facts concerning Begin and his party; and of urging all concerned not to support this latest manifestation of fascism.

Signed by

Albert Einstein and 27 other Jewish Leaders.

If we were to substitute Ariel Sharon for Menachem Begin and the Likud Party for the Freedom Party, there is no difference whatsoever to the fascist nature of the present regime in Israel; after all, Begin did become the Prime Minister of Israel and Sharon has blood on his hands for the massacre of Palestinians in Sabra and Shatila refugee camps and the thousands since then.

Given the above historical facts, why has the United States been so subservient to the political agenda of the Zionists since the First World War?

How did the Zionists exercise such political control over the political process in the United States and in Europe?

I shall endeavor to provide some answers to the above questions in the next few chapters.

ENDNOTES:

1. Nur Masalha, citing *The Voice of Jerusalem*, (1920, London: William Heinemann) p. 104
2. Nur Masalha, citing Yosef Grony, *Zionism and the Arabs: 1882-1948*, (1987, Oxford, Clarendon Press)
3. Nur Masalha, citing speech delivered at a meeting of the French Zionist Federation, Paris March 28, 1914, quoted from *The Letters and Papers of Chaim Weizmann*, Vol. 1, Series B, Paper 24, Israel University Press, 1983
4. Nur Masalha, citing *The Struggle for the State: the Zionist Policy 1936-1948*
5. Nur Masalha, citing "The Address to the English Zionist Federation", 1919, Jewish Chronicle, May 20, 1921, in Arie Bober, ed., *The Other Israel*, (1972, New York, Garden City, Double Day)
6. Nur Masalha, citing Yosef Grony, *Zionism and the Arabs: 1882-1948*, (1987, Oxford, Clarendon Press)
7. Nur Masalha, citing Raphael Patai, Ed, *The Complete Diaries of Theodore Herzl*, Vol. I, Harry Zohn trans., (1960, New York, Herzl Press and T. Yoseloff)
8. Nur Masalha, citing Yosef Grony, quoting Beilinson's article "Right Over Palestine" in Davar, December 4, 1929
9. Nur Masalha, citing Yosef Grony.
10. Nur Masalha, citing Israel Zangwill, *Speeches, Articles and Letters*, (1937, London, The Soncino Press)
11. Nur Masalha, citing Nedava, *Tochniyot Helufei Ochlosin*, p164-165 quoting Levi's manuscript
12. Nur Masalha, citing Teveth, *Ben-Gurion and the Palestinian Arabs*, (1985, Oxford, Oxford University Press)
13. Nur Masalha, citing Protocol of the Jewish Agency Executive Meeting on June 7, 1938 in Jerusalem, Vol. 28, No 51, Central Zionist Archives. See also Morris, *The Birth of the Palestinian Refugee Problem*, p 24
14. Nur Masalha, citing Lenni Brenner, *The Iron Wall — Zionist Revisionism from Jabotinsky to Shamir*, (1984, London, Zed Books)
15. Nur Masalha, citing Joseph Schechtman, *The Jabotinsky Story: Fighter and Prophet*, (1956, New York: Thomas Yoseloff). See also "The Shahak Papers", No 31, Collection on Jabotinsky: His Life and Excerpts from his Writings.

171

16. Nur Masalha, citing Ya'acov Shavit, "The Attitude of Zionist Revisionism towards the Arabs" in *Zionism and the Arab Question*. See also Joseph Schechtman, *Rebel and Statesman: The Vladimir Jabotinsky Story, The Early Years*, (1956, New York, T. Yoseloff)

17. Nur Masalha, citing Doar Hayom (Jerusalem) April 28 1930. See also *Sefer Ussishkin [The book of Ussishkin]*, p. 223

18. Nur Masalha, citing Benny Morris, *Israel Border Wars, 1949-1956*, (1993, Oxford, Clarendon Press)

19. Nur Masalha, quoting Israel State Archives, Foreign Ministry, 2463/2

20. Nur Masalha, citing Motti Golani, *Israel In Search of a War: The Sinai Campaign, 1955-1956*, (1998, Brighton, Sussex Academic Press)

21. Nur Masalha, citing Avi Schlaim, "Israel, the Great Powers and the Middle East Crisis of 1958", Journal of Imperial and Commonwealth History 27, No. 2, p.178, (May 1999)

22. Nur Masalha, citing Moshe Dayan, *Milestones: an Autobiography*, (1976, Edanim and Dvir), describing how Ben-Gurion argued at the Sevres Conference.

23. Nur Masalha, citing Moshe Dayan, *A New Map, Other Relationships*, (1969, Ma'ariv)

24. Nur Masalha, citing Ben Ami, *Sefer Eretz Yisrael Hashlemah*, p. 312-313

25. Nur Masalha, citing Ben Ami p. 349-350

26. Nur Masalha, citing Haumah, No. 88, p. 20-26, (Autumn 1987)

27. Nur Masalha, citing De'ot (Opinions), No 35, quoted in Uri Davis and Norton Mezvinsky, *Documents from Israel 1967-1973*, (1975, London: Ithaca Press)

28. Nur Masalha, quoting excerpts from the interview were published in Moledet, No 8, p. 6, (June 1989)

29. Nur Masalha, citing Sunday Times (London), June 15, 1969; John K. Cooley, *Green March, Black September*, (1973, London: Franak Cass)

30. Nur Masalha, citing Schindler, *Israel, Likud and the Zionist Dream*, (1995, London: I.B. Tauris)

31. Nur Masalha, citing Davar, July 3, 1967.

32. Nur Masalha, citing Eric Silver, *Begin: A Biography*, (1984, London: Weidenfeld and Nicholson)

33. Nur Masalha, quoting excerpts from Speech in New York Times, October 6, 1981. See also Yitzhak Shamir, "Israel's Role in a Changing Middle East," Foreign Affairs, (Spring 1982)

34. Nur Masalha, citing Elfi Pallis, "The Likud Party: A Primer", Journal of Studies 21, No. 2, (Winter 1992)

35. Nur Masalha, citing Ian Lustick, "The Fetish of Jerusalem: A Hegemonic Analysis" in Michael Barnett, Ed., *Israel in Comparative Perspective*, (1996, New York: State University of New York Press)

36. Nur Masalha, citing Elfi Pallis.

37. Nur Masalha, citing Samuel Katz, *Battleground: Facts and Fantasy in Palestine*, (1973, London: W.H. Allen); Michael Palumbo, *Imperial Israel*, (1990, London: Bloomsbury)

38. Nur Masalha, citing Shlomo Lev-Ami, *Did Zionism Fail?* (1988, Tel Aviv: Ami Press)

39. Nur Masalha, citing Amos Perlmutter, "Begin's Rhetoric, Sharon's Tactics", Foreign Affairs, (Fall 1982)

40. Nur Masalha, citing Harold Saunders, "An Israeli-Palestinian Peace", Foreign Affairs (Fall 1982)

41. Nur Masalha, citing Al Hamishmar, June 6, 1980

42. Nur Masalha, citing Elfi Pallis.

43. Nur Masalha, citing Oded Yinon, "A Strategy for Israel in the 1980s", Kivunim (Jerusalem No 8, Feb 1982) Periodical of the World Zionist Organization.

44. Nur Masalha, citing Oded Yinon.

45. Nur Masalha, citing Ariel Dvarim Kehavayatam

46. Nur Masalha, citing Urit Shohat in Haaretz, May 13, 1985 Supplement

172

47. Nur Masalha, citing Meir Kahane, *Lesikim Be'eneikhim*

48. *Eretz Yisrael:* Hebrew, land of Israel.

49. Although the Letter was dated September 21, 2003, it was published in the Washington Post on October 5, 2003. Source: www.jewsagainstzionism.com

50. Orthodox Jews believe that the name of God is too sacred to be uttered or written. Hence, "G-d" for "God".

51. Alfred M. Lilienthal, *What Price Israel?* (2003, Infinity Publishing) 50th Anniversary Ed.

52. Benjamin Freedman, "Facts are Facts". Source: www.biblebelievers.com

53. Alfred Lilienthal, Chapter 12, p. 162

54. Ibid.,The indigenous American Population, the Indians belonged to the Mongolian race.

55. Ibid,The indigenous people before the arrival of the Europeans.

56. Louis Finkelstein, *The Pharisees: The Sociological Background of Their Faith*, A Golden Jubilee Volume, (1938, Philadelphia: The Jewish Publication Society of America)

57. Alfred Lilienthal, p. 70

58. "What is Race", a pamphlet published by UNESCO (Paris 1952), Appendix III

59. Ruth Benedict and Gene Weltfish, *The Races of Mankind*, (1945, New York: Viking)

60. Lilienthal, p 168, citing Heinrich Graetz, *History of Jews* and S.M. Dubnow, *History of Jews in Russia and Poland*.

61. Jawi is the Malay language written in Arabic script.

62. When Freedman wrote the article "Facts are Facts" there were only 48 states.

63. Albert Einstein, Letter to Editors of the New York Times, December 4, 1948

Part 3

The Keystone of the Zionist Empire Edifice

*"The Work is at a standstill. On what account?
For want of a Keystone for the Sacred Arch."*

11

The Zionist Imperial Edifice Part I — The Two Pillars

The British Zionists labored long and hard to erect the Zionist Imperial Edifice. Persistent efforts over 150 years have brought them to the stage where what remains to be done is to place the Keystone between the two contiguous arch-stones in the Catenarian Arch which compresses and binds the whole structure together.

However, before proceeding to examine how the Zionists hewn the Keystone, let us recollect and examine how the Twin Pillars of the Zionist Imperial Edifice were constructed. The establishment of Israel may be said to symbolize one of the pillars, the First Pillar, which construction was interrupted until after the Second World War. The total control of Empire Finance via the establishment of the Federal Reserve System in the United States was the Second Pillar, and though the two proceeded simultaneously, the Second Pillar was completed first. To this we shall revert later. Let us recap how the First Pillar was constructed.

We have in the preceding chapters seen how through political blackmail, an agreement was reached to establish the Zionist State of Israel. Lloyd George, the British Prime Minister, in **Memoirs of the Peace Conference**[1] wrote:

"It was believed that if Great Britain declared for the fulfillment of Zionist aspirations in Palestine under her own pledge, one effect would be to bring Russian Jewry to the cause of the entente.

"It was believed, also, that such a declaration would have a potent influence upon world Jewry outside Russia, and secure

177

for the entente the aid of Jewish financial interest. In America, their aid in this respect would have a special value when the allies had almost exhausted the gold and marketable securities available for American purchase.

"Such were the chief considerations which, in 1917, impelled the British Government towards <u>making a contract with Jewry</u>." (Emphasis added)

Corroboration is to be found in the pamphlet, entitled **"Great Britain, the Jews and Palestine"** by Samuel Landman, who was the secretary to Chaim Weizmann of the World Zionist Organization.[2] He wrote:

"... the only way to induce the American President to come to war was to secure the cooperation of Zionist Jews by promising them Palestine, and thus enlist and mobilize the hitherto unsuspectedly powerful forces of Zionist Jews in America and elsewhere in favor of the Allies on a quid pro quo contract basis. The Balfour Declaration, in the words of Prof. H.M.V. Temperley, was a 'definite contract between the British Government and Jewry.[3]' The main consideration given by the Jewish people (represented at the time by the leaders of the Zionist organization) was their help in bringing President Woodrow Wilson to the aid of the Allies."

How did the Zionists wield such power and influence over the president? Simple! At the material time, the close advisers of President Wilson were Supreme Court Justice Brandeis, Bernard Baruch and Rabbi Stephen Wise. Americans will be surprised to know that American Zionists owe their loyalty first to Zionism and Israel, and not to America, even though they are citizens of the U.S. Let me share a secret about Justice Brandeis. He is a Zionist and has admitted that his first loyalty is to Zionism. Justice Brandeis wrote:[4]

"Let us recognize that we Jews are a distinct nationality of which every Jew whatever his country, his station, or shade of belief, is necessarily a member. To this end we must organize. Organize, in the first place, so that the world may have proof of the extent and the intensity of our desire for liberty. Organize, in the second place, so that our resources may become known and be made available. Organize, organize, organize until every Jew must stand up and be counted — counted with us, or prove him-

self, wittingly or unwittingly, of the few who are against their own people."

Should we be surprised that Nazi Germany behaved as they did in the Second World War? It was conceded by Samuel Landman that, *"the fact that it was Jewish help that brought the U.S.A. into the war on the side of the Allies has rankled ever since in Germany — especially Nazi minds — and has contributed in no small measure to the prominence which anti-Semitism occupied in the Nazi program.*[5]*"*

Yet Jewish propaganda has it that the Nazis hated Jews because they were "Jews" as if there were no basis for their animosity. In fact, world Zionism without provocation in the early 1930s declared war on Germany. David A. Brown, the President of the American Hebrew in 1934, told Robert E. Edmondson, *"We Jews are going to bring war on Germany.*[6]*"* Vladimir Jabotinsky, in Mascha Rjetsch, January, 1934, vented his hatred for Germany, by declaring:

"The fight against Germany has now been waged for months by every Jewish community, on every conference, in all labor unions and by every single Jew in the world. There are reasons for the assumption that our share in this fight is of general importance. We shall start a spiritual and material war of the whole world against Germany. Germany is striving to become once again a great nation, and to recover her lost territories as well as her colonies. But our Jewish interests call for the complete destruction of Germany."

In the Daily Express of March 4, 1934, the headlines trumpeted: *"Judea declares War on Germany."*

Similar rabid expression of Zionist hatred was voiced by the Jewish Professor A. Kulisher in 1937, when he openly called for the destruction of Germany. This is what he said:

"Germany is the enemy of Judaism and must be pursued with deadly hatred. The goal of Judaism of today is: a merciless campaign against all German peoples and the complete destruction of the nation. We demand a complete blockade of trade, the importation of raw materials stopped and retaliation towards every German, woman and child."

Jewish newspapers echoed similar sentiments, one of which had no qualms in confessing that one of its aim was the annihilation of the German people:

"The millions of Jews who live in America, England and France, North and South Africa, and, not to forget those in Palestine, are determined to bring the war of annihilation against Germany to its final end.[7] *"*

So the Jews are not the innocent victims as Jewish propaganda have made them out to be for the last sixty years. Further corroboration for this design can be found in the Jewish Chronicle, May 8, 1942 — *"We have been at war with Hitler since the first day that he gained power"*; and January 22, 1943 — *"The Yishuv was at war with Hitler long before Britain and America.*[8] *"*

We can therefore see a similar duplicity in the Second World War, and once again, Zionist financial interests ensured the defeat of Germany. The bargain that was agreed in 1917 (to establish a Zionist State of Israel) was finally implemented, and in 1948, the State of Israel was established. It was officially proclaimed in Tel Aviv at midnight, May 14, 1948. Eleven minutes later, President Truman conveyed the U.S. recognition of Israel which was the quid pro quo for Zionists' support for Truman's re-election. And although the odds were 20 to 1 against his election, Truman defeated Governor Dewey convincingly.

While in school, we have been taught that the Second World War was about democracy and the fight against fascism. However, it is interesting to note that from the Zionist point of view, *"the Second World War is being fought for the defense of the fundamentals of Judaism.*[9] *"* And in an article in the New York Times of October, 1940, it was reported that Arthur Greenwood, a member without portfolio in the British War Cabinet assured the Jews of the United States that when victory was achieved an effort would be made to found a new world order on the ideals of "Justice and Peace". This was further corroborated by the article in TIME magazine of August 16, 1948, which quoted Ben-Gurion as having said that *"the United Nations ideal is a Jewish Ideal."*

To those who still doubt that the Zionists are the masterminds behind World War II, and that the war served to further the Zionist agenda, there can be no stronger evidence than the speech given by Chaim Weizmann, President of the World Jewish Congress on

December 3, 1942, in New York City where he unashamedly admitted that:

"We are not denying and we are not afraid to confess, this war is our war and that it is waged for the liberation of Jewry... stronger than all fronts together is our front, that of Jewry. We are not only giving this war our financial support on which the entire war production is based. We are not only providing our full propaganda power which is the moral energy that keeps this war going. The guarantee of victory is predominantly based on weakening the enemy forces, on destroying them in their own country, within the resistance. And we are the Trojan horse in the enemy's fortress. Thousands of Jews living in Europe constitute the principal factor in the destruction of our enemy. There, our front is a fact and the most valuable aid for victory."

It is by the blood of millions, shed during the Second World War that the First Pillar of the Zionist Imperial Edifice was built. Eustace Mullins in his foreword to the book *War! War! War!* reminds us that the great massacres of the war occurred not in battlefields, but in peaceful neighborhoods. Since the Jews were the architects of the war, they were merely following the dictate of the Book of Esther, which directs the Jews to massacre women and children, and all those who dare oppose them. The atomic bomb developed by the Jews was tested in Hiroshima and Nagasaki, exterminating hundreds of thousands of civilians. Terror and genocide became the legitimate weapons to impose the agenda of the Zionist Anglo-American Empire.

The above quotations reveal a startling admission of the war aims of the Zionists for the Second World War. Given that the avowed aim was the complete destruction of Germany and her people, men, women and children, in furtherance to the Zionist agenda, we must of necessity re-evaluate the entire history of the Second World War. The so-called Jewish Holocaust must likewise be re-examined and I hereby challenge any Zionist historian to furnish irrefutable proof that six million Jews were killed by Nazi Germany. For too long this magic figure of six million has been bandied about and the world is expected to accept this without question. History must also evaluate how many Germans were killed as a result of the Zionist conspiracy to wage war on Germany. In the circumstances, how can we reconcile the avowed aims of world Jewry and Zionism for fomenting the Second World War, so as to ensure the implementation of the 1917 agreement in the creation of the Zionist State of Israel and the Jewish propaganda that Israel was necessary for the remnants of European Jews killed by Nazi Germany — a homeland for a people without a land. My conviction that the history of the Second World War must be re-visited was strengthened when in the course of my research I came across a speech by Sir Hartle Shawcross, who was the British Chief Prosecutor at the Nuremberg Trials and later Attorney General wherein he said:

"Step by step, I have arrived at the conviction that the aims of Communism in Europe are sinister and fatal. At the Nuremberg trials, I, together with my Russian colleague, condemned Nazi aggression and Terror. I believe now that Hitler and the German people did not want war. But we, (England), declared war on Germany, intent on destroying it, in accordance with our principle of Balance of Power, and we were encouraged by the 'Americans' [Jews] around Roosevelt. We ignored Hitler's pleadings, not to enter into war. Now we are forced to realize that Hitler was right. He offered us the cooperation of Germany: instead, since 1945, we have been facing the immense power of the Soviet Empire. I feel ashamed and humiliated to see that the aims we accused Hitler of, are being relentlessly pursued now, only under a different label.[10]*"*

The people of Asia and Africa were not part of this European adventure, yet today, we are dragged into various Zionist Anglo-American inspired conflicts, the various undeclared wars and right-wing coups against democratically elected governments. There is no doubt, and going by historical experiences, that the principal threat to world peace today is Zionist Israel and her principal ally, the Zionist Anglo-American Establishment. Had Israel not been established, we would not have the genocidal occupation of Palestine by the fascist Zionist army; there would be a state of Palestine, a multicultural, multiracial and multireligious community living in peace and harmony; there would be no reasons for the 1967 Six Day War, the 1973 Yom Kippur War, the First Gulf War and the present illegal invasion and occupation of Iraq. All the wars in the Middle East can be traced to one source and one source alone — Zionist Israel and her imperial ambitions.

We must not entertain any illusions about Zionism, the Zionist State of Israel and Talmudism. In Part IV we shall examine in more detail the Zionist Anglo-American Empire ambitions for the 21st century.

The Second Pillar, the financial pillar was likewise constructed by the sweat and blood of millions. The need to control a nation's finances was explained by Anselm Rothschild[11] who said: *"Give me the power to issue and control the money of a nation and I care not who makes the laws."* The need for such financial controls is further explained by Professor Carroll Quigley in his remarkable book, *Tragedy and Hope: A History of The World in Our Time*:

"The powers of financial capitalism had another far-reaching aim, nothing less than to create a world system of financial control in private hands able to dominate the political system of each country and the economy of the world as a whole. This system was to be controlled in a feudalist fashion by the central banks of the world acting in concert, by secret agreements, arrived at in frequent private meetings and conferences... The growth of financial capitalism made possible a centralization of world economic control and use of this power for the direct benefit of financiers and the indirect injury of all other economic groups."

The Architect and Master Overseer for the design and construction of the Second Pillar was the Rothschild banking family. But the ruthless power of the Rothschild family was backed by the entire world Jewry. According to Professor Werner Sombart, the name of Rothschild means more than the firm. It means all Jewdom. For only with the help of compatriots could the Rothschilds have reached their position of power which dominates all others. It is also said that the Rothschilds have power over agencies inaccessible to other mortals.[12] In the circumstances, it is incumbent on us to study how the Rothschild family weaved their web of power and how they have sustained it till today.

The founder of the Rothschild financial empire was Mayer Amschel Bauer who was born in 1743, the son of Moses Amschel Bauer, a moneylender and goldsmith. At an early age, Mayer learned from his father the intricacies of money-lending which laid the foundation for his later banking expertise. Soon after the death of his father, Mayer joined a bank, owned by the Oppenheimers in Hanover. He rose rapidly and was made a junior partner. He then returned to Frankfurt and re-established the business started by his father. Using the friendship and patronage of General von Estorff, he gained access to the court of Prince William of Hanau. From then on, the young banker became adviser and banker to a long line of princes and Head of States. But it was from Prince William that the banker made his first fortune.

Mayer Amschel changed his surname to Rothschild[13] from the Red Shield that used to hang over the door of his father's money-lending firm, a representation of the Red Flag, the emblem of the revolutionary Jews in Eastern Europe. Mayer Rothschild had five sons, Amschel, Salomon, Nathan, Kalman (Karl) and Jacob (James), and each was entrusted with a branch of the family banking empire. Amschel was in charge in Berlin, Salomon in Vienna, James was in Paris and Karl was posted to Naples. Nathan took charge of the London operations, where the headquarters was situated.

The Jewish Encyclopaedia 1905, reveals how Nathan multiplied the family fortune from the money which his father took from Prince William. He invested in *"gold from the East India Company knowing that it was needed for Wellington's peninsula campaign... and made no less than four profits (1) on the sale of Wellington's paper (which he bought at 50 cents on the dollar) and collected at par; (2) on the sale of gold to Wellington; (3) on its repurchase; and (4) on forwarding it to Portugal. This was the beginning of the great fortunes of the House."*

There were other spectacular exploits, like how the family made another fortune by misleading the London Stock Exchange that the British lost the Battle of Waterloo, thereby causing the massive unloading of consuls, slumping to five cents on the dollar. The Rothschild intelligence network knew all along that Britain had defeated the French, but had suppressed the news. When the price of the consuls hit rock bottom, an order was issued to buy every consul in sight. When the official news reached London, that Wellington defeated the French, the price of the consuls soared. Overnight the Rothschilds became the dominant financial power in England. However, for the purposes of this book it is sufficient once again to quote The Jewish Encyclopaedia[14] which described the novel, *Coningsby* by British Prime Minister Benjamin Disraeli as the *"ideal portrait"* of the Rothschild family financial empire. This was how Disraeli portrayed Nathan Rothschild:

"The Lord and Money master of the money markets of the world, and of course virtually lord and master of everything else. He literally held the revenues of Southern Italy in pawn, and monarchs and ministers of all countries courted his advice and were guided by his suggestions."

The essence of financial power is debt! This is the secret of Rothschilds' financial power. And national debts are best created by wars. This is why throughout the ages, the financiers and international bankers financed both sides of any conflict, as in any event, both the victor and the vanquished would be indebted to the bankers.

Having captured and asserted total control of the finances of Europe, the Rothschild cast their eyes on America, which by this time had developed a remarkable system of financial management, which to a large extent was different from that of Europe. The new system posed a threat to the international bankers as it would curb the bankers' ability to create debt. The Times of London could not have painted a better picture of the impending collision between the Rothschild financial empire and the New Republic when it wrote:

"If that mischievous financial policy which had its origin in the North American Republic should become indurated down to a fixture, then that government will furnish its own money without cost. It will pay off its debts and be without a debt [to the international banker]. It will become prosperous beyond precedent in the history of civilized governments of the world. The brains and wealth of all countries will go to North America. That government must be destroyed or it will destroy every monarch on the globe.[15]"

In the beginning of the chapter, I made reference to the establishment of the Federal Reserve System (the Fed) as the Second Pillar. The history of the Fed is the history of how international bankers under the leadership of the Rothschild empire assumed total control of the finances of the United States. To this we shall now turn our attention.

I must at this juncture acknowledge the great American patriot whose persistence and courage over the last forty years have exposed the conspiracy that led to the formation of the Federal Reserve System. He is none other than Eustace Mullins who in 1952 published the pioneering work, *Mullins On The Federal Reserve*, which was commissioned by the great American poet and patriot Ezra

Pound.[16] The information disclosed in this chapter is essentially from Mr. Mullins's seminal work. I have learned more about international finance and banking from this treatise than any textbooks that I have studied as an economics student at the university and ever since, notwithstanding disagreements on some of his conclusions.

The American Revolution won for the American people political independence and freedom from Britain, but not financial freedom. Thomas Jefferson warned:

"If the American People ever allow the banks to control the issuance of their currency, first by inflation and then by deflation, the banks and corporations that will grow up around them will deprive the people of all property, until their children will wake up homeless on the continent their fathers occupied. The issuing moneys should be taken from the banks and restored to Congress and the people to whom it belongs."

The battle for the financial independence of the American Republic was, according to Congressman Louis McFadden, one of the greatest battles fought against the Zionist British financial empire.[17] The first attempt to create a privately owned Federal Bank was initiated by Alexander Hamilton in collusion with foreign financial interests and in 1791 Congress chartered the bank for 20 years. The bank was called the Bank for the United States. The bank was essentially controlled by foreign investors and for their benefit. At the end of its 20 year term in 1811, its charter was not renewed by Congress. The foreign banking interests persisted in their efforts and in 1816 a second national bank was given a Federal Charter. This bank was controlled by the Rothschilds through their front men, John Jacob Astor, Stephen Girard, David Parish and Nicholas Biddle. However, this attempt to control the republic's finances was short lived, as it was closed down by President Andrew Jackson when he vetoed the Bill which would have renewed its charter in 1836. He warned the American people:

"The bold efforts the present bank has made to control the government, the distress it has wantonly caused, are but premonitions of the fate which awaits the American people should they be deluded into a perpetuation of this institution or the establishment of another like it."

The President was so infuriated by the bankers that he called them:

"You are a den of vipers. I intend to rout you out and by the eternal God I will rout you out. If the people only understood the rank injustice of our money and banking system, there would be a revolution before morning."

From that time onwards, the international banking cartel headed by the Rothschilds plotted to seize control once again the finances of the United States. As stated earlier, debt is the essence of financial power and provoking wars was the surest way in creating national debts. The first step the Rothschild Empire took was to provide huge loans at exorbitant interest to state banks, especially to Southern state banks and to create a crisis. When these banks failed, as a result of gross mismanagement, the European financiers put pressure on the Federal government to assume the debts of these failed banks. This issue soon evolved into a constitutional issue, that of "State Rights" as against the Federal Authority and the constitutional crisis that followed was one of the major reasons for the Civil War, a war financed mainly by the Rothschild family. At the close of the Civil War, the Union was indebted to the tune of about $3 billion and the Confederacy some $2 billion. But this was insufficient to bankrupt and destroy the United States.

The period between 1869[18] and 1913, witnessed one of the most carefully planned subversion of a nation ever mounted by modern financial interests. The dirty work was carried out by Kuhn, Loeb and Co, J.P. Morgan and Co., and the Rockefellers, all connected to the Rothschild. This tie-up was revealed by Newsweek, February 1, 1936:

"Abraham Kuhn and Solomon Loeb were general merchandise merchants in Lafayette, Indiana, in 1850. As usual in newly settled regions, most transactions were on credit. They soon found out that they were bankers. In 1867, they established Kuhn, Loeb and Co., bankers, in New York City, and took in a young German immigrant, Jacob Schiff, as partner. Young Schiff had important connections in Europe. After ten years, Jacob Schiff was head of Kuhn, Loeb and Co., Kuhn having retired. Under Schiff's guidance, the house brought European capital into contact with American industry.[19]"

The European connections referred to were none other than the Rothschilds and their German representatives, the Warburgs of Hamburg and Amsterdam. And it was this European cartel that was responsible for the rapid rise of the Rockefellers in the oil industry, the Harrimans, in the railroads and Andrew Carnegie in the steel industry.

To appreciate the power and influence of this financial cabal, I need only to quote Carroll Quigley's monumental work, **Tragedy and Hope**.

"The structure of financial controls created by the tycoons of 'Big Banking' and 'Big Business' in the period 1880-1993 was of extraordinary complexity, one business fief being built on another, both being allied with semi-independent associates, the whole rearing upward into two pinnacles of economic and financial power, of which one, centered in New York, was headed by J.P. Morgan and Company, and the other in Ohio, was headed by the Rockefeller family. When these two cooperated, as they generally did, they would influence the economic life of the country to a large degree and could almost control its political life, at least on the Federal level."

With their financial power firmly established, they were ready to take on Congress and the first salvo was sounded in 1907, when Jacob Schiff in a speech to the New York Chamber of Commerce warned: *"unless we have a central bank with adequate control of credit resources, this country is going to undergo the most severe and far-reaching money panic in its history."*

True to the warning, a financial panic occurred in 1907 which sent shock waves throughout America, and the public demanded reforms to the financial system. This laid the basis for the international banking cabal to weave their web of deceit. Eustace Mullins gives a graphic description how seven power financial figures set about putting their plan into action. On the night of November 22, 1910, the United States' leading financiers left the railway station at Hoboken, New Jersey on a secret mission. They were headed for Jekyll Island, Georgia. The delegation was headed by Senator Nelson Aldrich, head of the National Monetary Commission, which was formed by President Theodore Roosevelt in 1908, following the 1907 panic, and a business associate of J.P. Morgan and father-in-law of John D. Rockefeller; Abraham Piat Andrew, Assistant Secretary of the U.S. Treasury and Special Assistant to the National Monetary Commission; Frank Vanderlip, President of the National City Bank of New York, reputed to be the most powerful bank at that time and said to be representing Kuhn, Loeb and Company; Henry P. Davidson, senior partner of J.P. Morgan Company and generally regarded as Morgan's personal emissary; Charles D. Norton, President of J.P. Morgan dominated First National Bank of New York; Benjamin Strong, representing J.P. Morgan's Bankers trust Company; Paul M. Warburg, partner of Kuhn, Loeb and Company.

The choice of Jekyll Island made sense not only because it was isolated, but it was the private preserve of the people who drafted the plan for the Fed. It was reported in the New York Times on May 3, 1931, that the members of the Jekyll Island Club represented one-sixth of the total wealth of the world. Bertie Charles Forbes who later founded the Forbes magazine wrote about the gathering in a likeness that parodies fiction:

"...sneaking onto an island deserted by all but a few servants, living there a full week under such rigid secrecy that the names of not one of them was once mentioned lest the servants learned the identity and disclose to the world this strangest, most secret expedition in the history of American finance... Nelson (Aldrich) had confided .... that he was to keep them locked up in Jekyll Island, out of the rest of the world, until they had evolved and compiled a scientific currency system for the United States, the real birth of the present Federal Reserve System.."

Such absolute secrecy as was demanded of the members of the delegation was corroborated by Vanderlip himself who wrote an article for the Saturday Evening Post, on February 9, 1935:

"If it were to be exposed publicly that our particular group had gotten together and written a banking bill, that bill would have no chance whatever of passage by Congress.[20]"

Here is an express admission of the sordid duplicity of the consortium — to draft a piece of legislation that would govern their financial activities. What is not obvious to the public is that the system recommended by the conspirators ensured a monopoly for the banking houses of the Rothschild, J.P. Morgan and company, Kuhn, Loeb and Company, Rockefeller and the Warburgs of the finances of the United States of America. It is indeed remarkable that the competitors in the banking industry, agreed to collude to ensure their stranglehold on the U.S. finances — the most powerful monopoly ever created.

For those who still harbor doubts and entertain the idea that I am a conspiracy theorist, I would like to close this part of the chapter with a series of quotations which, I believe, would put to rest any further debate on the significance of the construction of the Second Pillar of the Zionist Imperial Edifice in the overall scheme of things.

"This [Federal Reserve act] establishes the most gigantic trust on earth. When the President [Wilson] signs this bill, the invisible government of the monetary power will be legalized... the worst legislative crime of the age is perpetrated by this banking and currency bill.

"From now on, depressions will be scientifically created.

"The financial system has been turned over to the Federal Reserve Board. That Board administers the finance system by authority of a purely profiteering group. The system is private, conducted for the sole purpose of obtaining the greatest profits from the use of other people's money."
— Congressman Charles A. Lindbergh Sr.

"Most Americans have no real understanding of the operation of the international moneylenders. The accounts of the Federal Reserve System have never been audited. It operates outside the control of Congress and manipulates the credit of the United States."
— Senator Barry Goldwater

"We have, in this country, one of the most corrupt institutions the world has ever known. I refer to the Federal Reserve Board. This evil institution has impoverished the people of the United States and has practically bankrupted our government. It has done this through the corrupt practices of the moneyed vultures who control it.

"Some people think the Federal Reserve Banks are the United States government's institutions. They are not government institutions. They are private credit monopolies which prey upon the people of the United States for the benefit of themselves and their foreign swindlers."
— Congressman Louis T. McFadden, Chairman of the Committee on Banking & Currency (12 years) June 10, 1932.[21]

"These 12 corporations together cover the whole country and monopolize and use for private gain every dollar of the public currency."

— Mr. Crozier of Cincinnati, before Senate Banking & Currency Committee, 1913.

The status of the Federal Reserve as a private institution and not a Federal agency was tested in Court. One Mr. Lewis who was injured by a Federal Reserve vehicle sued the U.S. Government. On April 17, 1982, the court ruled:

"The regional Federal Reserve Banks are not government agencies, but are independent, privately owned and locally controlled corporations... that since the Federal Reserve System and its twelve branch banks are private corporations, the federal government could not be held liable." (Lewis v U.S., 608F 2d 1239 (1982) 9th Circuit)

Yet, we have books on the Fed which maintain this myth. These authors serve the interest of the Fed by misleading the general public. One particular book comes to mind, **Secrets of the Temple: How the Federal Reserve Runs the Country**, by William Greider.[22] Although the title seems to suggest that the book intends to expose the truth about the Fed, the contrary is the case. This is how Greider misleads the people by stating half-truths:

"The Federal Reserve System was an odd arrangement, a unique marriage of public supervision and private interests, deliberately set apart from the elected government, _though still part of it_."

Yet in the very next sentence, Greider contradicts himself:

"The Fed enjoyed privileges extended to no other agency in Washington — it raised its own revenue, drafted its own operating budget and submitted neither to Congress for approval."

One of the difficulties in exposing the hidden power of the Fed is explaining to the people that the Federal Reserve Banks create money out of nothing, literally out of thin air. Each time, such an assertion is made the usual retort is "bullshit!" As a result of the inability by so many people to comprehend this duplicity of the Fed, I had spent a considerable period of time tracking down authoritative statements

191

on this point and I was fortunate to have found the following admissions:

"When you and I write a check there must be sufficient funds in our account to cover the check, but when the Federal Reserve writes a check, there is no bank deposit on which that check is drawn. When the Federal Reserve writes a check, it is creating money."

— Boston Federal Reserve Bank

"Neither paper currency nor deposits have value as commodities, intrinsically, a 'dollar' bill is just a piece of paper. Deposits are merely book entries."

— Chicago Federal Reserve Bank

"The Federal Reserve System pays the U.S. Treasury $20.60 per thousand notes — a little over 2 cents each — without regard to the face value of the note. Federal Reserve Notes incidentally are the only type of currency now produced for circulation. They are printed exclusively by the Treasury's Bureau of Engraving and Printing, and the $20.60 per thousand price reflects the Bureau's full cost of production. Federal Reserve Notes are printed in 01, 02, 05, 10, 20, 50 and 100 dollar denomination only; notes of 500, 1000, 5000 and 10,000 denominations were last printed in 1945."

— Donald J. Winn, Asst to Board of Governors

The next few quotations will be eye openers for many readers. The first is from President Woodrow Wilson who you may recall signed into law the Federal Reserve Act 1913, but subsequently realized the folly of his action. This is what he wrote:

"A great industrial nation is controlled by its system of credit. Our system of credit is concentrated in the hands of a few men. We have come to be one of the worst ruled, one of the most completely controlled and dominated governments in the world — no longer a government of free opinion, no longer a government by conviction and vote of the majority, but a government by the opinion and duress of small groups of dominant men."

The second is from John Maynard Keynes who wrote in the ***Consequences of Peace***[23] that:

"Should government refrain from regulation [taxation], the worthlessness of the money becomes apparent and the fraud can no longer be concealed."

And finally, the brutal truth from Sir Josiah Stamp, Governor of the Bank of England in the 1920s:

"Banking was conceived in inequity and was born in sin. The bankers own the earth. Take it away from them, but leave them the power to create deposits, and with a flick of the pen they will create enough deposits to buy it back again. However, take it away from them, and all the great fortunes like mine will disappear and they ought to disappear, for this would be a happier and better world to live in. But if you wish to remain the slaves of bankers and pay the costs of your own slavery, let them continue to create deposits."

The Rothschild brothers once boasted that the few who understand the system, will either be so interested from its profits or so dependent on its favors, that there will be no opposition from that class. That such was the case is evident from the observation of Senator John Danforth, in great shame, said:

"I have never seen more Senators express discontent with their jobs... I think the major cause is that, deep down in our hearts, we have been accomplices in doing something terrible and unforgivable to our wonderful country. Deep down in our hearts, we know we have given our children a legacy of bankruptcy. We have defrauded our country to get ourselves elected."

When I finished writing the first draft of this chapter, I forwarded it to a few friends to find out whether they understood what I had written, in particular the statement by Senator John Danforth that Congress had defrauded the country. My friends replied that while they understood the principles, they wanted to know, in simple terms, how the scam was carried out, without the technical jargon. I shall now endeavor to explain in simple terms how the scam is being carried out.[24]

Let's take the following scenario. The President of the United States has just launched a war against a foreign country and had initially estimated that it would cost a mere $50 billion. As a result of complications, e.g. citizens of the target country rose en masse to resist the invasion, the cost of the war escalated tremendously. The occupation of the country and the efforts to suppress the resistance now cost $100 billion, but the U.S. Government has no money to pay for the additional costs. What the government does is to issue what is

193

generally referred to as "government bonds" or "Bills" with a face value of $100 billion which is essentially an "IOU". That is to say an acknowledgement by the government to the holder of the bond (the person/institution who has purchased the said bond) that the principal will be repaid within a certain period at a fixed interest. People will buy these bonds, because they trust that the government will honor the pledge of repayment.

Let's say that investors (both local and foreign) took up only $50 billion worth of bonds. There is therefore a shortfall of $50 billion. What happens is this: The U.S. government goes to the Fed and asks it to take up the shortfall. No problem. The Fed issues a check for $50 billion. Just like that, out of thin air, as authorized by the Federal Reserve Act. Recall the earlier quotation from the Boston Federal Reserve Bank:

"When you and I write a check there must be sufficient funds in our account to cover the check, but when the Federal Reserve writes a check there is no bank deposit on which that check is drawn. When the Federal Reserve writes a check, it is creating money."

What happens next is that the Treasury official deposits the check into the government's account which will indicate in the statement of accounts a deposit of $50 billion. Suddenly, the government now has $50 billion to spend. But this amount of borrowed money must be repaid to all bond holders. This the government does by taxing the people, as without taxation, the borrowed money cannot be repaid. Recall once again the quotation by John Maynard Keynes:

"Should government refrain from regulation [taxation], the worthlessness of the money becomes apparent and the fraud can no longer be concealed."

The next stage of money creation takes place when the U.S. government pays Halliburton $10 billion for services rendered in the war effort. This $10 billion is deposited in Halliburton's account in its bank, say Citibank. Under the law, banks need only to keep in reserve 10% of any deposit, in this case $1 billion.

The other $9 billion can be used by the banks to loan money to its customers which collects interests. So what we have here is a situation where in step one, the Fed creates money out of thin air and collects interests on it; in the second stage, that same money is routed to a commercial bank, and is then used by that bank to create loans that earn further interests. This money is not backed by any asset like gold or silver. It is just a paper. It is not redeemable.

From a personal level, when a bank lends you money (which was created out nothing), it demands security from you by way of a mortgage of your house or other assets. Should you default, the bank will sell your house, in repayment of monies owing that has no value in the first place! That is why, Sir Josiah Stamp said:

"Banking was conceived in inequity and was born in sin. The Bankers own the earth... If you wish to remain the slaves of Bankers and pay the cost of your own slavery, let them continue to create deposits."

Henry Ford was equally blunt when he said:

"It is well that the people of the nation do not understand our banking and monetary system, for if they did, I believe there would be a revolution before tomorrow morning."

The next point that we need to understand is why currencies are no longer backed by gold as it was previously. The answer is really simple. If a 20 dollar note is redeemable for an equivalent value in gold, the amount of currency in circulation will be determined by the amount of gold held by the government. Money cannot be created out of thin air. Let's say that a government has only $20 billion worth of gold but has printed $100 billion worth of currency in various denominations.

If just holders of $40 billion of these notes were to redeem them for gold, there would be insufficient gold to meet the demand. In essence, a fraud was perpetrated on the holders of these notes and the country is in actual fact bankrupt. This was what happened in the 1970s when President Nixon declared that the US dollar was no longer redeemable for gold, as there was just not enough gold to meet the trillions of paper money circulating in the world's financial system. If the U.S. did not have the most lethal war machine to enforce its dictates, its economy would have collapsed and the country would have ended up a banana republic long ago.

The U.S. since 1913 has been indebted to the Zionists international banking cabal and politically has no choice but to follow the dictates of this cabal. The betrayal by the 1913 Congress to the Zionist Financial Cabal as admitted by Senator John Danforth has ruined the United States.

ENDNOTES:

1. *Memoirs of the Peace Conference*, (1972, H. Fertig), p. 726

2. He was also Hon. Secretary of the Joint Zionist Council of the United Kingdom in 1912, Joint Editor of the "Zionist" in 1913-1914 and author of the pamphlets "History of Zionism" and "Zionism, Its Organization and Institutions".

3. *History of the Peace Conference in Paris*, Vol 6, p173

4. Visit http://tinyuri.com/pvq3 for details of his writings.

5. Samuel Landman, *Great Britain, the Jews and Palestine*

6. Robert E. Edmondson, *Testify*, p 188

7. The Jewish newspaper, Central Blad Voor Israeliten in Nederland, September 13, 1939.

8. Moishe Shertok, in a speech at the British Zionist Conference in 1943 and reported in the Jewish Chronicle, January 22, 1943.

9. See the Jewish Chronicle, October 8, 1942. Statement by Rabbi Felix Mendelssohn

10. Sir Hartle Shawcross, "Ashamed and Humiliated": speech given at Stourbridge in March 12, 1948 and reported by AP and the Times (London)

11. Anselm Rothschild, quoted on the back cover of Eustace Mullin's *The Federal Reserve Conspiracy*, (1954, Christian Education Association, 2nd Ed.)

12. Jewish Chronicles, September 7, 1935

13. Rothschild is German for "Red-shield", from *roth* "red" + *schild* "shield"

14. The Jewish Encyclopaedia, Vol. 10, p 501-502

15. For a more detail discussion see Des Griffins, *Descent into Slavery* (1980 Emissary Publications)

16. Eustace Mullins, *Mullins On The Federal Reserve* (1952, New York: Kasper and Horton). Eustace Mullins is a veteran of the U.S. Air Force, with 38 months of active service during World War II. He was educated in Washington at Lee University, New York University, Ohio University, the University of North Dakota, the Escuelas des Bellas Artes, San Miguel de Allende, Mexico, and the Institute of Contemporary Arts, Washington, D.C. His *London Connection* is an updated version of the original book.

17. Speech by Louis McFadden on May 23, 1933 in Congress.

18. In 1869, the Credit Strengthening Act was passed by Congress and signed into law by the new President Grant, which allowed the Rothschild and his cabal to collect an additional $275 million over and above the principal and interest for the bonds that hey held and controlled.

19. Cited in *Descent into Slavery* by Des Griffin.

20. See also Vanderlip's autobiography, *From Farm Boy to Financier* (1935, New York: A Appleton Century). Also cited by Edward Griffin in *The Creature from Jekyll Island* (1994, American Media)

21. Congressional Record 12595-12603, 1932

22. William Greider, *Secrets of the Temple: How the Federal Reserve Runs the Country* (1987, New York: Touchstones Book)

23. John Maynard Keynes, *Consequences of Peace* (1920, New York: Harcourt Brace Jovanovich)

24. Adapted from Edward Griffin's *Creature from Jekyll Island*.

12

The Zionist Imperial Edifice Part II — The Spear of Conquest

When I started out as an attorney 29 years ago, I did not have the luxury of choosing the type of work and clients that I wanted to represent. I was game for any case that brought in good fees. On one occasion, a senior member of a local triad enquired whether I was willing to represent one of his lieutenants who was charged for assaulting a member of a rival triad. The victim was badly smashed up. His lieutenant had defied the order not to take such an action and he was now out on a limb. I was curious, as I thought the triads have enforcers to do precisely such work. I sought an explanation. His answer was simple enough. It was more effective to use the uniformed forces; they can conduct raids and close down rivals' joints and it would be legitimate; rival enforcers could be arrested on a tip-off and it would be legitimate; there would be no basis for retaliation. It was the long arm of the law that did the damage. In extreme cases, different rules apply and different responses would be adopted. Triads don't like the spotlight and if others can do the dirty work, why not.

The rationale of the triads for getting someone to do the dirty work is not unique. It is the principal method of warfare perfected by the Zionists and when extreme situations demand extreme measures, the Zionists send out their own enforcers. In this chapter we shall explore how the Zionists get the world's uniformed forces to do their dirty work to further their imperialist agenda.

In the preceding chapters, we have seen how on two occasions, during the First and Second World Wars, the Zionists were able to manipulate the U.S. to intervene in the global conflicts in exchange for the agreement to set up the Zionist State of Israel. The events in the Middle East since 1990 are further examples of Zionists getting oth-

197

ers to do the dirty work. If we want to defeat Zionism, we need to study and understand how they have succeeded so well in getting others to do the dirty work, more so after the Vietnam debacle.

The horrendous cost of the Vietnam War — which killed nearly 59,000 Americans and wounded over 350,000 and millions of civilian casualties — has prompted many top military leaders to review previous military doctrines. They vowed "never again". As a result, a new military doctrine evolved: the United States would not commit forces unless its national or allies' interests were threatened; there should be clearly defined military and political objectives; U.S. troops would not be committed unless Congress and the American public were likewise committed; and war would be the last resort. Colin Powell, as Chairman of the Joint Chiefs of Staff added two further qualifications: always use overwhelming force, not proportional force, and there must be an exit strategy — when the fighting is over, the army gets out. At the operations level, General Creighton Abrams, the last U.S. Commander in Vietnam devised an operational strategy that in any future wars, the Army Reserve and National Guard would be committed as well. The rationale being every segment of American society, in small towns as well as cities, would be affected and would have to bear the cost of deaths and injuries, thereby making war more difficult. They would be more demanding to know the reasons for war.[1]

Yet in the last decade, these sound principles were jettisoned and even ridiculed, as when Madeleine Albright chided Colin Powell: ***"What's the point of having this superb military that you've always been talking about if we can't use it."*** The reply by the then Chairman of the Joint Chiefs of Staff, ***"American GIs are not toy soldiers to be moved around on some global game board"*** did not even merit any consideration. Madeleine Albright, a committed Zionist had a better appreciation of the role of the U.S. military as dictated by Zionist global interests. The U.S. army will be the Zionists' enforcers of their global agenda.

The Zionist strategy of using the United Nations and the U.S. military war machine (i.e. the uniformed forces) to serve Zionists' agenda was implemented in 1948 when the State of Israel was established, with somewhat mixed results. But this has not distracted the Zionists from pursuing this strategy for the simple reason that it is most cost effective and efficient from the point of view of their global resources. Many Zionists have written and spoken on this issue but I find the speech by Rabbi Rabinovich to the Emergency Council of European Rabbis in Budapest, Hungary, on January 12, 1952[1A] most illustrative and still pertinent to the present discussion. I seek your indulgence for quoting the speech at length as I would like to avoid the accusation of misrepresentation. My comments are in brackets.

"Greetings, my children: You have been called here to recapitulate the principal steps of our new program... The goal for which we have striven so concernedly for three thousand years is at last within our reach, and because its fulfillment is so apparent, it behooves us to increase our efforts and our caution tenfold. I can safely promise you that before ten years have passed, our race will take its rightful place in the world, with every Jew a King and every Gentile a slave. You remember the success of our propaganda campaign during the 1930s, which aroused anti-American passions in Germany at the same time we were arousing anti-German passions in America, a campaign which culminated in the Second World War."

[I hope you can see the parallels in the present War on Terrorism. Anti-Muslim passion aroused in the United States and, at the same time, anti-American sentiments spurred on in the Middle East as a result of 9-11 on the one hand, and the Iraq War on the other.]

"A similar propaganda campaign is now being waged intensively throughout the world. A war fever is being worked up in Russia by an incessant anti-American barrage while a nationwide anti-communist scare is sweeping America. This campaign is forcing all the smaller nations to choose between the partnership of Russia or an alliance with the United States."

[Likewise, Bush's challenge[2], "Over time, it's going to be important for nations to know they will be held accountable for inactivity. You are either with us or against us in the fight against terror," forcing small nations to take sides on the bogus War on Terrorism.]

"Our most pressing problem at the moment is to inflame the lagging militaristic spirit of Americans. The failure of the Universal Military Training Act was a great setback to our plans, but we assured that a suitable measure will be rushed through Congress immediately... The Russians as well as Asiatic peoples, are well under control and offer no objections to war, but we must wait to secure Americans. This we hope to do with the

199

issue of ANTI-SEMITISM, which worked as well in uniting the Americans against Germany... We will advance through new sources large sums of money to outspokenly anti-Semitic elements in America to increase their effectiveness, and we shall stage anti-Semitic outbreaks in several of their largest cities... Within five years, this program will achieve its objective, the Third World War, which will surpass in destruction all previous contests. Israel, of course will remain neutral, and when both sides are devastated and exhausted, we will arbitrate, sending our Control Commissions into all wrecked countries. This war will end for all times our struggle against the Gentiles.

"We shall embark upon an era of ten thousand years of peace and plenty, the Pax Judaica, and our race will rule undisputed over the world. Our superior intelligence will easily enable us to retain mastery over a world of dark peoples....

"We may have to repeat the grim days of World War II, when we were forced to let the Hitlerite bandits sacrifice some of our people, in order that we may have adequate documentation and witnesses to legally justify out trial and execution of the leaders of America and Russia as war criminals, after we have dictated the peace. I am sure you will need little preparation for such a duty, for sacrifice has always been a watchword of our people, and the DEATH OF A FEW THOUSAND LESSER JEWS in exchange for world leadership, is indeed A SMALL PRICE TO PAY. To convince you of the certainty of that leadership, let me point out to you how we HAVE TURNED ALL THE INVENTIONS OF THE WHITE MAN INTO WEAPONS AGAINST HIM. HIS PRINTING PRESSES AND RADIOS ARE THE MOUTHPIECES OF OUR DESIRES, AND HIS HEAVY INDUSTRY MANUFACTURERS THE INSTRUMENTS WHICH HE SENDS OUT TO ARM ASIA AND AFRICA AGAINST HIM.

"Our interests in Washington are greatly extending the Point Four Program for developing industry in backward areas of the world, so that after the industrial plants and cities of Europe and America are destroyed by atomic warfare, the Whites can offer no resistance against the large masses of the dark races, who will maintain an unchallenged technological superiority. And so, with the vision of world victory before you, go back to your countries and intensify your good work, until that

200

approaching day when Israel will reveal herself in all her glorious destiny as the light of the world."

One may argue that the vision of Rabbi Rabinovich no longer holds true, having been superseded by events that have since occurred or that he is a fanatic and a minority and his views were not reflective of Zionists in general. On the contrary, his views are very current and I intend to demonstrate that throughout the 1980s and 1990s more detailed plans were formulated to ensure the success of Rabbi Rabinovich's vision.

In 1982, an essay entitled "A Strategy for Israel in the Nineteen Eighties" by Oded Yinon was published in Hebrew in KIVUNIM.[3] In the Foreword to his translation of Oded Yinon's essay[4], Israel Shahak wrote that the essay represented the accurate and detailed plan of the Zionist regime for the Middle East. He states further that strong connection with Neoconservative thought in the USA is very prominent and while lip service is paid to the idea of the 'defense of the West' from Soviet power, the real aim of the author and the Israeli establishment is clear: To make an Imperial Israel into a world power. In other words, the aim of Sharon is to deceive the Americans after he has deceived the rest.

The strategy rest on two essential premises, namely: (1) Israel must become an Imperial power to survive; and (2) Israel must effect the break-up and division of the entire Middle East into smaller entities by the dissolution of all the existing states, along sectarian and tribal lines. This idea is not new as the memoirs of Moshe Sharett, the former Prime Minister of Israel reveals similar plans.[5] However, what is new, or rather what has been brought out into the open is the admission that Israel must prepare for nuclear warfare, which corroborates Rabbi Rabinovich's agenda. Oded Yinon has warned that the next *"great saga will demolish a large part of our world in a multidimensional global war, in comparison with which the past world wars will have been mere child's play. The war over resources in the world, the Arab monopoly on oil, and the need of the West to import most of its raw materials from the Third World, are transforming the world we know... We can imagine the dimensions of the global confrontation which will face us in the future."*

The Arab constituency should pay attention to the assessment by

Oded Yinon of the strategic implications of the Arab world in the context of Zionists global ambitions. And unless the Arab world and the Organization of Islamic Conference (OIC) wakes up to the realities of the present geopolitical situation, it can be said without fear of contradiction that Zionism would eventually triumph in the Middle East. The Arabs and Muslims may not like what I say here, but the arrogance and contempt of Oded Yinon is more than justified when he wrote:

"The Arab Moslem world ... is not the major strategic problem which we shall face in the eighties, despite the fact that it carries the main threat against Israel, due to its growing military might. The world [Arab], with its ethnic minorities, its factions and internal crisis, which is astonishingly self-destructive, as we can see in Lebanon, in non-Arab Iran and now also in Syria, is unable to deal successfully with its fundamental problems and does not therefore constitute a real threat against the State of Israel in the long run, but only in the short where its immediate military power has great import. In the long run, this world [Arab] will be unable to exist within its present framework in the areas around us without having to go through revolutionary changes. The Moslem Arab world is built like a temporary house of cards put together by foreigners (France and Britain in the nineteenth century), without the wishes and desires of its inhabitants having been taken into account. It was arbitrarily divided into 19 states, all made up of combinations of minorities and ethnic groups which are hostile to one another, so that every Arab Moslem state nowadays face ethnic social destruction from within, and in some a civil war is raging. In the Gulf states, Saudi Arabia, Libya and Egypt there is the largest accumulation of money and oil in the world, but those enjoying it are tiny elites who lack a wide base of support and self-confidence, something that no army can guarantee."

In essence, the above straightforward analysis confirms that the Arab world, in fact I could go to the extent of saying that the Muslim world is still being controlled by the time-tested "Divide and Rule" policy of the British Zionists. The internal tensions are further aggravated by the divide within Islam itself and the feudal bigoted practices so common in the region, which practices have spread throughout the Muslim *ummah*. The result is impotency and disillusion, and the inability of the intellectual elites to break out from this mental straitjacket. Is it any surprise then, that these states prostitute themselves to the

Zionist U.S. military for protection, not against the threat from Israel, but their very own people and their neighbors? It is apparent that the Zionists have exploited this advantage to maintain the unchallenged power and supremacy of Israel, and its ability to humiliate and dominate the Arab-Muslim world.

What Oded Yinon conceived in the 1980s with regard to Iraq has already come to pass. This was what he wrote back then:

"Iraq, rich in oil on the one hand and internally torn on the other, is <u>guaranteed as a candidate for Israel's target.</u> Its dissolution is even more important for us than Syria. Iraq is stronger than Syria. In the short run it is Iraqi power which constitutes the greatest threat to Israel. An Iraq-Iran war will tear Iraq apart and cause its downfall at home even before it is able to organize on a wide front against us. <u>Every kind of Inter-Arab confrontation will assist us in the short run and will shorten the way to the more important aim of breaking up Iraq into denominations as in Syria and in Lebanon.</u> In Iraq, a division into provinces along ethnic/religious lines as in Syria during Ottoman times is possible. So, three (or more) states will exist around the three major cities: Basra, Baghdad and Mosul, and Shi'ite areas in the south will separate from the Sunni and Kurdish north. It is possible that the present Iranian-Iraqi confrontation will deepen this polarization."

The recent U.S.-engineered elections in Iraq and the outcome have more or less confirmed this three-way split.

Given this open declaration of war against the Arab states in the Middle East and the methods to achieve the Zionists' objectives, the leaders of the Arab-Muslim world did not even attempt to foster a simple united front to confront this Zionist threat. Instead, they scheme to undermine each other and suppress their citizens' legitimate aspirations for dignity and respect and freedom from feudal institutions. In the conclusion to the essay, Oded Yinon asked, *"Why is it assumed that there is no special risk from the outside in the publication of such plans?"* And his own reply was:

"The Arab world has shown itself so far quite incapable of a detailed and rational analysis of Israel-Jewish society, and the Palestinians have been, on the average, no better than the rest. In such a situation, even those who are shouting about the dangers of Israeli expansionism (which are real enough) are doing this not because of factual and detailed knowledge, but because of belief in myth."

203

The answer provided by Yinon is an indictment of the entire leadership of the Arab-Muslim world and on reflection, by any measure is objectively correct. This may not sit well with the Arab establishment, but the truth must be said.

At each and every conference of the OIC and the Arab League, the leaders parade themselves before foreign media, displaying their so called Islamic credentials and supposed unity, only to return home to indulge in deals and compromises to perpetuate their rule. In wars, even enemies would admire the resilience, courage and determination of the opposing forces, should they be able to display such sterling qualities; for there is no shame in defeat if the battle was fought bravely and with honor. Sadly the heroism of the Palestinian people has been repeatedly undermined and betrayed by such leaders.

In the 1990s, another review of the various strategic options available to Israel was commissioned by the Israeli Institute for Advanced Strategic and Political Studies entitled **"A Clean Break: A New Strategy for Securing the Realm"**. The team included Richard Perle, James Colbert, Charles Fairbanks, Douglas Feith, Robert Lowenberg, David Wurmser and Meyrav Wurmser, leading neoconservatives in Bush's administration.

The thrust of the Report/Review is that Israel has the opportunity to make a clean break:[6] it can forge a peace process and strategy based on an entirely new intellectual foundation, one that restores strategy initiatives and provides the nation room to engage every possible energy on rebuilding Zionism, the starting point of which must be economic reforms. To secure Israel in the immediate future, the Report recommended:

1) Work closely with Turkey and Jordan to contain, destabilize, and rollback some of its most dangerous threats. This implies a clean break from the slogan, "comprehensive peace" to a traditional concept of strategy based on a balance of power;

2) Change the nature of its relations with the Palestinians, including upholding the right of hot pursuit for self-defense into all Palestinian areas and nurturing alternatives to Arafat's exclusive grip on Palestinian society; and

3) Forge a new basis for relations with the United States —

stressing self-reliance, maturity, strategic cooperation on areas of mutual concern, and furthering values inherent in the West. This can be done if Israel takes serious steps to terminate aid, which prevents economic reforms.

The Report also contained passages of a possible speech for Benjamin Netanyahu which ought to be read by everyone who has an interest in a just solution to the crisis in the Middle East, as it lays bare, without any pretensions, the New Strategy. This is reproduced below:

"We have for four years pursued peace based on a New Middle East. We in Israel cannot lay innocents abroad in a world that is not innocent. Peace depends on the character and behavior of our foes. We live in a dangerous neighborhood, with fragile states and bitter rivalries. Displaying moral ambivalence between the effort to build a Jewish State and the desire to annihilate it by trading 'land for peace' will not secure 'peace now.' Our claim to the land — to which we have clung in hope for 2000 years — is legitimate and noble. It is not within our own power, no matter how much we concede, to make peace unilaterally. Only the unconditional acceptance by Arabs of our rights, especially in their territorial dimensions, 'peace for peace', is a solid basis for the future.

"Negotiations with repressive regime like Syria's require cautious realism. One cannot sensibly assume the other side's good faith. It is dangerous for Israel to deal naively with a regime murderous of its own people, openly aggressive towards its neighbors, criminally involved with international drug traffickers and counterfeiters, and supportive of the most deadly terrorist organizations.

"We must distinguish soberly and clearly friend from foe. We must make sure that our friends across the Middle East never doubt the solidity or value of our friendship.

"We believe that the Palestinian Authority must be held to the same minimal standards of accountability as other recipients of U.S. foreign aid. A firm peace cannot tolerate repression and injustice. A regime that cannot fulfill the most rudimentary obligations to its own people cannot be counted upon to fulfill its obligations to its neighbors.

"Israel will not only contain its foes; it will transcend them."

205

Likewise the Arab-Muslim world should not be naive and assume the other side's good faith. The Zionists have declared their evil intentions and launched a propaganda campaign of lies and distortions. Yet there are some who covets Israel's friendship at the expense of Arab unity. Turkey and Jordan have been singled out as reliable collaborators in an effort to divide and rule. Yet the Arab world has not come out with a rational counter-strategy.

Once again, the contempt for the Arabs is obvious. But what is startling is how some of the Arab states have danced to Zionist Israel's tunes. The Report smugly revealed:

"Israel can shape its strategic environment, in cooperation with Turkey and Jordan, by weakening, containing, and even rolling back Syria. This effort can focus on removing Saddam Hussein from power in Iraq — an important Israeli strategic objective in its own right — as a means of foiling Syria's regional ambitions. Jordan has challenged Syria's regional ambitions recently by suggesting the restoration of the Hashemites in Iraq. This has triggered a Jordanian-Syria rivalry to which Assad has responded by stepping up efforts to destabilize the Hashemite Kingdom, including using infiltrations."

It is clear that Oded Yinon's prescription to exploit "every kind of inter-Arab confrontation" is working and the Arabs are none the wiser!

The Institute for Research: Middle Eastern Policy (IRMEP) in March 2003 came out with a Score Card on the success rate in the implementation of this new strategy by Israel. According to the findings, the Zionists scored almost full marks in all areas except "Domestic Economic Reforms" which is not really surprising, for why should Israel give up the enormous economic and military aid amounting to billions of dollars.

Exhibit 3 to the Score Card deserves serious study as it shows convincingly how the Zionists have succeeded in "recruiting" the U.S. to serve its interest.

The Neocon Policy Distribution & Implementation Network[7]

Groups	Messages	Medium	Members
Defense Cabal	Pre-emption/remaking the Middle East Aid for Israel/Weapons Development New Homeland Security Business Opportunities Legitimization of Israeli Occupation of Palestinian Territories	Think Tanks Defense Policy Board Defense Department Defense Contractors Talk Shows Investment Banks	Paul Wolfowitz Richard Perle Douglas Feith Elliot Abrams David Wirmser
Neocon Specialty Press	Danger of Islam Illegitimacy of Arab Governments Illegitimacy of "Land for Peace" Initiatives Primacy of the Defense of Israel	American Enterprise Institute JINSA Heritage Foundation Reports The Weekly Standard The New Republic Commentary (American-Jewish Committee)	David Brooks Lawrence Kaplan William Kristol Norman Podhoretz
Columnists	Palestinian Militants as "Terrorists" Linkage between 9-11 and all Arab governments Israelis as "Heroes" Critics of Israel as "Anti-Semites"	Wall Street Journal New York Times Washington Post editorial pages	Robert Kagan Charles Krauthammer Max Boot William Safire

The more I researched into how the Zionists were able to hijack the U.S. military to do their dirty work, the more impressed I was by the breadth and depth of the propaganda campaign conducted over a period just under ten years. The key was winning the ideological war and they had won with hardly any resistance. Thereafter, getting the Americans to sacrifice their brave young men and women was like taking candy from a child. Such was their mastery over the propaganda war. Let us now examine how the Zionists won this ideological war.

PHASE I:

Phase I was essentially to get the U.S. Power Elites to effect a dramatic change in U.S. foreign policy towards the Middle East in general and Iraq in particular, to abandon the policy of containment. To spearhead this phase, an organization called Project for A New American Century (PNAC) was entrusted with this responsibility. In a letter dated January 26, 1998 to President Bill Clinton, they wrote:

"We are writing to you because we are convinced that current American policy toward Iraq is not succeeding and that we may soon face a threat in the Middle East more serious than any we have known since the end of the Cold War. In your upcoming State of the Union Address, you have an opportunity to chart a clear and determined course for meeting this threat. We urge you to seize the opportunity, and to enunciate a new strategy that would secure the interests of the U.S. and our friends and allies around the world. The strategy should aim, above all, at the removal of Saddam Hussein's regime from power. We stand ready to offer our full support in this difficult but necessary endeavor.

"Given the magnitude of the threat, the current policy, which depends for its success upon the steadfastness of our coalition partners and upon cooperation of Saddam Hussein, is dangerously inadequate. The only acceptable strategy is one that eliminates the possibility that Iraq will be able to use or threaten to use weapons of mass destruction. In the near term, this means a willingness to undertake military action as diplomacy is clearly failing. In the long term it means removing Saddam Hussein and his regime from power. That now needs to become the aim of American foreign policy."

The signatories were, inter alia, Richard Perle, Paul Wolfowitz, John Bolton, William Kristol, R. James Woolsey, Elliot Abrams, Donald Rumsfeld, Richard Armitage, Robert Kagan and William Bennett. This scare tactic had the desired effect as on October, 1998, President Clinton signed into law the Iraq Liberation Act. A month later, in November, Clinton ordered a bombing campaign on Iraq. This was followed by a more intensive bombing campaign in December 16, 1998 by American and British forces. Many have forgotten that it was President Clinton, a democrat, who laid the legal basis domestically for a regime change and the removal of Saddam by means of the military.

Observe and remember: Create the necessary public opinion for change and then lay down the legislative basis for such a change. Conduct a trial run of military action and test the public response. Get an ally to come on board to internationalize the military action and test the public reaction again.

PHASE II:

Intensify the propaganda campaign to the next level and lay the groundwork to justify massive military action to preserve the security interest of the United States.

Observe and remember: The scare tactic is given another dimension.

In September, 2000, PNAC published a report entitled "Rebuilding America's Defense." No one seemed to question why there is a need for America to rebuild its defense, when the Cold War has ended, the Soviet Empire has collapsed and the U.S. is the sole superpower. But these three words illustrate psychological warfare at its very best — conditioning Americans to be prepared for the next global war against an enemy (Militant Islam) which they have created, and the need to preserve America's supreme military power. In broad terms, the Report built upon the defense strategy outlined by the Cheney Defense Department in the waning days of the Bush I administration. The Defense Policy Guidance (DPG) drafted in the early months of 1992, provided a blueprint for maintaining U.S. pre-eminence, precluding the rise of a great rival power, and shaping the international security order in line with American principles and interest. The Report achieved the desired effect by contrasting the strategies under Cold War conditions and the New Strategies for the 21st century.

209

Key Strategies[8]

Cold War	21st Century
Security System —Bipolar	Security System —Unipolar
Strategic Goal — Containment	Strategic Goal — Preserve Pax Americana
Military Mission — Deter Soviet Expansion	Military Mission — Secure and expand zones of peace; deter rise of new great power competitor; defend key regions and exploit transformation war
Main Military Threats — Potential Global Wars across many theatres	Main Military Threats — Potential theatre wars across the globe
Focus of Strategic Competition — Europe	Focus of Strategic Competition — East Asia

PHASE III:

Create a situation that will give rise to a "New Pearl Harbor". In *The Grand Chess Board*[9] Brzezinski postulated:

"...as America becomes an increasingly multicultural society, it may find it more difficult to fashion a consensus on foreign policy issues, except in the circumstances of a truly massive and widely perceived direct and external threat ... The pursuit of power and especially the economic costs and human sacrifice that the exercise of such power often requires are not generally congenial to democratic instincts. Democracy is inimical to imperial mobilization."

This sentiment was echoed by the authors of the report **"Rebuilding America's Defense"** who acknowledged that the *"process of transformation even if it brings revolutionary change, is likely to be a long one, absent some catastrophic and catalyzing event — like a new Pearl Harbor.*[10]*"* September 11, 2001 was the "New Pearl Harbor" that gave the Zionists the pretext to give President Bush the **Spear of Conquest.**

This phase entails emboldening the President to wield the **Spear**

of Conquest decisively, by appealing to religious and moral values — the battle between good and evil. On September 20, 2001, PNAC wrote such a letter, urging the President to wage total war. Additionally, the letter urged the President thus:

"...even if evidence does not link Iraq directly to the attack, any strategy aiming at the eradication of terrorism and its sponsors must include a determined effort to remove Saddam Hussein from power in Iraq. Failure to undertake such an effort will constitute an early and perhaps decisive surrender in the war on international terrorism."

PHASE IV:

The next crucial area of propaganda control is to ensure that Presidential speeches reflect the Zionist Agenda. To control the contents of President Bush's speeches, via the influence of his speech writers, was a major coup by the Zionists. Obviously, the control was exercised much earlier, but I have slotted it under Phase IV, to illustrate how such control, when synchronized with external influence like PNAC's letters and media editorials, has a tremendous indoctrinational effect on the President. All the President's speeches since his inauguration must be viewed in that perspective, especially the State of the Union speeches and those given at strategic functions, e.g., the Speech at West Point in June, 2002.

PHASE V:

This phase is most crucial — to convince the entire military that they have a just cause to go and slaughter men, women and children. The speech by President Bush at West Point in June, 2002, was the clincher. As the Commander-in-Chief, President Bush abused his position to hoodwink the military to engage in illegal wars. He said:

"Our security will require all Americans to be forward looking and resolute, to be ready for pre-emptive action when necessary to defend our liberty and to defend our lives... America has and intends to keep, military strengths beyond challenge."

Dick Cheney was also doing his part to whip up war fever. In a speech to the Veterans of Foreign Wars, he said:

"Regime change in Iraq would bring about a number of benefits to the region. When the gravest threats are eliminated, the

*freedom loving peoples of the region will have a chance to pro-
mote the values that can bring lasting peace. As for the reaction
of the Arab 'street', the Middle East expert Professor Fouad
Ajami predicts that after liberation, the streets in Basra and
Baghdad are 'sure to erupt in joy the same way the throngs in
Kabul greeted the Americans.' Extremists in the region would
have to rethink their strategy of Jihad."*

The point to be noted here is that it does not matter whether the
scenario presented reflects reality; what is important is to ensure total
compliance and adherence to the political line as laid down by the
propaganda chiefs. In this speech, we see the outline of the *"Reverse
Domino Theory"* in the Middle East — the knock-on effect of a
regime change in Iraq would usher in a new era of "democracy" in the
feudal monarchic environment of the Middle East. The crusade is on,
and everyone is jumping on the bandwagon, notwithstanding
Brzezinski's pointed observation that, *"democracy is inimical to
imperial mobilization..."*

The opportunism in exploiting 9-11 as the "New Pearl Harbor" is
evident and is confirmed in the article by Condoleezza Rice in Foreign
Affairs, 2000, when she said that, *"the United States has found it
exceedingly difficult to define its 'national interest' in the
absence of Soviet power."* But after 9-11, her attitude changed. In
July, 2002, she said:

*"I think September 11 was one of those earthquakes that
clarify and sharpens. Events are in sharper relief... I really think
that this period is analogous to 1945 to 1947, in that the events
so clearly demonstrated that there is a big global threat, and that
it's a big global threat to a lot of countries that you would not
have normally thought of being in the coalition. That has started
shifting the tectonic plates in international politics. And it's
important to try and seize on that and position America's interest and institutions and all of that before they harden again.*[11]*"*

PHASE VI:

In this phase, the strategy is to link the security of the United States
with that of Israel. This by any measure is a master stroke, without which
Israel would not have been able to hijack the U.S. military to be their

Spear of Conquest. PNAC wrote a most crucial letter dated January, 2002, to the President, planting the seed that it is time to draw blood.

"We write to thank you for your courageous leadership in the War on Terrorism and to offer our full support as you continue to protect the security and well-being of Americans and all freedom loving peoples around the world.

"No one should doubt that the United States and Israel share a common enemy. We are both targets of what you have correctly called an 'Axis of Evil.' Israel is targeted in part because it is our friend, and in part because it is an island of liberal, democratic principles — American principles — in a sea of tyranny, intolerance, and hatred.... You have declared war on international terrorism, Mr. President. Israel is fighting the same war.

"Mr. President, in that address, you put forth a most compelling vision of a world at peace, free from the threat of terrorism, where freedom flourishes. Israel's fight against terrorism is our fight. Israel's victory is an important part of our victory. For reasons both moral and strategic, we need to stand with Israel in its fight against terrorism."

This last paragraph ensures President Bush's agreement to permit American youths to be cannon fodder for Zionists' imperial objectives, under the guise of combating the bogus War on Terrorism — another master stroke and a brilliant strategic positioning by Israel. The State of Union speech by President Bush in January 29, 2002 confirmed that he was willing to be a party to the Zionist Agenda.

Observe and remember: The application of reverse psychology — planting the seed that wielding the Spear of Conquest is entirely President Bush's strategic initiative, and that Israel's strategic stance will always be that of a reliable ally standing side by side with the United States. Israel is displaying the classic role of the High Priest, whispering suggestions of grandeur, leadership and courage to a Pharaoh unskilled in foreign affairs; an agent provocateur within the inner sanctum of power. The U.S. slaughters Israel's enemies but Israel is completely protected from any potential flak and can in fact claim that its hands are clean.

The art of deviousness has been transformed by the Zionists into a Science!

PHASE VII:

The final blueprint for Zionist conquest came out in September 17, 2002, with the publication of the National Security Strategy (NSS). It has been described by some neocons, notably John Lewis Gaddis that this document represents the most sweeping shift in U.S. Grand Strategy since the Cold War. Three feel-good objectives were clearly defined to camouflage its imperial objectives:

1) America will defend the peace by fighting terrorists and tyrants;

2) We will preserve the peace by building good relations among great powers; and

3) We will extend the peace by encouraging free and open societies on every continent.

The president has a warped sense of humour. He goes all over the globe killing people and then tells them that he's doing it for peace. On a closer reading of the NSS, it is evident that it rests on three essential elements, namely:

1) **Dominance**
2) **Pre-emption**
3) **Political Transformation (Regime Change)**

What is chilling in the NSS is the intent to conduct open-ended wars. The bogus War on Terrorism is now given a new dimension:

"We make no distinction between terrorist and those who knowingly harbor or provide aid to them. The struggle against global terrorism is different from any other war in history. It will be fought on many fronts against a particularly elusive enemy over an extended period of time. Progress will come through the persistent accumulation of successes — some seen, some unseen."

Recently, we have seen how the U.S. manufactured false allegations against Syria and Iran that they have sponsored terrorists, possessed WMD, etc., to lay the groundwork for future invasions, as was the case with Iraq when she was unjustly held to be responsible for 9-11 and for allegedly having WMD.

The pretext for war is now couched in terms of eliminating rogue states and the way to go about this is by launching pre-emptive wars:

"We must be prepared to stop rogue states and their terror-ist clients before they are able to threaten or use weapons of mass destruction against the United States and our allies and friends. We must deter and defend against threat before it is unleashed... Given the goals of rogue states and terrorists, the United States can no longer rely on a reactive posture as we have in the past. The inability to deter a potential attacker, the immediacy of today's threats, and the magnitude of potential harm that could be caused by our adversaries' choice of weapons, do not permit that option. We cannot let our enemies strike first."

I am sure that some of you after reading the preceding para-graphs may question whether the Zionists have such power of influ-ence to hijack the U.S. military for its war aims. In the course of my research, I was fortunate enough to come across an article written by Stephen Sniegoski entitled "The War on Iraq: Conceived in Israel"[12] which substantiates my contention. In the opening paragraph of his article, Sniegoski drew attention to the fact that the diplomatic histori-an Paul W. Schroeder is of the view that if Israel's security were indeed the real American motive for war, it would represent something unique in history; it would be the first instance where a great power (in fact a superpower) would do the fighting as the proxy of a small client state.[13]

You will recall that I had in the preceding chapters highlighted how Britain made use of the United States. The great revisionist his-torian Charles Tansill maintained: *"the main objective of American foreign policy since 1900 has been the preservation of the British Empire.[14]"* Britain was able to achieve her goal through media propaganda and sympathizers in the United States and we are see-ing a repeat performance by the Zionists who obviously have been well-trained by Whitehall to replicate its "back door" policies.[15]

I would urge anyone who really wants to understand the geopo-litical implications of Zionist Israel's intentions in the Middle East to take time and read this brilliant essay. For the purpose of this book it is enough to quote a few passages from the essay. Sniegoski cites Kathleen and Bill Christison[16] as one of his sources for his assertion and I quote:

"The suggestion that the war with Iraq is being planned at Israel's behest, or at the instigation of policymakers whose main motivation is trying to create a secure environment for Israel, is strong. Many Israeli analysts believe this. The Israeli commentator Akiva Eldar recently observed frankly in a Ha'aretz column that [Richard] Perle, [Douglas] Feith, and their fellow strategists 'are walking a fine line between their loyalty to American governments and Israeli interests.' The suggestion of dual loyalties is not a verboten subject in the Israeli press, as it is in the United States. Peace activist Uri Avery, who knows Israeli Prime Minister Sharon well, has written that Sharon has long planned grandiose schemes for restructuring the Middle East and that 'the winds blowing now in Washington remind me of Sharon. I have absolutely no proof that the Bushies got their ideas from him. But the style is the same.'"

Referring to the Special Report, **"A Clean Break"** (which I had cited earlier on the preceding pages above), Sniegoski commented that, *"It is also remarkable that while in 1996 Israel was to 'shape its strategic environment' by removing her enemies, the same individuals are now proposing that the United States shape the Middle East environment by removing Israel's enemies. That is to say, the United States is to serve as Israel's proxy, to advance Israel's interests."*

In the late 1930s, Ben-Gurion wrote: *"What is inconceivable in normal times is possible in revolutionary times...."* September 11, as admitted by Condoleezza Rice was earth-shattering, and provided the "revolutionary times" in which Israel could undertake revolutionary measures unacceptable during normal times. Sniegoski drew our attention to the interview given by Benjamin Netanyahu when he was asked what the attack would do for U.S.-Israeli relations. He replied, *"it's very good"* and that it will, *"strengthen the bond between our two peoples, because we've experienced terror over so many decades, but the United States has now experienced a massive hemorrhaging of terror."*

Obviously, it is not the case that I am putting forward here that security of Israel and her Zionist imperial ambitions are the main reasons for the invasion of Iraq. There were other reasons as well, which I shall address later. What I have endeavored to do is to show how, when there are convergence of imperial interests, between the United

States and Israel, the latter has always been able to exploit such convergence to the maximum at relatively low cost to herself.

In October 29, 2002, William Kristol and Robert Kagan gave a chilling account in The Weekly Standard[17] of what would be the outcome for such convergence of imperial interest.

"When all is said and done, the conflict in Afghanistan will be to the War on Terrorism what the North Africa campaign was to World War II: an essential beginning on the path to victory. But compared to what looms over the horizon — a wide ranging war in locales from Central Asia to the Middle East and, unfortunately, back again to the United States — Afghanistan will prove but an opening battle... But this war will not end in Afghanistan. It is going to spread and engulf a number of countries in conflicts of varying intensity. It could well require the use of American military power in multiple places simultaneously. It is going to resemble the clash of civilization that everyone has hoped to avoid."

What has been most infuriating is that the Zionist Anglo-American establishment has been very open about their aims and intentions, going back at least ten years before the invasion of Iraq. While they were preparing the conditions for war, members of the Nonaligned Movement (NAM), Organization of Islamic Conference (OIC) and other regional groups neither paid attention to these rabid declarations of war nor made preparations to counter the war agenda. The former leaders of Malaysia and South Africa, Tun Dr. Mahathir Mohamad and Nelson Mandela respectively, were the notable exceptions. In the coming nuclear wars, only countries which have made preparations and taken strategic measures to safeguard their resources would survive, but I am not hopeful. Like the Tsunami that hit us recently, it will be too little too late, notwithstanding all the warnings.

ENDNOTES:

1. Joe Galloway, "Weinberger, Powell War Doctrines Now History", December 3, 2003 @ www.military.com

1A. Source: www.universalway.org/denile.html   See also www.clrc.net/rabinovich.html and Eustace Mullins, New History of the Jews.

2. November 6, 2001, in a Joint News Conference in Washington with President Chirac.

3. KIVUNIM (Directions), a Journal for Judaism and Zionism; Issue No 14 – winter, 5742, February 1982. Published by the Department of Publicity/The World Zionist Organization, Jerusalem.

4. The translation was published by the Association of Arab-American University Graduates Inc, Belmont, Massachusetts, 1982 as Special Document No 1, ed. Israel Shahak.

5. See Livia Rokach, *Israel's Sacred Terrorism* (1980 AAUG Publication). An analysis of the diaries of Moshe Sharett, the former Prime Minister of Israel.

6. The opportunity referred to in the Report was the new regime in Israel under Benjamin Netanyahu.

7. See www.irmep.org/Policy_Briefs. This is an incredible website.

8. @ www.irmep.org/Policy_Briefs

9. Zbigniew Brzezinski, *The Grand Chess Board: American Primacy and Its Geostrategic Imperatives*, (1997, New York: Basic Books)

10. PNAC, "Rebuilding America's Defense", p. 51

11. Nicholas Lemann, "The Next World Order", April 1, 2002, The New Yorker Magazine.

12. Source: www.radioislam.org/islam/english/iraq/waroniraq

13. Paul W. Schroeder, "Iraq: The Case Against Preemptive War," The American Conservative, October 21, 2002 @ www.amconmag.com/10_21/iraq.html

14. *Back Door to War*, p.3, (1952, Chicago University Press)

15. See Nicholas John Cull, *Selling War: The British Propaganda Campaign against American Neutrality in World War II*, (1995, Oxford University Press) and Thomas E. Mahl, *Desperate Deceptions: British Covert Operations in the United States 1939–44*, (1998, Washington: Brassy's)

16. Kathleen and Bill Christison, "A Rose By Another Name: The Bush Administration Dual Loyalties," Counterpunch, December 13, 2002 @ http://www.counterpunch.org/christison1213.html

17. Robert Kagan and William Kristol, "The Gathering Storm", The Weekly Standard, October 29, 2002 @ http://theweeklystandard.com

13

Propaganda for War

"I am running out of demons.
I am running out of villains" — Colin Powell[1]

Make no mistake about it. The essence of Empire Capitalism is economic plunder by wars as imperialist mobilization can only be sustained by a war economy. The fundamental problem in managing a war economy is how to convince the various economic stakeholders, in particular your average Joe, that spending $400 billion on armaments is more crucial than bread and butter, healthcare and education.

In the last sixty years, as I have pointed out in the preceding chapters, the United States has been engaged in wars of one kind or another. But what really sustained the power elites' control over the economy was the Cold War and the threat of nuclear annihilation. When the Cold War ended with the collapse of the Soviet Union, the rationale for a war economy literally evaporated and the quote by Colin Powell cited above reflects the desperation of the establishment to find an alternative villain to justify the continued investments in the wasteful and outlandish projects of the military-industrial complex. When you have an enemy, it is easy to mobilize the populace to face an impending threat, which becomes the national focus on the home front, that is, security for the homeland, and externally, an assertive foreign policy that serves as a camouflage for imperial plunder. The lesser economies were hijacked to serve the imperial agenda in exchange for the perceived comfort of collective defense and security.

When euphoria swept the Western world, celebrating the end of history, the war economy grinded to a halt when military budgets were slashed and intelligence services downsized. The intellectual elite and the political leadership were caught in a mental gridlock, as admitted by Condoleezza Rice, *"the United States has found it exceedingly difficult to define its 'national interests' in the absence of Soviet power."*

September 11, restored the equation that national interests = facing a national enemy. In the New Yorker Magazine of April 1, 2002, in an interview with Nicholas Lemann, Condoleezza Rice confessed that the United States was back in war mode:

"I think September 11 was one of those great earthquakes that clarify and sharpen. Events are in much sharper relief. Like Bush, she said that opposing terrorism and preventing the accumulation of weapons of mass destruction 'in the hands of irresponsible states' now define the national interest. Rice said that she had called together the senior staff people of the National Security Council and asked them to think seriously about 'how do you capitalize on these opportunities' to fundamentally change American doctrine, and shape the world, in the wake of September 11."

A parallel opportunistic mindset also gripped the Israeli political leadership as explained by the Israeli historian Martin van Creveld in the Daily Telegraph of April 28, 2002:[2]

"Sharon would have to wait for a suitable opportunity — such as an American offensive against Iraq. An uprising in Jordan, followed by the collapse of King Abdullah's regime, would also present such an opportunity — as would a spectacular act of terrorism inside Israel that killed hundreds.

"Should such circumstances arise, then Israel would mobilize with lightning speed — even now, much of its male population is on standby. First, the country's borders would be closed, a news blackout imposed, and all foreign journalists rounded up and confined to a hotel as guests of the Government. A force of 12 divisions, 11 of them armored, plus various territorial units suitable for occupation duties, would be deployed: five against Egypt, three against Syria, and one opposite Lebanon. This would leave three to face east as well as enough forces to put a tank inside every Arab-Israeli village just in case their population gets any funny ideas.

"The expulsion of the Palestinians would require only a few brigades. They would not drag people out of their houses but use of heavy artillery to drive them out; the damage caused to Jenin would look like a pinprick in comparison.

"Israeli military experts estimate that such a war could be over in just eight days. If the Arabs states do not intervene, it will end with the Palestinians expelled and Jordan in ruins. If they do intervene, the result will be the same, with the main Arab armies destroyed."

This is another example of the convergence of imperial objectives, but in this scenario, Israel is willing to commit its own forces against relatively weak opponents, while the U.S. bears the brunt of the Iraqi invasion. The outcome of this convergence, the Zionist/Israeli Anglo-American Pact for Middle East, was correctly predicted by Eric Margolis[3] as the updated version of the Sykes-Picot Treaty of 1916 when Britain and France carved up the Middle East. Eric's observation is uncanny:

"Iraq is to be placed under U.S. military rule. Iraq's leadership, notably Saddam Hussein and Tariq Aziz, will face U.S. drumhead courts martial and firing squads. The swift ruthless crushing of Iraq is expected to terrify other Arab states, Palestinians and Iran into obeying U.S. political dictates.

"Independent minded Syria will be ordered to cease support for Lebanon's Hezbollah, and allow Israel to dominate Jordan and Lebanon, or face invasion and 'regime change'. The U.S. will anyway undermine the ruling Ba'ath regime and young leader, Bashir Assad, replacing him with a French-based exile regime. France will get renewed influence in Syria as a consolation prize for losing out in Iraq to the Americans and Brits.

"Iran will be severely pressured to dismantle its nuclear and missile programs or face attack by U.S. forces. Israel's rightist Likud party, which guides much of the Bush administration's Mideast thinking, sees Iran, not demolished Iraq, as its principal foe and threat and is pressing Washington to attack Iran once Iraq is finished off. At a minimum, U.S. will encourage an uprising against Iran's Islamic regime, replacing it with either a royalist government or one drawn from U.S.-based Iranian exiles.

"Saudi Arabia will be allowed to keep the royal family in power, but compelled to become more responsive to U.S. demands and to clamp down on its increasing anti-American population. If this fails, the CIA is reportedly cultivating senior Saudi air force officers who could overthrow the royal family and bring in a compliant military regime like that of General Pervez Musharaff in Pakistan. Or, partition Saudi Arabia, making the oil-rich eastern region an American protectorate."

A substantial portion of Eric's analysis has already come to pass. What remains of the article is already unfolding before our very eyes, as the events in Iran and Lebanon in recent weeks bear testimony.

In trying to understand the propaganda for war, we must always bear in mind the following:

1) Democracy is inimical to imperial mobilization;
2) Imperial mobilization can only be sustained by a war economy; and
3) Noble and altruistic ideals are always used to justify wars.

Propaganda for war has three distinct phases or stages, namely:

1) **Before** the military campaign;
2) **During** the military campaign; and
3) **The Aftermath** of the military campaign.

The illegal invasion of Iraq is an appropriate case study.

BEFORE THE MILITARY CAMPAIGN

As the first step in its war preparations, the Pentagon under Rumsfeld established the Office of Strategic Intelligence (OSI) whose functions were, inter alia, to conduct disinformation campaigns in foreign countries.[4] Although the agency was disbanded after it was leaked to the media, it continued under different guises. Certain "truths" that needed fabrication were:

1. Iraq has weapons of mass destruction which constituted an imminent threat to the security of the United States;
2. Iraq is a haven for terrorists and collaborates with Al Qaeda;

3. Saddam was in some way connected with September 11; and

4. Saddam is a tyrant and oppresses the people by, inter alia, gassing them.

In the circumstances, the required actions would entail:

1. U.S. must invade to remove the WMD before the smoking gun becomes a mushroom cloud;

2. U.S. must prevent the repeat of 9-11 and the spread of terrorism;

3. There is a need for regime change; and

4. Democracy must be restored in Iraq.

These so called "truths" are then syndicated to pro-Bush regime news agencies and they in turn transmit the same to the various print media and television and radio stations. So effective was the propaganda that the majority of the mass media of the Third World just downloaded these "truths" without any verification, even to the extent of adopting the same headlines. The target audience was totally brainwashed; the propaganda war was won even before it started.

All the abovementioned "truths" were employed to serve the pretext for war, which was self-preservation and defense in the face of an imminent threat. Absent this pretext, no war can be waged. Herman Goering explained:

"It is easy. All you have to do is to tell the people they are being attacked, and denounce the peacemakers for lack of patriotism and exposing the country to danger."

Self-defense is the best camouflage for the real and underlying strategic economic objectives of war against another state. Once this is grasped, it is easy to appreciate the slanted headlines and the accompanying stories — to legitimize the war even though it was not sanctioned by the United Nations.

The overall guidelines were laid own in the National Security Strategy (NSS) and the spin doctors essentially worked within those parameters. I quote the relevant passages:

"The war against terrorists of global reach is a global enterprise of uncertain duration. America will act against such

emerging threats before they are fully formed. Rogue states and terrorists do not seek to attack us using conventional means. They know such attacks would fail. Instead they rely on acts of terror and, potentially, the use of weapons of mass destruction....

"The targets of these attacks are our military forces and our civilian population, in direct violation of one of the principal norms of the laws of warfare. As was demonstrated by the losses of September 11, 2001, mass civilian casualties is the specific objective of terrorists and these losses would be exponentially more severe if terrorists acquired and used weapons of mass destruction....

"The United States has long maintained the option of preemptive actions to counter a sufficient threat to our national security. The greater the threat, the greater the risk of inaction — and the more compelling the case for taking anticipatory action to defend ourselves. To forestall or prevent such hostile acts by our adversaries, the United States will, if necessary, act pre-emptively."

The parameters set for war propaganda is exactly as those outlined by Herman Goering. It was the same ruthless justification that led to the wanton carpet bombings of Vietnamese cities of Hanoi and Haiphong and the undeclared war on Cambodia in the 1960s and 1970s. So powerful is this form of propaganda that ordinary Americans who would normally condemn such barbaric actions, would sheepishly submit to such atrocities committed on their behalf. Such propaganda messages work on the simple logic: **either they get killed or you get killed**. All the values you were brought up to value and cherish get thrown out of the window on account of self-preservation and survival.

And if that is not enough, and just in case there are still some who are caught in the morality/conscience straitjacket, the call to serve God and other noble ideals would remove any lingering resistance. And if these messages can be shown in graphic visuals, all the better and as media baron Randolph Hearst counselled, *"You furnish the pictures, I'll furnish the war."* War propaganda is elevated to war entertainment and reality shows, running 24 hours a day, for as long as it takes, directly to your house and offices.

Another propaganda device, a favorite of Ariel Sharon, is attributing to the enemy the crimes they are doing to others (especially the target country of their propaganda). Once your enemy has been labeled a 'war criminal' or any other derogatory label, the propaganda war is as good as over. Professor John McMurthy succinctly observes:

"U.S. state justifications always project onto the designated enemy what the U.S. security state is doing. If it loudly condemns another weaker state's 'weapons of mass destruction', 'chemical or biological weapons', 'violation of international laws', or 'attempts to impose its will by terror', then we can deduce that this is exactly what the U.S. is planning more of, but is diverting attention from by accusing others. Test this principle with every international accusation the U.S. makes next and you will find that it is invariable confirmed.

"So exactly does the U.S. security state projects its own violent policies on to others that one can tell what vicious policy it is about to escalate next by the intensity with which the other is accused of the crime ... and how we can make sense of the official U.S. fixation on 'global terrorism' today."

<u>**Test Run:**</u>

1) Iraq repeatedly violates international law by failing to observe UN resolutions.

Contrast: U.S. launched an illegal invasion of Iraq in violation of international law.

2) Iraq is a terrorist state and supports terrorists.

Contrast: Operation Shock and Awe, the indiscriminate bombing of Baghdad and other cities just before the commencement of the invasion; the atrocities at Abu Ghraib prison and Guantanamo Bay.

3) Iraq has accumulated a massive arsenal of WMD, ready to be launched in 45 minutes.

Contrast: U.S. has the world's largest stockpile of nuclear weapons and is the world's largest producer of anthrax and other biological and chemical weapons.

It is clear from the above analysis, that one of the aims of such propaganda is to demonize the enemy and it is usually narrowed to one target — the leader of the enemy or the inner circle. Thus they will be variously labeled as 'the tyrant', the 'dictator', the 'Pharaoh', 'the Cabal', 'the regime', 'the war criminals', etc. In contrast, the Bush regime is presented as 'guardians for peace and security' and the 'protectors of democracy'. Thus in the NSS, Bush proclaimed with a poker face:

"The great struggles of the 20th century... [has shown] a single sustainable model for success: freedom, democracy and free enterprise.... A time of opportunity for America... the United States will use this moment of opportunity to extend the benefits of freedom across the globe. We will actively work to bring the hope of democracy, development, free markets and free trade to every corner of the world. Today, the United States enjoy a position of unparalleled military strength."

This is but a blueprint for imperial hegemony and worldwide plunder. Good sound bites to hide the real intentions. And in conclusion, Bush assured the world that:

"We will defend the peace by fighting terrorists and tyrants.

"We will preserve the peace by building good relations among great powers.

"We extend the peace by encouraging free and open societies on every continent."

But what do we observe in reality?

The Bush regime invades Iraq in violation of international law and thus far had slaughtered over 100,000 Iraqi civilians and destroyed the economy of Iraq.

The Bush regime declares that it will launch pre-emptive wars and act unilaterally and will ignore the United Nations.

The Bush regime, emboldened by its criminal invasion of Iraq, now threatens Syria and Iran, and is colluding with Israel to subvert and foment internal strife in Lebanon. It has already subverted the majority of the countries in ASEAN by planting agents of influence in the corridors of power of these administrations, and is conspiring to launch a second round of financial devastation in Asia with one or two countries as Trojan horses. Anyone who still refuses to accept the hidden messages of these glorious sound bites should read the confession of Irving Kristol given to Corey Robin in 2000, of his inner longings for imperial plunder:[5]

"What's the point of being the greatest, most powerful nation in the world and not having an imperial role? I think it would be natural for the United States to play a far more important role in world affairs... to command and to give orders as what is to be done. People need that. There are many parts of the world — Africa in particular — where an authority willing to use troops can make a difference...."

In reading any newspaper or propaganda material coming from the Zionist Anglo-American War Cabal, look out for the following words and phrases. They would be inserted and used to create legitimacy and to overcome your doubts and win you over to their side in support of the war.

- Official sources disclosed; reliable information received; intelligence received, etc.

- Majority of analysts have agreed; polls have indicated; for reasons of security which cannot be disclosed, it is confirmed that, etc.

- We have done all we could to resolve the impasse; Diplomacy has failed; All options are on the table, we cannot discount any; we have the smoking gun, etc.

- Communication intercepts have revealed; documents retrieved have indicated, it is likely, sources have confirmed; experts believe, etc.

- We must spare no efforts to defeat our enemies; we must make sacrifices; we must be prepared, etc.

DURING THE MILITARY CAMPAIGN

The propaganda is now directed at the troops to secure support for them. Hence, the inexplicable stance of many British Members of Parliament (MPs) and U.S. Congressman who opposed the war, but nevertheless express support for the troops. There will be specially crafted stories of heroic exploits and events and incidents may even be staged. Special efforts would be made to promote military hardware, to tout the superiority of weapons system as part of the psychological warfare to demoralize the enemy. War films produced before the war would be screened during the conflict, and the main theme would be patriotism. Every effort would be made to shield the public from the true costs of the war, especially in terms of the number of soldiers killed and wounded in action.

Continuing from the campaign to demonize the enemy, the enemy soldiers are portrayed to be especially brutal and not adhering to the Geneva Conventions; resistance to the U.S. is characterized as terrorism and appropriate labels are used such as terrorists, insurgents, militants, subversives; and anything that will demonstrate counteraction to the U.S. military as unlawful, inhuman, and to portray enemy soldiers as unlawful combatants, terrorists, etc. Damage to civilian properties is kept from the media and the extent of civilian deaths is kept ambiguous or not acknowledged. The following words and phrases come to mind:

- Collateral damage; clean war; surgical strikes; precision bombs; etc.
- Deliberate sabotage; brutal and senseless killings by insurgents; terrorists demands; we will not be held to ransom; etc.
- Our soldiers are trained to the highest standards; misconduct of a few soldiers acting out of frustration; we will investigate and bring those found guilty to justice; etc.
- We have no intentions to stay even a day longer than is necessary; our soldiers are doing a fine job; they are restoring democracy; we are doing everything to ensure humanitarian aid gets through; the people are better off now than before; etc.

Commentary throughout the military campaign would centre on the theme: "Good must triumph over Evil." There will be no "shades of grey," as every conceivable picture must be contrasted in terms of black and white, good versus bad. While setbacks are downplayed, success would be exaggerated and highlighted prodigiously. A different reality has to be projected to the home audience. Exhortations to make sacrifices for the greater good intensify and antiwar activists are marginalized to suppress antiwar sentiments when body bags starts arriving in the U.S.

THE AFTERMATH OF THE MILITARY CAMPAIGN

The theme is one of "Good having triumphed over Evil". Whatever sacrifices in human terms is depicted as being worthy. Antiwar activists are portrayed as cowards, unpatriotic, and supporters of the enemy's cause. Freedom and liberation from the oppressive tyrant is drummed into the heads of everyone. Staged euphoria and celebrations, as in the case of the toppling of Saddam's statue, and children giving flowers to the troops serve to silence war critics. The following words and phrases become common:

- Peace has now been restored; mission accomplished; the peace dividend; etc.

- Reconstruction; rebuilding the war-torn economy; the suffering is over; free at last; etc.

- A new era for democracy; the post-Saddam era; a fresh start; the people will have elections; reforms; etc.

To cover up the war crimes, every effort is made to show that the victims are indeed grateful. Such is their perverse logic that the British Minister of Defense was quoted as having said that, ***"one day the mothers of children killed or maimed by British cluster bombs will thank Britain for their use.***[6]***"*** The wanton looting that took place soon after U.S. troops entered Baghdad was described by Donald Rumsfeld as freedom — freedom to commit crimes.

Recently, I came across a brilliant article entitled "Thirteen Techniques for truth Suppression" by David Martin,[7] which ought to be read by everyone. I append below his summary of the techniques highlighted in the article. Study the techniques, and the next time you read the newspaper, check out how many of these techniques have been applied.

1. Dummy up. If it's not reported, if it is not news, it didn't happen.

2. Wax indignant. This is also known as the "how dare you?" gambit.

3. Characterize the charges as "rumors" or better yet, "wild rumors." If in spite of news blackout, the public is still able to learn about the suspicious facts, it can only be through rumors.

4. Knock down straw men. Deal only with the weakest aspect of the weakest charges.

5. Call skeptics names like "conspiracy theorists", "nut", "crackpot", and of course "rumor-monger".

6. Impugn motives. Attempt to marginalize the critics by suggesting strongly that they are not really interested in the truth but are simply pursuing a partisan political agenda or are out to make money.

7. Invoke authority. Here the controlled press and the sham opposition can be very useful.

8. Dismiss the "charges" as old news.

9. Come half-clean. This is known as "confession and avoidance" or "taking the limited hang-out route." This way, you create the impression of candor and honesty while you admit only to relatively harmless, less-than-criminal "mistakes".

10. Characterize the crimes as impossibly complex and the truth as ultimately unknowable.

11. Reason backward, using the deductive method with a vengeance. With thoroughly rigorous deduction, troublesome evidence is irrelevant. For example: we have a completely free press. If they know of evidence that the Bureau of Alcohol, Tobacco and Firearms (BATF) had prior knowledge of the Oklahoma City bombing they would have reported it. They haven't reported it, so there was no prior knowledge by BATF. Another variation on this theme involves the likelihood of a conspiracy leaker and a press that would report it.

12. Require the skeptics to solve the crime completely.

13. Change the subject. This technique includes reporting a distraction.

The most insidious and harrowing techniques of propaganda warfare is the planting of evidence to provoke and justify the launching of wars of aggression. Various stories have cropped up now and again over the last twenty years, but the establishment has been able to palm them off quite successfully as "conspiracy theories", "hoaxes" or "rumors", and by using a combination of the techniques previously mentioned. It was therefore most timely that the Veteran Intelligence Professionals for Sanity (VIPS), a group of intelligence officers, mostly from the analytical branch of the CIA, have come forward to confirm and explain how such operations were carried out. In the article entitled, **"Weapons of Mass Distraction: Where? Find? Plant?"** David MacMichael and Ray McGovern, a CIA analyst for 27 years, gave a chilling account of such operations.[8]

The authors were prompted to expose these operations because of President Bush's refusal to allow weapons inspectors to joint in the hunt for the alleged WMD in Iraq after the invasion. This aroused the suspicions of many in the intelligence services and political analysts that the refusal was to avoid the scandal of not finding any WMD, because there was none in the first place, and that the Bush regime may resort to planting WMD or evidence linking to WMD. A good starting point in this discussion is the observation that:

"Were the Bush administration to decide in favor of a planting or similar operation, it would not have to start from scratch as far as experience is concerned. Moreover, many of the historical examples that follow bear an uncanny resemblance to factors and circumstances in play today. Likely or not in the present circumstances, there is ample precedent for such covert action operations."

The intelligence officers then proceeded to give five specific operations. Faked evidence was the hallmark of post-World War II covert operations in Latin America.

1) In 1954, such an operation was instrumental in overthrowing the Arbenz government in Guatemala. To justify the invasion of Guatemala, the CIA planted a cache of Soviet-made weapons and alleged that the arms were being used by the Arbenz to overthrow the Nicaraguan government.

2) On the eve of the Bay of Pigs operation in 1961, Alabama National Guard B-26 bombers attacked a Cuban Air Force base in Havana. The American government denied having authorized such an operation. Two of the aircrafts deployed were shot down and four guardsmen were killed in the operation. When Cuba attempted to return the bodies to the families, the U.S. government refused to accept the remains until 1978.

231

3) The Gulf of Tonkin Incident was a fabricated incident, in which Vietnam was alleged to have attacked U.S. warships. This was the pretext that President Johnson used to widen the war in Vietnam. More directly relevant to the search for WMD in Iraq was the search for alleged munitions dumps in Cambodia which the U.S. suspected was used to aid the Vietnamese struggle. This was the pretext to bomb the living daylights out of Cambodia. The colonel in charge of logistics for the raid surprised other members of the raiding party by loading large amounts of North Vietnamese uniforms, weapons, communications equipment, etc. He explained to the members that since it would be necessary to discover North Vietnamese supplies to justify the bombings and incursions into neutral Cambodia, it behooved them to be prepared to carry some back.

4) During William Casey's tenure as CIA Director, planting evidence went to new heights in Central America. The object was to demonstrate the opposition to fascist regimes were sponsored by the Soviets. In January 1981, it was alleged that four dugout canoes were "discovered" on a Salvadorian beach which were supposed to have ferried Nicaraguan guerrillas to support rebels in El Salvador. No such boats were found. But this "evidence" enabled Reagan to lift the arms embargo imposed by President Carter after El Salvadorian guards had raped and murdered three nuns. Thereafter a reign of terror prevailed in El Salvador. There was also an attempt to plant evidence to show that Cuba and Nicaragua were involved in the drug trade. But the opposite turned out to be the case. The U.S. instead was caught in its own Iran-Contra scandal.

5) Fabricated evidence was also used to justify the First Gulf War. A heart-rending testimony was staged whereby a sobbing 15-year-old girl called Nayirah testified to a Congressional Committee that Iraqi soldiers were killing babies by taking them out of the incubators and leaving them on the floor to die. The true identity of the young girl was not disclosed until two years later when it was discovered that she was actually the daughter of the Kuwaiti Ambassador in Washington. However, following that testi-

mony, Congress voted to allow the use of force against Iraq on January 12, 1991.

For those who have not been exposed to propaganda warfare, and have a lingering doubt that the above discussion seems too good to be true, I would like, once again to draw your attention to the document entitled **"Israeli Communications Priority 2003**⁹**"** which sets out Israel's strategy for waging its propaganda war so as to bring about a convergence of interests between the United States and Israel. Propaganda warfare is for real, and I quote:

"America is dominated by developments in Iraq. This is a unique opportunity for Israelis to deliver a message of support and unity at a time of great international anxiety. For a year, a solid year, Israel should be invoking the name of Saddam Hussein and how Israel was always behind American efforts to rid the world of this ruthless dictator and liberate their people. Saddam will remain a powerful symbol of terror for Americans for a long time to come. The language of this document will work, but it will work best when it is accompanied with passion and compassion. Too many supporters of Israel speak out in anger or shout when faced with opposition. Listeners are more likely to accept arguments if they like how you express them. They will bless these words but they will truly accept them if, and only if, they accept you."

To counter the Zionist Anglo-American Empire's war propaganda, we need to master propaganda warfare and a good starting point is to study the propaganda successes of the Israelis. We must adopt their thoroughness with which they plan their propaganda campaign. Rapid response will be crucial in such warfare, as every lie and manufactured "truths" must be discredited immediately and a counterattack launched. This is sorely missing in the front line states confronting the Zionist war agenda.

If there is one book that you should read on propaganda, it is Jacques Ellul's *Propaganda: The Formation of Men's Attitude*.¹⁰ Reading it the umpteenth time is as refreshing as I first read it. The introduction by Konrad Kellan sums up well the essence of the book:

"Most people are easy prey for propaganda, because of their firm but entirely erroneous conviction that it is composed only of lies and 'tall stories' and that conversely, what is true

cannot be propaganda. But modern propaganda has long disdained the ridiculous lies of the past and outmoded forms of propaganda. It operates instead with many different kinds of truths — half-truth, limited truth, truth out of context. Even Goebbels always insisted that Wehrmacht communiqués be as accurate as possible."

Be vigilant!

ENDNOTES:

1. Cited in David N. Gibbs, "Washington's New Interventionism: US Hegemony and Inter-Imperialist Rivalries.", Monthly Review, September 2001.

2. Martin van Creveld, "Sharon's Plan is to drive Palestinians across Jordan", Daily Telegraph, April 28, 2002

3. Eric Margolis, "Bush's Mideast Plan: Conquer and Divide", Toronto Sun, December 8, 2002.

4. BBC News, February 20, 2002.

5. Corey Robin, "Grand Designs: How 9-11 Unified Conservatives in Pursuit of Empire", Washington Post, May 2, 2004.

6. The Independent, April 5, 2003.

7. Source: http://home.earthlink.net

8. David MacMichael and Ray McGovern, "Weapons of Mass Distraction: Where? Find? Plant?" April 26, 2003 @ www.guerillanews.com/intelligence/doc1785.html

9. Refer to chapter 8 for the entire document.

10. Jacques Ellul, *Propaganda: The Formation of Men's Attitude*, (1973, Vintage Books)

Part 4

Agenda Fast-Forward

"What is inconceivable in normal times is possible in revolutionary times; and if at this time the opportunity is missed and what is possible in such great hours is not carried out — a whole world is lost."

— David Ben-Gurion

14

The Road to Jerusalem Leads through Baghdad

As a political analyst for thirty years, of which fifteen have been devoted to the study of Zionists' world strategy, I had on many occasions relied on my intuition to pursue a line of investigation. Other times, a mere statement from a key player would set me on a relentless hunt and I am seldom disappointed with the outcomes of these investigations.

In 2002, two statements made six months apart kept me thinking for days on end, and which led me to look for other evidence that the Zionists' global strategy which had remained more or less consistent in the last 45 years was to be abandoned in a dramatic way.

The first statement was made in April 1, 2002, by Condoleezza Rice in an interview with Norman Lemann in the New Yorker magazine. It was reported as follows:

"'I think September 11 was one of those great earthquakes that clarify and sharpen. Events are in much sharper relief.' Like Bush, she said that opposing terrorism and preventing the accumulation of weapons of mass destruction 'in the hands of irresponsible states' now define the national interest. Rice said that she had called together the senior staff people of the National Security Council and asked them to think seriously about 'how do you capitalize on these opportunities' to fundamentally change American doctrine, and shape the world, in the wake of September 11." (Emphasis added)

For six months, I couldn't figure out what was going to happen. The second piece of information that caught my attention was the article by William Kristol and Robert Kagan on October 29, 2002 in the Weekly Standard.

"When all is said and done, the conflict in Afghanistan will be to the War on Terrorism what the North Africa campaign was to World War II: <u>an essential beginning on the path to victory</u>. But compared to what looms over the horizon — a wide-ranging war in locales from Central Asia to the Middle East and, unfortunately, back again to the United States — <u>Afghanistan will prove but an opening battle</u> .... But this war will not end in Afghanistan. It is going to spread and engulf a number of countries in conflicts of varying intensity. It could well require the use of American military power in multiple places simultaneously. It is going to resemble the clash of civilizations that everyone has hoped to avoid." (Emphasis added)

I stared at this paragraph for about an hour, stunned and numbed, but at the same time, the whole picture came before me crystal clear. Yes indeed, Afghanistan would be the opening battle. But more importantly, after Afghanistan, the Zionist Anglo-American Empire would **fast-forward their agenda to establish a New Jerusalem, and the "Third Temple." And to achieve this objective within the new time frame, the previous modus operandi would have to be abandoned; the UN would have to be abandoned.**

In Chapter 12, I detailed how the Zionists hijacked the U.S. military, but I deliberately left out why they switched their global military strategy until now. Since 1948, the founding of the Zionist fascist State of Israel, the Zionists have always sought international legitimacy and the United Nations, in particular the Security Council, was the external protector of Israel, albeit with the connivance of the United States. Any resolution critical of Israel was vetoed by the U.S. It was obvious that the Zionists' global ambitions were to be achieved via the United Nations and the Security Council sanctioned military aggressions against her enemies. It was not a secret, as it was openly admitted as such. I had already made several references in the preceding chapters. In fact the strategy of relying on an international organization was adopted much earlier. Let us recap.

"The League of Nations is a Jewish conception."

— **Israel Zangwill**[1]

"The League of Nations is a Jewish idea. We created it after a fight of twenty five years."   — **Nahum Sokolow**[2]

"The United Nations ideal is a Jewish Ideal."
— **David Ben-Gurion**[3]

"We shall have World Government, whether or not we like it. The only question is whether World Government will be achieved by conquest or consent."   — **James P. Warburg**[4]

"Today, America would be outraged if UN troops entered Los Angeles to restore order [referring to the 1991 LA Riot]. Tomorrow they will be grateful. This is especially true if they were told that there were an outside threat from beyond, whether real or promulgated that threatened our very existence. It is then that all peoples of the world will plead to deliver them from evil. The one thing every man fears is the unknown. When presented with this scenario, individual rights will be willingly relinquished for the guarantee of their well-being granted to them by the World Government."   — **Dr. Henry Kissinger**[5]

After the war in Afghanistan, the Zionists were convinced that their cherished dream of world domination through the one world government of the United Nations would in fact delay or retard their agenda. It was too cumbersome. The Zionists could dispense with the façade of the United Nations for legitimacy because they realized that they have absolute control of the U.S. financial and military muscle, but had not taken advantage of it.

This realization came much earlier, but there was no opportunity to exploit this dominance. This was reflected in the manner in which Madeleine Albright chided Colin Powell:

"What's the point of having this superb military you've always been talking about if we can't use it."

It is apparent that the Zionists were prepared to bypass the façade of the United Nations and act unilaterally on the strength of U.S. military soon after the War Council in October, 2002, as was disclosed obliquely by William Kristol and Robert Kagan in their article in the Weekly Standard in the same month. The reference to the Afghan war and the hint, *"it could well require the use of American military power in multiple places simultaneously"* was the clincher!

The debate within the Security Council regarding the implications of resolution 1441 was essentially an open quarrel between two factions of the International Zionist Movement. It was the final debate and test of will. The European Zionists organized around the Bilderberg group did not share the confidence of the Anglo-American Zionists that the agenda could be fast-forwarded or that the objectives could be achieved solely on the strength of United States' military power, notwithstanding that it was the world's only superpower. The European experience of two world wars warranted a more cautious approach. The factor that tipped the scale was Israel. Being the front line state her view was pivotal and she expressed full confidence in the necessity to fast-forward the agenda, as these were not normal times, but revolutionary times and the opportunity presented should be exploited. Sharon had no wish to repeat the mistake of Ben-Gurion in 1948 in not pressing the advantage. 9-11, the New Pearl Harbor, must be exploited to launch the next world war and the establishment of New Jerusalem.

Recall that the original time line was twice delayed: the State of Israel was supposed to have been established in 1917/1918 but was delayed till 1948. In 1952, Rabbi Rabinovich proclaimed that the Zionist's three-thousand-year goal was within reach, and expressed the confidence that it could be achieved via World War III.

"Within five years, this program will achieve its objective, the Third World War, which will surpass in destruction all previous contests. We shall embark upon an era of ten thousand years of peace and plenty, the Pax Judaica, and our race will rule undisputed over the world."

But it was not to be, as the Cold War did not translate into a "Hot War" and the horrendous devastation that was hoped for by the Rabbi. In a sense that delay was a blessing in disguise as the collapse of the Soviet Union had reduced the costs for embarking this Zionist adventure. Having achieved total dominance, the Zionist Anglo-American faction saw no credible resistance from China, the only potential power that would be able to mount a challenge, but that would be years away, at the minimum two decades, in the future.

From the Zionist Anglo-American perspective, pre-emption and unilateral action make sense and would be cost-effective, i.e., World War IV[6] without the massive costs of World War II or the Cold War in real terms. It was, according to their war planners, world domination

on the cheap. To them, the Arab-Muslim world was mere tribal nui-
sance, easily blackmailed by nuclear threats and destabilized through
a combination of corruption of the ruling cliques and subversion via
special operations. Intelligence indicated that the Arab world could be
easily divided along sectarian lines and religious bigotry, exploiting
existing Sunni/Shiite mistrust. The first phase of subjugating the Arabs
would be a walk in the park. It was just too tempting to bypass imperial hegemony at Wal-Mart prices! Recall that the initial estimate for
the Iraq adventure was about $50 billion and the conventional wisdom
was that the marines would be showered with flowers, and welcomed
as liberators.

Any lingering doubts about the dramatic change in the global
strategy were dispelled when I read the "Israeli Communications
Priorities 2003", prepared by the Luntz Research Companies & the
Israel Project for the Wexner Foundation. There were other pointers —
PNAC's "Rebuilding America's Defense" and the National Security
Strategy (NSS) which I had already mentioned earlier, but this was
special. It was *the Manual* to win the coming wars at the propaganda
level. And propaganda wars always preceded the military campaigns,
thus, its significance. Judge for yourself the following statements:

*"In the past, we have urged a lower profile for Israel out of
fear that the American people would blame Israel for what was
happening in the rest of the Middle East. Now is the time to link
America's success in dealing with terrorism and dictators from
a position of strength to Israel's ongoing efforts to eradicate terrorism on and within its borders. In the current political environment, you have little to lose and a lot to gain by aligning with
America.*

*"The fact that Israel has remained relatively silent for the
three months preceding the war and for three weeks of the war
was absolutely correct strategy — and according to all the
polling done, it worked. But as the military conflict comes to a
close, it is now time for Israel to lay out its own 'road map' for the
future which includes unqualified support for America and
unqualified commitment to an ongoing war against terrorism.*

*"There are some who would say that Saddam Hussein is
already old news. They don't understand history. They don't
understand communication. They don't understand how to integrate and leverage history and communication for the benefit of*

241

Israel. The day we allow Saddam to take his eventual place in the trash heap of history is <u>the day we loose our strongest weapon in the linguistic defense of Israel</u>." (Emphasis added)

A sense of urgency never displayed before, as well as a time line, is detectable in the strategy. The planners were very emphatic when they said, *"For a year — a Solid Year — you should be invoking the name of Saddam Hussein and how Israel was always behind American efforts to rid the world of this ruthless dictator and liberate their people."*

Previously, Rabbi Rabinovich had a five-year plan to provoke a World War but that was delayed. It took too long and fizzled out. Israelis are not prone to repeat a mistake. It then occurred to me why Bush was set up to win the 2000 elections, and as stated in the Introduction, the Zionists and their partners, the Neocons needed a bastard to do the dirty work and to fast-forward the agenda. The Democrats had delayed the agenda by a decade and the *Spear of Conquest got rusty,* and the soldiers got fat in the belly. The evidence was right before my eyes but I missed it completely.

After the 1997 financial crisis, I concentrated on the economic time bombs that would be put in place for the second round of devastation. Malaysia survived the first round, but barely. I was blindsided by the various controversial issues of globalization. Clinton did declare, "Its economics, Stupid!" 30 years of believing that imperialism will never change, that imperial mobilization can only be sustained by a war economy, somehow got fuzzy, distracted by the aftermath of the 1997 financial crisis. China and Malaysia survived the crisis. Surely, when the financial WMD failed to wreak the expected devastation, they would revert to the time-tested wars of aggression. I missed it by a long mile.

Let's examine the evidence — did the Spear get rusty and were the soldiers getting fat in the belly? And more importantly, who were complaining about the state of affairs? To be honest, given the unprecedented economic advances under the Clinton administration and the exuberance that was generated, one was hard-pressed to find dissidents. But they were there and they did make it known that getting fat was not a good idea for an imperial power. Clinton's global economic program caused many to believe that globalization and imperialist's concept of free trade would supplant the need for gun boats. The chiding by Madeleine Albright of Colin Powell for not using the U.S. military power was to some extent indicative of the Zionist's irritation within Clinton's inner circle. In essence, the dissidents took the view that economic prosperity and peace, ironically has its downside. The world was still a dangerous place and America needed to wave the flag and send in the marines to remind potential challengers not to cross the red line.

The Indicators

1) **William Kristol:** He asserted that the failure of the Bush I administration to finish the job in 1991 had resulted in a "lack of awe for the U.S" in the Middle East, an absence of respect that fostered contempt of the U.S. among Arabs and encouraged the rise of the Al Qaeda terrorist organization. The 2nd Iraq War would address those mistakes. The fall of Mr. Hussein would be an "inspiration" for Iranians to be free of their dictatorial mullahs.[7] He looked back in disgust at the previous decade as a squandered opportunity. Americans and their political leaders have spent the years since 1991 lavishing gifts of an "illusory peace dividend" upon themselves and frittering away the opportunity to strengthen and extend an international order uniquely favorable to the United States. What was needed today is not better management of the status quo, but a fundamental change in the way our leaders and the public think about America's role in the world. The U.S. should conceive itself as at once a European power, an Asian power, a Middle Eastern power and, of course a Western Hemispheric power.[8]

2) **Charles Krauthammer:** The goal of American foreign policy should have been to turn the "unipolar moment" into a unipolar era.[9]

3) **Paul Wolfowitz:** He lamented that prior to the election of George Bush, we were living in ambiguity. Even though more than a decade has passed since the Berlin Wall came down, we shall have no better name for the world in which we live than the "post-Cold War era." Although many have aspired to play the role of the next George Kennan by defining American strategy for this new era that does not yet have a name, no one so far succeeded. But one thing seems clear: we can't succeed at the task of defining a new strategy if we ignore the historical record of the basis on which the old strategy was developed and defended, how it was implemented over a long period of time despite various obstacles and criticisms. And why it was eventually victorious. In 1992, a draft memo … suggested that a "dominant

consideration" in U.S. defense strategy should be "to prevent any hostile power from dominating a region whose resources would, under consolidated control, be sufficient to generate global power.[10]"

4) **Norman Podhoretz:** He vented his frustration that the broad coalition assembled by the United States, together with the imprimatur we had sought and acquired from the United Nations, resulted not in the consummation of a decisive victory but in an act of military and political coitus interruptus. Having driven Saddam Hussein out of Kuwait — which was all we had a "mandate" to do from our allies and the UN — we did not then push on to drive him out of Baghdad. Nor, in the event, did we even render him incapable of building the weapons of mass destruction he now possesses.[11]

5) **Former CIA Director James Woolsey:** He really spoke his mind and was blunt —The United States was engaged in World War IV and this could continue for years. He pointed out that the new war would be against three enemies: the religious rulers of Iran, the 'fascists' of Iraq and Syria and Islamic extremists like Al Qaeda. They have waged wars against the U.S. for several years and it was time to take stock of the situation. He sounded a warning: *"We want you nervous. We want you to realize now, for the fourth time in a hundred years, this country and its allies are on the march and that we are on the side of those whom you — the Mubaraks, the Saudi Royal family — most fear: we're on the side of your own people.[12]"*

Max Boot sums up the concerns of the war cabal very well when he wrote:

"A short pause to rest, to regroup, and recharge is fine, even necessary. But turning away from the world's dangers for long would be a mistake, possibly a fatal one. The war against Islamist terrorism and proliferation of weapons of mass destruction is not over.... World War II was not finished after El Alamein and Midway, or even after D-Day and Iwo Jima. Much remained to be done before the monstrous evils of Fascism and Nazism were defeated. So it is today. In a world where North Korea may already have nuclear weapons, and Iran less than two years away from having them; in a world where Al Qaeda continues to plot, and states like Syria continue to support transnational terrorist groups; in a world where U.S. security depends on

alliances with shaky dictatorships like Pakistan, Egypt, and even Saudi Arabia — in such a world, much remains to be done before America can feel safe.

"If we revert to our pre-9-11 passivity, if we return to the 1990s' policy of pretending globalization will solve all problems, if we place our faith once again in accommodation and 'stability', then we may awake before long to a disaster worse than 9-11.

"The first priority lies in Iraq. We must not repeat the mistake of the First Gulf War, when we confused battlefield victory with long term political success.... Unfortunately this viewpoint is not popular within the State Department, the CIA, or even among many at the Pentagon — the very people who have to implement the policy on the ground. To avoid the taint of being imperial occupiers, better that we should hand off power... to the United Nations or some other organization.

"That is a temptation to be resisted. The U.N.'s record in running Kosovo, Bosnia, Cambodia, and other international protectorates inspires little confidence." [13]

World War IV has started and it is for real. Make no mistake about it. Every antiwar activist should make it a point to read Norman Podhoretz's:[14]

1) "How to Win World War IV"
2) "World War IV: How It Started, What It Means, and Why We have to Win"
3) "The War Against World War IV"

To fulfill the Zionist dream of a New Jerusalem and the building of the Third Temple, the Zionist Anglo-American War Cabal needs a world war. And if one of the leading Zionist ideologue tells us that World War IV has started and why they should win, we do not have the luxury to indulge in frivolous debates and intellectual masturbation whether the Bush regime will go beyond Iraq. Wake up folks, the U.S. has already spent some $400 billion on its war efforts. This sounds a lot of money but to the war planners it is still under 3.5 percent of the GDP, which is less than the cost of the entire Cold War. And they want more, much more and they will get it to ensure victory.

Read and digest what Max Boot has to say on this.

"Even after 9-11, some Americans might shrink from this task. But Afghanistan and Iraq have shown that the mission is achievable. <u>Iraq should not be seen as an aberration, but rather as another important step in a longer campaign to make the world safe for democracy.</u> Sophisticates may laugh at Woodrow Wilson's objective, but it was the right one; the problem was that he was unable to mobilize the American society to achieve it. Franklin Delano Roosevelt, Harry Truman, Ronald Reagan, and George W. Bush have been more successful in pursuing this noble vision. We have already vanquished Nazism and Communism; <u>only one of the twentieth century's evil ideologies — Fascism, this time in its Islamic variant — remains to be defeated for liberalism to breathe easier. Victory is almost in sight.</u> We ought not to return to passivity now.[15]*"* (Emphasis added)

We may be forgiven by our children for not being able to see the dramatic change in the Zionist Global strategy prior to 9-11, but we will not be forgiven for shirking our duties and responsibilities to defeat the Zionist War Cabal, now that they have openly declared their intentions, have acted on them and are ensuring its victory. Victory for the Zionists according to Rabbi Rabinovich means:

"This war will end for all times our struggle against the Gentiles. We shall embark upon an era of ten thousand years of peace and plenty, the Pax Judaica, and our race will rule undisputed over the world. Our superior intelligence will easily enable us to retain mastery over a world of dark peoples."

This is the Zionist variant of Fascism and Nazism!

Are we too late to mount a world wide Resistance by way of a "People's War"? There may yet be hope left for the Resistance. But we must first examine and analyze how the Zionists started World War IV and their strategies for winning the war.

The war in Iraq was pivotal in their overall war strategy, as it was widely held that there can be no victory, if it ends with Saddam Hussein in power — **the Road to Jerusalem leads through Baghdad**. Eliot A. Cohen a leading military strategist warned as much when he counselled that should the U.S. fail to take the challenges, sooner or later, it is sure to find Iraq's terror on its doorstep. He further explained that the Cold War was World War III and reminded us that not all global conflicts entail the movement of multimillion soldiers or conventional front lines on a map. World War IV will have similar features with the Cold War: it will be global; it will involve a mixture of violent and non-violent efforts; that it will require mobilization of skill, expertise and resources, if not of vast numbers of soldiers; that it may go on for a long time, and that it has ideological roots.[16]

Eliot Cohen did not mince his words, and unlike others, did not skirt the issue by couching it in terms of "terrorism". To him the real enemy in World War IV is "Militant Islam". We must now get to the meat of the matter — the Zionists' perception of Islam. According to Norman Podhoretz:

"Militant Islam today represents a revival of the expansionism by the sword that carried the new religion from its birthplace in Arabia in the 7th century C.E. through North Africa, the Balkans, Spain, and as far West as the gates of Vienna in the 1680s. In the East, it swept through, among other countries, India, Iran, Afghanistan, and Indonesia, and also penetrated southward into the African lands that became Nigeria and Sudan.

"Never in those places did Islam undergo anything resembling the various forms of modernization and reform that took place within Christianity and Judaism. The lone exception was Turkey after World War I, under the secularist Kemal Atatürk. But the expectation that Turkey would set a model for the future was not fulfilled. It is true that there are rival traditions — Sunni, Shi'a, Wahabbi — in the many other predominantly Muslim states, but all these sects are equally orthodox.

"Certainly not all Muslims are terrorists. Like any other collection of human beings, they can as individuals be good or evil, kind or cruel, intelligent or stupid, sweet or sour. But it would be dishonest to ignore the plain truth that Islam has become an especially fertile breeding-ground of terrorism in our time. This can only mean that there is something in the religion itself that legitimizes the likes of Osama Bin Laden, and indeed there is: the obligation imposed by the Koran to wage Holy War, or Jihad, against the 'infidels'.[17]"

Norman Podhoretz asked a question: "What hope is there for winning the war we are fighting against Militant Islam and the terrorism it uses as its main weapon against us?" His answer was to introduce long delayed reforms and modernization of Islam, as it will enable its adherents to have greater freedom and prosperity and to make peace with the existence of Israel. Additionally, the boundaries of the Arab world ought to be realigned or reconfigured. The rationale being:

"Big wars, to say it again, usually end with the world being reshaped in forms unanticipated when they begin... the Middle East we know today was not created by a mandate from heaven, and the miserable despotisms there did not evolve through some unstoppable natural or historical process. As it happened most of the states in question were conjured into existence less than a hundred years ago out of the ruins of the defeated Ottoman Empire in World War I. Their boundaries were drawn by the victorious British and French with the stroke of an often arbitrary pen, and their hapless peoples were handed over in due course to one tyrant after another. There is thus no warrant to assume that these states will last forever in their present forms, or that the only alternatives to them are necessarily worse.[18]*"*

Podhoretz made it plain that the true purport of the Bush Doctrine pointed just as clearly to World War IV as the Truman Doctrine had to World War III and although Bush did not explicitly give the name World War IV to the coming wars, it left no doubt that the future struggles were a continuation of the previous two world wars. Regarding the Middle East, we should re-read that speech of President Bush on September 20, 2001, and its subsequent reaffirmation on June 2, 2004, at the commencement address at the Air Force Academy.

"For decades, free nations tolerated oppression in the Middle East for the sake of stability. In practice, this approach brought little stability and much oppression, so I have changed this policy. Some who call themselves realists question whether the spread of democracy in the Middle East should be any concern of ours. But the realists in this case have lost contact with a fundamental reality: America has always been less secure when freedom is in retreat; America is always more secured when freedom is on the march."

Once we remove the rhetoric about "freedom", "democracy", etc., what you get is a blunt blueprint for imperial mobilization and plunder. When a bully sits around doing nothing, getting fat and sloppy for close to ten years, the fear is that smaller bullies may get funny ideas. A big bully must never let up the pressure, it must continue to dominate and beat up the next potential bully.

This is how Norman Podhoretz puts it in intellectual jargon:

"The first Pillar of the Bush Doctrine, then, was built on a _repudiation_ *of moral relativism and an entirely unapologetic assertion of the need for and the possibility of moral judgement in the realm of world affairs.*[19]*"* (Emphasis added)

Bush feared that his Middle East turf could be repossessed by the "small bullies" Iran and Syria, two members of his "Axis of Evil". Bush's world view is not unlike that of the triads or mafias. In the straightforward "turf language", he is the boss and no one pisses on his turf. The language may be undiplomatic or impolite but I can assure you that Bush and his intellectuals in the war cabal understand fully what I am getting at. I have studied Bush Jr., for a long time. This is what he said about straight-talking. Judge for yourself:

"Some worry it is somehow undiplomatic or impolite to speak the language of right or wrong. I disagree...."

The second Pillar of the Doctrine was couched in the following terms, which also provides the modus operandi in handling the Muslim Arabs:

"The 'swamps' in which this murderous plague [i.e. terrorism] bred were swamps not of poverty and hunger but of political oppression. It was only by 'draining' them, through a strategy of 'regime change,' that we would be making ourselves safe from the threat of terrorism and simultaneously giving the peoples of the 'entire Islamic world' the freedoms 'they want and deserve'.[20]*"*

The first front of World War IV was the war in Afghanistan and this was justified as a retaliatory strike against the terrorists who attacked the U.S. on September 11. Like sharks, the smell of blood was irresistible. When B-52s and 15,000 lbs "Daisy Cutter" bombs were unleashed, the war cabal celebrated the banishment of the ghost of Vietnam. And when the bombs exploded just above the ground, wiping out everything for hundreds of yards, it was sweet satisfaction to the sadistic Zionists that a terrifying psychological impact would overwhelm the Arab street. There were also the smart bombs!

The third Pillar of the doctrine was elaborated in stark terms by President Bush in his State of the Union speech in January, 2002. Having tasted blood, and fresh from the adventure in Afghanistan, the war cabal wanted nothing less than going for the kill. President Bush said:

"We'll be deliberate, yet time is not on our side. I will not wait on events, while dangers gather. I will not stand by, as peril draws closer and closer. The United States of America will not permit the world's most dangerous regimes to threaten us with the world's most destructive weapons."

Pre-emptive wars would be unleashed. The sheriff and his posse will ride out in search of the outlaws. The U.S. Calvary was called out in support of the Sheriff, when in the speech at the West Point on June 2, 2002, Bush made the bugle call that, *"we must take the battle to the enemy, disrupt his plans, and confront the worst threats before they emerge. In the world we have entered, the only path to safety is the path of action. And this nation will act."* Brent Scowcroft in a vain attempt to deter Bush opined that war against Iraq would be seen by the Arab street as America turning its backs on the Palestinian-Israeli conflict and ignoring a key interest of the Muslim world. The Zionists were furious as they considered such rhetoric as an euphemism for putting pressure on Israel to resolve the Palestinian conflict. Scowcroft was accused of insinuating that Sharon was a greater threat to the U.S. than Saddam Hussein and that he had provided a respectable rationale for the hostility towards Israel.

It comes as no surprise therefore that the fourth Pillar relates to the Palestine–Israel conflict. To remove the sting, Bush postulated the possibility of a Palestinian state when he said, *"The United States will not support the establishment of a Palestinian state until its leaders engage in a sustained fight against terrorists and dismantle their infrastructure."* But it did not wash with the Arab world, when everyday men, women and children were being hunted down and massacred. The putrid smell of decomposing bodies buried under rubbles and homes levelled to the ground by Zionist war criminals using American made bulldozers tells a different story. But for the Bushies, the fairy tale must continue to spin lest Sharon gets nasty and upsets the apple cart.

Come March 2005, it will be two years since the invasion of Iraq. Are the Zionists as hell-bent as before in moving the agenda forward? I believe so and they may in fact be more in a hurry than before, as any delay would complicate matters. The events unfolding in Iran and Lebanon are the surest indicators that the time line has not changed. Fast-forwarding the agenda is on schedule. The antiwar resistance movement must accept the fact that Bush did get the endorsement for his fascist doctrine. The sooner this is accepted, the sooner the realization will sink in that much more work is needed to turn the tide. Absent this reality check, the resistance will fail, as the entire counter-strategy would be based on the wrong premise. Even if I am wrong in this assessment, it is more prudent to plan on the basis of the worst scenario than indulge in excessive optimism. Get it right — Kerry and Bush, as I have indicated earlier in this book, serves the Zionist War Cabal. Kerry was dumped because he could not be trusted to do the dirty work and complete the job. In any event, the United States is not the issue. The telescopic sight has, in the last forty-five years, been pointed at the wrong target.

America is not the target. Period! We must not make war with America.

Shift the telescopic sight to the right target and everything falls into place and the right strategy will evolve to ensure victory over the Zionist Anglo-American Empire headquartered in London and Tel Aviv, — the twin pillars[21] of the Zionist Imperial Edifice — not Washington or New York.

September 11 is the greatest gift to the Zionist Anglo-American War Cabal and has set back, at least for ten years, the resistance to the Zionist global agenda. Absent September 11, there would be no New Pearl Harbor and there would be no pretext to launch World War IV. The Zionists would not have dared to fast-forward their agenda. For fifty glorious years, the heroic Palestinian people took the fight to the Zionists, curtailing and containing the Zionist War Cabal's appetite for naked aggression and imperial wars. While the more reckless Zionists were willing to provoke and turn the Cold War to a "Hot War" during the first three decades after World War II, the cooler heads of the opportunist faction of the cabal counselled restrain. This was because, in the ensuing conflagration, there was no guarantee that they could wipe out the Palestinians, at least not until they could subvert the U.S. and hijack its military to do its bidding. The experiment in

251

Korea and Vietnam showed that the military could be hijacked, but to use the *Spear of Conquest* for total war, it would have to wait for a New Pearl Harbor.

ENDNOTES:

1. Quoted in the Jewish Guardian, June 11, 1920
2. Speech at the Carlsbad Zionist Congress, August 27, 1922. Quoted in E.N. Santuary's *Are these things so?* p. 213
3. Time, August 16, 1948
4. Speech before the U.S. Senate, February 17, 1950
5. Speech at the Bilderbeger Conference, Evian, France 1991
6. Some political pundits, such as Norman Podhoretz, consider the Cold War as the Third World War.
7. Source: www.politicalstrategy.org/archives
8. Source: *Present Dangers: Crisis and Opportunity in American Foreign and Defense Policy*, ed. Robert Kagan and William Kristol, (2000, Encounter Books)
9. Cited by Robert Kagan and William Kristol in the Introduction to *Present Dangers*.
10. Source: *Present Dangers*, ed. Robert Kagan and William Kristol
11. The Commentary Magazine, February, 2002
12. Source: www.politicalstrategy.org/archives
13. Max Boot, "What Next? The Foreign Policy Agenda beyond Iraq", The Weekly Standard, May 5, 2003.
14. Visit www.commentarymagazine.com to subscribe and download.
15. Max Boot, "What Next? The Foreign Policy Agenda Beyond Iraq", Weekly Standard, May 5, 2003
16. Norman Podhoretz, "World War IV: How It Started, What It Means, and Why We Have to Win" Commentary Magazine, September 2004
17. Ibid.
18. Ibid.
19. Ibid.
20. Ibid.
21. The Temple of Solomon at Jerusalem had two pillars at the entrance which were named Boaz and Jachin.

15

A New Map for the 21st Century
Part I — Understanding Ideological
Strategies

That there will be a new world map for the 21st century is a foregone conclusion. What remains to be seen is where and how the borders are realigned. Too far fetched? Look at the world map now and compare it to the one before the collapse of the Soviet Union and the case which I am putting before you is all too obvious. The realignment of the borders would not be confined to the Middle East, though that would be the starting point. This would be followed, not necessarily in any sequence, by the realignment in Asia, Africa and Latin America, the hot spots being Western and Southern Africa, Columbia and Venezuela, Southeast Asia, Northeast Asia and a second round of break-up in the Asian Central Republics.

The Middle East was carved out after the First World War; Eastern Europe and parts of Asia were divided following World War II; and the Soviet Empire was dissected after the end of the Cold War (or World War III). So why shouldn't there be a major carve-up after World War IV?

The principal area of contention is only whether the realignment favors the Zionist Anglo-American War Cabal or the Worldwide People's Resistance. Like Bush, I too believe in the triumph of Good over Evil, but where we differ is our choice of what is "Good" and what is "Evil." Like Bush, the choice is equally clear: **either you are with us or against us**, and if you are aligned with the Zionist Anglo-American War Cabal which intends to unleash state terrorism and nuclear wars against innocent men, women and children, regardless of race, creed or culture, let it be said here and now, that we will stay the course, we will not flinch, we will be resolute until total victory — until the blood of the Palestinian martyrs have been avenged and repaid. Never in its history has the world owed so much to a nation for its survival and freedom from slavery — from Zionist slavery. History will one day hand down its judgement — soon, I hope — that it was the national sacrifice of the entire Palestinian people that defeated Zionism.

On that day, a New Jerusalem would be established, but not in the image of the Zionist Anglo-American Empire; freedom bells will ring across the entire globe in celebration of a new coming — the true brotherhood of humanity, grounded on love and compassion and homage to the One True Living God. To the East we shall turn our gaze and, with elevated hands, give thanks to the Almighty for the bounty which we shall receive.

But before we can touch the Holy Ground, we must survive and win World War IV. And like Norman Podhoretz, we must teach our children and our children's children why World War IV started, how it started, what it means, and why we have to win. If they are prepared to go the distance and wage a long war, we too must be prepared for a long-drawn-out resistance until total victory.

We must now look at the world map and see for ourselves where the Zionist Anglo-American War Cabal has placed their front lines. The First Front at Afghanistan has already been established for the Central Asian theatre; the Second Front in Iraq as a stepping stone for the Middle East theatre is likewise established. They have had a head start, two swift initial battleground victories. But we must not make the mistake in construing that these temporary setbacks amount to a lost war. In spite of overwhelming firepower, the resistance have held their lines and the beginnings of a People's War have emerged.

The people's resistance in the other theatres of war must make preparations now before the Zionist War Cabal opens new fronts before we are ready. We must now identify where these fronts are to be located. Our tasks have been made easier because of their arrogance. The Zionists, having hijacked the U.S. military, their **Spear of Conquest**, are so arrogant as to display their entire war plans. Recall the earlier contempt by Oded Yinon for the Arabs in disclosing his agenda for the Middle East. He declared that the Arabs were too tribal and stupid to mount an effective resistance. There is always a first time for everything — they have repeated their earlier mistake.

First the smug disclosure by Norman Podhoretz, in the 3 articles referred to in chapter 14, and secondly by Thomas P.M. Barnett in his book, ***The Pentagon's New Map: War and Peace in the 21st Century***.[1] Treat the three articles by Norman Podhoretz referred to above and this book as your "War Bible." Study it and devise the relevant strategies for your respective front lines and then, when opportunity presents itself, unleash your "People's War".

Thirdly, they have willingly exposed their deepest assets within the U.S. administration, which have been subverting the American Republic for Zionist interests. Stanley Fisher, the former Chief Economist of the World Bank and First Deputy Managing Director of the IMF and currently Vice-Chairman of Citigroup, has now been appointed as the Governor of the Bank of Israel (to look after and revamp the depleting Zionist War Chest). Can you imagine, he has to give up his U.S. citizenship and take up Israeli citizenship? His acceptance was not a charitable gesture; he was commanded by the Zionist leadership. These are indeed desperate financial times. This closet Zionist was revealed to have written more articles in Hebrew for the *Riv'on Hayisraeli Lekalkala* (Israel Economic Quarterly) than all the other 14 Israeli candidates combined. A statement issued by the Israel Prime Minister's Office said:

"Stanley Fisher is an American Jew, and a Hebrew speaker. He has long standing connections with the state and the economy of Israel. Among other things, he was involved, as a member of the U.S. administration, with the stabilization plans of the Israel economy in the mid-1980s. He studied at the Hebrew University, Jerusalem. He advised the Israeli government in formulating its economic reform program in 1985, when hyperinflation was raging and which helped tame inflation from hundreds of percentages a year to 10–20 percent.[2]"

He is also a member of the Bilderberg group and the Council on Foreign Relations (CFR). Do not forget that there is also a war on the economic and financial front, but more of that later. This appointment tells us a lot of their plans for financial warfare.

This man has been described by Hanah Kim in Ha'aretz, January 11, thus:

"Fisher is slated to be the policeman who will prevent political changes — if such do take place in Israel — from affecting the economic policy that Netanyahu is orchestrating. He is, in fact, something of a mercenary, even if he really is a 'warm Jew' as he has been described over the past few days. A mercenary is employed when the internal elements are no longer sure of their strength."

And according to Professor Danny Gutwein of Haifa University, Fisher's role will be the "High Commissioner" of globalization to Israel — sort of a globalized equivalent to Great Britain's high commissioner in pre-1948 Palestine.[3] Fondly recalling his education in Britain, at the London School of Economics, Fisher said, *"For us, England was the centre of the Universe."*

Be prepared for betrayal by the corrupt and greedy leaders from the front line states in the Middle East and within ASEAN. Israeli intelligence officers based in Australia have already mounted operations against countries they consider hostile to their interests. The guy in control of those operations was Amir Lati, masquerading as a diplomat. He is a nasty bit of shit! They come in all forms, from travel agents "scouting locations for package tours" to "business consultants" and they do target women in sensitive places. They often pass off as Arabs or Muslim traders. You are forewarned!

Another asset that has been taken out of the closet is Ambassador Dennis Ross, the supposed neutral and objective peacemaker between the Palestinian Authority and the Israeli regime. He has been appointed the first Chairman of a new Jerusalem-based think tank, the Institute for Jewish People Policy Planning, funded and founded by the Jewish Agency. He is also currently Director and Ziegler distinguished fellow of the Washington Institute for Near East Policy. Is it any wonder that President Arafat was always short-changed and left to hang out on a limb? The Israelis knew every nuance of the Palestinian Authority's proposals for peace before Arafat could even start measuring the size of the real estate. The pretense of having negotiations for peace is no longer required. World War IV has already started and if I may adapt Clinton's expressive style, **"Its war, Stupid!"**

Then we have Harvard Law Professor, Alan Dershowitz, the "great libertarian" coming out of the woodwork. Since the commencement of hostilities, he has been championing the use of torture, in fact, to the extent of recommending the legalization of torture. On November 8, 2001, in a commentary in the Los Angeles Times, he exposed his fascist core by suggesting, *"I have no doubt that if an actual ticking bomb were to arise, our law enforcement authorities would torture. The real debate is whether such torture should take place outside our legal system or within it. The answer to this seems clear: If we are to have torture, it should be authorized by law."* For a further discussion on this issue, please refer to chapter four of this book. Look out for more draconian laws in the United States beyond the PATRIOT Act I & II. I bet you didn't know that this fascist legislation stands for "**U**niting and **S**trengthening **A**merica by **P**roviding **A**ppropriate **T**ools **R**equired to **I**ntercept and **O**bstruct **T**errorism."

The Zionists are in a real hurry. To bring in from the cold, three strategic assets, thus far buried deep within the U.S. corridors of power is telling. Remember the Wexner Foundation's Communications Priority time line? They set it at ONE YEAR!!!

Unfortunately, the war is not going too well for the Zionists.[4] The one year has yet to bring in the anticipated war booty. Take comfort in that, but remain vigilant and use the present impasse to rebuild, rearm and rejuvenate your ranks.

Indications:

1) Peter Goss was appointed Director of CIA with the mandate to clean the company of officials who were not too enthusiastic about the Bush Doctrine.

2) Colin Powell out, Condoleezza Rice in. The State Department has been described as the "most insubordinate" in American history.

3) Frustration at continuing lack of international support which prompted Bush to lash out:

   "The objective of the UN and other institutions must be collective security and not endless debate. For the sake of peace, when those bodies promise serious consequences, serious consequences must follow."

4) A split of some sorts with poodle Blair over Palestine, when Bush, after the November, 2004, elections, rejected Blair's Middle East proposals. Israel's pressure is mounting on Bush

and he is feeling the heat. He would rather sacrifice Blair's ego than annoy Sharon. Nothing substantial has changed.

5) The appointment of John Negroponte as the all-powerful Director of National Intelligence. Although the strategy remains the same, ground tactics have changed, as a result of spectacular successes of the resistance in Iraq. Covert operations and dirty tricks (Operation Phoenix revisited, etc.,) will be reintroduced on a grand scale, that's for sure! The war has entered a new phase. Following from Sharon's policy of extrajudicial killings of Palestinian leaders, and the feeble backlash from the world community, the next phase of the war will be very ugly and brutal. A senior strategist in Washington was quoted as saying:

"We are in no position to take military action just now and, in any case, the odds are stacked against us. Iran is on the point of developing nuclear weapons and Syria is a patron of terrorism. Both have created a powerful alliance, both need to be brought round and both need to mend their ways. If they are not open to negotiations, we'll have to take a more indirect approach.[5]*"*

Make no mistake, this is CIA-speak for the worst type of covert operations.

6) That there was a dramatic change in the global strategy by the Zionists as discussed earlier is corroborated by the differences within the ranks of Zionists in the United States, with the CFR faction losing out to the Neocon faction. Podhoretz revealed the estrangement:

"Here — housed in bodies like the Council on Foreign Relations, the Brookings Institution, and the Carnegie Endowment, and surrounded by the populous community of non-government organizations (NGOs) — live the liberal internationalists, with their virtually religious commitment to negotiations as the best, or indeed the only, way to resolve conflicts; their relentless faith in the UN (which they stubbornly persist in seeing as the great instrument of collective security even though its record is marked by an 'unwillingness to get serious about preventing deadly violence'); and their corre-

sponding squeamishness about military force. Among their most sophisticated spokesmen are Stanley Hoffman of Harvard, Charles A. Kupchan of the CFR, and G. John Ikenberry of Georgetown.

"Under Jimmy Carter (whose Secretary of State, Cyrus Vance, was a devout member of this school) and to a lesser extent under Bill Clinton, the liberal internationalists were at the very heart of American Foreign Policy. But while George W. Bush has thrown a rhetorical bone or two in their direction, and has even done them the kindness of making a few ceremonial bows to the UN, he has for all practical purposes written off the liberal-internationalists school. Nor he has been coy about this. As he declared in a speech at West Point on June 1, 2002: 'We cannot defend America and our friends by hoping for the best. We cannot put our faith in the world of tyrants, who solemnly sign nonproliferation treaties, and then systematically break them.'"

Notwithstanding the above indicators, the Resistance should not have any illusions. The Zionists are as determined as ever. Norman Podhoretz takes the view that Bush will not reverse his course in his second term and that he will continue striving to implement the doctrine bearing his name throughout the greater Middle East. I am in total agreement with him. Dick Cheney, Rumsfeld and the rest of the war cabal are still there. They have been bruised a bit, but they are made of meaner stuff. That's a given.

Take heed that Norman Podhoretz has openly declared that he supports the stand taken by Charles Kessler, editor of the Claremont Review in waging a ruthless war. Kessler wrote:

"If democratization is to succeed in the regimes of the Islamic world, a necessary precondition is to beat these regimes into complete submission and then occupy them for decades — not just months or years but for decades. Even then our troops may have to stay and die indefinitely on behalf of a mission...."

I cannot stress enough how important it is to study and understand fully Norman Podhoretz's strategies and ideas. For God's sake, he is the Founding Father of the Neocon Movement. You must know your enemy better than yourself.

What I am going to say in the next few paragraphs will confound and even upset many resistance forces in the Third World. It is this: World War IV unleashed by the Zionists cannot be defeated without the heroic struggles of the American patriots against the barbarians inside their gates. And there are indeed many Americans who are quietly building up their defenses in preparation for the final battle inside the United States. That is why I said earlier, the **TARGET IS NOT AMERICA**.

The Zionists have already hijacked the U.S. military but they know that unless they can impose absolute fascist control, the American patriots holding true to their Constitution and the Declaration of Independence will launch the Second American Revolution to restore freedom in America and reverse the coup d'état that gave George Bush the presidency. Already a growing number of soldiers returning from Iraq have seen through the fraud of the Iraq War and are organizing to resist further calls to serve as cannon fodder.

If you think all this is just garble, check this out.

You need not know the dedicated American patriots who will be in the front lines fighting the enemies inside their gates. Suffice to say, a retired CIA officer, Ray McGovern (1963–1990) in a recent article has warned that what Zionists have in store for these dedicated patriots and the good American people is ugly, very ugly.[6] Ray explained that the United States is turning into a police state and the key indicators are the recent appointments by President Bush.

1) Alberto Gonzales as the Attorney General: the lawyer who advised the president he could ignore the U.S. War Crimes Act and the Geneva Conventions on Torture and by his memo as to what is permissible in the interrogation of prisoners of war, led to the torture scandal at Abu Ghraib, Baghdad and Guantanamo Bay, Cuba.

2) Michael Chertoff, as Secretary of Homeland Security: the lawyer condoned the incarceration of 762 innocent immigrants (mostly Arabs and of South Asian descent) for several months as "suspected terrorists", and like Gonzales, condoned the use of torture.

3) John Negroponte, as Director of National Intelligence: currently U.S. Ambassador to Baghdad. He is best-known as the Ambassador to Honduras who was involved to his eyeball with the Contras in their effort to overthrow the duly elected government of Nicaragua in the 1980s, and who condoned the use of torture and death squads by the Honduras fascist military Junta._

Let us examine a bit of the background of John Negroponte. While as Ambassador to Honduras, he supported Battalion 316, the Honduran intelligence unit trained by the CIA that slaughtered at least 184 people. One of those was the former secretary to Archbishop Oscar Romero of El Salvador, himself a victim of CIA-funded death squad. The secretary who fled to Honduras was abducted by the Battalion and was thrown out of a helicopter to her death. Another victim was Oscar Reyes who was brutally tortured. He testified, ***"...on my wife, they used electrical shock in her vagina. It was so bad that she had permanent damage to her ovaries and she had to have a hysterectomy.***[7]*"* At the time of the Iraq War, Negroponte was the U.S. Ambassador to the UN where he led the war brigade and bullied small nations in supporting the illegal invasion.

Prior to the creation of the office of the Director of National Intelligence, the CIA and the FBI have been kept separate and distinct for a very good reason — first and foremost, to protect civil liberties. But now, the DNI will have under him the entire CIA (whose operatives are skilled in breaking foreign laws) and the FBI whose agents are trained not to violate constitutional protections. Mr. McGovern warned and reminded Americans about Operation COINTELPRO during the Vietnam War when lines of jurisdiction were blurred and were given carte blanche to pursue antiwar dissidents in the United States. They are now using the PATRIOT Act I & II to hunt down the patriots who mount resistance against America's Zionist enemies inside their gates.

I fear for the American patriots who are fighting this war, but I have faith in their loyalty to their Constitution and their integrity. That is why I am going to share something with you, in the hope that you will understand and support my appeal that we must stand shoulder to shoulder with the true American patriots.

The Zionists are going to unleash a fascist war inside America to ensure that the hijacked army will continue to do its bidding. **The Bush regime will reintroduce "Operation Gladio" under a new guise.** Operation Gladio was the covert operation of terrorism and deceit planned and controlled by the western intelligence services (essentially the CIA and MI6) against their own citizens, which was exposed in 1991. Gladio is Latin for sword. And, appropriately, Operation Gladio was the sword that slaughtered hundreds of innocent people on train stations, supermarkets, restaurants and offices via so-called terrorist attacks which were later blamed on the left-wing groups. The rationale is beyond rational comprehension and evil to the very core: to attack civilian men, women and children — innocent bystanders — in the political intrigues weaved by the secret services **so that the people, in a state of terror, would turn to the State for security and protection,** which would then introduce draconian laws with minimum or no resistance at all, and at the same time introduce Fascism via the back door. That's how the PATRIOT ACT I & II were introduced — via the back door.

The original objective of Operation Gladio was to create cells to carry out sabotage behind enemy lines in the event of a Soviet invasion of Europe. However, political masters with sinister aims subverted the organization and transformed it into a tool for repression and manipulation. Right-wing groups, underground figures, agent provocateurs and secret military and intelligence units conducted terrorist attacks all over Europe: in Italy, France, West Germany, Spain and Portugal. These units were also used in the military coup in Greece. There is a Pentagon document — Field Manual FM30-31B — which lays out in detail how terrorist attacks are to be conducted against countries and governments that are ineffective in combating communist propaganda and subversion. Such attacks allow the media to whip up hysteria against real and perceived enemies. Pause and think about this snippet from the Manual:

"When the revolutionaries temporarily renounce the use of force... US army intelligence must have the means of launching special operations which will convince Host Country Governments and public opinion of the reality of the insurgent danger...."

In simple terms, when our enemies want to heat things up, to make the hot war explosive, Special Forces Terror is let loose.[8] This is not some kind of story from a spy novel to tickle you over the weekend. None other than William Colby himself, former Director of the CIA, has confirmed the existence of Operation Gladio.[9]

The resistance in Iraq targets occupation troops. False flag operations by the security services (U.S. and British and local assets) target civilians in the hope that the Iraqis will look to the occupation forces to enforce security and stability, thus legitimizing the otherwise unpopular occupation. But this strategy has failed thus far.

Already it has been leaked out that the U.S. may be considering ***"also the use of the 'Salvador Option'"***, i.e., the use of death squads in Iraq to stem the growing resistance to the occupation and in other countries. The twist is that these operations will be run from the bowels of the Pentagon, not the CIA, because Peter Goss, the new director does not trust them enough to do the dirty work.

When resistance within the U.S. grows, a new and improved Operation Gladio or Salvador Option would be unleashed on the American people, and "Muslim fanatics" would take the blame. This is a given. That is why John Negroponte was slotted for Director of National Intelligence. When it happens, the previous Operation Gladio would be 'amateur football' when compared to the waves of terrorist attacks planned for the future.

The next time you read of a terrorist attack in the media, don't jump to a conclusion immediately. Analyze the *facts* and surrounding circumstances, the *timing* of the incident, the *victim*(s) and his/her recent statements or policy, who gets the blame *in less than 24 hours*, which *newspaper* screams the loudest as to the perpetrator and finally ask who *BENEFITS* most from the outrage. Apply these guidelines to the recent bombing and murder of the former Prime Minister of Lebanon. This is a crash course in counter-propaganda. So learn it fast and research — and research until you get it right!

The resistance in America is therefore an important front in this war, and I thank you for your understanding and support of the American patriots who are also fighting a very difficult war against Zionism.

ENDNOTES:

1. Thomas P.M. Barnett, *The Pentagon's New Map: War and Peace in the 21st Century*, (2004, New York: G.P. Putnam & Sons). The in-depth analysis is given in Chapter Sixteen.

2. Source: Dei'ah Ve Dibur (Information and Insight), January 12, 2005 @ www.chareidi. shemayisrael.com

3. Cited in Steven Meyer and Dean Andromidas, "Shultz Hit Man, Fisher to Head Bank of Israel" EIR, January 21, 2005

4. Norman Podhoretz, "The War Against World War IV, the Commentary Magazine, February 2005. The indications cited are taken from the article.

5. Cited by Trevor Royle in "New Front on the War on Terror", The Sunday Herald, February 20, 2005.

6. Ray McGovern, "Hail, Hail The Gang's All Here." February 18, 2005 @ www.TomPaine. com

7. See "America's Amnesia" The Progressive, July 2004

8. Dr. Daniele Ganser, *NATO's Secret Armies. Operation Gladio and Terrorism in Western Europe*, (2005, London, Frank Cass). Dr. Ganser is based with the Centre for Security Studies at the Federal Institute of Technology, Zurich.

9. Lila Lajiva, "The Pentagon's NATO Option" @ www.commondreams.org

16

A New Map for the 21st Century Part II — A New Military Theory

In the previous two chapters we explored the ideological strategies for World War IV, from the perspective of a Zionist ideologue, Norman Podhoretz, and have made an effort to understand its implications and consequences. In this chapter, we shall examine the new military theory for World War IV as explained by Thomas P.M. Barnett, in his book, *The Pentagon's New Map: War and Peace in the 21st Century*. Professor Barnett is the senior strategic researcher and professor at the U.S. Naval War College. Professor Barnett has been doing this work for a long time, testing various theories and finally (from his perspective anyway) hit mother lode — the Grand Strategy for World War IV. In chapter 15, I mentioned that the three articles by the Father of the Neocons, Norman Podhoretz, on World War IV and this book should be our "War Bible." If we fail to understand and appreciate the war plans and the strategies which they have so generously disclosed to us, we will not be able to launch an effective defense and counterattack.

I am not here to debate whether the basis of his theory is right or wrong. His war strategies and tactics have already been adopted by Rumsfeld's backroom boys, those mean little bastards, who care not for publicity, but are the real meat grinders. More importantly, empathize with them and get into their heads, into their bowels, and into their very soul so much so that you could literally smell their breath (after spraying with a deodorant). When you can think like them, you can then outwit them. Absent this strenuous mental exercise, they're going to barbecue the whole lot of us with their new weapons — zing and zap! But don't be discouraged.

To make things really simple, I shall be quoting those passages in his book and his ideas published elsewhere in great length so that his Core Messages will not be misinterpreted and or watered down. My comments are in brackets.

The Premise for the New Military Theory

The military theory before the New Military Theory:

"When the Cold War ended, we thought the world had changed. It had — but not in the way we thought. The United States had spent so much energy during those years trying to prevent the horror of global war that it forgot the dream of global peace."

[Forget the rhetoric about global peace, but try to appreciate where he is coming from.]

"As far as most Pentagon's strategists were concerned, America's status as the world's sole military superpower was something to preserve, not something to exploit, and because the future was unknowable, they assumed we needed to hedge against all possibilities, all threats, and all futures. America was better served adopting a wait-and-see strategy. They decided, one that assumed some grand enemy would arise in the distant future."

[Consistent with the views of Condoleezza Rice who said that prior to 9-11, things were a bit fuzzy and Colin Powell's exasperation that he needed to find new villains.]

"It was better than wasting precious resources trying to manage a messy world in the near term. The grand strategy was to avoid all grand strategies."

[Madeleine Albright felt differently and that is why she chided Colin Powell for not using America's superb military. No doubt there were intense debates within the corridors of power.]

"Until September 11, 2001, the closest thing the Pentagon had to a comprehensive view of the world was simply to call it 'chaos' and 'uncertainty,' two words that implied the impossibility of capturing the big picture perspective of the world's potential futures. Since September 11, at least we have an enemy to attach to all this 'chaos' and 'uncertainty' but that still leave us describing horrible futures to be prevented, not positive ones to be created.

266

"America drifted through the roaring nineties, blissfully unaware that globalization was speeding ahead with no one at the wheel. The Clinton administration spent its time tending to the emerging financial and technological architecture of the global economy, pushing worldwide connectivity for all it was worth in those heady days, assuming that eventually it would reach even the most disconnected societies. Did we as a nation truly understand the political and security ramifications of encouraging all this connectivity? Could we understand how some people might view this process of cultural assimilation as a mortal threat? As something worth fighting against? Was a clash of civilizations inevitable?"

[This is consistent with Rice's comments cited above. Recall also the frustrations expressed by Kagan and Kristol and that of Norman Podhoretz – the "wasted decade" and Clinton's distractions. Recall also the polemics between the Neocons and the Liberal Internationalists. Notice the convergence of the Zionist Neocon's world view and that of Pentagon's planners, of which Barnett played a leading role. This reveals a deep and effective penetration at both the ideological and operation levels.]

"Globalization seemed to be remaking the world, but meanwhile the U.S. military seemed to be doing nothing more than baby-sitting chronic security situations on the margin. Inside the Pentagon the new rubric 'military operations other than war,' as if to signify the lack of strategic meaning."

[The Zionist agenda was delayed. The **Spear of Conquest was getting rusty**, and the rest, fat on the bellies. In essence Zionist Imperial agenda was somehow diverted or distracted.]

"Today the role of the Defense Department in the U.S. national security is being radically reshaped by new missions arising in response to new international security environment. It is tempting to view this radical <u>redefinition of the use of U.S. military power around the world</u> as merely the work of senior officials in the Bush administration, but that is to confuse the midwife with the miracle of birth." (Emphasis added)

[Confirms my observations in preceding chapters of the dramatic shift in global military strategy, and more importantly that the military has been hijacked for Zionist global agenda. This was done not by the external front men of the Bush administration, but the hidden manipulators deep in the bowels of the military-industrial complex.]

"...is the heart of the work that I have been doing since the end of the Cold War."

[Clear admission that the hijacking was planned a long time ago and that plans were needed to fast-forward the hidden agenda.]

"What I found there in the late 1990s was neither 'chaos' or 'uncertainty' but the <u>defining conflict of our age</u> — a historical struggle that screamed out for a new American vision of a future worth creating.

"I was approached by senior executives of the Wall Street bond firm Cantor Fitzgerald. They asked me to oversee a unique research partnership between the firm and the college (the Naval War College) that would later <u>yield a series of high powered war games involving national security policy makers, Wall Street heavy weights and academic experts.</u>" (Emphasis added)

[You might want to ask why Wall Street is so interested in military affairs and high powered war games. Welcome to the real world of the military-industrial-financial complex. They set the agenda, they direct the execution and the front men, the President and his posse are told to ride out and do the dirty work.]

"Our shared goal was to explore how globalization was remaking global security environment — in other words, the Pentagon's New Map."

[I have stated repeatedly that Empire Capitalism is grounded on Wars and Imperial mobilization and plunder can only be sustained by a war economy. If confirmation is needed from a key representative of the Imperial War Cabal of my thesis, this is it.[1]]

"Those war games were conducted atop World Trade Centre One; the resulting briefings were offered throughout the Pentagon. <u>When both buildings came under attack on 9-11 my research immediately shifted from Grand Theory to Grand Strategy.</u>" (Emphasis added)

[Bingo! Bingo! Insidious military and war planning hiding under

268

civilian cover and civilian environment. When Bush launched the "Shock and Awe" campaign targeting civilian structures, the rationale was that Saddam was conducting military actions from civilian structures. As such they have become legitimate targets. These structures are to be considered military structures and must be destroyed. In all the investigation of the 9-11 attacks, political pundits have completely glossed over this blatant covert activity right inside the Twin Towers. What was astonishing was the open confession that when they had perfected the theory through high powered war games, they turbo-charged to implement it. The agenda was fast forwarded **because the pretext had presented itself in the shape and form of the New Pearl Harbor.** Those heavy weights at Wall Street knew what it was all about; they funded it, sought the right guys to research it, then war-planned it. This is Empire Capitalism working overtime.

The 9-11 investigation community may have entered into a dead end. My investigation into 9-11 will be published in due course, as it is not within the scope of this book and its purpose to delve deep into this issue as my reference to 9-11 was to reiterate that it was exploited as the New Pearl Harbor to launch World War IV. **But let me say here and now, and being the first to say so, that any investigation into the 9-11 Military Campaign (and I have deliberately chosen this expression) should pursue Cantor Fitzgerald's overt support for funding the joint research with the U.S. Naval War College and the subsequent high-powered war games conducted atop Tower I, with subsequent support from other heavy weights of Wall Street and other vested interests. The money made from the insider trading just prior to September 11 is a drop in the ocean and merely a dress rehearsal for the biggest score in the history of Empire Capitalism. The relevant airline stocks are not even strategic stocks in the overall scheme of things. Without the subsequent bailout, they would have gone under and the effect on the economy would be zilch!**

Cantor Fitzgerald had $50 trillion in automated trades the year preceding 9-11. Not millions, not billions, but trillions. Unfortunately they lost 2/3 of the entire force in the 9-11 military campaign.[2] Prof. Barnett has been rather coy about those series of war games. However he did mention about the meltdown by Y2K computer bug followed by terrorist attacks designed to exploit the chaos. Who were the other big heavyweights from Wall Street???]

Who is this guy, Prof. Barnett???

"Our task was as ambitious as it was direct: refocus the Pentagon's strategic vision of future wars. As the 'vision guy', my job was to generate and deliver a compelling brief that would mobilize the Defense Department toward generating the future fighting force demanded by the post 9-11 strategic environment. <u>Over time, senior military officials began citing the brief as a Rosetta Stone for the Bush Administration's new national security strategy</u>.[3]*"* (Emphasis added)

[This guy developed the military strategy for World War IV and was the overseer in its implementation. But the findings came out to the public domain after the fact and the Mission beyond reversal by some lingering chicken hawks. He had already sewn up the entire Pentagon to his world view and grand strategy. Wall Street liked it, they smelled blood and money – and the order went out to Bush, Cheney and Rumsfeld — "Go get them, and kick their butts. Then you can have your Halliburton chow."]

Why is Prof. Barnett's Grand Strategy so important?

"I was asked by a visiting delegation of security officials from Singapore how my vision of future war differs from traditional Pentagon perspectives. My answer was 'Pentagon strategists typically view war within the context of war. I view war within the context of everything else.' This book will be mostly about the 'everything else' associated with war in the twenty-first century or that essential connectivity between war and peace that defines globalization's advance. This vision constitutes a seismic shift in how we think of the military's place in American society, in how our military functions in the world, and in how we think of America's relationship to the world. All such 'contracts' are currently being renegotiated, whether we realize it or not. As citizens of this American Union, we all need to understand better the stakes at hand, for it is not the danger just ahead that we underestimate, but the opportunity that lies beyond — the opportunity to make globalization truly global."

[In essence, Prof Barnett has formulated a Grand Strategy for a truly Global Imperial Empire and a military doctrine to ensure its attainment; his Grand Strategy is the successor to the Grand Strategy of Containment during the Cold War.]

The Grand Strategy

"Our next war in the Gulf will mark a historical tipping point — the moment when Washington takes real ownership of strategic security in the age of globalization. That is why the public debate about this war has been so important: It forces Americans to come to terms with what I believe is the new security paradigm that shapes this age, namely Disconnectedness defines danger. Saddam Hussein's outlaw regime is dangerously disconnected from the globalizing world, from its rule sets, its norms, and all the ties that bind countries together in mutually assured dependence.

"The problem with most discussion of globalization is that too many experts treat it as a binary outcome: either it is great and sweeping the planet or it is horrid and failing humanity everywhere. Neither view really works, because globalization as a historical process is simply too big and too complex for such summary judgments. Instead, this new world must be defined by where globalization has truly taken root and where it has not."

[The next paragraph is important as it sets out the basis for his Grand Strategy.]

"Show me where globalization is thick with network connectivity, financial transactions, liberal media flows, and collective security, and I will show you regions featuring stable governments, rising standards of living, and more deaths by suicide than murder. <u>*These parts of the world I call the Functioning Core, or Core.*</u> *But show me where globalization is thinning or just plain absent, and I will show you regions plagued by politically repressive regimes, widespread poverty and disease, routine mass murder and — most important — the chronic conflicts that incubate the next generation of global terrorist.* <u>*These part of the world I call the Non-Integrating Gap, or Gap.*</u>*"* (Emphasis added)

[Essentially the Prof. has divided the world into the haves and the have-nots, the First World and the Third World. There is no originality here except the new terms for the division. There is no necessity for debate here. But what is interesting is that those countries in the Gap are all rich in resources. Therefore the world will be divided along "resource boundaries."]

"The reason I support going to war in Iraq is not simply that Saddam Hussein is a cut throat Stalinist willing to kill anyone to stay in power, not because that regime has clearly supported terrorist networks over the years. <u>The real reason I support a war like this is that the resulting long term military commitment will finally force America to deal with the entire Gap as a strategic threat environment.</u>" (Emphasis added)

[Read this once again and think hard. But before I give my comments, I will quote another passage to facilitate completeness. When you read the next passage, you will get disgusted with the Nazi mindset, but try not to let it overwhelm you.]

"Since September 11, 2001, it has gotten a lot harder for even experts to speak authoritatively about the rule sets governing war and peace, primarily because it seems as if the world has left one era behind and entered another that feels very different and unfamiliar. It is almost as if we were playing football one minute and then the game suddenly switched to soccer — the two sides in this conflict do not seem to be keeping score in the same way, or even playing by similar rule sets. If this 'global War on Terrorism' is something new, then it will naturally generate a new rule set concerning war and peace, or one that replaces the old rule set that governed America's Cold War with the Soviet Union."

[Operation Gladio and the Salvador Option are all terrorist campaigns conducted by the American and the British secret services since the 1960s. They have been using terror tactics when it suited them. It was their rule set. But when the opponent adopts similar tactics in defense, it is alleged that the rules of the game has changed. It is no longer football, but soccer. In the next passage, the Prof. explains why it is so.]

"My purpose in writing this book is to explain how I think these new rule sets for war and peace will actually work in the years ahead. To do that, I will need to take you inside the game that is U.S. security planning, <u>because America is the biggest rule</u>

<u>*maker in the business of global security affairs. I have to make*</u> <u>*you a student of the game so that you can appreciate just how*</u> <u>*much the rule sets have changed since 9-11."*</u> (Emphasis added)

[I hope by now you understand why I am writing my book in the style that I have written. This is not just an intellectual challenge. He is telling the Pentagon how to whack us and our families on behalf of the Zionist Anglo-American Power Elites. Just as he is writing his book to tell his goons how to play his game according to his rules, I am writing to tell the Worldwide Resistance not to play his game according to his rule. So America is the biggest rule maker, and therefore he can be the referee, linesmen and score keeper. Dear Prof. I must apologize that we are not willing to play a game stacked in your favor. General Patton, when asked by his German counter-part to surrender during the Battle of the Bulge, sent a note back with just one word, "Nuts!" What an appropriate response indeed to a stupid offer.]

"Whenever rules are clear, because most players in that system agree they're good, there's not as much enforcement required, because most participants simply decide on their own that playing by the rules is the best course of action. But where you don't find generally agreed-upon rules, or where rules are out of whack or misaligned across social sectors, then you're talking about the future of instability, the potential for misperceptions leading to conflicts, and the clash of competing rule sets. It's simple as that: The fewer the rules, the more war you have.

"Growing a community of like minded states is simply a matter of identifying the difference between 'good' and 'bad' regimes, and rallying the former to work collectively to encourage the latter to change their ways, applying military power when diplomacy alone does not do the trick.

"Enunciating that rule set is the most immediate task in this global War on Terrorism, and promoting the global spread of that security rule set through our use of military force overseas (e.g. pre-emptive war against regimes that openly transgress the rule set) is our most important long term goal in this struggle."

[International relations are now reduced to a set of rules enun-

273

ciated by Big Brother and the relationship is grounded on a simple premise — conform and follow the rules, failing which you will be clobbered by the U.S. military. The recent tour of Europe by Ms Rice and followed by President Bush is to remind Europe that post Saddam Hussein, there will be further changes and new rule sets are to be followed. However, Europe seems to think otherwise and have decided that they will have their own rule sets. A question for the professor, "Are these countries drifting from the Core or what?" The Professor gets more specific.]

"In the era of globalization, we draw that line between those parts of the world that are actively integrating their national economies into the global economy, or what I call globalization's Functioning Core, and those that are failing to integrate themselves into that larger economic community and the rule sets it generates, or those states I identify as constituting the Non-Integrating Gap. A country's potential to warrant a U.S. military response is inversely related to its globalization connectivity.

"But just as important as 'getting them where they live' is stopping the ability of these terrorist networks to access the Core via the 'seam states' that lie along the Gap's bloody boundaries. It is along this seam that the Core will seek to suppress bad things coming out of the Gap. Which are some of these classic seam states? Mexico, Brazil, South Africa, Morocco, Algeria, Greece, Turkey, Pakistan, Thailand, Malaysia, the Philippines, and Indonesia come to mind." (Emphasis added)

[Members of ASEAN, take heed. You have been identified for military action, when nasty things spill over from the Gap to your turf, defined as "seam states"; these nasty things cannot be allowed to go beyond the seam states to infect the Core! Just like the fascist Israeli thugs, they want to come to our homes to kill and humiliate. They are not looking for terrorists, there aren't any! They are unleashing state terrorism. Just look at the pictures that came out from Jenin and Fallujah.]

Finally, we now come to the last segment of the Grand Strategy.

"If we step back for a minute and consider the broader implications of this new global map, then U.S. national security strategy would seem to be: 1) Increase the Core's immune

*system capabilities for responding to September 11- like sys-
tem perturbations; 2) Work the seam states to firewall the Core
from the Gap's worst exports, such as terror, drugs and pan-
demics; and most important, 3) Shrink the Gap.*"

[To work the seams, build the firewall and to shrink the Gap,
Prof. Barnett proposes that instead a single all encompassing army
or force the future military would have two separate forces with very
different objectives. The first, he calls "Leviathan", the cowboys who
will do all the hard and dirty work of conquering and destroying
enemy forces etc. which must be able to be deployed rapidly. This
force consists of stealth submarines, long range bombers, latest
high-tech weaponry and in his own words, soldiers who are **"young,
unmarried and... pissed off."** The second, not strictly military,
which he terms as "System Administrators" (their principal role) is to
bring dysfunctional states to comply with the "rule sets" laid down by
Big Brother, via nation building operations previously seen in the
Balkans, East Africa and now trying very hard in Iraq. They are not
necessarily deployed after a war, but could be sent out to the seam
states and the Gap during "peacetime" (whatever that means) to
build local security forces and infrastructure, euphemism for
Paramilitary forces and fascist goons to hunt down potential opponents and to keep the seam states in high tension and so preoccu-
pied internally that they cannot mount any resistance and do any
damage to the Core. How do you think, Deputy Sheriff Howard got
his idea to roam in Southeast Asia from his base in the out-backs of
Australia? Additionally, Prof. Barnett recently told a group of senior
officers, **"You guys can do two or three Iraq wars a year, no
problem, but you can't do one occupation.**4 **"**

The endgame scenario is painted by the Prof. in very stark
terms, and leaders of the third world, what he calls the seam states
and the Gap should take heed.]

*"Show me a part of the world that is secure in its peace
and I will show you a strong or growing ties between local mil-
itaries and the U.S. military. Show me regions where major war
is inconceivable and I will show you permanent U.S. military
bases and long term security alliances. Show me the strongest
investment relationships in the global economy and I will show
you two post war military occupations that remade Europe and
Japan following World War II."* (Emphasis added)

[The United States whose efforts to control the Straits of Malacca by stationing its war ships there on the excuse of combating piracy and terrorism on the high seas was thwarted by the rigorous opposition from Malaysia and Indonesia, has now found a back door via the unfortunate but timely Tsunami disaster. The United States and Indonesia (having been pressured and coerced) are "seeking" to use their cooperation in dealing with the Tsunami crisis as a springboard to restore closer military ties after a decade of limited contact. When Deputy Secretary Paul Wolfowitz comes a calling supposedly to visit hard hit areas, and suggest that Congressional restrictions on arm sales should be re-evaluated, be prepared. Those who have short memories, please recall that Wolfowitz was the U.S. ambassador to Jakarta from 1986–1989 in the Reagan administration. He was quoted as saying that *"cutting off contact with Indonesian officers only makes the problem worse."* The new President of Indonesia, Susilo Bambang Yudhoyono is a former general who was trained at the U.S. Army's Command and General Staff College at Fort Leavenworth, Kansas. Admiral Thomas Fargo, the head of the Pacific Command is seeking to have Pentagon's approval to expand a series of conferences his command has sponsored with the Indonesian army on civil-military relations, and other forms of training. Take them to mean, training for internal suppression.]

"Making this effort means reshaping our military establishment to mirror image the challenge that we face. Think about it. Global war is not in the offing, primarily because of our huge nuclear stockpile renders such war unthinkable — for anyone. Meanwhile classic state-on-state wars are becoming fairly rare. So if the United States is in the process of 'transforming' its military to meet the threats of tomorrow, what should it end up looking like? In my mind, we fight fire with fire. If we live in a world increasingly populated by Super-Empowered Individuals, we field a military of Super-Empowered individuals."

[The term "Super-Empowered Individuals" is the euphemism for Death Squads and Special Forces Operations — updated versions of Operation Phoenix, Operation Gladio, the Salvador Option, Tiger Force, etc.[5] More frightening will be the broadening of the practice of "extraordinary rendition" to cover any dissidents and not only suspected terrorists. In such operations, the CIA and British secret service will kidnap suspects and fly them in unmarked planes to regimes which have sophisticated machinery for torture and make use of the information obtained. Former British ambassador to Uzbekistan, Craig Murray revealed that he witnessed such rendition in Uzbekistan. The regime's dictator is known to boil his victims alive. He also confirmed that this is also taking place in Egypt and Saudi Arabia, CIA client regimes.[6]]

So here is the Professor's deal. Open up your country for Zionist Anglo-American plunder and rape according to the globalization "rule sets" laid down by Big Brother or else the U.S. military will come and get you. And when they do, they will occupy your country and whack the living daylights out of you. To save yourself one whole lot of aggravation, there is an easy way out — surrender your sovereignty, enter into a long term slavery agreement and let the U.S. military secure their loot, by having bases in your neighborhood. And in return, your women won't get abused and you may have a chance to eat the leftover, and if they are generous enough, a decent meal.

Finally, don't you ever believe the bit about not using nuclear weapons in the coming wars! Remember he said that the U.S. is the biggest rule maker and will change the rules when situation demands a change.

Following from the above, I envisaged the revival of the **CIA-SIS "TPAJAX"** plan (the covert operation that overthrew Prime Minister Mossadeq of Iran in June 1953) to destabilize Iran and foment an upheaval to overthrow the Clerics in power. A possibility is to install the son of the previous Shah to continue the legacy. The modus operandi would be replicated all over the Middle East and within the ASEAN region in due course. I have no doubts that initial stages of preparation have already being put in place. The CIA and SIS will be working overtime. I have also in mind operation **PBFORTUNE,** the covert campaign that overthrew the Arbenz government in Guatemala to address the situation in Latin America, especially Venezuela.

In the circumstances, it is incumbent that potential resistance and democratic forces should be familiar with the overall planning of such operations, so as to be able to pre-empt such operations, plan countermeasures and protect their duly elected governments. Study the blueprint and **observe how it might be adapted** by the Zionist Anglo-American intelligence services to your local theatre of operations. Then warn the democratic forces in your country.

The CIA-SIS "TPAJAX" Plan[7]

The Overthrow of Mossadeq of Iran, June 1953

1.   Preliminary Action

A.   Interim Financing of Operation

    1. CIA will supply $35,000 to General Fazlullah Zahedi.

    2. SIS will supply $25,000 to Zahedi

    3. SIS indigenous channels will be used to supply above funds to Zahedi

    4. CIA will attempt to subsidize key military leaders if necessary.

B.   Acquisition of Shah's Cooperation

    1. Stage 1: Convince Shah that UK and US have joint aim and to remove pathological fear of British intrigues against him.

    a. US Ambassador Henderson to call on the Shah to assure him of US – UK common aid and the British is supporting him and not Mossadeq.

    b. Henderson to say to the Shah that a special US representative will soon to be introduced to him for presentation of joint US-UK plan.

    2. Stage 2: Special US representative will visit the Shah and present the following:

    a. Presentation to the Shah

       • Both governments consider oil question secondary.

       • Major issue is to maintain independence of Iran and keep her from the Soviet orbit. To do this Mossadeq must be removed.

       • Present dynasty is best bulwark for national sovereignty.

- While Mossadeq in power, no aid for Iran from the United States.

- Mossadeq must go.

- US-UK financial aid will be forthcoming to successor government.

- Acceptable oil settlement will be offered but successor government will not be rushed into it.

b. Demands on the Shah

1. You must take leadership in the overthrow of Mossadeq.

2. If not, you bear responsibility of collapse of country.

3. If not, Shah's dynasty will fall and US-UK backing of you will cease.

4. Who do you want to head successor government? (Try and manoeuvre Shah into naming Zahedi).

5. Warning not to discuss approach.

6. Plan of operation with Zahedi will be discussed with you.

II <u>Arrangement with Zahedi</u>

A. After agreement with the Shah per above, inform Zahedi he is chosen to head successor government with US-UK support.

B. Agree on specific plan for action and timetable for action. There are two ways to put Zahedi in office:

1. Quasi-legally, whereby the Shah names Zahedi Prime Minister by royal *fatwa*.

2. Military coup. Quasi-legal method to be tried first. If successful, at least part of the machinery for military coup will be brought into action. If it fails, military coup will follow in matter of hours.

III <u>Relations with Majlis (Iranian Parliament)</u>

Important for quasi-legal effort. To prepare for such effort, deputies must be purchased.

A. Basic is to secure 41 votes against Mossadeq and assure

quorum for quasi-legal move by being able to depend on 53 deputies in Majlis. (SIS considers 20 deputies now not controlled must be purchased.)

B. Approach to deputies to be done by SIS indigenous group. CIA will backstop where necessary by pressures on Majlis deputies and will provide part of the funds.

IV Relations with Religious Leaders

Religious leaders should:

A. Spread word of their disapproval of Mossadeq

B. As required, stage political demonstrations under religious cover.

C. Reinforce backbone of the Shah.

D. Make strong assurances over radio and in Mosques after coup that new government will faithful to Muslim principles. Possibly as quid pro quo prominent cleric Borujedi would be offered ministry without portfolio or consider implementing neglected article in constitution providing body of five *mullahs* (religious leaders) to pass on orthodoxy of religion.

V. Relations with Bazaar [control morhetrilace]

Bazaar contacts to be used to spread anti-government rumors and possibly close bazaar as anti-government expression.

VI. Tudeh [Iranian Communist Party][8]

Zahedi must expect violent reaction from Tudeh and be prepared to meet with superior violence.

A. Arrest at least 100 Party and Front Group leaders.

B. Sealed off South Tehran to prevent influx Tudeh demonstrations.

C. Via black leaflets direct Tudeh not to take any action.

VII. Press and Propaganda Programs

A. Prior to coup, intensify anti-Mossadeq propaganda.

B. Zahedi should quickly appoint effective chief of government press and propaganda as well;

1. Brief all foreign correspondents.

2. Release advance prepared US and UK official statements.

3. Make maximum use of radio Tehran.

VIII.   Relations with Tribes[9]

A. Coup will provoke no reaction from Bakhtiari, Kurds, Baluchi, Zolfaghari, Manassani, Boor, Ahmndi, and Khamseh tribal groups.

B. Major problem is neutralization of Qashqa'i tribal leaders.[10]

IX. Mechanics of Quasi-Legal Overthrow

A. At this moment the view with most favor is the so called (...) plan — where by mass demonstrators seek religious refuge in Majlis grounds. Elements available to religious leaders would be joined by those supplied by bazaar merchants, up to 4,000 supplied by SIS controlled group, and additional elements supplied through CIA.[11]

B. Would be widely publicized that this refuge movement on rest on the basis of popular dissatisfaction with Mossadeq government as follows:

1. That Mossadeq government basically anti-religious as most clearly demonstrated by ties between Mossadeq and Tudeh; and Mossadeq and USSR. Just prior to movement CIA would give widest publicity to all fabricated documents proving secret agreement between Mossadeq and Tudeh.

2. That Mossadeq is leading the country into complete economic collapse through his unsympathetic dictatorship. Just prior to movement CIA might have capability to print masses of excellent imitation currency...

C. Religious refuge to take place at the dawn of the coup day. Immediately followed by effort to have Majlis pass a motion to censure the government. This is to be followed by the dismissal of Mossadeq and the appointment of Zahedi as successor. If successful, the coup would be completed by early afternoon. Failing success, the coup would be mounted later that evening.

[Please note that the above plan, as per original, was written in an informal, sort of shorthand style. This explains some of the fragmented sentences and errors.]

Study the plan and ask yourself, whether over the years, variants have been applied in other parts of the world. This will come as a surprise to many Muslims - that the SIS and CIA have such control over religious groups. I have observed so often that the Muslim street is taken so easily by inflammatory rhetoric by some of the planted SIS controlled Mullahs. In fact I would say that religious groups of **any denomination** are the easiest groups to infiltrate and subvert, because their members wear their religion as a badge and naively place more emphasis on form than content. The mindset is that if one is clothed in some religious garb and is knowledgeable of some rituals then they are devout followers of that **particular religion**. Better still if you can speak the lingo. That is why the Mossad has been so successful in infiltrating various resistance groups in the Middle East and the ranks of Evangelical Christian groups. Small Christian groups are sprouting all over, sowing confusion, and one of their propaganda line, is that "only those who are completely submersed in water during a specific ritual is deemed "baptized" and a true Christian. Otherwise these "un-baptized" Christians will burn in hell!

Get it out of your minds that religious leaders cannot be purchased. And you should not ever, ever underestimate the tenacity of the SIS, more then the CIA to be deliberate and persistent in building such sleeper cells over a long period of time, in anticipation of future uses. Otherwise, how can you explain the certainty and confidence of the coup-plotters that the coup would be over by afternoon and even if there is a hitch, by sunset?

Short Note

Take the Professor seriously. There was a two day retreat in Washington, where top generals, admirals and colonels from the Pentagon's Joint Chiefs gathered to listen to the Professor. Also present was the Deputy Director of Operations of Central Command, the army colonel who led the "Thunder Run" into Baghdad and the air force general, one of only a handful of U.S. fighter pilots to have shot down an enemy plane in combat over the past two decades. After the retreat one army colonel remarked about the situation in Iraq: ***"Right now all we've got is a hammer and we are driving that screw into the wall with our hammer, as best we can. But it won't set right. What we really need is a screw driver.*[12]***"** After the meeting, the group led by a team of one and two stars admirals and generals decided to recommend that the good Professor brief senior four stars generals at another retreat.

Query

The force is going to hammer and screw the living daylights out of us. **What have we got planned to stop them from hammering and screwing us?**

Answer

People's War. Nothing can defeat People's War, if you really understand it. The key is not "How to fight?" but "Why are we fighting?" The professor addresses the former, but my interest is in the latter. Anyone can be trained and taught how to fight. The best soldiers, the most efficient killing machines, will stop killing when he sees no good reason for killing. They will even rebel. Recall the "fragging" of officers by soldiers during the Vietnam War.[13] Every one has a "pain threshold," beyond which insanity sets in. Knowing why you are fighting - that you are fighting for a just cause, defending your country, fighting to prevent your country from being plundered and raped - you will quickly learn how to fight and will fight skillfully. The entire nation is the army and the logistic base to counter aggression and repel the invaders. They are truly the Super-Empowered Individuals, not the kind described by the good professor.

The Zionist Anglo-American armed forces, being Imperialist armed forces serving the cause of Empire Capitalism, by its very nature will not be able to appreciate this fundamental principle of warfare. The mindset of a rapist and plunderer is obviously different from those who are going to resist. You don't need to be a rocket scientist or a highly paid gung-ho professor to tell you this.

Consider this statement by former US Marine Officer, Lieutenant General James Watt, who dismissed photographic evidence of the brutal massacre of Iraqi civilians at a wedding party — 27 of the Rakat family and relatives were killed, including musicians engaged to celebrate this joyous occasion; 11 of the dead were women and 14 were children.

This fascist goon said:

"It's fun to shoot people. You go to Afghanistan. You've got guys who slap women around for five years because they don't wear a veil. You know, guys like that ain't got no manhood anyway, so it's a hell lot of fun to shoot them."

Such a leader can never lead an effective army to win any war, more so a war of aggression against innocent people. This is a given! Likewise, the resistance should not give any cause to such fascist to justify their war crimes and confuse the American people whose support is indispensable to the resistance. This has nothing to do with religion. This is part of propaganda warfare, and to ensure that our cause is just and in full compliance with international laws on wars.

ENDNOTES:

1. Find time to read this excellent book on war by Chris Hedges, *War is a Force That Gives Us Meaning*, (2003, New York: Anchor Books)

2. Source: Christian Science Monitor, September 17, 2001

3. The Rosetta Stone, a black basalt bearing inscriptions that provided the key to the deciphering of Egyptian hieroglyphs, and thus to modern Egyptology. It was found near Rosetta (Rashid) by a French soldier on July, 1799, during Napoleon's occupation of Egypt.

4. Greg Jaffe, "At the Pentagon, Quirky PowerPoint Carries Big Punch", May 11, 2004, Wall Street Journal.

5. Please revert to Chapter 4 for a detailed discussion.

6. The Independent, Raymond Whitaker, February, 2005

7. *The Cold War: A History in Documents and Eyewitness Accounts*, ed. Jussi M. Hanhimaki and Odd Arne Westad, (2004, Oxford: Oxford University Press)

8. In the present context, the key opposition party in your country.

9. In other countries, this would mean minority groups and other important indigenous groups. Watch out for strong influence of these groups as signs.

10. Coup plotters will neutralize any potential resistance no matter how small or insignificant, as if left unchecked, it can grow to be a problem.

11. The recent battle for Najaf by the occupying forces in Iraq has elements of this plan.

12. Wall Street Journal, May 11, 2004.

13. The term "fragging" refers to disgruntled soldiers throwing grenades at their officers.

17

Who is the Enemy?

AMERICA IS NOT THE ENEMY. The countries as defined by Professor Barnett as being in the Gap — in Latin America, Western, Central and Southern Africa and South-East Asia are not enemies or threats to the United States, or to the world for that matter.

The power that hijacked the U.S. military is the **ENEMY and the ENEMY is ZIONIST ISRAEL POWER ELITES, and their MASTERS.** They have now seized the ***Spear of Conquest.*** Zionist Israel is the global enemy to all peace loving peoples of the world. Just as we distinguished between the American people from the Zionist Anglo-American War Cabal, we must also make similar distinction between Zionists and genuine peace makers.

The "Jews" are not our enemies. By this I mean "Jews" who reject Zionism and are not Zionists. And as explained in preceding chapters, the word "Jew" is a linguistic term and bears no racial connotation. A believer in Judaism is not necessarily a Zionist. Absent this clarification, we will be aiming at the wrong target.

Unfortunately, after the Cold War, and in order to advance its Agenda, **the Zionist Anglo-American Power Elites**[1] realized that they must have a universally identifiable enemy. Absent such an enemy, it would be highly impossible to mobilize the American people for imperial wars, hidden behind the veil of national security and defense. It was very hard, after the Cold War to identify China, because China was making waves in transforming her economy and everyone wanted a piece of her pie. She had no army fighting wars overseas, no surrogates to stir trouble in other people's back yard. The West was perceived to have won the ideological war; we had arrived at "the end of history" and liberal democracy was bringing in the goodies. And according to the Professor Barnett, China is in fact a critical part of the "Integrated Core" and not part of the seam states or the Gap. So it would be a hard sell to turn China into an "Evil Empire."

The "Black People" in Africa was considered too primitive by the Zionist to be a threat. They would serve another purpose but their numbers have to be reduced first, through manipulated famines, inter-tribal wars, pestilence and AIDS.[2] They would be useful in the subsequent wars against the White Gentiles.

That left only one candidate. This candidate has always been reserved as such by the Zionist in the event that future conventional wars on the scale of the previous two world wars could not be successfully provoked. They tried to turn the Cold War into a "Hot War" but failed.

Ultimately, the Zionists knew within their hearts, who would be the ultimate enemy. So why bother to postpone the final reckoning. Might as well fast forward the global agenda!

From biblical times, the contest was already framed by the Pharisees theologically and ideologically as that of:

ERETZ ISHMAEL v ERETZ YISRAEL

The establishment of Israel in 1948 by the British Zionists was the first step in bringing about this Final Battle. The history of the Zionist movement since 1948 is about one preparation after another to ensure victory when this war is finally fought. But the war could not be fought until and unless they have seized the **Spear of Conquest.** They have done so now.

In the past, when this "enemy" of the Zionist was united under one Supreme Leader, they were unbeatable. The Zionists saw how their "enemy" dominated and occupied from what is now known as the Central Republics in the East to Spain in the West; its influence spread even further. But Jews have lived peacefully under their rule. And when this "enemy" divided into two main factions soon after the demise of their Supreme Leader, they were still able to maintain their domination; and in the modern world it was known as the Ottoman Empire. When Zionism reared its ugly head, it lusted for Eretz Yisrael.

The onset of the First World War gave the Zionist the first real opportunity to inflict a fatal blow. After World War I was over, the Zionist having lured the United States to be the cannon fodder for their cause was able to collude with Britain and France to carve up the entire Ottoman Empire into pieces, like broken china. This was how Norman Podhoretz described the division of the spoils of war by Britain and France:

"The Middle East we know today was not created by a mandate from heaven and the miserable despotisms there did not evolve through some unstoppable natural or historical process. As it happened most of the states in question were <u>*conjured into existence*</u> *less than a hundred years ago out of the ruins of the defeated Ottoman Empire in World War I. Their boundaries were drawn by the victorious British and French with the stroke of an often arbitrary pen, and their hapless people were handed over in due course to one tyrant after another. There is thus no warrant to assume that these states will last forever in their present forms, or that the only alternatives to them are necessarily worse.[3]"* (Emphasis added)

But their dream for Eretz Yisrael could not be realized. They had to wait for World War II to demand that the bargain struck in 1917 be honored.

There was never a distinction between Eretz Ishmael and Eretz Yisrael in the Holy Land. In a moving Preface to the Book, *What Price Israel?* by Alfred M. Lilienthal, to commemorate the 50th Anniversary Edition, Fahda Binte Saud, the daughter of the late King Saud wrote:

"Contrary to Zionist claims, there never was any ancient and deep-rooted hatred of Arabs for Jews before the partition of Palestine, just as there never was any hatred between Abraham's sons, Ishmael and Isaac, who each became the forefathers of the Arab and Hebrew peoples.

"Sadly, many in the West are still deluded by this unfortunate Zionist propaganda, that only the Jews and not Arabs were blessed by God. Tragically, this false animosity is today fuelling the clash of civilization."

But how did the Zionists get away with this lie for so long, you may want to ask? Simple! People don't read. They don't read the Holy Books, the very basis of their faith in their religion. The Zionist knows that and that's why they have spend such a considerable amount of money, in the billions and over such a protracted period of time to seize control of all the world's major news media, radio and television, and publishing houses. And through constant repetition of such lies in the news, films, novels, etc., they were able to indoctrinate and manipulate our minds.[4]

We are told in the Bible, in Genesis: 25:9 that both Ishmael and Isaac buried Abraham in the Machpelah Cave. And in Genesis: 36:3-4, it was told that Esau, Isaac's firstborn and Jacob's brother, married Ishmael's daughter Bashemath.

And in the Qur'ân in Sûrah 2 (Al Baqarâh), Verse 133, that at the death bed of Jacob, it was recorded that:

> *Were ye witnesses when death appeared before Jacob? Behold, he said to his sons: "What will ye worship after me?" They said: "We will worship thy God and the God of thy forefathers, of Abraham, Ishmael and Isaac — the One [true] God: to Him we bow in [Islam].*[5]

But the Zionists have rejected the teachings of the Holy Books and substituted instead the worship of Israel, as the agenda. In the Introduction to his book, Alfred Lilienthal, a Jew, courageously exposed that, *"Zionism has often been innocently defined as a movement to provide a homeland and refuge for Jews in need of safety in the land where their ancestors lived in ancient times. That definition only sounds good until we realize that almost a million Palestinian Arabs already living there had to be displaced and made homeless in the process. Incredibly, even today so many years later, many Americans and others worldwide still believe that it was 'a land without a people for a people without a land.' It was not!"*

Until it was pointed our by Alfred Lilienthal, I was not aware that Israel was a nation without a written constitution and more importantly **a state without officially declared borders.** This is significant and points to the lie that the Zionists want to live in peace with its neighbors. How can that be when Israel reserves to itself the right to decide whether its neighbor's land is up for grabs, and be incorporated into its homestead?

This one point exposes Zionist Israel's imperial ambitions to ultimately conquer the whole of the Middle East and to extend its boundaries from the Nile to the Euphrates. For if Israel were to declare its borders now, it will be stopped from asserting otherwise and under international law disallowed to claim any larger and wider borders. The Zionist logic goes something like this. They come to the neighborhood and ask for a house, a shelter for their homeless. After a while, they complain that the premises are too cramped for comfort, so they go and break down the adjoining wall and move in to the neighbor's premises; then their relatives from afar joins the party and they break down more walls and muscle into more houses, on the basis of some God given right. Before too long, they own the entire bloodied neighborhood. In time, they will complain that the neighbors across the two rivers are pissing into "their" rivers and then they will demand the lands beyond the river as well!

Before proceeding further, I would like to quote one more passage from Alfred Lilienthal's book, and coming from a Jew (who is not a Zionist) who opposes the establishment of the Zionist state of Israel, it should be an eye opener for many:

"I know that some of my colleagues for justice for the Palestinians would like to believe that American imperialism controls Israel rather than that Israel controls American foreign policy in the Middle East through the network of ultra-Zionist sympathizers within the U.S. who place their concerns for Israel above their concerns for America itself. Without the state of Israel having come into existence in 1948 – there would be no need for a war on terror. Other conflicts would be going on around the world, including in the Mid-East region, since human nature seems to have such a talent for strife. But this particular 'clash of civilizations' between the West and Islam is primarily a tragic outcome of U.S. support for Israel.[6]"

I know it is not easy to overcome fifty years of Zionist propaganda and some of you may, after reading the last quote, concede that the Zionist may have hijacked the U.S. foreign policy to the extent of controlling it, but that does not follow that the Zionists have hijacked the U.S. Military.

Fortunately for those who are fighting for truth and justice, there is a very brave American, a former Congressman who had served honorably for 22 years and who was a senior member of the House

Middle East Committee who will vouch that the U.S. military has been hijacked by the Zionists. He is none other than the extraordinary truth seeker, the Hon. Paul Findley, author of the book, ***They Dare Speak Out: People and Institution Confront Israel's Lobby***.[7] This is what he wrote about penetration of the Defense Department:

"The penetration is all the more remarkable because much of it is carried out by U.S. citizens on behalf of a foreign government. The practical effect is to give Israel its own network of sources, through which it is able to learn almost anything it wishes about decisions or resources of the U.S. government. When making procurement demands, Israel can display better knowledge of Defense Department inventories than the Pentagon itself."

I need only cite two instances as examples of the hijacking of the U.S. military. Richard Helms, the Director of the CIA during the 1967 Arab-Israeli War recalled an occasion when an Israeli arms request was filled with the wrong items. Israeli officials resubmitted the request **complete with all the supposedly top-secret code numbers.** The director was of the view that during that period, no important secret was kept from Israel and that they always got what they wanted.

Admiral Moorer was the Chairman of the Joint Chief of Staff at the time of the 1973 Arab-Israeli conflict — the Yom Kippur War. Israel's defense attaché, Mordecai Gur, who later became Commander-in-Chief of Israeli forces, demanded that the U.S. supply Israel with aircrafts equipped with the latest high technology air-to-surface anti-tank missile called "Maverick." At the material time, the U.S. had only one squadron that was so equipped. And so the Admiral declined the request on the ground that Congress would not allow it. Mordecai Gur told the Admiral, "You get us the plane and I will take care of Congress." Sure enough, and not too long, America's only squadron equipped with the missiles were shipped to Israel.

If you have read carefully the previous sixteen chapters, I am confident that you would agree that Israel is the lynchpin in any counter-strategy to defeat the Zionist in World War IV. If I may put it in another way — **the Achilles heel of the Zionist Anglo-American Power Elites is Israel.** An incredible myth has been created as to the invincibility of the Zionist War Machine and this was built mainly on the sweeping victory of the 1967 war and the 1973 conflict. In both cases, had the U.S. not helped Israel, that myth would have been punctured. That Israel was able to get away with this strategic propaganda victory is due to the abject failure of Arab front line states to harness the resources of the people to wage a people's war against Israel.

History will in time pass judgement as to who were the victors, and who the losers, in the 1973 Arab-Israeli War. That aspect bears no consideration in the present discussion. Earlier, I had referred to the ability of the Israelis to arm twist Admiral Moorer, Chairman of the Joint Chiefs of Staff to divert the only U.S. squadron of aircrafts equipped with the latest air-to-surface anti-tank missile to Israel in the midst of war. Let's examine how critical this was to the Israelis, in checking the advances made by the Egyptians (who were subsequently manipulated by Russia and the U.S. for their own selfish geopolitical agenda). Consider the following from Kissinger:[8]

"We can't let Israel lose. If the Soviet side wins, we will be in a very bad shape. I then told Haig that if the ceasefire initiative collapsed, we would have to step up the airlift to the maximum capacity using all available planes, no matter what the risk of confrontation…."

What Kissinger has admitted in his memoirs was that he was prepared to risk a confrontation with the Soviets, even at the risk of a World War. He was ever the faithful servant to the Zionist Anglo-American Power Elites. Kissinger elaborated further:

"Conciliation is meaningful only if one is thought to have an alternative. We could not know, when we decided to engage in massive re-supply, whether Arab states would take out their frustration in bitter hostility or whether the Soviet Union would pick up the challenge and organize a block of countries working against our interests throughout the region. But we had no alternative anyway. If the Soviet-armed states won, the Soviets would control the post war diplomacy. <u>If Israel did not force a decision, it would enmesh in a war of attrition in which courage and ingenuity even in Israeli measure could not overcome a population ratio of thirty to one arrayed against it.</u>[9]" (Emphasis added)

The situation was dire for Israel and the situation was vividly described by Richard Ned Lebow and Janice Gross Stein:[10]

"...American officials began to question their earlier expectations of a quick, crushing Israeli victory. They learned that a large Israeli counterattack against Egyptian forces the previous day had failed to dislodge Egyptian armies. Israel's military attaché in Washington told Kissinger that Israel had suffered over a thousand casualties, and had lost five hundred tanks and forty nine aircraft, heavy losses for the Israel Defense Forces. Ambassador Dinitz asked for an urgent meeting with Kissinger to press for accelerated deliveries of weaponry... Prime Minister Golda Meir considered the situation so desperate that she asked Dinitz to arrange a secret visit to Washington so that she can meet personally with President Nixon to impress upon him Israel's urgent need for American aid. Defense Minister Dayan ordered an operational check of missiles capable of delivering nuclear weapons."

What would be the significance of such massive military aid to Israel? Ambassador Dinitz was very frank when he said to Kissinger:

"I must tell you: Our decision whether to start a new offensive or not depends on our power. We thought we would have by now in Israel the implements to do it – the bombs, the missiles etc.[11] "

So what Kissinger did was to mount a brilliant deception to gain time for the unprecedented re-supply of arms to strengthen the Israelis and ensure a different outcome of the war. This was how he described it:

"Informing Dinitz of our decision to operate the airlift <u>at maximum capacity and exclusively with American military planes,</u> I urged that Israel accelerate its military offensives so that they could be completed within forty-eight hours of the issue going to the Security Council – whenever that was. We could not stall much longer than that, and we would not be able to justify vetoing what many nations knew we had advocated a short time ago..."(Emphasis added)

What American had advocated was a ceasefire. But Kissinger wanted an Israeli advantage on the battleground first before pushing a ceasefire in the Security Council. If such a resolution was tabled before the massive airlift and the Egyptian army in a position of ascendancy, all would be lost for Zionist ambitions for the region. This was the dastardly act of Kissinger, yet in subsequent years, leaders of the Muslim *ummah* considered him to be an honest broker for peace in the Palestinian-Israeli conflicts.

So if Moshe Dayan, the then Defense Minister of Israel was prepared to let loose nuclear weapons, in the event the massive resupply would not check the Egyptian army, can we have any more doubts that Israel would resort to such weapons if their final push to fast forward their global agenda is being thwarted?

However, we should not be afraid of this eventuality. In fact from a strategic point of view, politically, such an action by the Israelis would ensure their ultimate isolation and defeat. **This is the strategic Israeli catch-22.** This is the main reason why the Zionist Anglo-American War Cabal is screaming and spreading the propaganda, firstly that Saddam Hussein and now Iran have weapons of mass destruction. And why they have goaded Georgie Boy Bush to pre-emptively attack Iraq and now are goading Georgie again to pre-emptively attack Iran. Their strategic thinking is this — in any nuclear war, Israel being a small piece of real estate and a small population (recall Kissinger's prognosis of the impossibility of overcoming a demographic imbalance of 30:1 against Israel) it cannot win such a war. Let's posit the scenario: Israel nukes Tehran, and there is a response, and Tel Aviv gets zap by whatever WMD, what then? Where is Israel going to nuke next, when the whole Arab Muslim world is on the boil? Cairo? Amman? Beirut? Damascus? Riyadh? Baghdad?

Given such a scenario, "suicide bombers" attacks in the past would be mere pin pricks, when compared to the human waves strapped with bombs and armed with every conceivable kind of weaponry ripping through the settlements all over Israel. Israel would be drenched in blood. Nuclear bombs will have no relevance in the Gaza, in the West Bank and in the very heart of Israel.

And do you know why? The pain threshold of the Palestinian is that point when pain has no meaning at all. At that point they have broken through the pain barrier and freedom beckons them. In death, they would be released from oppression and they know for certain, their death and sacrifice for final victory have assured their children and their children's children and all future generations their National Homeland and justice. And at last a new era of peace. That is why I said previously that when the deed is done and all is over, the World would bow in shame for turning its back on the Palestinians for over fifty years. This is one agenda.

There is another agenda. Think. What will be the pain threshold for the U.S.? Will it be the same as the Palestinians? Would the American people really get involved in a nuclear war started by the madman Sharon for a Zionist agenda that benefits no one, least the Americans thousands of miles away? Would they be willing to be nuked and or wiped out by some other lesser WMDs launched as an act of self-defense by the victims of the Zionist pre-emptive war, as the price for retaliating on behalf of Zionist Israel? If the U.S. nukes any country in a pre-emptive action in support of Israel, the U.S. would by any measure be committing suicide. The situation would not be one that will secure victory and or rescue Israel from the jaws of defeat. It would only accelerate the collapse of the Zionist Anglo-American Empire.

Like the earlier scenario for Israel, which city or country would the U.S. want to nuke? Riyadh? Beirut? Amman? Damascus? Cairo? Would the American people tolerate this madness? How would this madness serve U.S. interests?

It all finally boils downs to the ultimate **PAIN THRESHOLD!** If the Bush regime, acting recklessly for the Zionist Anglo-American War Cabal indulge in such brinkmanship, there would be a military coup in America and if that fails, rest assured there would be a Second American Revolution. And the good Professor Barnett's war-games based war strategies, would be jettisoned even before you could count up to one!

In such a scenario, where is the threat from the Gap and or the seam states?

Professor Barnett's Grand Strategy is indeed a **brilliant diversionary strategy** — to draw away the focus on the issues that threatens the Core's existence within the Core itself to some non-lethal threat (by any measure in military terms) from the Gap, exaggerated to the level of Force 10 or higher on the Richter scale.

From a purely military and strategic point of view, such attacks as the 9-11 on the twin towers serve no real purpose, if in fact it was planned by "Islamic Terrorists" (a theory which I do not for one moment subscribe). The "collateral damage" even if the number was much higher, was still within the U.S. pain threshold. Even Pearl Harbor, a military target did not in the long run affect the War's outcome in favor of Japan. Japan was suckered into attacking Pearl Harbor to whip up war hysteria to enable Roosevelt to railroad America into the War in Europe. The Zionist has already admitted that they were the mastermind behind this deception.

Obviously, if the military campaign on September 11, served another agenda, the pretext to launch World War IV, it was a brilliant strategy.

While the damage to the real estate was relatively costly, it hardly inflicted lasting damage to the financial system or the real economy. Recall that the New York Stock Exchange was up and running again within two weeks. The Military-Industrial Complex has been given a new lease of life and since then has raked in billions in war profits. I had already mentioned that Wall Street had already taken into account such a contingency and in fact wargamed on that premises, as admitted by Professor Barnett. The war games engineered by sophisticated computer programs funded massively by Cantor Fitzgerald initially, and other Wall Street heavy weights subsequently, laid the groundwork for the defense of such an eventuality.

The alleged Y2K threat was the biggest hoax perpetrated by the power elites. The whole exercise was a massive war game and it went on for almost a year. All possible outcomes were configured, tested and outcomes evaluated. They were confident that the system would be able to take a major hit and survived. But you see this was all on computers, like the computer games you buy from the shops. And like the pharmaceutical industry, there is a need to move from laboratory tests to clinical trials where humans will be the guinea pigs. The military campaign conducted on 9-11 was the equivalent of the pharmaceutical clinical trials, and I can assure you, the results matched all the outcomes of the war games to 0.000000000001 percent.

But, let's get back to Israel.

If there is no financial lifeline from the U.S. to Zionist Israel, the latter would be in deep shit. In fact, the Israeli economy is now in intensive care and that is why they had to send in the financial rescue A-Team in the person of Stanley Fisher, former Chief economist to the World Bank and deputy Managing Director of the IMF, to head the Bank of Israel.

In short, Israel is a financial liability and the U.S. military's Achilles Heel and that's where the Worldwide Resistance should focus their attention. We must now examine the various strategies and tactics available to the Worldwide Resistance to defeat the Zionist Anglo-American War Cabal! This we shall discuss in the next chapter.

ENDNOTES:

1. Please do not confuse this entity with America. This entity is beyond borders and is not confined to any borders. It answers to no one but itself.

2. See the incredible ground breaking and courageous work by Boyd E. Graves J.D., *State Origin:The Evidence of the Laboratory Birth of Aids*, (2001, National Organization for the Advancement of Humanity & Zygote Media)

3. Norman Podhoretz, "World War IV."

4. Denise Winn, *The Manipulated Mind: Brainwashing, Conditioning and Indoctrination*, (2000, Malor Books). See also John Marks, *The Search for the Manchurian Candidate: the CIA and Mind Control*, (1979, New York: W.W. Norton & Company) and Colin A. Ross MD, *Bluebird: Deliberate Creation of Multiple Personality by Psychiatrists* (2000, Manitou Communications Inc.)

5. Passage taken from *The Holy Qur'an: Text, Translation and Commentary* by Abdullah Yusuf Ali (Amana Publications, USA.)

6. Alfred M. Lilienthal, *What Price Israel?*, 50th Anniversary Edition. (2003, Infinity Publications)

7. (2003, Lawrence Hill Books). He is also the author of *Silent No More: Confronting America's False Images of Islam*, and *Deliberate Deceptions: Facing the Facts about the US-Israeli Relationship*.

8. Henry Kissinger, *Years of Upheaval*, (1982, London: George Weidenfield & Nicholson Ltd)

9. Ibid.

10. *We All Lost the Cold War* (1994, Princeton University Press) p. 189

11. Kissinger, *Years of Upheaval*, p. 512.

Part 5

The New Map
for the 21st Century —
But Not the Pentagon's

18

The House of Cards — All Deuces

For too long, the world wide resistance have been barking up the wrong tree. You will recall that in my introduction and subsequent chapters, I had highlighted that there is a WMD more power than any nuclear weapon ever created by rocket scientists. The world has experienced three World Wars, the First World War, World War II and the Cold War (which some political pundits have termed the Third World War). Each time, the basic political structure and the underlying economic system remained unaffected as a whole — Empire Capitalism.[1]

This is so basic and obvious, staring right into our eyes and yet we miss it time after time, because our attention and focus have always been diverted by some other irrelevant economic agenda conceived by the Zionist Anglo-American Financial Cabal, the sister of its war cabal. The two go hand in hand. Make no mistake about that. Recently, an obscure Malaysian economist was elevated to a key economic position at the United Nations. Take it from me there is an agenda here. A new spin will come out very soon on how the third world ought to reform its financial system allegedly from being a miserable country in the Gap to that of a proud country, an integral part of the Integrated Core. They think we are stupid and have short memories. The financial crisis of 1997 was a major campaign to destroy the targeted economies, and is still fresh in our minds, but more of that later.

Let's recap some basic ideas.

The essence of Empire Capitalism is economic plunder by wars of aggression. Financial plunder by hedge funds repre-

sents a new strategy. However, mobilization for imperial wars of aggression can only be sustained by a war economy. When we studied economics, we are taught that one fundamental economic principle is the need for effective utilization of economic and financial resources to produce goods and services for the growing economy. To put it simply, any misallocation will upset the apple cart and the economy will suffer bouts of inflation, severe unemployment etc. This is conventional wisdom in our textbooks, and up to a point is correct. The reality of a war economy is a different matrix altogether.

Tell me good professors at Harvard, Cambridge etc., why disproportionate allocation of finite resources for wars of aggression is good for any economy, if wars are not in the equation at all. I can accept a small but adequate allocation for the constabulary to maintain internal law and order, but massive allocation for war against manufactured enemies is plain daylight robbery for the war profiteers. Students, who have volunteered to undergo mental torture in these institutions, I would be most obliged if you could find for me a basic text book that examines critically this misallocation of resources to the Military-Industrial Complex and its effects on a national economy.

If this short but brutal awakening is not enough for you, wait till you get to the end of this chapter, when we examine leading luminaries of Empire Capitalism have to say on this issue. All writers on this issue, when confronted with such a challenge (to get the mind out of the proverbial strait jacket), have the difficulty of deciding where to kick off the debate. For me this is as good as any — the 1967 essay by Alan Greenspan, scion of the Zionist Anglo-American Financial War Cabal.

We are told that the present financial system is good for the world economy, engineered by brilliant minds on par with rocket scientist to meet the challenges of globalization (have to admit, these spin doctors are good. They can always conjure such macro images with just one word). These high priests of the financial world tell us, "Watch my lips — gold is not good for you. Fiat money is the way."

Is that correct? You be the judge.

I wonder how many have read, and if they had, still remember Alan Greenspan's essay, "Gold and Economic Freedom.[2]" I bet it never occurred to you to associate gold with freedom. Strange, how through indoctrination and mind manipulation, we often associate gold with pawn shops, money lenders, avarice and all things bad and ugly, when it should be associated with all things nice, sugar and spice — freedom!

So here we go, in Greenspan very own words. My comments are in brackets.

"An almost hysterical antagonism toward the gold standard is one issue which unites statists of all persuasions. They seem to sense — perhaps more clearly and subtly than many consistent defenders of laissez-faire — that gold and economic freedom are inseparable....

"Money is the common denominator of all economic transactions. It is that commodity which serves as a medium of exchange, is universally acceptable to all participants in an exchange economy as payment for their goods and services, and can, therefore, be used as a standard of market value and as a store of value, i.e. as a means of saving.

"The existence of such a commodity is a precondition of a division of labor economy. If men did not have some <u>commodity of objective value</u> which was generally acceptable as money, they would have to resort to primitive barter.... If men had no means to store value, i.e. to save neither long-range planning nor exchange would be possible." (Emphasis added)

[Gold is a commodity. Paper money is not a commodity. When this article was written, the world's reserve currency, the mighty U.S. dollar was backed by gold. So was the British pound until they screwed up. And later when the U.S. screwed up, they dumped the gold, but of this later.]

"What medium of exchange will be acceptable to all participants in an economy is not determined arbitrarily. First the medium of exchange should be durable. A metal is generally chosen because it is homogenous and divisible: every unit is the same as every other and it can be blended or formed in any quantity. Precious jewels for example, are neither homogenous nor divisible. More important, the commodity chosen must be a luxury. Luxury goods are always in demand and will always be acceptable. The term "luxury good" implies scarcity and high unit value.

301

"Since the beginning of World War I, it [i.e. gold] has been virtually the sole international standard of exchange. If all goods and services were to be paid in gold, large payments would be difficult to execute, and this would tend to limit the extent of a society's division of labor and specialization. Thus a logical extension of the creation of a medium of exchange is the development of a banking system and credit instruments (bank notes and deposits) which act as a substitute for, but convertible into, gold." (Emphasis added)

[This was the rationale for the convertibility and don't we ever forget this. And there is a further reason for this. See below. The next passage is crucial.]

"When banks loans money to finance productive and profitable endeavors, the loans are paid off rapidly... but when business ventures... are less profitable and loans slow to pay off, bankers soon find that their loans outstanding are excessive relative to their gold reserves, and they begin to curtail new lending... Thus, under the gold standard, a free banking system stands as a protector of an economy's stability and balanced growth."

[In simple terms, the bank's ability to create money and extend credit is limited and curtailed by the amount of gold reserves they have. This applies equally to Central Banks. On the international level, the effect is explained as follows.]

"Free international gold standard serves to foster a worldwide division of labor and the broadest international trade. Even though the units of exchange (the dollar, the pound, the franc, etc.,) differ from country to country, when all are defined in terms of gold the economies of the different countries act as one. Credit, interest rates, and prices tend to follow similar patterns in all countries.

For example, if banks in one country extend credit liberally, interest rates in that country will tend to fall, inducing depositors to shift their gold to higher-interest paying banks in other countries. This will immediately cause a shortage of bank reserves in the 'easy money' country, inducing tighter credit standards and a return to competitively higher interest rates again."

[Thus the gold standard also acts as a restraining factor, as in the case of banks, to discipline governments who are corrupt and who prints money inconsistent with the needs of the economy. If such governments are not restrained, the end result would be "banana republics."

The following passages have to be reproduced in full because Alan Greenspan himself realized the danger of the Fed and what harm it can do to the economy. This was before he sold his soul to Big Money on Wall Street.]

"But the process of cure was misdiagnosed as the disease: if shortage of bank reserves was causing a business decline — argued economic interventionists — why not find a way of supplying increased reserves to the banks as they never need be short! If banks can continue to loan money indefinitely — it was claimed — there need never be slumps in business. And so the Federal Reserve System was organized in 1913. It consisted of twelve regional Federal Reserve Banks... in addition to gold, credit extended by the Federal Reserve banks (paper reserves) could serve as legal tender to pay deposits."

[This resulted in paper money flooding the economy. The Great Depression was one of the major consequences and was graphically explained by Greenspan.]

"The excess credit which the Fed pumped into the economy spilled over into the stock market — triggering a fantastic speculative boom. By 1929 the speculative imbalances had become so overwhelming... that the American economy collapsed. Great Britain fared even worse... she abandoned the gold standard completely in 1931, tearing asunder what remained of the fabric of confidence and inducing a worldwide series of bank failures. The world economies plunged into the Great Depression of the 1930s.

"Under a gold standard, the amount of credit that an economy can support is determined by the economy's tangible assets, <u>since every credit instrument is ultimately a claim on some tangible assets</u>. But government bonds are not backed by tangible wealth, only by government's promise to pay out of future tax revenues, and cannot be easily absorbed by financial

303

markets. A large volume of new government bonds can be sold to the public at progressively higher interest rates. Thus, government deficit spending under a gold standard is severely limited." (Emphasis added)

[This one passage explains better than the rubbish that comes out of Wall Street Journal, the Economists, etc., of the problem faced by the present Bush regime. They can get away with such a huge deficit simply because there is no one who is willing to expose this fraud — borrowing with money created out of thin air, by a mere stroke of a pen, in extending credits, and the printing presses, as when the supply of paper money is increased.

And finally, Greenspan's punch line. His words, not mine.]

"The law of supply and demand is not to be conned. As the supply of money (of claims) increases relative to supply of tangible assets in the economy, prices must eventually rise. Thus the earnings saved by the productive members of the society lose value in terms of goods... In the absence of the gold standard, there is no way to protect savings from confiscation through inflation. There is no safe store of value. If there were, the government would have to make its holding illegal, as was done in the case of gold." (Emphasis added)

[This was done in America. Gold was outlawed by President Roosevelt.]

"If every one decided, for example, to convert all his bank deposits to silver or copper or any other good, and thereafter declined to accept check as payment for goods, bank deposits would lose their purchasing power and government created bank credit would be worthless as a claim on goods. This is the shabby secret of the welfare statists' tirades against gold. Gold stands in the way of this insidious process... If one grasps this, one has no difficulty in understanding the statists' antagonism toward the gold Standard." (Emphasis added)

I rest my case.

I would like to share something with you, notwithstanding it might nauseate you. But it is for your own good. You may just be able to save your entire savings, your matrimonial home and any other assets which are not at risk, at the moment.

The Big Boys have already prepared for this eventuality. Recall what I told you earlier — they have sold out, took their cash, converted them into safe assets, gave huge amounts of "a girl's best friend" to their girlfriends to buy their silence for now, and paid cash for their secret hideaway in some island. You would suppose that they might have had second thoughts about islands after the Asia Tsunami disaster, but fear not, plans for such contingencies would already be in place by now.

Something caught my eye way back in 2004 which confirmed the above scenario that the Big Boys in Wall Street have made preparations for the coming financial wipeout. In fact they wargamed it and analyzed all the possible outcomes. Here it is:

"In 1998, Thomas Barnett, an obscure Defense Department analyst,[3] *teamed up with senior executives at the Wall Street firm Cantor Fitzgerald LP to study how globalization was changing national security. One scenario they studied was a meltdown caused by the Y2K computer bug followed by terrorist attacks ..."*

This is a quote from an article from the Wall Street Journal, May 11, 2004. Take note, that Y2K was only one of the scenarios. There were other war games but those were not disclosed. Y2K was the biggest hoax in history, but it served its purpose, that is, to enable a worldwide war game to be conducted. And a great amount of the costs were, believe it or not, paid by the world's tax payers, because governments were hoodwinked to conduct extensive studies, etc. This is the last time I am going to say it. **Wall Street have wargamed all the meltdown scenarios and are prepared for it. If they were not, how could they have resume trading within two weeks of 9-11?**

Just imagine that your business was destroyed by Tsunami. All records wiped out, key personnel killed and financial data lost in Cyber space. Till today, after months, your business have yet to get back on its feet, what more up and running, which was what happened in Aceh, Indonesia, and many parts of South India and Sri Lanka. Let me say it here again, the coming global financial meltdown will dwarf Tsunami in terms of the scale of devastation. We are talking in trillions, not billions. This is a given.

But that does not mean that they can avert the coming disaster <u>if the worldwide resistance knows how to attack the system</u>. <u>Thus far the wounds were self-inflicted, the result of their own avarice and what Alan Greenspan called "the irrational exuberance</u>."

Wall Street is scared to death, if the system is attacked and is praying that no one knows the Achilles Heel of the system. You can stop reading the Wall Street Journal, the Financial Times and all the other leading financial news daily. You only get confused and out of focus. And talking to those who are of the intellectual bent, they have become so diffident, that they are thinking of going back to business school to catch up on new thinking and latest theories.

So let us move on.

The issue is not just the dollarization of the oil trade. Changing the currency of the trade to that of Euro and any other currency is **merely a short-term** measure to address the depreciating dollar, and a tactical response to the unilateralism of the United States. **Undoubtedly, it is the correct policy.** Of course it will have an impact. I am not denying this at all. That argument applies equally to the diversification of a country's reserve, now mainly denominated in U.S. dollar. Again, it will only address short and medium term issues.

The thing about falling in love with the Euro reflects a **major disconnect** — the failure to appreciate that the Euro serves the same function as the US dollar. It is also a fiat money. To drive home the point, I am going to be upfront and frank. It's like swapping a Dixie chick for a French poodle. So what! First we gambled with green chips (the greenback) and now we are gambling with blue chips (the Euro) but they are all plastic gambling chips! Fiat money is paper money. It is plastic chips!

In the long term it is jumping from the frying pan into the fire. Both belong to the same system, and the same system will continue to dominate our economies. If we do not address the systemic issues and analyze its fundamental weaknesses, in time the present Dollar problem will turn into the Euro problem. The European economy is also grounded on Empire Capitalism. But that does not prevent us from entering into temporary alliance, in the short to middle term to isolate the Bush regime. But let us not be naive as well. France and Germany and for that matter Russia has no real love for us. It is a matter of balance of power.

Only one world leader thus far had the courage and the tenacity to consistently call for the reform of the entire financial architecture. He is none other then the former Prime Minister of Malaysia, Tun Dr. Mahathir Mohamad. Alone he defied the international financiers and bankers to preserve the independence of Malaysia, the dignity and welfare of his people and beat off the attempts by foreign elements to oust him by way of a palace coup. Notwithstanding his recommendations to diversify dollar reserves, to end the dollarization of the oil trade, and the use of gold dinars for trade, Tun Dr. Mahathir Mohamad has been relentless in calling for a major overhaul of the world's financial system as the only viable solution to the financial chaos that is sweeping the globe. Long term problems demand long term solutions.

That is why I decided to quote at great length Greenspan's essay of 1967 as the starting point. His present cover-up does not invalidate the earlier exposure and the truth of the matter. In fact, it reinforces his earlier arguments, because nothing has changed since 1967. What has changed is the intense rivalry between the Maritime powers and the Continental powers. Applying dialectics, the present scenario within the Western world is one of "non-antagonistic contradictions within the First World." According to Zbigniew Brzezinski[4] a truly global power must dominate the entire Eurasian continent, which assumes that the "Old Europe" would just sit back and be dominated. Not likely!

However, the problem of fiat money has been compounded by the worldwide derivatives market. Warren Buffet in a letter dated March, 2003 to the shareholders of Berkshire Hathaway,[5] warned:

"Charlie and I are one mind in how we feel about derivatives and the trading activities that go with them: We view them as time bombs, both for the parties that deal in them and the economic system.... In our view, however, derivatives are financial weapons of mass destruction, carrying dangers that while now latent, are potentially lethal."

Derivatives trading system is the Achilles Heel of Empire Capitalism. The myth is that if you are not a rocket scientist, you can never understand this complex trading system. We are fortunate that we have Warren Buffet to explain to us in simple language. This is

307

how he explains it. My comments are in brackets.

"Essentially, these instruments call for money to change hands at some future date, with the amount to be determined by one or more referenced items, such as interest rates, stock prices or currency values. If, for example, you are either long or short an S & P 500 futures contract, you are a party to a very simple derivatives transaction — with your gain or loss derived from movements in the index. Derivatives contracts are of varying duration (running sometimes to 20 or more years) and their value is often tied to several variables.

"The range of derivatives contracts is limited only by the imagination of man (or sometimes, so it seems madmen). At Enron, for example, newsprint and broad band derivatives, due to be settled many years in the future, were put on the books. Or say you want to write a contract speculating on the number of twins to be born in Nebraska in 2020. No problem – at a price, you will easily find an obliging party."

[What Buffet is saying is that you can literally gamble on anything. The derivatives market is the biggest casino in the world. He also exposed Enron's fraudulent accounting — future unrealized earnings written into the books. He then explains how this can happen and why.]

"I can assure you marking errors in the derivatives business have not been symmetrical. Almost invariably, they have favored either the trader who was eyeing a multi-million dollar bonus or the CEO who wanted to report impressive 'earnings' (or both). The bonuses were paid and the CEO profited from his options. Only much later did shareholders learn that the reported earnings were a sham."

[Outright cheating. And the culprits are mainly the traders and CEOs who gets away with the money. This is trillion dollar casino market. Financial goons come to our country to demand transparency and what not, but back in their home country, they behave worst than crooks.

The next passage is a bit tricky technically but I need to quote it, because, it exposes another fraud technique. Bear with me.]

"Those who trade derivatives are usually paid (in whole or

part) on 'earnings' calculated by mark-to-market accounting. But often there is no real market (think about the contract involving twins) and mark-to-model is utilized. This substitution can bring on large scale mischief. In the twins scenario, for example, the two parties to the contract might well use differing models allowing both to show substantial profits for many years. In extreme cases, mark-to-model degenerates into what I would call mark-to-myth."

[What Buffet is saying is that because you can gamble on anything, there is no real market to evaluate the price. The expression "mark-to-market" means there is a real market. "Marking" means "pricing", thus, marking to market, means pricing according to the real market. So these gamblers create what is known as a model market, hence the expression, "mark-to-model." Therefore in a model market, you can conjure all kind of assumptions to justify a particular set of prices. But the fraud is in the accounting of it. In case of party A, he can tell his company that he will be making so much "earnings" based purely on his imaginary assumptions, and no one would be wiser and these assumptions would be different from the opposite party who is gambling within him. Just try and gamble on how many twins Nebraska will have in 2020. Such a situation is not unlike many of Enron's trades where you will have mythical prices. Hence, the expression, "mark-to-myth" — price according to myths!

Even banks are into these types of frauds, as observed by Buffet.]

"When Charlie and I finish reading the long footnotes detailing the derivatives activities of major banks, the only thing we understand is that we don't understand how much risk the institution is running. <u>The derivatives genie is now well out of the bottle, and these instruments will almost certainly multiply in variety and number until some event makes their toxicity clear. Central banks and governments have so far found no effective way to control, or even monitor, the risk posed by these contracts.</u>" (Emphasis added)___

[Major Banks are involved and I have enumerated them in Chapter 1, where I had revealed that exposures for these banks are in trillions. It is just not possible for them to settle these huge exposures. Buffet next explains the impact of the collapse of LTCM.]

"Indeed in 1998, the leveraged and derivatives-heavy activities of a single hedge fund, Long Term Capital Management, caused the Federal Reserve anxieties so severe that it hastily orchestrated a rescue effort. In later Congressional testimony, Fed officials acknowledged that, had they not intervened, <u>the outstanding trades of LTCM... could well have posed a serious threat to the stability of American markets. In other words, the Fed acted because its leaders were fearful of what might have happened to other financial institutions had the LTCM domino toppled. This was far from the worst case scenario....</u>" (Emphasis added)

The OCC Bank Derivatives Report for the 3rd Quarter of 2004, reported that the notional value of derivatives held by U.S. Banks rose to a record US$84.2 trillion (note: not billions but trillions) from $81 trillion in the 2nd quarter. The report stated that derivatives volumes continued to be dominated by interest-rate contracts, which grew $2.4 trillion during the quarter to $73 trillion or 87% of the total derivatives volumes. The total bank risk exposure through these financial instruments rose to $804 billion, up from the previous $752 billion.

However, something interesting is happening in the gold market. Although the price of gold has risen over the last two years, it does not reflect in any way its true value. If there were no manipulation in the market by the Rothschild control cartel, the price of gold would have rocketed to at least $1,000 per ounce. Why are they keeping the price as low as possible? Recall Greenspan's essay at the beginning of this chapter on the role of gold.

In summary, suppressing the price of gold has made it a cheap resource capital for the New York Bullion banks, which borrow it at very low costs, sometime as little as 1% of its value, per year. Bet you don't know about this. These banks borrow gold from Central Banks and are sold. The proceeds are then invested in all sorts of securities in the financial market, including derivatives that give a better return, i.e. more 1% per year. This is called in the trade as "Gold Carry Trade". If gold prices are allowed to sky rocket according to market forces, the effective interest rate of gold would not be 1% but very much higher. Therefore, when it suits them, these financial robbers demand a cartel market for control, and when they want to plunder new markets, they demand free access.

Additionally, keeping the price of gold artificially low, gives a false impression as to the real value and strength of the Dollar as a reserve currency. This is to induce the ordinary folks in believing all is hunky-dory and to have continued faith in paper money, fiat money. As stated earlier, if people lose faith, the US dollar is worthless – toilet paper will have better value. It is all a big con game. The gold market is rigged and that is why small investors running to gold as a shelter (which is a correct strategy, provided the market is not rigged) get clobbered time after time, in the result they lose confidence in gold as a store of value and hang on to toilet paper! According to GATA, too much gold is being consumed at too cheap a price and that massive amounts of derivatives are being used to suppress the gold price. If this situation is not corrected, there will be a derivative crisis which will add to the problems faced by the big banks. This is a double whammy of gigantic proportions.

There is therefore a currency war going on. It follows that if one of their strategies is to suppress gold prices to prop up dollar value artificially, then the opposite must hold true, accumulate gold to expose the weakness of the dollar. It is not enough to diversify into other currencies, as pointed out earlier. Diversifying into gold and silver is the key and will enable countries presently held to ransom by the weak dollar to better protect its reserves both in the short term and in the long run.

In conclusion to this discussion, I hope that I have made my point. LTCM is not even the worst-case scenario and it would have destroyed the entire American financial system. What if Citigroup or JPMorgan Chase suffered the same fate? Any more doubts that it would be a financial Tsunami?

Warren Buffet has warned that these are "financial weapons of mass destruction." Being an astute investor, the world's number one investor, if he had feared that the shift from dollar to euro in the oil trades would devastate the economy, he would have said so, but he has not. He has in fact as pointed out in Chapter I, diversified some of his dollar holdings. As long as the world needs the U.S. market for their exports, these trades will be in dollars. The dollar may even depreciate as much as 30-40 percent, it would not trigger the financial collapse of the U.S. The major financial institutions are controlled by the Zionist and they are most exposed here. If they collapse, even the Fed would not be able to mount a rescue. In the final analysis, that and that alone will usher in a new financial architecture, where gold will play a dominant role again.

Warren Buffet has pointed out to us in unambiguous terms, the Achilles Heel of the empire's financial system. It is not within the scope of this book to detail the mechanics of the trades that can trigger the time bomb. Suffice to say here that it would take no more than $500 million to bring the system down. I know, because I once talked to a team of financial wizards who told me that it can be done.

ENDNOTES:

1. The Soviet Empire and its economic system is the mirror image of Western Empire Capitalism.
2. This was written in 1967, when he was yet to be corrupted and lured by the cabal to do the dirty work at the Fed.
3. He's not obscure anymore. He is the good Professor that came out with the Grand Strategy to whack us.
4. *The Grand Chessboard: American Primacy and its Geostrategic Imperatives*, (1997, Basic Books)
5. Source: http://www.berkshirehathaway.com

19

Where Have All the BMWs, Mercs and Lexuses Gone?

Be prepared to ride bicycles. Yes, not even motorcycles, but back to the basic bicycles, and you can kiss goodbyes to the BMWs, Mercs, Lexuses, and gas-guzzler SUVs.

I am sorry to have spoilt your breakfast,[1] but the truth must be told. Let me share something with you about bicycles. Sometime back I came across a book[2] that set me awake the whole night. Scared the shit out of me! First reaction, screw the author, no way I am going to give up my turbo that zooms 0–100 in just under 6 seconds and, of course, a whole lot of gas. Scorching and burning rubber at 200 kph gives you a false sense of freedom but you come back to reality soon enough. The following evening, I picked up the book again and read it once more. Holy Smoke, that guy made a lot of sense! Since then I began to have more respect for bicycles — and it is sexy!

When cheap Russian oil was turned off after the collapse of the Soviet Union, something horrible happened to Cuba:

"Cuba has become an undeveloped country. Bicycles are replacing automobiles. Horse drawn carts replacing delivery trucks. Oxen are replacing tractors. Factories are shut down and urban industrial workers resettled in rural areas to engage in labor intensive agriculture. Food consumption is shifting from meat and processed products to potatoes, bananas and other staples.[3]"

Obviously, Cuba has recovered from those terrible days. My point is that, if Cuba which was not a first world country and its economy which was less dependent on oil had to go through such a traumatic adjustment, what more the industrialized countries and those recently developed countries who can now afford the luxury of consumerism.

Let me now gently walk you through the "Peak Oil" maze and try to make some sense to what I consider to be the number 1 resource issue of the 21st century. But let me first, set out straight away the parameters of my arguments. If the analysis of the leading experts is true then we are going to be up to our necks in deep shit. If, on the other hand, it is propaganda, another pretext (the economic equivalent of Pearl Harbor) to extend the present imperial plunder, we are also going to be in deep shit. Professor Barnett's "leviathans" will come to our countries to kick ass and get our oil as well!

Let's proceed.

According to Campbell, the world is **not running out of oil,** and not for a long time. **What is running out is cheap oil, and soon.** Relatively speaking, it will still be cheap to produce but it will **be expensive to buy** because it will be increasingly scarce and controlled by a few Middle East countries. Back in 1997, this guy saw it coming because he thought about it: *"I wonder if the US government would fire missiles at Iraq if it properly understood the resource constraints."* Wow!

Have I GOT your attention now?

Campbell goes on to say:

"Some may think that the end of cheap oil-based energy, which has fuelled our consumer age, is a Doomsday message. The Coming Oil Crisis will be just that because the transition will not be easy, but I sometimes think that the world needs a change in direction in any case. From the ashes of the oil crisis may arise a better and more sustainable planet. It must at least become more sustainable as Mankind lives out his allotted life-span in the fossil record. Whether or not it is better depends on how well we manage the transition. We don't have long to prepare."

So did this warning catch the attention of the Neocons, as Campbell wondered?

Matthew Simmons is the adviser to Dick Cheney, a member of

the top secret National Energy Policy Development Group (NEPDG), member of Council on Foreign Relations, and adviser to President George W. Bush. Therefore his views ought to grip our attention.

"Is peaking an important question or issue? First of all if you start out by saying usable energy is the world's most critical resource then obviously it is an important issue. Without energy we have no sustainable water, no sustainable food and no sustainable healthcare. <u>What peaking does mean, in energy terms, is that once you've peaked, further growth in supply is over.</u> So is this issue important, I think the answer is an emphatic yes. Why does this issue invoke such controversy? Well, I think for several reasons, first of all, the term "peaking" unfortunately, does suggest a bleak future. It also suggests high future energy prices and neither are pleasant thoughts. I think it is human nature, basically to say that we really like to have pleasant thoughts. The crying wolf is abandoned unless the wolf turns out to be already at the front door, and by then, the cry is generally too late. And crisis, are basically problems, by definition, that have been ignored. And all the great crisis were ignored until it became too late to do anything about it." (Emphasis added)

The world's greatest concentration of oil reserves is confined to a "golden triangle" running from Kirkuk, in Northern Iraq, through Iran to the United Arab Emirates, then west through Saudi Arabia's central oil fields, then northwards and back up to Kirkuk.

Matthew Simmons has warned that *"<u>the world has no plan B</u>."*

In a Report entitled "Strategic Energy Policy Challenges for the 21st Century", prepared by the Independent Task Force sponsored by the James A. Baker III Institute for Public Policy of Rice University and the Council on Foreign Relations, it was stated that:

"There are no easy Solomonic solutions to energy crisis, only hard policy trade-offs between legitimate and competing interests... strong economic growth across the globe and new global demands for more energy, <u>have meant the end of sustained surplus capacity in hydrocarbon fuels and the beginning of capacity limitations.</u>

"In fact, the world is currently <u>precariously close to utilizing all of its available global oil production capacity,</u> raising the chances of an oil-supply crisis with more substantial consequences than seen in three decades.

"Emerging technologies are <u>not yet commercially viable</u> to fill shortages and will not be for some time. Nor is surplus energy capacity available at this time to meet such demands. Indeed the situation is <u>worse than the oil shocks of the past because of the present energy situation.</u>

"These choices will affect other U.S. policy objectives: U.S. policy towards the Middle East; U.S. policy toward the former Soviet Union and China; the fight against international terrorism, environmental policy and international trade policy, including our position on the European Union (E.U.) Energy Charter, economic sanctions, North American Free Trade Agreement (NAFTA), and foreign trade credits and aid." (Emphasis added)

This document is a "must read" and if the worldwide resistance fails to grasp the implications of the conclusions stated in this report, we will not be able to have the relevant policy options to counter this threat to our societies.

The Report frankly admitted that any major disruption would cause catastrophic damage to the world's economy: an accident on the Alaska pipeline that brings the bulk of North Slope crude oil to market would have the same impact as a revolution cutting off supplies from a major Middle East producer. An attack on the California electric power grid could cripple the state's economy for years, affecting all of the economies of the Pacific basin. A revolution in Indonesia would paralyze the liquefied natural gas (LNG) import dependent economies of South Korea and Japan, affecting domestic politics and all of their trading partners. While oil is still readily available on international markets, prices have doubled from the levels that helped spur rapid economic growth through much of the 1990s. And with spare capacity scarce and Middle East tension high, chances are greater than at any point in the last two decades of an oil supply disruption that would even more severely test the nation's security and prosperity. The situation is, by analogy, like travelling in a car with broken shock absorbers at very high speeds such as 90 miles an hour. As long as the paving on the highways is perfectly smooth, no injury to the driver will result from the poor decision of not spending money to fix the car. But if the car confronts a large bump or pothole, the injury to the driver could be severe regardless of whether he was wearing seatbelts.

The authors and I do think alike in using analogies. So guys, stop complaining.

A. M. Samsam Bakhtiari of the National Iranian Oil Company at the ASPO Conference in Paris, May 2003 observed:

"In order to investigate the Middle East's long term production capacity, the forecast and scenarios developed by the following experts or institutions were reviewed: a) Dr. Campbell; b) the major international institutions (IEA, EIA, OPEC); c) the major oil companies; d) the major international banks; e) the specialized press; f) prominent economists and consultants; g) the simulations of the 'World Oil Production Capacity' (WOCAP) model. The most significant results were derived from Dr. Campbell's prediction and WOCAP model. Both of these show Middle Eastern producers going through a long 'bumpy plateau' between 2003 and 2020 with a gradual ramping down during the second decade. _____*

"And although the region's oil represents 40% of global reserves and roughly two thirds of proved reserves, there are limits to its output. For those believing, that for Middle East oil "sky is the limit," some shattering surprises might result over the next two decades."

We need also to consider non-OPEC oil supply. We can safely say that the good days are over for this sector. Two leading commentators[4] observed that there is little prospect for long term growth and a strong likelihood that over the next few years the trend will flatten and then decline irrevocably.

Although oil from the Caspian region loomed large in the Afghanistan War, the results from explorations have been rather disappointing. Kashagan, which is in a similar geological setting to the Tengiz oilfields was the promised mother lode, but having drilled three deep wells at great costs, the reserves are now estimated to be a fraction of its original estimates. This was discovered in the last 18 months. BP-Statoil has pulled out already.

To round up the debate on "Peak Oil" allow me to quote Richard Heinberg,[5] author of *The Party's Over — Oil, War and the Fate of*

Industrial Societies, who had summed up well the future scenario:

"Clearly we need to find substitutes for oil. But an analysis of the current energy alternatives is not reassuring. Solar and wind are renewable, but we now get less than one percent of our national energy budget from them; rapid growth will be necessary if they are to replace even a significant fraction of the energy shortfall from post peak oil. Nuclear power is dogged by the unsolved problem of radioactive waste disposal. <u>Hydrogen is not an energy source at all, but an energy carrier: it takes more energy to produce a given quantity of hydrogen than the hydrogen itself will yield.</u> Moreover, nearly all commercially produced hydrogen now comes from natural gas – whose production will peak only a few years after oil begins its historic decline. Unconventional petroleum resources — so-called 'heavy oil', 'oil sands', and 'shale oil' — are plentiful but extremely costly to extract, a fact that no technical innovation is likely to change.

"The hard math of energy resource analysis yields an uncomfortable but unavoidable prospect: even if efforts are intensified now to switch to alternative energy sources, after the oil peak, industrial nations will have less energy available to do useful work — including the manufacturing and transporting of goods, the growing of food, and the heating of homes.

"To be sure, we should be investing in alternatives and converting our industrial infrastructure to use them. If there is any solution to industrial societies' approaching energy crisis, renewables, plus conservation will provide it. Yet in order to achieve a smooth transition from non-renewables to renewables, decades will be needed — and <u>we do not have decades before the peaks in the extraction rates of oil and natural gas occur.</u> Moreover, even in the best case, the transition will require the massive shifting of investments from other sectors of the economy (such as military) toward energy research and conservation. And the available alternatives will likely be unable to support the kinds of transportation, food, and dwelling infrastructure we now have; <u>thus the transition will entail an almost complete redesign of industrial societies."</u>
(Emphasis added)

The future scenario will be bloody, as resource wars will multiply and escalate. Paul Wolfowitz said as much at the 2003 Asian Security Conference:

"For reasons that have a lot to do with the U.S. government bureaucracy, we settled on the one issue that everyone could agree on: weapons of mass destruction ... Look, the primary difference – to put it a little too simply – between North Korea and Iraq is that <u>we have virtually no options with Iraq because the country floats on a sea of oil</u>." (Emphasis added)

In anticipation of the need for such wars, the U.S. must secure the sea-lanes and "swing oil producing countries." This explains Paul Wolfowitz statement in Singapore for the need to redeploy their Far East and Pacific armed forces. It is my belief that **Singapore will be converted into an Island Aircraft Carrier.** For all intent and purposes this has already taken place. From this vantage point, the U.S. will intimidate the ASEAN oil producing countries in the South China seas – especially the contested areas of the Spratly Islands. Singapore will be the U.S. dagger and Australia its strategic rear in this new theatre of war. The U.S. will have Australia as the Deputy Sheriff directing Singapore, the local policeman. As a result of the Tsunami disaster, the U.S. by stationing troops under the pretext of aid to Aceh has found a back door to controlling the northern choke point of the Malacca Straits. In the circumstances, the stability of Myanmar will be an important staging area, to counterbalance U.S. intentions in this area. With respect I disagree with the present ASEAN's policy to force a situation in Myanmar whereby the government is made to accommodate U.S. interests via the surrender of power to the opposition parties. Singapore is in a very strong position to control the southern choke point. The reclamation works around the islands of Singapore should be viewed as serving this strategic purpose. Malaysia will be squeezed from three sides, north, West and South. All major ports of Malaysia's are located along the West coasts. Just look at the map!

Have Malaysia and Indonesia (targeted Muslim states as admitted by Professor Barnett) adopted the correct response and policies to address this potential and growing threat to their sovereignty and resources? The history of U.S. domination and control via CIA of Indonesia's domestic politics will be a severe challenge to its people who are still recovering from the 1997 financial crisis and the Tsunami disaster. Sadly, for them the options are few. The only consolation is that this time round, the people are better informed and central control is not as absolute as before. In the case of Malaysia, continuation of Tun Dr. Mahathir Mohamad administration's policies in the critical areas will enable Malaysia to be adequately prepared for the anticipated scenario. The present administration has pledged that it will continue with the previous administration's policies, and adapting, when necessary, to changes in circumstances. Singapore has already made its intentions clear and has made its moves. Malaysia must be vigilant. Singapore has put its feet inside the gate. When the U.S. unleashed the coming resource wars in this part of the world, we must not have "enemies within our gates!"

"The Road to Beijing is Through Kuala Lumpur" and the preferred path at this stage is through infiltration of the financial and corporate sectors, Malaysia's weakest link in its Chain of Defense. When Tun Dr. Mahathir Mohamad defeated the international financial war cabal, during the Asian Financial Crisis, the Zionist international financiers realized that any future subversion of Malaysia must begin with this sector. On the previous occasion, because of the determined and resolute leadership by the administration, subversion by corruption of financial and corporate leaders was very difficult. They almost succeeded. They are having a second go and testing whether the previous resistance was collective and systemic or merely the resilient and determined leadership of an individual.

Malaysians have to ask two simple questions: "In the event of any U.S. aggression in whatever form against Malaysia, can you count on Singapore to be on your side as an ally? What was your experience during the 1997 financial crisis? Obviously, Malaysia's response will depend on the answer to the two questions.

And so long as ASEAN members stick together on the broad issues and Malaysia makes use of the opportunity as the current Chair of the Nonaligned Movement (NAM) and the Organization of Islamic Conference (OIC) to rally the entire Muslim *ummah* there is hope and Malaysia will not be an easy meat to chew up. Having resolved its domestic agenda in 2004, Malaysia must move on vigorously in 2005 in the international arena to secure a minimum platform for adoption by members of the UN not to condone any military action allegedly to prevent the proliferation of weapons of mass destruction, and that any nation which allows its territory and airspace and or agreed to send its armed forces in aid of any unsanctioned military action by the Security Council, is deemed to have committed war crimes in like manner as the country that has launched an illegal war.

The force of international law must be brought to bear on any country that has waged a war of aggression. And together with any country that aids and abets such aggression they must be brought before a War Crimes Tribunal immediately when the act of aggression is being committed.

I am in total agreement with Professor Barnett for the rules of the game to be changed. The international community must establish new "Rule Sets" (to borrow the Professor's terminology) to punish any player that commits war crimes. The punishment is simple. By collective agreement announced through the United Nations General Assembly, not the Security Council (as it will be scuttled by the veto power) the world must declare that the offending nation's currency is no longer recognized as "legal tender" for trade. I term this initiative **"THE CURRENCY SANCTIONS."** The issue here is not whether it can be enforced, but the potential damage to the financial markets of the offending nations; that such a resolution would even come before the General Assembly. Confidence in the reserve currency and allied currencies will plummet. This is "People's Power" in international relations.[6]

When a nation is in debt and needs to import massive amounts of goods, for too long, the conventional wisdom has it that because the country is the buyer, it calls the shots. Absolute rubbish!!! It is a seller's market when the buyer is in debt. Examine this fundamental Principle of Bargains at the micro level, and you know it is true.

The Zionists did that, when they launched a worldwide boycott of German goods just before the Second World War, as a leverage to impose their Zionist Agenda on Germany. Germany succumbed. The Zionist did not even have Israel yet, but mobilize they did and it was bloody effective. Just the Muslim *ummah* alone, imposing this **"TRADE-CUM-CURRENCY SANCTION"** will ensure that the myth is forever punctured. The Emperor will be exposed as having no clothes. If there is one thing that I wish most to come out of this book, in the short to mid term is that **THE CURRENCY SANCTION** initiative will be considered and pursued with vigour. The Zionist Anglo-American Empire has tried to wipe us out through the immense power of the hedge funds. All we had were defensive measures like **CAPITAL AND EXCHANGE CONTROLS.** We did not have any offensive instruments with which to counter-attack. **THE CURREN-CY SANCTION INITIATIVE** is the offensive weapon and it is the flip side to the Hedge Fund's strategy to depreciate currencies by massive sell-down. While this hedge fund strategy requires huge capital, our offensive campaign is essentially psychological warfare by the Third World Collective. Such a campaign in conjunction with the **DERIVATIVES GUERRILLA WARFARE** (discussed in Chapter 18) would cost less then $500 million.

Recall, the small country Malaysia being bullied by "Mother England" two decades back. When Malaysia responded by adopting the policy "Buy British Last" the critical financial and commercial establishments that have billions at stake in the Malaysian trade disassociated themselves from the bully policies of Margaret Thatcher and went to the extent of putting out full page advertisements in the leading national dailies to emphasize the point. The sovereignty and dignity of Malaysia was restored. Subsequently a new sense of mutual respect and equality governed future relations. A simple **ANNOUNCEMENT by Tun Dr. Mahathir Mohamad** and the shock waves were felt immediately 13,000 miles away.

It is the ultimate poker game and George Bush knows it. Any disruption in supplies, meltdown takes place. Are you really saying that it can't be done? Why, is bad boy Bush going to nuke every trading nation? He will be impeached within a week and thrown out of office, or a coup will see to it that sanity prevails.

These are legitimate counter measures and within the ambit of international laws. In any event, trade is a two-way relationship. The buyer need not buy the oil, the computer chips, and the whole range of consumer goods at bargain prices at Wall Mart, sourced from the third world, if he doesn't want to. After all the buyer tells everyone that he wants free trade and free markets. Right! He is free to buy and the third world is free to sell at the price and the currency for the bargain.

Think through before dismissing it with a wave of a hand.

I have engaged in international trades over the years, importing and exporting and choice of currency is always an option not the rule. It's negotiable. Oil is already beginning to be traded in Euros and countries are diversifying their foreign reserves. It depends on the circumstances and who has a better leverage. In the past decades, exploiting the anxieties of the Cold War, America was able to compel countries to adopt the mighty dollar as the currency for trade, in exchange for its protection. Half of the world's exports were denominated in dollars and two thirds of all official exchange reserves were likewise in dollars. But with the coming of age of the Euro, a new equation has emerged. This is because the Euro-Zone has a bigger share of global trade than the U.S. And while the U.S. has a huge current account deficit with no foreseeable reduction in the near future, at least a decade and the Euro-Zone having a more balance account, exchange risks will weigh in heavily. One of the arguments for the dollarization of oil is that the U.S. is a major importer, despite being a major producer. However, this is a skewered view, because looking at the statistics Euro-Zone is a bigger importer of oil and petroleum products than the U.S.

The weak link in the Defense Chain of the Bully is that the Bully (the regime) is not the buyer. It's the hard working people and corporations that are paying through letters of credit, money transfer, bills of exchange, etc., from Arizona, from Wyoming, from California, from Florida, from New York, etc. They are doing the trades.

The more the U.S. insists on acting unilaterally, the more so we should use all the avenues of the United Nations General Assembly as a tactical convenience, to isolate the Zionist Anglo-American agenda. That is why one of my prescriptions is to impose **CURRENCY SANCTIONS,** a unique but effective global **weapon of mass destruction.** The worldwide resistance must make it known to the Zionist Anglo-American War Cabal that they are not immune to pain, that they too have a **PAIN THRESHOLD** and we know how to trigger that switch. And just as Professor Barnett recommended to the Pentagon's Brass, that they must fight fire with fire, so must we. We too have "virtually no option" but to defend ourselves when the Zionists have made their intentions clear. We have no nuclear, chemical and/or biological weapons at all. In addition they have the hedge funds, the financial mercenaries. We now have our equivalent.

Can you see the links in the gravy chain? If the importer cannot get his imports, his wholesaler cannot get his imports, the factory cannot get its imports, goods cannot be produced; when the retailer

323

cannot get the imports, the consumers get zilch! Ouch! Then grand-ma gets annoyed — Bully Bush will be out of the equation.

When you are being whacked, should we not also adopt Madeleine Albright's advice that it is no use talking about the superb U.S. military, and not use it. It is no use having such weapons in our hands if we do not deploy it in legitimate defense and counterattack **if and when we are attacked. We will not follow Bush and pre-cipitate pre-emptive actions. We do not accept the Hobbesian logic, but when they want to devour us, we shall respond accordingly and with deliberation and resoluteness.** The alter-native is surrender and total submission. This is the choice which the world wide resistance must decide. **It is not a call that I can make. I am just laying down the cold hard options, like Professor Barnett.**

To borrow Bush's expression, it is about time, someone "put all the options on the table." For too long, the leaders of the Third World and the Muslim *ummah* have been playing tweeddledee, tweeddle-dum with the perpetrators of State Terrorism at the expense of more then 500,000 Iraqi children and thousands more in the occupied Palestine slaughtered by the Butcher Sharon. I say enough is enough to State Terrorism.

ENDNOTES:

1. Would you believe it, I wrote this chapter at 5.30 a.m., while having my breakfast too?
2. C. J. Campbell, *The Coming Oil Crisis*, (1997, Multi-Science Publishing Company)
3. M.Falcoff, "Cuba in Our Mind", National Interest, 1995, quoting Preeg & Levine, 1993.
4. C. J. Campbell, *The Coming Oil Crisis*, citing Maarten van Mourik & Richard K. Sheperd, "Non-OPEC Oil Supply: Economic and Policy Option"
5. 2003, New Society Publishers. He is also the author of *Power Down: Options and Actions for a Post Carbon World,* (2004, New Society Publishers).
6. See further discussion in the next chapter and America's aversion of the UN, and why.

20

The Bogus War on Terrorism

We live in a dangerous world — "a world threatened by terrorists, in particular Muslim Terrorists. Islam is the ideology that drives these wretched militants." This is the warped message and image that the Zionist spin doctors have planted in the minds of anyone who reads any newspaper or watches the television, since September 11. **We have also discovered a new Axis of Evil.**

How did the Zionists score such a dramatic victory in the psychological warfare against Islam? The following analysis seeks to answer the question.

For the good part of fifty years post-World War II, we had the Cold War (World War III) and Communism was public enemy number one, **the evil** that must be wiped out. The Soviet Union was labeled the **'Evil Empire'** by President Ronald Reagan. Wars, brutal wars were waged in the name of freedom and democracy, with millions slaughtered, invariably the civilians of the target country. The Vietnam War was the ultimate proxy war fought allegedly between forces of good against the forces of evil. It was also a war that was projected as one between "believers" (the so call democratic Christian West) and the "atheists" (the Yellow Communist hordes of the East). More bombs were dropped in Vietnam than in the whole of World War II, yet the US and her assembled allies failed to defeat a peasant army.

The West was traumatized and lost its moral compass with the defeat of the United States in Vietnam. But proxy wars continued in Africa, South America and Middle East, to perpetuate the imperialist agenda that the war against evil and non-believers must continue.

However, with the collapse of the Soviet Union and her satellites, **'Western Moral Superiority'** was resurrected. One would have thought that with the end of the Cold War, world peace would ensue. It was not to be. The fact that there was no lasting peace ought to have triggered alarm bells, but the Third World was so brainwashed, that they could not comprehend that **wars and hegemony are the essential nature of Empire Capitalism, Imperialism and Colonialism.** It is indeed incredible that so many third world leaders and thinkers of all hues take the view that Western democracies and their values are the guardians of peace and prosperity, notwithstanding the **declared intentions** of the Imperialist powers throughout the ages.

What is more incredible in the present context is the attitude of the so-called "moderate" Muslims (whatever that means) who pin their faith and hopes on Western regimes to win the so-called "War on Terrorism". Uncritically, they rally behind the United States and Britain to wage a War on Terrorism. September 11 was sufficient justification to embark on this new crusade against the **Evil of the 21st century — Terrorism.** The term "crusade" has since been abandoned by President Bush, but not the intent. **It is as if terrorism did not exist prior to September 11.**

How the third world in general and the Muslim countries in particular can be so naive to believe that the War on Terrorism is anything but **the cover for renewed Zionist Anglo-American Imperialist aggression against resource rich third world countries?**

Leaders of Muslim countries strived to out perform each other in waging the heinous War on Terrorism and exhibit the credentials that they are "moderate" and civilized in the hope that they may find favor with the United States and other Western regimes, thus securing their very own survival. **In this cesspool of deceit and hypocrisy, the corruption of Islam and the betrayal of the *ummah* by its leaders are being perpetuated.**

The Muslims in general and the Arabs in particular are in a state of frustration and impotence and despair. It need not be so as lessons can be learned from the successful struggles of other people in the recent past.

Why is it that during the Vietnam War, the People's Liberation Army (PLA) was only derogatorily referred to as "Vietcongs" and not terrorists when they inflicted more than 50,000 fatalities and a quarter million wounded on the American forces? **More than a million civilians were killed during the war by the United States.**

It may be that the Vietnamese was fighting a "War of Liberation" and therefore a "Just War". Though the US puppet regime's first President (Diem) was a Catholic and the majority of the people were Buddhist, **religious overtones was absent, notwithstanding US attempts to manipulate the issue.**

It is equally obvious that had the Vietnamese lost the war, they would have been labeled "Communist terrorists", "insurgents", "diehard followers of Ho Chi Minh," etc., and war crime tribunals and show trials would have been the order of the day!

What lessons can the *ummah* learn from this heroic experience of the Vietnamese people?

Why is it that the Serb and Croatian armed forces and para-military units that committed ethnic cleansings and genocide against the Bosnians were not referred to as "terrorists?" The leaders who were captured were accused of committing war crimes but were given the benefit of a trial to prove their innocence. Somehow the heinous crimes of war criminals are a notch lower in the scale of criminality so as to be distinguished from that of **'real terrorists', Muslim terrorists, in particular 'suicide bombers.'** Why do we uncritically accept this labeling of the heroic fighters of the Palestinian Liberation Armed Forces. They don't have planes, tanks and drones to deliver the bombs and missiles. So they deliver themselves. What is the difference between a pilot on a mission to deliver bombs, knowing that he will get killed when his plane is shot down, or a battalion is commanded to charge the enemy's lines during a war? The soldiers obey knowing that they will be killed. Are not these soldiers committing "suicide"? **Yet this kind of imperialist logic is accepted without more!** And our mass media day in, day out repeat this heinous logic thus supplanting Zionist propaganda.

Afghans and other nationals captured and incarcerated in the Guantanamo Bay military camp are referred to variously as "terrorists" and "enemy combatants" not "Prisoners of War" (POWs) and denied of all judicial process and subjected to torture. **More than 8 thousand Afghan civilians died when the US sought revenge for September 11.**

What lessons can the *ummah* learn from this terrifying experience?

Why is it that the Japanese who raped and massacred more than 500,000 Chinese civilians in the *Rape of Nanking* and Manchuria during World War II were never referred to as "terrorists"? It may be that Japan was rehabilitated by the U.S. after the war and her war criminals recruited to serve the wider interest of the West to contain the then "New Evil" — Communist Russia and China. The Japanese hordes that destroyed Pearl Harbor were transformed overnight into 'strategic allies'. **Evil, like beauty, is in the eyes of the beholder.**

What lessons can the *ummah* learn from this Imperialist whitewash?

In spite of the pain and suffering, the humiliation and wanton destruction at the hands of the Americans and the Japanese, the Vietnamese and Chinese people did not seek revenge, though victorious. They maintained their humanity and dignity. In the course of their struggles for liberation, they did not dwell on past humiliations and defeats and or past glories. National liberation and salvation drove them to overcome all odds, **not perverse religious hangups.**

The clarion call to action was not and never was, 'Taoists Unite' or 'Buddhists Unite'. Being victims of rape and plunder by Christian Imperialists, they knew only too well that religion can be corrupted to serve different agendas and is **inherently divisive,** as all major religions are splintered in one form or another.

What lessons can the *ummah* learn from this historical past?

States condemn the use of terror when directed at them but justify the use of terror against all and sundry when its monopoly of power is threatened. Somehow terrorism by non-state organizations is more heinous and grotesque than state terrorism. **What perverse logic!** But this is the logic that finds favor with the third world, notwithstanding the fact that their people are being oppressed, impoverished and plundered.

Terror is a **method of warfare** throughout the ages, and the weapon of first choice by imperialist powers.

Only the gullible accepts the proposition that only armies are engaged in wars, not civilians. And only the blind fails to see that in **all wars,** the **civilians** are always the main **casualty.** No wars can be conducted successfully without the fullest support of the public (civilians). This is trite. When civilians are demoralized and withdraw their support, no army can sustain a war. The U.S. defeat in the Vietnam War is the case in point. **Hence, the need to terrorize and demoralize the civilians.**

All wars target civilians, and the weapon of choice is **terror.** And all wars have always been fought on the footing of "Good versus Evil" whichever side one belongs. **The victorious will always justify that all means are legitimate to defeat evil, whereas the defeated will have to suffer the fate of being labeled 'war criminals', 'terrorists' and 'criminals.'**

Consider:

The 'Shock and Awe' terror campaign in the recent Iraq War. More bombs were dropped in the first three days than the entire First Gulf War. The authors of this strategy were forthright in declaring that the stated purpose was **to terrorize the Iraqi people.**

The indiscriminate use of 'Mother of All Bombs" (the 15,000 lbs Daisy Cutter) in the recent Afghan war against the Talibans in Tora Bora. **The crater is the size of a football field.**

The 'Target Killings' of Palestinians in Gaza and the West Bank. **The demolition of homes by bulldozers and burying alive the inhabitants.** However, Israel is hailed as the only democracy in the Middle East.

The blanket shelling and bombing with Depleted Uranium in the first Gulf War. **Napalm bombs, Cluster bombs and anti-personnel bombs are intended to demoralize the surviving soldiers and families of the victims when exposed to the mangled bodies.**

The ethnic cleansing campaign by Serbs against the Bosnians in the then Yugoslavia. **Old and young slaughtered and buried in mass graves.**

Carpet bombings by B52 bombers from 60,000 feet high over towns and villages during the Vietnam War. **Total destruction of villages and rice fields. Unexploded ordinance continue to kill and maim civilians when accidentally triggered off by children till today.**

The My Lai Massacre and the CIA's Operation Phoenix in Vietnam and Cambodia. **An entire village massacred by a platoon of US Marines. Death-squads dispatched to hunt down civilians supporting liberation fighters.**

V-2 rocket attacks on Coventry and other British cities by Nazi Germany. **The Coventry Cathedral was totally destroyed. Saturation bombing was a daily occurrence and was called the 'Blitz.'**

The total destruction and wasting of Stalingrad and Leningrad on the Eastern Front by Nazi Germany. **The two cities were reduced to rubbles.**

The rape and massacre of Nanking and Manchuria by Japanese Imperial army. **Over 500,000 adults and children were murdered.**

The total destruction of German cities and towns by Allied forces in the closing stages of World War II. **Revenge was sweet for the Allied forces, but terror no less.**

The Nuclear destruction of Hiroshima and Nagasaki, the **most horrendous mass killing in the history of mankind.**

The pogroms by the Zionist Stern Gang and Irgun against the Arabs during the time of the British Protectorate of Palestine. **But Ariel Sharon and all previous Israeli prime ministers are men of peace.**

The use of mustard gas against the Iraqis by the British in the 1920s. **Saddam Hussein is evil. The British....?**

Civilians were the main collateral damage in all the above examples.

Suicide bombers — **mosquito bites in comparison.**

Yet in all the above examples, the perpetrators were never referred to as "terrorists" notwithstanding their weapon of choice was "terrorism." But the victims who defended and counter-attacked, are labeled terrorists and condemned as such.

Interestingly, all the major combatants who were engaged in the abovementioned terror tactics other than Germany and Japan have always referred themselves as "Allied Forces", a positive connotation.

Consider the Following Terms:

The Allied Forces
The Coalition of the Willing
We must defeat the perpetrators of evil
Freedom Loving People
Democratic Forces
Self Defense Force *(even when engaged in wars of aggression)*
Jewish Settlers *(not unlawful occupiers)*
Peace Loving people
Peacekeeping Force
Government/Administration

Contrast:

Axis Army
Terrorists
Muslim militants
Remnants
Diehards
Extremists
Fundamentalists
Insurgents
Common criminals
Murderers
War Criminals
Tyrants
Regime
Rogue States
Axis of Evil
Evil Empire
The Palestinian Question *(Can a people struggling for Liberation be reduced to a Question?)*

The world grieved for the victims of September 11. More recently, the world was invited to observe the Day of Mourning in Italy and Spain when 14 Italians and 7 Spanish aggressors were killed in Iraq. But the Iraqis and Palestinians cannot even bury their dead.

Mass media of the Muslim countries, uncritically parrots or adopts all the above derogatory terms when reference is made to the armed struggle of the heroic people of Iraq and Palestine for liberation! **Yet Muslims the world over moan and groan that they have been labeled unfairly!!!**

331

How strange that Muslim media does not consider the Palestinian fighters as "National Liberation Fighters" nor the killing of Palestinians as genocide. While attempts have been made to indict Ariel Sharon as a war criminal in the West, not one Muslim country has the courage to establish a War Crimes Tribunal against the Zionist murderers and the War Cabal of the Neocons along the lines of the Bertrand Russell's War Crimes Tribunal during the Vietnam War. Progressive American citizens, the likes of Ramsay Clarke and Senator Byrd even have the moral courage to refer the acts of the Neocons as war crimes. But leaders of the Muslim world find comfort in a vigil of pathetic silence.

Young intelligent Christian youths have volunteered to go to Rafah, Jenin, Nablus and confront head on the bulldozers, snipers and tanks of the Israeli armed forces in solidarity with the Palestinians.

Some have already paid with their lives – recently one American girl was ran over by a bulldozer and buried alive and in another incident, a British youth was shot in the head. However, Muslim youths in general are content to participate in the occasional demonstrations and the solicitation of donations. I still recall when at the age of 18, participating in anti-war campaigns in Europe and when the world's youths rallied to oppose the war in Vietnam, Muslim youths were conspicuously in the minority or absent!

The Vietnam experience is before their very eyes, but the *ummah* refuses to learn the lessons paid in blood.

"War on Terrorism" — what a misnomer! How can terrorism be the 'enemy' and or the 'evil' that needs to be defeated? Terrorism **is not** an entity, a state or an ideology. It is a **method,** more precisely a method of warfare that has been in use since time immemorial! **It is an essential part of warfare.** Anyone who says otherwise knows nothing about warfare, weapons of war and the reasons for war. I had earlier cited various examples of the use of terror in the major conflicts of the 20th and 21st century. **Terrorism can never be defeated, since it is a method of choice in warfare.**

The fact that Muslim countries have been rather reticent in condemning state terrorism (but all too eager to hunt down non-state agents of terror) reflects clearly the political reality. **States are founded on the exclusive right to employ violence in all forms,** including the right to kill. This is fundamental to state power. They also employ religion, ideology and laws to demonize and de-legitimize any recourse to violence by non-state agents or organizations. When a state employs the instruments of violence against its own population, we call it tyranny. When a state relies on instruments of violence against another country, we justify it as defending national security, another oppressor's logic.

"If you kill one person, it is murder. If you kill a hundred thousand, it is foreign policy." —Anonymous

The caption itself, "War on Terror" is but a propaganda sound bite and serves the purpose of pre-empting the psychological war that is required to defeat the **intended enemy** — in the present context, Muslim nations rich in oil reserves.

To a large extent, the Muslim countries have already lost the psychological warfare, as the mindset has been established — **The US and Britain are fighting terrorists. Those who are opposing them regardless of their circumstances are terrorists and will be labeled as such.** The resistance to the unlawful war in Iraq from the outset has been stigmatized as being illegitimate, for the simple reason that the US and Britain have been cast as the "good guys." When the mass media of Muslim nations adopt the propaganda sound bites of the Western controlled media (as illustrated above), there is no way in the short to middle term that the heroic people of Iraq and Palestine can cast off the unjust 'terrorist' label. To date it has been exposed that the Iraq War was planned well before September 11 and the latter was the mere excuse to wage an imperialist war to secure oil for the United States, **but more importantly to implement Zionist agenda for the Middle East, under the guise of fighting terrorism**. If there was no Osama Bin Laden, the US would have invented one. Yet instead of resisting Imperialist conquest, Muslim leaders are rallying their people to fight a War on Terrorism for and on behalf of President Bush and his war cabal!

Have we learned nothing from the Vietnam War?

From the very beginning, when they were only a ragtag collective of fighters, the Vietnamese always referred to their military organization as the 'National Liberation Army' in all their propaganda machinery. In the result, two armies were squared off against each other. Hence, when the US used terror attacks and invited similar counter-attacks, they could not whine and complaint. Both sides knew that ultimately who gets labeled as "terrorists" and or "war criminals" depended upon who won the war. The Vietnamese never let the world forget that they were fighting a war of liberation and their army was a Liberation Army.

The war criminals, Nixon and Kissinger did not agree to any peaceful settlement of the Vietnam conflict until the tide of war turned against the United States. The Paris Peace Talks was the US exit strategy when her terror campaign failed to intimidate the Vietnamese people and when her armed forces suffered horrific and mounting casualties. It is trite to state that no aggressor or occupying power would relinquish the fruits of war.

In 1971, Anwar Sadat offered a Peace Treaty to Israel, but the United States (in particular Kissinger) counselled Israel to reject the offer. Yet in 1973, after the October war, when the Israeli army was nearly annihilated, did Israel agreed to a peace treaty with Egypt on terms less favorable than in 1971. Even then, it was secured under the protection of the US Nuclear umbrella and continued military assistance for Israel.

Given the above scenario and the avowed aim of the present American administration to implement the **National Security Strategy** — the use of military might to maintain world hegemony for and on behalf of Zionism, Muslim nations and the *ummah* will not have peace if they continue to rely on the false promises of the US, her Western allies and corrupt Muslim states.

What a bleak picture!

What is the strategy for victory?

Stop Corrupting Religion!

How can we stop the corruption of religion? Most of the major religions are divided into two main schools of thought (e.g. Catholics v Protestants; Sunnis v Shiites, etc.,) each asserting that they represent the correct interpretation of the original teachings. What constitutes the Original Teachings? Debate abounds. In the next chapter we will discuss how the Zionists are using this divide to secure their objectives.

To frame the proposition in the proper perspective, I invite Muslims, Hindus and Buddhists, etc., to ask Christians: **"What are** the essentials of Christianity?" I can assure my Muslim friends that the answer will be as diverse as the pebbles to be found on a beach.

My Christian friends have debated on this and here are some sample responses:

"It is the Ten Commandments."
"The Sermon on the Mount by Jesus."
"The Holy Trinity — The Holy Father, The Son and the Holy Spirit."
"The Immaculate Conception of Jesus."
"Jesus' death and his Resurrection."
"Love thy Neighbor."
"A combination of the above."

I am sure that my Muslim friends will have as diverse a response as that of my Christian friends when invited to debate what constitutes the original teachings of Islam. Debating what constitutes the essentials of any given religion can itself be divisive. If the world cannot agree on such mundane matters as to which is more important, the singer or the song, the lyrics or the tune, how can communities agree with confidence on matters relating to religion. **We should adopt a more pertinent and pragmatic approach to understand how a given religion is corrupted to serve the interest and agendas of Zionism, Imperialism, and Colonialism.**

An ideology or teaching is corrupted for a particular purpose. **The usual argument put forward is that the end justifies the means.** Thus we have the spectacle of some anti-abortionists (pro-life) murdering doctors who perform abortions on the grounds that a young life (the foetus) has been violently terminated!

Communism was depicted as the Evil of the 20th century to serve the interest of the merchants of death — the 'Military-Industrial Complex'. **Islamic terrorism is being projected as the evil of the 21st century** to serve the same interest of the merchants of death – the Halliburtons, Bechtel Corporation, Boeing and Lockheed, British Aerospace etc. Without **"Islamic terrorists"** at their disposals, the merchants of death would not have an enemy to justify the allocation of hundreds of billions to the armaments industry. Wars are needed to keep churning weaponry to replace the outdated and destroyed equipment.

The Imperialist Formula of the Zionists Anglo-American War

335

Cabal is simple.

Thesis — Corrupted Christianity
Antithesis — Corrupted Islam
Synthesis — Zionist Anglo-American New World Order

Once we grasp and fully appreciate the dimension and implications of the formula, everything falls into its logical place. If the *ummah* dismiss the said formula as some mumbo jumbo and or conspiracy theory, a heavy price will be paid by the Muslim nations.

Muslim must first learn how Christianity has been corrupted and subverted in the service of Imperial Powers. Just as terrorism is a method of warfare (not an objective in itself or an ideology), Christianity has been subverted and used as a weapon of subjugation by the imperial and colonial powers. Christian Zionism is the corruption of Christianity. This is elementary history.

Today the parallels are there for all to see. Islam is being distorted by the Zionists and agents of Zionism for its political agendas. Al Qaeda and Osama Bin Laden serve the interests of Zionism when they hold themselves as the true followers of Islam. By portraying a "Corrupted Islam" the Zionists can hide their corruption of Christianity by Christian Zionists. **As in the case of the War on Terrorism, the Christian Zionists condemn terrorism, but hide the fact that they are the worst perpetrators of terror together with Israeli Zionists. The recent statement by the US General Boykin illustrates the point I am making.**

Once the *ummah* understands how Christianity has been corrupted by Zionism, they can stop the corruption of Islam by these same forces.

The Corruption of Christianity

If the *ummah* fails to understand this crucial issue, they can never overcome the conspiracies of the Christian Zionists and the Zionist Anglo-American War Cabal. This new Imperialism is without any rivals and can command more capital and lethal weapons than the old imperial powers could imagine. A crucial difference this time round is that the New Imperialists have pursued their schemes and agendas under the cover of international legitimacy – the United Nations Security Council, the World Bank, IMF, WTO and any other international organizations that further their interest.

(1) A Glaring Example of Corruption

It is asserted that the founding of Israel cannot be challenged because it was founded on a 'divine promise' made some 2,500 years ago in the Old Testament. Christian Zionists in America are a potent force behind the establishment of Zionism and continue to be so at the present time. Consider the following:

'We should prepare to go over to the offensive. Our aim is to smash Lebanon, Trans-Jordan and Syria. The weak point is Lebanon, for the Moslem regime is artificial and easy for us to undermine. We shall establish a Christian state there, and then we will smash the Arab Legion, eliminate Trans-Jordan; Syria will fall to us. We then bomb and move on and take Port Said, Alexandria and Sinai.'

— David Ben-Gurion to the General Staff, May, 1948.

Can you and would you (if you had not read the quote) believe that a Jew (a Zionist at that) would not only agree but actually conspired to establish a Christian state in Lebanon? What kind of Christian state would that be if not a state founded on a corrupted Christian Faith?

Israel Koenig correctly pointed out that nowhere in the Torah, Jewish Faith or the Bible does it say that in the establishment of the State of Israel, Israelis are allowed to use terror, assassinations, intimidation, land confiscation and the cutting of all social services to rid the land of its Arab population. In fact the Torah forbids the creation of the state of Israel.

"Is it logical for God to mandate a nation (Israel) and demand the killing and oppression of the Palestinians to fulfill his prophecy?[1] "

The fact that so many religious leaders and other progressives have not asked this fundamental question as the basis to refute Christian Zionists' and Zionists' assertions of their allegedly divine right is indeed revealing — a reflection of theological impotence if not intellectual bankruptcy!

(2) The Corruption Index[2]

The Corruption Index is a tool to determine the degree a given religion has been corrupted to serve a specific agenda, whether religious or political. I can anticipate the screams of protest that such an approach is simply not possible. The usual arguments being: different religions have different institutions, rituals, teachings, history, etc.

My reply is simple. All religions have one common message. I am grateful to Charles Kimball for choosing the Jewish Torah as the starting point and invite all my Muslim, Christian, Hindu, Buddhist, Sikh, Bahai and Taoist friends to contemplate whether or not their religion share the basic precept as contained in the Torah.

In the first century there was a famous rabbi called Hillel. He was approached by a non-believer who said to the rabbi, "If you can teach me the whole of the Torah while I stand on one foot, you can make me a Jew." Hillel replied without hesitation, "What is hateful to you, do not do to your neighbor. This is the whole Torah; the rest is commentary. Go and study."

Jesus taught: "Love Thy Neighbor."

The Corruption Index measures to what extent a particular religion deviates from this universal teaching — the one essential and fundamental teaching common to all religion. The basic premise being — What thoughts and actions will help me practice this universal injunction? What thoughts and actions will inhibit me from achieving neighborliness?

Before proceeding further, I now invite all my friends to consider a passage from the Qur'ân in Sûrah 5 (Al Mâ'idah), Verse 48:[3]

> ***...if God had willed, He would have made you one nation, but that (He) may test you in what He has given you; so compete in good deeds. The return of you (all) is to God; then He will inform you about that in which you used to differ.***

Thus the Quran exhorts all who believe in God, Muslims and non-Muslims alike that their differences should make them **"compete in good deeds"** rather than in mutual hostility.

The Corruption Index consists of four criteria, namely:

(a) Absolute Truths

When adherents of each religion assert that their religion contains the absolute truths, and all others are falsehoods, we have corrupted to that extent our religion. Thus it is so easy to divide and rule — **absolute truth is not only the wedge between religions, but within a religious community as well.**

According to the Quran, only God can *"inform you about that in which you used to differ."*

Those who use religion as a weapon understand this fundamental principle and exploit this issue to their advantage to achieve their agendas. Imperialist wars under the guise of religious wars were waged and continue to be waged allegedly in defense of absolute truths, precisely because many political and religious leaders of **all denominations** failed to understand this Quranic revelation, and allow their religion to be exploited by the Zionist propaganda machine.

It has been said that more wars have been waged, more people killed, and these days more evil perpetrated in the name of religion than any other institutional force in human history.

(b) *Narrow Mindset*

It follows that if one takes a dogmatic position as what the "truth" is in one's religion one tends to exclude constructive debates and comparative analysis. We don't even bother to read the Holy Books of other religions so as to avoid misunderstanding as to their true teachings. We closet our minds in a little world. We are prevented from learning the teachings of other religions. **Fear sets in — the fear that we will be corrupted by the teachings of the other religions.** In the result, communities became inclusive, depicting followers of other faiths as heathens, non-believers and even enemies. Surely the Spanish Inquisition has taught us the danger of such rigid narrow mindset. But President Bush (a self-professed 'Born Again Christian') demands "Either you are with us or with the terrorists!"

No one dares question and or challenge this silly and illogical proposition, when all religions teach the same basic precepts and tenets about God and our neighbor. Promoting narrow mindset or insular thinking is another useful method to divide and rule for whatever ends!

How can there be peace and understanding when we cannot even talk to one another and or fear the other. *"We must take the view that it is possible to be faithful to one's religion —*

339

Christianity, Hinduism, Islam, Buddhism, etc., — and at the same time acknowledge the humility of one's limited experience and that our personal relationship with our God does not and cannot exclude and exhaust other possibilities.[4]*"*

(c) Blind Obedience

A logical consequence of the preceding mindset is the demand for blind obedience to the teachings of one's religion as **interpreted by its clerics**. When blind obedience to religious precepts is pervasive within a community, **it is the beginning of the corruption of the religion for ulterior motives. It is the clearest symptom of corruption.**

When followers commit mass suicide in blind obedience, as in the case of the Rev. Jim Jones and the People's Temple in Guyana, we have an example as to how religion can be corrupted. The Aum Shinrikyo, whose followers released sarin toxic gas into the Japanese metropolitan subway, is another example.

When God exhorts us to 'compete in good works', this necessitates the creative use of our intellect, as opposed to blind obedience. This is what Buddha said as he lay on his deathbed:

"Do not accept what you hear by report, do not accept tradition, do not accept a statement because it is found in our books, nor because it is in accord with your belief, nor because it is the saying of your teacher. Be ye lamps unto yourselves. Those who, either now or after I am dead, shall rely upon themselves only and not look for assistance to anyone besides themselves, it is they who shall reach the very top most height."

(d) Superiority/Inferiority Complex

If on reading the quotation below, taken from a speech by Pat Robertson, one of the most right wing Christian-Zionist, we are angry and shocked, why then do we tolerate such nonsense in our own religion and community?

Pat Robertson speaking to the Christian Coalition National Convention 1993 said:

"Our culture is superior because our religion is Christianity and that is the truth that sets men free.

"There is no neutral ground, no sphere of activity outside

God's rule. One is either following God in all aspects of life or not following God at all. One is either engaged in Godly politics or is participating in the anti-God structures that now threaten the home, the school, and the church...."

Such arrogance can also be the result of inferiority complex and or fear. The need to be assertive when threatened can give rise to such rabid ravings. We need to accept that one of the consequences of September 11 and Al Qaeda is the present American psyche — **fear of 'Muslim Terrorists' and the revenge mindset.** The fascist statement of General Boykin is reflective of such a mindset when he said:

"Satan wants to destroy this nation, he wants to destroy us as a nation, and he wants to destroy us as a Christian army.

"The Muslim world hates America because we are a nation of believers."

Does not my fellow Muslim, Hindu, Buddhist and Taoist friends recognize the same kind of rigid, rabid ravings of some of their religious and political leaders in their communities? We have our General Boykin within our very own communities.

When Baruch Goldstein, an American medical doctor living in the Jewish settlement of Kiryat Arba entered the Holy Mosque in Hebron and massacred the congregation and was thereafter hailed as the hero *"who gave his life for the Jewish people, the Torah and the nation of Israel,"* can we not see how and what a corrupted religion can do to its own adherents as well as to other faiths?

When people are called upon to commit violence on their neighbors, we know in our hearts that something is awfully wrong and dangerous — **our religion has been corrupted.**

The Christians are fighting back, fighting against those who have corrupted Christianity and used the perverted teachings to wage wars on their neighbors. In October 1986, on the occasion of the World Day of Prayer for Peace, Pope John Paul rallied his flock with the clarion call:

"The fact that we came together in Assisi to pray, to fast and to walk in silence — and this, in support of peace which is always so fragile and threatened, perhaps more than ever – has been, as it were, a clear sign of the profound unity of those who

seek in religion spiritual and transcendent values that respond to the great questions of the human heart, despite concrete divisions. The Day of Assisi, showing the Catholic Church holding hands of brother Christians, and showing us all joining hands with the brothers of other religions, was a visible expression of these statements of the Second Vatican Council. With this day, and by means of it, we have succeeded by the grace of God, in realizing this conviction of ours about the unity of the origin and goal of the human family, and about the meaning and value of non-Christian religions — without the least shadow and confusion or syncretism."

Notwithstanding this clarion call by Pope John Paul, we have recently witnessed the rabid ravings of Falwell, Pat Robertson and others. Dare we hope that we can and shall unite to fight against the corruption of all religions so that the human family shall live as one, do good work and love our neighbors?

Christianity has been corrupted to the detriment of Christians. Islam has also been corrupted to the detriment of Muslims. **When these two great religions are being corrupted to the point of no return, we shall unwittingly be a party to the Grand Design by Christian Zionists and Zionists for World Domination and their New World Order.** This synthesis cannot materialize without the "thesis (corrupted Christianity) and the antithesis (corrupted Islam). If we fail to challenge dogmas and presuppositions, and think anew and openly confront the clerics of Armageddon, we shall have failed in our duty to God, to our country, and to our people.

'When you are standing on the edge of a cliff, progress is not defined as one step forward.[5]

ENDNOTES:

1. Charles Kimball, *When Religion Becomes Evil,* (2002, Harpers Collins).

2. Ibid., adapted from Charles Kimball's "Five Signs" when a religion becomes evil.

3. *The Translation of the Meaning of the Noble Qur'an with Commentaries* by Muhammad Muhsin Khan (Saudi Arabia, King Fahd Press).

4. Charles Kimball, *When Religion Becomes Evil,* (2002, Harpers Collins). This is a must read book. The Corruption Index is adapted from the author's "five warning signs" when religion becomes evil.

5. Ibid.

21

Hopefully a Better Neighborhood

What Paul Wolfowitz disclosed at the 2003 Asian Security Conference that, *"for reasons that have a lot to do with U.S. government bureaucracy, we settled on the one issue that everyone could agree on: weapons of mass destruction ... Look, the primary difference – to put it a little too simply – between North Korea and Iraq is that <u>we have virtually no options with Iraq because the country floats on a sea of oil...</u>"* is most revealing. It reflects the kind of Thucydides-Hobbesian logic[1] that we should act only in our self interest, without regard to others. This produces the bully mentality — a way of life that is solitary, nasty, brutish and short; a mafia existence. The only solution for the lesser being is to come to terms with the stronger, surrender our individual interest, in order to have the advantages of safety and security. Is it any surprise that Professor Barnett refers to his Two Force New Military, the first of which, he calls the "Leviathan" the military thugs.

And since Wolfowitz was addressing a gathering of like-minded persons (after all, it was held in Singapore), it reminded me of the Melian Dialogue[2] — the dialogue between the Athenian generals Cleomedes and Tisias and the magistrates of the island state of Melos. Thucydides observed, *"they that have odds of power exact as much as they can, and the weak yield to such conditions as they can get."* In the Hobbesian derivative, human nature is such that we are driven by what is feasible and what is necessary, *"and from hence it comes to pass that where an invader hath no more to fear than another man's single power, if one plant, sow, build, or possess a convenient seat, others may probably be expected to come prepared with forces united to dispossess and deprive him not only the fruit of his labor, but also of his life or liberty. And the invader again is in like danger."* In short, the Bush regime will conquer when they can.

Unlike the "intellectuals" within the Neocon War Cabal, with Wolfowitz, there is no Hindustani song and dance routine round a tree. He gives it to you straight — no sound bites, no salad dressings.

What I am trying to say is that in the next ten to fifteen years or so, the mindset that directs U.S. foreign policy, regardless whether it is a Republican or a Democratic regime, will be that of Paul Wolfowitz — the "virtually no option" mindset. And he is absolutely right, what with the oil and gas problems and the declining dollar. Too bad it is not our cup of tea, but that's how it goes. In fact we should be grateful for this typical American frankness, unlike poodle Blair who can give you at least five different interpretations for the four letter word.

It is ideologically consistent with the new military theory and grand strategy laid out by Professor Barnett.

Why the emphatic, "virtually no options"? Simple! It is peak oil and the financial house of cards. The U.S. is technically bankrupt and needs to feed its aging population but has no money to pay for all the huge bills. Bush is already preparing to plunder the Social Security and transfer the multi-billion loot to his cronies at Wall Street.

Still on this side of the equation, but from the perspective of a different neighborhood, the Old Europe — they are also in demand for the scarce resources. And although they have the money to pay for the goodies, for now anyway, Big Bully has told his neighbors that he wants to grab the loot first and will not countenance any impertinence whatsoever — the new "rule sets". During the Cold War, it used to be one big party — pot luck so to speak. Not any more. To borrow Wolfowitz's frankness, and "to put it a little too simply," it is going to be a big quarrel among the looters — **contradictions within the First World, tensions inherent in Empire Capitalism.**

In the testimony for and on behalf of the Project for the New American Century (PNAC) before the Senate Foreign Relations Committee on April 8, 2003 less than a month after the invasion of Iraq, on the "Future of NATO", William Kristol gave us a hint of the contradictions and tensions between the Maritime Powers (the U.S. and Britain) and the Continental Powers (the Old Europe).

"But what of the future of NATO and, more generally, of the trans-Atlantic relationship? Obviously, there are questions about the health of the Alliance. The first thing I would say is that it is <u>too late to paper over these questions and pretend that all is well.</u> The problem with the Alliance go beyond European preferences for the charm of President Clinton over the directness of President Bush and beyond the American preference for the policy of Chancellor Kohl over those of Chancellor Schroeder.

"The Bush administration is not responsible for the current crisis in the Alliance.

"Who, or what, is? The answer to "who" is France and sec- ondarily, Germany. The answer to "what" is the new post 9-11 world to which the U.S. has reacted in one way, and France and Germany in another." (Emphasis added)

On first reading of the text of the speech, one may be excused for not grasping fully the extent of the differences, albeit at the moment, the contradictions are non-antagonistic. To a large extent, this is because of President Chirac's leadership, but it still irks the Neocons. In the later part of the text, one gets the full measure of the Hobbesian logic which drives the Zionist Neocon Agenda. Let's get back to the speech.

"This is not the place for France-bashing. But it is the place to tell the truth. At best, the government of France is uninterested in the trans-Atlantic alliance. At worse, it wants to weaken it. France priority lies with the European Union and/or the UN — not NATO. And there is no question that many in Paris desire to see a France-led European Union as a counterweight to U.S. power. Germany, a troubled nation with economic and demographic dif- ficulties, and an understandable aversion to the exercise of mili- tary and nation-state power, has followed France's lead. The European as a whole has embraced a view of the world that is post nationalist, post-historical, and extremely reluctant to use military force ever in a just cause.

"The United States is different. The 'distinctly American Internationalism' the President has articulated in speeches and in the White House's National Security Strategy — and with which I am in basic agreement — is quite far removed from the 'European' view of the world in both the nature of the threats we face and cer- tainly what strategies to employ to deal with them."

Thus the difference is not the matter of not "eating French fries" as some American news media have frivolously portrayed. Neither is it one of failure to communicate. It is two fundamental world views that now separate the Atlantic — once again it reflects the underlying substratum that had always distinguished the victorious Maritime Powers and the Continental Powers, the former from a historical perspective have always being more aggressive.

To the question, "how do we bridge the gap?" Kristol was equally forthright and his prescription was one of circumventing wherever and whenever possible "Old Europe" and to establish new structures and institutions that will facilitate U.S. objectives in Europe.

"We... might want to explore new institutional arrangements that allow us to work in particular ways with our new allies in Central and Eastern Europe, and our friends elsewhere in Europe, as well. We can't confine ourselves to Cold War structures. Institutional creativity is needed for a new world. There may also be ways to institutionalize our friendship, and common interests, with democracies like Turkey, Israel, and India, in conjunction with NATO or outside of NATO. Nor, I trust do we want to hand over U.S. interest or decision making to the United Nations — an organization that seeks to speak for the 'international community' but actually reflects the particular state interests of its Security Council members.... But at the end of the day, our priority has to be dealing with these dangers, not placating allies who are more concerned with the exercise of American power than the threats we face." (Emphasis added)

The contradictions have also impacted on other strategic interests of both camps. Since 1999, France and Germany have established military assistance and cooperation with Russia with a view to protect their converging economic interests in the Middle East in the face of Anglo-American attempts to dislodge them from their respective spheres of influence. This is acutely reflected in the oil sector. Arraigned on the one side is the BP-Amoco, Chevron-Texaco, Exxon-Mobil/Shell alliance which is pitted against Total-Fina Elf which is allied with Russian oil interests for Middle East oil. The field is getting crowded and there is just not enough to go around.[3] The invasion of Iraq has literally pushed the European oil alliance out of the equation in that area of contention.[4]

The rivalry has now also extended to the competition for global currency supremacy, with the dollar wary of the Euro's attempts to dislodge its current status. Whichever side loses out, they can kiss goodbye to their gravy chain. The disruption to the respective economies would be catastrophic. The issue here is not why they cannot cooperate to share the spoil. It is just that the remaining spoil is insufficient to sustain both powers — it is either all or nothing, because the effect of just having half of the cake is marginally less devastating than no cake at all.

"It is virtually no option at all! Stupid."

To some the above is too bleak a scenario, notwithstanding the occasional hiccups in the Atlantic Alliance. That was my reaction too, until I read the prophetic essay by Charles Kupchan entitled **"The End of the West"** way back in 2002, which anticipated William Kristol's belligerency.[5] In essence, Kupchan has warned that the next clash of civilization will not be between the West and the rest, but between the United States and Europe. He laments that Americans remain largely oblivious. Let's examine his grounds in support of his contention, which in many ways coincides with my own views, that the contradictions within the First World will in due course be antagonistic contradictions.

"The terrorist attack in New York and Washington certainly punctured the sense of security that arose from the end of the Cold War and the triumph of the West, but they have done little to compromise U.S. hegemony... That encapsulates the conventional wisdom — and it is woefully off the mark. Not only is American primacy far less durable than it appears, but it is already beginning to diminish. And the rising challenger is not China or the Islamic world but the European Union, an emerging polity that is in the process of marshalling the impressive resources and historical ambitions of Europe's separate nation-states.

"The EU's annual economic output has reached about $8 trillion, compared with America's $10 trillion, and the euro will soon threaten the dollar's global dominance. The transatlantic rivalry that has already begun will inevitably intensify. Centers of power by their nature compete for position, influence and prestige.

"The U.S. Federal Reserve and the European Central Bank are destined to vie for control of the international monetary system. Washington and Brussels will just as likely lock horns over the Middle East, Europe will resist rather then backstop U.S. lead-

ership, perhaps paralyzing the World Bank, the United Nations and other institutions that since World War II have relied on transatlantic cooperation to function effectively. A once united West appears well on its way to separating into competing halves.... That the EU and the United States might part ways would seem to border on the unthinkable.

"The two have parted company on matters of statecraft. American live by the rules of real politics, viewing military threat, coercion, and war as essential tools of diplomacy ... Europeans see America's reliance on the use of force as simplistic, self-serving, and a product of its excessive power; America see the EU's firm commitment to multilateral institutions as naïve, self righteous, and a product of its military weakness.

"As Europe increasingly holds its own and the United States continues to shrug off compromise, the international institutions that have helped to promote peace and prosperity since World War II will inevitably falter.

"History is coming full circle. After breaking away from the British Empire, the United States came together as an unitary federation, emerged as a leading nation, and eventually eclipsed Europe's great powers. It is now Europe's turn to ascend and break away from an America that refuses to surrender its privileges of primacy. Europe will inevitably rise as America's principal competitor. Should Washington and Brussels begin to recognize the dangers of the growing gulf between them, they may be able to contain their budding rivalry. Should they fail, however, to prepare for life after Pax Americana, they will ensure that the coming clash of civilizations will not be between the West and the rest but within a West divided against itself."

While I subscribe to the overall assessment of the contradictions within the West, I part ways with Kupchan on issues relating to the growing and irreversible tensions in the Middle East. In exploiting the Islamic issue and the "War on Terrorism" both sides have helped create the "Al Qaeda Monster" and may live to regret it.

Having allied itself with the U.S. in the competition for resources in the region against the E.U., Israel deftly exploited this antagonism to further its own agenda to the extent that the United States is willing to sacrifice the trans-Atlantic alliance and place Israel's interest ahead of its own. And as long as America is led by the nose by Zionist Israel, the gap between the Maritime Powers and the Continental Powers will widen further. That is why I am saying Israel is the lynchpin to the coming wars. The events have now reached a stage whereby nothing within the horizon suggests any viable solution, save one. To this I shall now turn my attention.

By any measure and from whatever perspective, the present state of affairs is unsustainable, not unlike that of a hijacked runaway train, with a full load of passengers, nuclear armed and heading towards an explosive end. The hijackers have demanded that unless they get want they want, there will be a nasty explosion at the end of the run. There is no way to evacuate the millions away from the city. But the train will pass through a stretch of desert where if the train is derailed, the effect of the mushroom cloud could be contained.

In this analogy the runaway train is Israel and the Neocons, the hijackers are the International Zionists and the city is the United States.

There is therefore a Hobbesian choice to be made by the Bush regime — Israel or America.

If it's a matter of control for the oil resources in the Middle East, there is absolutely no justification for the destabilization of the entire Middle East, more so after the invasion of Iraq. The present plans to attack Iran, Syria and the orchestrated sectarian strife in Lebanon following the assassination of Rafik Hariri, the former Prime Minister, serve a different agenda and it is not in America's interests. Saudi Arabia and all the other oil producing Gulf States are in one way or another beholden to the U.S. and cannot in any conceivable way pose a threat to the security interests of America. There is only one beneficiary in the overall scheme, and that is Israel.

The destabilization of the Middle East and the current plans for the carving up of the area along sectarian and religious lines reflect clearly the Oded Yinon plan of the 1980s, and the strategy of Netanyahu's "Clean Break" for the establishment of Greater Eretz Yisrael, stretching from the Nile to the Euphrates. A study by the Rand Corporation, a leading U.S. Zionist think tank, entitled "U.S. Strategy in the Muslim World After 9-11[6]" advocates that the present divide between Sunni and Shia, Arabs and non-Arabs should be exploited to secure U.S. interest in the Muslim world. Read that to mean Israel's interest in the Muslim world.

One of the main objectives was to identify the "key cleavages" and fault lines among sectarian, ethnic, regional, and national lines and assess how these cleavages afford opportunities to the United States. The study maintained that the moves by Tehran and Riyadh for rapprochement allows the U.S. to align its policy with Shia aspirations for greater religious freedom and political expression and a say in their own affairs in countries controlled by others. The study calls for reforms of Madrasas and mosques and that there should be appointed and paid professional imams in all mosques to suppress anti-Western and anti-American feelings. There is also the recommendation that there should be an increase in military-to-military relations and this will be of particular importance to any U.S. shaping strategy in the Muslim world. Rebuilding a core of U.S. trained officers in key Muslim countries is a critical need. Programs such as International Military Education and Training (IMET) not only ensure that future military leaders are exposed to American military values and practices, but can also translate into increased U.S. influence and access.

In short, the Zionists are preparing for future coups and these U.S. trained and indoctrinated officers will be in the front line to execute the coup, replicating the modus operandi in the overthrow of Mossadeq in Iran. Such time bombs are unnecessary and in fact fuel the already explosive situation. Recruiting Muslims to do Israel's dirty work is a time-tested and effective weapon to divide the Muslim ranks.

Given the above scenario, and the growing resentment in the region, further wars in the Middle East are inevitable, and they will be nuclear as the Bush regime has already advocated its use over the last three years, and more recently by Defense Secretary Rumsfeld. Rumsfeld calls these tactical nuclear bombs bunker busters to mislead the public that the nuclear fallout would be limited, as it is only meant to destroy bunkers. If depleted uranium munitions used in the 1991 First Gulf War are still causing severe health and environmental problems in Iraq, what more nuclear bombs, even if they are tactical nuclear bombs. Syria and Iran in the Middle East and North Korea is right in coming to the conclusion, following the devastation of Iraq, that nonproliferation does not mean nonproliferation, but rather the disarming of a nation's legitimate defense capabilities to facilitate easy conquests. There is virtually no option — either be armed and be prepared or be conquered like Iraq.

The recent provocations against Iran and Syria as I see it, is a bait to force these two countries to take pre-emptive military measures which would result in a massive retaliation by U.S. without the need to prove possession of WMD as justification, as in the case of Iraq. And as admitted by Wolfowitz, WMDs was merely an excuse. Alternatively, Israel would launch an air strike thus provoking retaliation from Iran, and they expect that Iran will blame the U.S. for it. When Iran targets American interests, the U.S. will use that as an excuse for a massive counterattack, thus bypassing the need to establish Iran's WMD.

There can be no doubts that the Zionist Anglo-American War Cabal will attack Iran and Syria. Following the earlier modus operandi, and in line with the Iraq Liberation Act of 1998, Senator Rick Santorum recently introduced the Iran Freedom and Support Act, 2005, in the U.S. Senate. The Syria Accountability Act was given passage earlier. Knowing that there is no international legitimacy for such military actions, the U.S. Senate in collusion with the Bush regime is trying to pass off these wars as being legal because they are waged in accordance with U.S. laws. However, it is settled law that domestic laws have no extraterritorial effect. There are specific international laws governing military conflicts, the Charter of the United Nations, the Geneva Conventions, etc., and these must be complied with, failing which, the United States will be deemed to have committed war crimes.

In the circumstances, the United States might not launch an attack, but will connive with Israel. How Iran response to such an attack is crucial. If Israel launches any air strikes against Iran, Iran should only response by hitting Israeli targets. **IN ANY FUTURE WARS IN THE MIDDLE EAST, THE FOCUS OF THE RESISTANCE'S ACTIONS SHOULD BE DIRECTED AT ISRAEL, NOT AMERICA, notwithstanding it's connivance with Israel. WHY?**

We must give a Hobbesian choice to the people of the United States.

It would be very difficult for the American public to support a war started by Israel, notwithstanding it was at the urging of the U.S. The situation has changed from the last time, when Israel destroyed Iraq's nuclear facilities in the 1980s. World opinion against Israel would make it easier for the resistance to propose measures that will isolate Israel and strangle her economy.

We must **NOT ALLOW ZIONIST ISRAEL** to frame the issue as one relating to **AMERICAN SECURITY** — **the issue should be**

351

whether America should support an unprovoked attack by Israel against either Iran or Syria, and commit a WAR CRIME? Remember that in the Communications Priority 2003, prepared for the Wexner Foundation, Israel was advised that they must portray that their security is synonymous with the security of the United States. We must ensure the **DISCONNECT** between the two.

Absent American public support for U.S. intervention, there will be no repeat of the massive arms airlift as in the 1973 Arab-Israeli war. Israel would rather exercise the Samson option then surrender. This will mark the beginning of the end of Zionist Anglo-American War Cabal's global agenda. Zionist Israel's defeat would be costly as the entire Holy Land would be devastated. The Samson option and the use of tactical nuclear weapons will see to that.

I have come almost to the end of my book. I believe that I have successfully shown that the Zionist Anglo-American Empire is a paper tiger. The empire can only bully small states with weak armies, like Iraq. Yet the heavy weight has failed after ten brutal rounds to knock out the flyweight Iraq. On the contrary and to the surprise of many, the flyweight has traded blow for blow and gave a reasonable account of itself. After Korea and Vietnam, the imperialist powers still don't get it — that they cannot win a people's war.

I believe that I have also succeeded in showing that the Zionist Anglo-American War Cabal has hijacked the U.S. military, as their **Spear of Conquest.** I want to leave no doubt whatsoever about this. So please consider the following – Ariel Sharon's speech at the Herzliya Conference in 2004, an annual gathering of Israel's financial, political and academic aristocracy.[7]

"America is in our pocket. President Bush supports all of Sharon's positions, including those that are diametrically opposed to Bush's own former positions. Europe has resigned itself to him. The great of the world are standing in line to visit us, starting with Tony Blair, Egypt and the other Arab states are cozying to us. Our international position has improved beyond recognition. The economy is advancing by leaps and bounds, our society is flourishing. Apart from the right wing lunatic fringe, there is no opposition left. The Labor party is joining the government and will support all its steps..."

Such a boast, but not all is so rosy for Israel, especially her economy, as otherwise she would not have appointed Stanley Fisher to be the head of Bank of Israel. Sharon has to do a Hollywood show to hoodwink Israeli citizens who are suffering under the weight of the Intifada. However, there can be no doubts that Bush is dancing to his tune. And that is why I have repeatedly said that Israel is the lynchpin, and the American people must be given the Hobbesian Choice:

EITHER AMERICA'S SURVIVAL AND SECURITY OR ISRAEL'S ZIONIST AGENDA

The genie is out of the bottle, and there is nothing the Zionist can do about the genie. I have fulfilled my vow to the Palestinian and Iraqi children made in 2003. I am no longer burdened by the weight of the vow. The deed is done. The genie is out of the bottle. The day will come when I shall touch the Holy Ground with the children of Jenin, Nablus, and Bethlehem and other brave towns.

What then is the future scenario? There will be a New World Map, that's for sure, but it will not be the Pentagon's New Map. New boundaries will emerge in the Middle East, for the world will come to accept that neither the entity Eretz Yisrael or Eretz Ishmael have exclusive or historical claims to the real estate, called Palestine. A new state will emerge called Palestine, the original name to the entire Holy Land where Arabs and Jews, absent the Zionists, will live in peace but not before the Islamic Revolution that will sweep away all the puppet regimes installed by the Zionist Anglo-American War Cabal through so-called democratic elections, that will replace most of the absolute rulers in the region in the next few years, a pattern that will follow the American funded Ukraine elections.

It is indeed strange that the U.S., France and Saudi Arabia are leading the chorus for Syria to withdraw its troops from Lebanon, when the U.S. war machine and its fascist goons are occupying Iraq. When Israel was defeated in Lebanon and the Zionist occupation was ended, it was Syria that helped in restoring some sort of order among the warring factions. The murder of Rafik Hariri, the former prime minister of Lebanon by the Mossad, is but the 3rd step in the Zionist plan to fast forward their agenda,[8] without which a war against Iran would not be possible. Once Syria withdraws its troops from Lebanon, Israel's northern flank would be neutralized. Saudi Arabia, Egypt and Jordan having sold their souls to the Zionist Anglo-American Power Elites in exchange for protection and the continuation of their corrupt regimes, will watch on the sidelines when the U.S. and Israel attacks Syria and Iran. But these stupid regimes will soon learn that they are merely delaying their own passing, as ultimately they too would have to go — either by U.S./Israel manipulation or Islamic Revolution.

The downfall of Sharon will come after the military occupation of Syria and Iran and when he sets his eyes on Saudi Arabia. The people in the Middle East under the yoke of the various puppet regimes will realize soon enough that their so called democracy was merely a smokescreen for Sharon's regional hegemony. And the people of the Middle East will be shocked when they find out that Sharon's fantasy extends beyond the Nile and the Euphrates. Sharon will openly declare that the Zionist hegemony will extend from Mauritania to Afghanistan.[9] And that is why there will be no genuine peace between Israel and the Palestinians. This issue will only be resolved after a total war in the Middle East and in the final defeat of Israel. Many political pundits will find this conclusion, difficult to accept. This is because they have forgotten the military defeat of the Israelis in Lebanon.[10] For the next ten years, occupation and Islamic Revolution will ravage the entire Middle East, until the surrender of Zionist Israel. And when the Islamic Revolution has cleansed the Middle East of all corrupt puppet regimes, an era of Islamic Renaissance will transform the entire Middle East and the bond of unity forged by fire will bury the present schism between the Shias and the Sunnis.

America will pay a heavy price.

Having funded and aided in the Middle East wars, and the brutal suppression of the Arab masses, she will be compelled to give refuge to those surviving Zionists fleeing from their "Promised Land" as a compromise for peace and under the pressure of the Zionist lobbies in America to save the Zionists from total annihilation in Palestine. They will be down but not out and will continue to lust for another Eretz Yisrael. From deep inside the bowels of America, this cancer will spread. The Zionist Anglo-American Power Elites will change their strategy from one of hijacking the foreign policy and military of the U.S. to one of total domination of the U.S. government in all aspects. This game will play out in the next twenty years. Like Troy, the United States will be destroyed from within.

The end of hostilities in the Middle East will give rise to a new international institution, established to ensure a more equitable distribution of scarce resources to prevent and contain future resource wars at least in the foreseeable two decades. The world's economies have to make painful adjustments and restructure their societies to address the chronic shortage of oil and petroleum products as well as other scarce resources.

One of the most significant developments in the latter half of the 21st century will be the Regional Mindset as opposed to the Global Mindset, as regional trade will be more than sufficient to meet the expectations of the various domestic economies within the respective regions. Globalization as we know it today will be an abstraction. Empire Capitalism's tentacles will no longer have global reach.

This is a direct consequence of the restructuring and redesigning of our societies in the face of diminishing natural resources. In place of globalization, there will intra-regional trade, as trade will be more efficient through regional mechanisms. ASEAN plus 3 is a good model. The consumer society will slowly recede as it has shown to be wasteful and inefficient in the allocation of resources. This is a step in the right direction but beyond this I am not willing to venture as it is not within the scope of this book.

There will be a lull, an interlude before the next round of bloodletting occurs again. This is also inevitable. Why? As long as there are standing armies, and the major economies of the West and the East have substantial allocations to their respective military-industrial complex, the cycle will repeat itself. Europe is on the ascendancy again, as correctly observed by Kupchan and Europe's capitalism is in essence Empire Capitalism albeit less predatory, not because its nature has changed, but its economic and military strength would not be able to reach the heights of dominance once possessed by the United States. China and India will not be easy meat and the Asian market will in the later half of the 21st century equal in size to that of the European market and would have surpassed the United States. Whether there will be a major war in Asia will depend to a large extent on China-Japan relations. The two countries must work together to provide security for Asia. And that is why it is so important for Japan not to be seduced by the U.S. to be the the latter's proxy to confront China. The U.S. economically will not be able to wage war against China on its own and will require the assistance of Japan and Taiwan. Japan and Taiwan must re-examine their current policy of having to rely on the U.S. for their security. Japan has no reason to fear China unless she has hegemonic designs on Asia. Asians can solve their differences, if any, without outside interference and should not be used as cannon fodder for the Zionist Anglo-American War Cabal. To prevent a nuclear war in Asia, Korea must be reunited, as a peaceful Korean peninsula will deny the Zionist Anglo-American War Cabal a crucial flank in any war against China. That leaves just one wild card in the deck — Taiwan.

The Zionist Anglo-American War Cabal will continue to manipulate Taiwan to provoke China. That is the nature of war cabals, to meddle and create instability so as to justify its presence in the region on the pretext of providing security to the region and to counter China's growing economic strength. If Asia wants peace, then it has to act in concert to isolate Taiwan economically through economic sanctions should Taiwan persist in its path as agent provocateur for the Zionist Anglo-American War Cabal. A weak Taiwan will not be able to sustain a war economy; and another flank against China will be disarmed. In such a scenario, where the threat of war is eliminated, China and Japan can then concentrate on providing the leadership to transform Asia. It would not serve Japan's interests to pursue any hegemonic policies in Asia as a junior partner to the U.S. China must also do its part in assuring the region that it has no hegemonic ambitions. China and Japan must embark on an ambitious economic program for Asia as their combines foreign reserves should be invested in Asia to establish a vibrant Asian Market. ASEAN + 3 and the economic spin-offs is the surest guarantee for a peaceful Asia in the 21st century.

If Asia succeeds in pulling together, it may very well be spared the ravages of World War IV that has already started in the Middle East. The success of Asia will have a profound effect on Latin America and Africa, as trade between the Latin American regional bloc and the African bloc with Asia will relieve the former from overdependance on the U.S. and Europe for economic survival. The WTO in its present form will become irrelevant, to be replaced by more equitable regional mechanisms.

The need for a Big Brother for protection against global enemies as in the days of the Cold War and the War on Terrorism will be exposed for what it is — a pretext to maintain imperial hegemony. The world has no need for big bullies. Regional trade and security and the collective responsibility for economic prosperity will be the bulwark against foreign and hegemonic agendas. Asians in the 21st century must ensure that the Zionist Anglo-American Axis as well as the emerging European continental powers will not be able, under any pretext, to launch any war of aggression in Asia.

The regional signboard should be "Global Empires and Collaborators Not Allowed in Asia."

The Zionist Anglo-American Empire will be the last global empire, if not by 2015, certainly by 2020.

ENDNOTES:

1. Thomas Hobbes, *The Leviathan*, see chapters 13 and 14 and Hobbes Thucydides: ed. Richard Slatter (New Brunswick, 1975), *The History of the Peloponnesian War*
2. Michael Walzer, *Just and Unjust Wars*, (1977, Basic Books)
3. Eric Wadell, "The Battle for Oil," Global Outlook , Issue No 3, Winter 2003.
4. Washington Post, September 15, 2002
5. Charles Kupchan, "The End of the West", The Atlantic Monthly, November, 2002. Norman Podhoretz arrogantly dismisses Kupchan as a "Liberal Internationalist,"in his essay, "War Against World War IV", Commentary, February, 2005. He is a member of the Council on Foreign Relations.
6. Source: http://www.rand.org/publications/RB/RB/151
7. Uri Avery, "The Mountain and the Mouse: Sharon's Vision for Israel and the Palestinians Exposed", December 19, 2004, @ www.redress.btinernet.co.uk/uavnery110.htm. A free translation by Uri Avery.
8. I have previously indicated that 9-11 was the 1st step and the Iraqi invasion, the 2nd step.
9. Israel Shahak, *Open Secrets: Israel Nuclear and Foreign Policies*, (1997, Pluto Books) p. 32
10. Ibid. p. 63

Postscript

When I completed the manuscript on February 22, 2005, I had not expected that Phase II of the Zionist Anglo-American Agenda for the Middle East to be implemented so quickly, as they were still bogged down in Iraq. More so when Major Isaiah Wilson, the official historian of the U.S. Army (who also served as a war planner for the 101st Airborne Division) had issued a report which concluded that the U.S. army's failure to occupy and stabilize Iraq in 2003 soon after the invasion has resulted in a situation whereby the U.S. Army had lost its dominance and has yet to regain that position.[1] The report also revealed that there was no adequate operational plan for stability and support operations. Wilson said that army planners failed to understand or accept that there would be Iraqi resistance and deemed the military performance in Iraq mediocre and that the army could lose the war.

Therefore, I had to revise the previous chapter to bring the reader up to speed on the events in Lebanon. But as events turned out, Bush is not only sticking to the Agenda, but fast-forwarding it at a greater speed then envisaged. The orchestrated demonstrations by the Zionist Anglo-American War Cabal with the connivance of France against Syria was well executed, and it is obvious that the plans were already in place before the murder of Rafik Hariri, most probably by Israeli intelligence services working in concert with local opposition elements. French, Israeli and American interests converged in Lebanon. Just because France opposed the Iraq War, it does not mean that she has no neocolonial ambitions in the Middle East. Imperial powers oppose and collude with each other all the time, depending on the circumstances and the interests involved. Make no mistake about that. If they can't get in by the front door, they will try to sneak in by the back.

The funding of the opposition demonstrations and the coming

elections in Lebanon follows the modus operandi used in Ukraine's recent elections and in the funding of opposition forces against President Chavez of Venezuela.

In the circumstances, we should examine critically, how such "democratic coups" are financed and implemented and what front organizations are being employed. Such is the double standard that when other countries support a government which is opposed by the Zionist Anglo-American Empire, it is interference and corruption, but when cash is doled out openly and liberally by organizations funded by the U.S., it is to promote democracy. It has been revealed[2] that the Bush regime has spent more than $65 million in the past two years to fund political organizations in Ukraine, and especially Viktor Yushchenko. This is part of the $1 billion which the State Department spends each year in building "democracy worldwide". The monies are funnelled through organizations such as the Eurasia Foundation or through other front organizations aligned with the Republicans and the Democrats. These organizations also provide election training, fund human rights forums, and liaise with news outlets to further their agenda.

White House press secretary, Scott McClellan admitted as much when he said, ***"There's accountability in place. We make sure that the money is being used for the purposes for which it is assigned or designated."***

A sinister ploy adopted by the Zionist Anglo-American War Cabal is to fund exit polls which will invariably show that their puppet has won the election, notwithstanding results may indicate otherwise, and thus laying the propaganda groundwork for accusing their opponents of election fraud. These exit polls are usually funded by U.S. Embassies and various American Foundations, the principal ones being:

1) The National Endowment for Democracy (NED) which receives money directly from Congress;

2) The Eurasia Foundation which receives money from the State Department;

3) The Renaissance Foundation which is funded by George Soros;

4) The National Democratic Institute (NDI), headed by the Zionist Madeleine Albright, which received nearly $48 million from the State Department for "Democracy Building" programs; and

359

5) The International Republican Institute (IRI), funded by the Republican Party, and is chaired by Senator John McCain.

In Iraq, the Dawa Party and the Supreme Council for the Islamic Revolution are backed by such foundations and serve U.S. interests. So beware of such organizations that boast Islamic credentials. According to IRI's website, these prominent parties were being trained together with smaller organizations to promote a "civil society". Some $80 million was allocated to train collaborators. The IRI funded the armed coup against President Chavez of Venezuela as well as the violent overthrow of the democratically elected Haitian President Jean-Bertrand Aristide.

Another U.S. organization, the AFL-CIO (the U.S. Labor Federation) is complicit in NED's dirty work. The American Institute for Free Labor (AIFLD), the predecessor of AFL-CIO was instrumental in the overthrow of democratically elected governments in Guyana in 1963, Brazil in 1964, the Dominican Republic in 1965 and Chile in 1973. Allen Weinstein, an NED founder confessed in 1991[3] that *"A lot of what we do today was done covertly 25 years ago by the CIA."* NED was responsible for the manipulations of elections in Nicaragua in 1990, Mongolia in 1996 and the overthrow of democratically elected candidates in Bulgaria in 1990 and Albania in 1991-92. The NED is supported by the right wing think tank, the Heritage Foundation, and the oil and defense establishments: Chevron, Exxon, Mobil, Texaco, and the disgraced Enron.

If these foundations are in your country, this is the surest sign that they are preparing a coup dressed up in "democratic elections" and they would have bought various candidates and funded local NGOs to do their bidding. Infiltrate these organizations and observe how they fund and recruit local supporters; collect documentary evidence. Monitor their personnel conducting exit polls and follow the money trail and nail down the public relations firms that they have engaged for their campaigns; follow through with the production house and printers that have been assigned to produce the final propaganda product. Once all these information are in hand, patriots in your country can then mount a counter-attack and foil the coup, and when they are about to strike just before the elections, expose the corruption and the coup's master-minds.

Obviously, now that they are being exposed, they may create new foundations to cover their tracks, but they cannot hide their activities. If new organizations are sprouting and working with local NGOs on issues relating to elections, freedom, environment, human rights, climate change etc., target them for investigation and **follow the money trail as outlined above.**

Mark Almond, the Cold War bagman revealed in an article[4] how he financed and organized such coups in the 1980s. This is how he described it:

"Throughout the 1980s, in the build-up to the 1989's velvet revolutions, a small army of volunteers – and, let's be frank, spies – cooperated to promote what became People Power. A network of inter-locking foundations and charities mushroomed to organize the logistics of transferring millions of dollars to dissidents. The money came overwhelmingly from NATO states and covert allies such as 'neutral' Sweden.

"The hangover from People Power is shock therapy. Each successive crowd is sold a multimedia vision of Euro-Atlantic prosperity by western-funded 'independent' media to get them on the streets.

Our media portrayed Prague dissidents as selfless academics who were reduced to poverty for their principles, when they were in fact receiving $600 monthly stipends. Now they sit in the front row of the new Euro-Atlantic ruling class. The dowdy do-gooder who seemed so devoted to making sure that every penny of her 'charity' got to a needy recipient is now a facilitator for investors in our old stamping grounds. The end of history was the birth of consultancy.

"Grown cynical, the dissident types who embezzled the cash to fund, say, a hotel in the Buda Hills did less harm than those that launched politico-media careers. In Poland, the ex-dissident Adam Michnik's Agora media empire — worth 400m today — grew out of the underground publishing world of Solidarity, funded by the CIA in the 1980s. His newspaper backed the Iraq War, despite its huge unpopularity among Poles.

"People Power is, it turns out, more about closing things than about open society. It shuts factories but, worse still, minds. Its advocates demand a free market in everything — except opinion. The current ideology of the New World Order ideologues, many of whom are renegade communists, is Market-Leninism —

that combination of dogmatic economic model with Machiavellian methods to grasp the levers of power.

"People Power was coined in 1986, when Washington decided Ferdinand Marcos had to go. But it was events in Iran in 1953 that set the template. Then, Anglo-American money stirred up anti-Mossadeq crowds to demand the restoration of the Shah. The New York Times's correspondent trumpeted the victory of the people over communism, even though he had given $50,000 and the CIA-drafted text of the anti-Mossadeq declaration to the coup leaders himself. Is today's version of People Power similarly economical with the truth?"

Dr. Peter Ackerman, the author of **Strategic Non-Violent Conflict**, is of the view that taking out regimes can be achieved without military means, in certain circumstances. In a speech at the State Department on June 29, 2004 entitled, **"Between Hard and Soft Power: The Rise of Civilian Based Struggle and Democratic Change"** he proposed using youth movements to bring down Iran and North Korea.[5] He has been working with top U.S. weapons designer, Lawrence Livermore Laboratories, on developing new communication strategies that could be used in youth movement insurgencies. Col. Robert Helvey, President of the Albert Einstein Institution has been advocating non-violence as a form of warfare. He trained and organized Myanmarese students to work behind Aung San Suu Kyi, and was responsible for the training of Hong Kong students who were subsequently used in the Tiananmen Square incident of June 1989. He is now believed to be acting as adviser to the Falun Gong, a quasi-religious movement in China.

Such youth groups have been established in Eastern Europe, notably Zubr in Belarus in January 2001, Kmara in Georgia, in April 2003, Pora in Ukraine in June 2004. The overthrow of Georgian President, Eduard Schevardnadze was accomplished in 2003, using the Kmara as a critical part of the operations. In the circumstances, the opposition demonstrations in Lebanon must be viewed in the above context. It is indeed interesting to note that the March issue of The Economist had as its lead story, "Democracy Stirs in the Middle East." Buoyed by their previous successes, they were counting the chickens before they were hatched. However, the Zionist Anglo-American War Cabal had a rude awakening on March 8, 2005, when over 500,000 Lebanese took to the streets in support of Syria and denouncing the subversion of Lebanon by the Zionist Anglo-American War Cabal. The demonstrators gathered in one of Beirut's major open areas, the Riad Al-Solh Square, and they came from all over Lebanon. They shouted slogans in support of Syria and President Bashar Al-Assad and condemned the interference of the U.S., France and Israel, and the UN resolution 1559.

The gathering was a strategic victory for Hezbullah and the Islamic Revolution in the Middle East. The discipline and organizational skills displayed must have unnerved the Zionist Anglo-American War Cabal. And even though three U.S. carrier groups are speeding towards the Middle East, any adventure by the war cabal would end up very bloody and hasten the departure of corrupt and decadent regimes in the region. We will also witness the second defeat of Israel at the hands of Hezbullah, God willing.

We must also be aware of the deceit of France and resolution 1559. To this international conspiracy, I shall return later. But at this juncture, it is imperative that Muslims and non-Muslims study the speech of Sheikh Sayyed Hassan Nasrallah, the Secretary General of the Hezbullah. I append below the key excerpts of the translation of that speech:[6]

"We in the Lebanese forces and parties, when we made the calls, we did not doubt or suspect that you would meet them because you have been, always and in the past years, in the fields of sacrifices along with the injured, the former detainees and their families, as well families of martyrs of the resistance and the army.

"You in this mass demonstration, went beyond all doubts today, rendering talks about loopholes here and there useless. We live in a free and democratic country where each of us has the right to express oneself, but within the limits of politeness and courtesy. In reply to insults that were circulated in public squares, I tell the world, which heard these words through television sets, and the Syrian Leadership and people: We, the polite, loyal and civil Lebanese people, apologize for every insult.

"Dear brothers and sisters, we gather here today to express our support for the goals we outlined in the news conference, the most important of which thanking Assad's Syria, Hafez Assad's Syria, Bashar Assad's Syria, the resisting Syrian people and the

steadfastness of the Syrian army who accompanied us, and still does, throughout the years of defense and resistance.

"We gather here today to remind the world and to remind our countrymen that this square that gather us or that square that gathers you in Martyrs' Square, were destroyed by Israel and internal wars, but were united and preserved by Syria and the blood of its officers and soldiers. Beirut was destroyed by Ariel Sharon and protected by Hafez Assad, but we are not ungrateful people. If anyone was ungrateful, he has disobeyed the Lebanese manners.

"To Syria we repeat what Syrian President Bashar Assad said: you do not have a materialistic military presence in Lebanon, you are present in the souls, in the hearts, in the minds, in the past, in the present and in the future, and no one can drive out Syria from Lebanon's mind, or Lebanon's heart or Lebanon's future.

"Second: We here support all the outcomes of the Higher Lebanese-Syrian Council that was held yesterday and stress that any plan for Syria's stay or withdrawal from Lebanon must comply with the Taif Accord solely.

"We have come here to voice to the world our opposition to the United Nations Security Council Resolution 1559.

"I address French President Jacque Chirac and I ask him: If you loved Lebanon and care for its independence and freedom, you should consider the different points of view. Aren't these people among the Lebanese citizens that you love? These Lebanese are telling you: we want to preserve our historical and special relations with Syria; we insist on the Palestinian refugees' return to their land; we refuse resolution 1559. These Lebanese people urge you to stop supporting a resolution refused by the majority of the Lebanese.

"Isn't that the principle of democracy in the West? If Lebanese democracy means accord, so where is the accord on Resolution 1559?

"I address U.S. President George W. Bush, Ms Condoleezza Rice and the American-Lebanese field leader David Satterfield: Your plans aiming at dividing the country are wrong. Lebanon *cannot be divided nor defeated. Lebanon will not change its name, or its history, or its identity. Lebanon will not throw its hearts to your soldiers' dogs to eat it.*

"Lebanon will remain the country of Arabism, the country of nationalism, the country of resistance. Lebanon is the nation itself.

"I am asking you and you can reply loudly in order to let your voices be heard by the commander of the U.S. forces in the region, John Abizaid: Are you afraid of the United States fleets? These fleets came here in the past and were defeated, and they will be defeated again if they return. I tell the Americans: Do not interfere in our domestic affairs. Let your Ambassador rest in his embassy in Awkar and leave us. We, as Lebanese, care for our country, our national unity and our civil peace. Be gone with your plans for upheaval."

Before quoting the remainder of the speech, I would like to say here that Sunni regimes all over should be ashamed of their cowardice and hypocrisy. When fellow Muslim brothers and sisters are being threatened, they turn their backs in silence, with some even colluding and conniving with the Zionists. If these regimes fail to change, the fire of Islamic Revolution would ensure their demise and their end would be bloody. The Zionists have declared this to be World War IV and the Final Battle. Everyone has to make a decision — either be in the front lines or face the ultimate justice for those who betray the heroic struggle against Zionism.

Nasrallah concludes with this warning:

"I address Israel, Sharon, Mofaz and Silvan Shalom: forget your hopes and quit dreaming of your ambitions in Lebanon. There is no place for you here. In 1982, you were at the zenith and our country was emerging from war. However, we resisted and fought for our liberation, and we defeated you. We, today, as Lebanese, with our unity, with our determination, with our soldiers, with our resistance, are stronger than we have ever been in the past.

"You, as Israelis are being defeated by our brothers, the Palestinians. What you couldn't get through war, you can never get through political strategies. Death to Israel!

"I thank you, the loyal, the devoted and the good. Long live the people, long live Lebanon, long live the Resistance and long live Syria."

Sunni regimes in the Middle East and their brand of political Islam are increasingly being perceived as having betrayed the *ummah* and have served their usefulness to the Zionist Anglo-American War Cabal and that is why they are being slowly squeezed out of the equation. But their substitutes are no better, notwithstanding their so called democratic credentials. Like the various puppet regimes installed in Vietnam, they will fail to command legitimacy and will be swept away into the dustbin of history. The worldwide resistance should not be afraid of the situation that is unfolding in the Middle East. They should welcome the opportunity. There is no better time to strike the mortal blow against Zionism than now. That is why the haste in calling for the implementation of UN Security Council Resolution 1559.

Read the speech by Nasrallah again, especially his address to President Jacque Chirac, President Bush and Ariel Sharon. Why the need for resolution 1559 when there is the Taif Agreement between Lebanon and Syria? And as pointed out by Nasrallah, it was Syria that helped the Lebanese people to secure peace and stability after the Zionist invasion of Lebanon. It was here in Lebanon that the fascist Sharon was defeated. Sharon had dreams to carve up Lebanon into little pieces, but this was thwarted by the heroic resistance of the Hezbullah and the Syrian armed forces. But Bush and Chirac want to divide Lebanon on sectarian lines, as they are doing so now in Iraq.

It is therefore crucial that we are acquainted with the provisions of the Taif Agreement, freely entered into by Lebanon and Syria and at the material time fully endorsed by the entire Arab world.

Some of the key provisions are as follows:

1) Lebanon is a sovereign, free and independent country and a final homeland for all its citizens.

2) It is Arab in belonging and identity. It is an active and founding member of the Arab League and is committed to the League's charter. It is an active and founding member of the United Nations Organization and is committed to its charter. Lebanon is a member of the Nonaligned Movement (NAM).

3) Lebanon is a democratic parliamentary republic founded   on

respect for public liberties, especially the freedom of expression and belief, on social justice, and on equality in rights and duties among all citizens, without discrimination or preference.

4) Lebanon's soil is united and it belongs to all Lebanese. Every Lebanese is entitled to live in and enjoy any part of the country under the supremacy of the law. The people may not be categorized on the basis of any affiliation whatsoever and there shall be no fragmentation, no partition, and no repatriation of Palestinians in Lebanon.

5) No authority violating the common co-existence charter shall be legitimate.

6) Abolishing political sectarianism is a fundamental national objective.

7) Taking all steps necessary to liberate all Lebanese territories from Israeli occupation.

8) Lebanon, with its Arab identity, is tied to all Arab countries by true fraternal relations. Between Lebanon and Syria there is special relationship that derives its strength from the roots of blood relationships, history, and joint fraternal interests. This is the concept on which the two countries coordination and cooperation is founded, and which will be embodied by the agreements between the two countries in all areas, in a manner that accomplishes the two fraternal countries' interests within the framework of the sovereignty and independence of each of them.

We cannot but be suspicious of the intentions of France, the U.S. and Israel, at this juncture, in their interference in the affairs of Lebanon under resolution 1559, supposedly to ensure the sovereignty of Lebanon, when it was Israel, supported by the U.S. that invaded the country, butchered its people and almost torn the country asunder. The current interference is nothing but the implementation of the Oded Yinon Plan and Netanyahu's Clean Break strategies to break up Arab states for Zionist conquest.

But what about the Iran's alleged nuclear bombs? My answer is: So what! It is strictly a non-issue from a military perspective. Any attempt by Iran to use nuclear weapons or to transfer such weapons to non-state actors would invite a massive retaliation from the U.S. So why is Israel so nervous? She boasts of having some 200 nuclear bombs and could easily obliterate Tehran. The nuclear scare and global terrorism is but an excuse for the Zionists to hijack the American military to invade all the Arab states to incapacitate their conventional forces. Israel knows only too well that when the Islamic Revolution sweeps across the entire Middle East, she won't have a chance to holding on even to Tel Aviv. Like President Nyuyen Van Thieu, Sharon and his remnants would have to scramble on board helicopters to take them out to the carriers parked in the Mediterranean Sea to ferry them to the United States. Such a scenario is driving Sharon, Netanyahu, Shimon Peres, Paul Wolfowitz and the Anti-Defamation League nuts.

There is also another angle. If any Arab state were to acquire nuclear weapons, the world would demand that the Middle East be turned into a nuclear-free zone. That means Israel has to give up its weapons and her dream of regional hegemony stretching from Mauritania to Afghanistan.

America will then be caught in a dilemma. The United States and the American people have to make a Hobbesian choice — America or Israel. Israel having hijacked the American war machine to do its bidding will also be confronted with a Hobbesian choice — give up her nuclear weapons and the U.S. war machine or loose the support of the American people. In any event, Zionist Israel would have to forgo her hegemonic dream of Eretz Yisrael from Mauritania to Afghanistan. That is why I am saying that the lynchpin to world peace or nuclear war is Zionist Israel. We must focus on Israel. That is why it is important that an Arab state should acquire nuclear weapons, for without which neither the U.S. nor Zionist Israel would have to contend with a Hobbesian choice. Iran's acquisition of nuclear weapons is not nuclear proliferation, but rather the guarantee of a nuclear-free Middle East and genuine peace for the entire region.

We are fighting against Fascism — Zionist Fascism — and a nuclear-armed fascist regime!

Let us have no illusions as to the fascist nature of the Bush-Sharon regimes. So when Senator Robert Byrd equates Bush with Hitler, we should all wake up to this reality. Senator Byrd warned the American people that Bush's moves to destroy time-honored senate rules parallel Hitler's ramming fascist legislation through the Reichstag.

"Hitler never abandoned the cloak of legality," said Byrd. *"He recognized the enormous psychological value of having the law on his side. Instead, he turned the law inside out and made illegality legal.*[7]*"* Hiding behind resolution 1559, is the Zionist Anglo-American strategy to legalize the break-up of Lebanon: Phase II of Zionist world conquest.

Hitler's central slogan: *"Ein Volk, Ein Reich, Ein Fuhrer"*—"One People, One Government, One Dictator" — reflects accurately the Zionist Anglo-American War Cabal's plans for America and their agenda for world conquest.

Hitler was drunk with power and thought that he could wage a war on two fronts. He was wrong and paid the price. Sharon has similar dreams and will pay the same price. **Sharon and Hitler are but the different sides of the same fascist coin!**

Matthias
18th March, 2005
Kuala Lumpur

ENDNOTES:

1. Source: www.WorldTribune.com
2. Matt Kelley, the Associated Press, "U.S. Money has Helped Opposition in Ukraine" December 11, 2004
3. Source: Against the Current: www.solidarity-us.org
4. Mark Almond, "The Price of People Power", December 7, 2004, The Guardian.
5. See Jonathan Mowat, "Coup d'Etat in Disguise: Washington's New World Order 'Democratization' Template", February 9, 2005
6. Source: www.cggl.org/scripts/document.asp?id=4625
7. Source: Harvey Wasserman, "Senator Byrd is Correct to Equate Bush with Hitler", March 7, 2005, Columbus Free Press. See also www.commondreams.org

Appendix

Palestine Liberation Organization
Palestinian National Authority
Negotiations Affairs Department
www.nad-plo.org

منظمة التحرير الفلسطينية
السلطة الوطنية الفلسطينية
دائرة شؤون المفاوضات

FCAMP DAVID PEACE PROPOSALS OF JULY, 2000

FREQUENTLY ASKED QUESTIONS

For a Map of the Camp David Proposal: www.nad-plo.org/maps/map13.html

1. Why did the Palestinians reject the Camp David Peace Proposal?

    For a true and lasting peace between the Israeli and Palestinian peoples, there must be two viable and independent states living as equal neighbors. Israel's Camp David proposal, which was never set forth in writing, denied the Palestinian state viability and independence by dividing Palestinian territory into four separate cantons entirely surrounded, and therefore controlled, by Israel. The Camp David proposal also denied Palestinians control over their own borders, airspace and water resources while legitimizing and expanding illegal Israeli colonies in Palestinian territory. Israel's Camp David proposal presented a 'repackaging' of military occupation, not an end to military occupation.

2. Didn't Israel's proposal give the Palestinians almost all of the territories occupied by Israel in 1967?

    No. Israel sought to annex almost 9% of the Occupied Palestinian Territories and in exchange offered from Israel's own territory only the equivalent of 1% of the Occupied Palestinian Territories. In addition, Israel sought control over an additional 10% of the Occupied Palestinian Territories in the form of a "long-term lease". However, the issue is not one of percentages — the issue is one of viability and independence. In a prison for example, 95% of the prison compound is ostensibly for the prisoners — cells, cafeterias, gym and medical facilities but the remaining 5% is all that is needed for the prison guards to maintain control over the prisoner population. Similarly, the Camp David proposal, while admittedly making Palestinian prison cells larger, failed to end Israeli control over the Palestinian population.

3. Did the Palestinians accept the idea of a land swap?

    The Palestinians were (and are) prepared to consider any idea that is consistent with a fair peace based on international law and equality of the Israeli and Palestinian peoples. The Palestinians did consider the idea of a land swap but proposed that such land swap must be based on a one-to-one ratio, with land of equal value and in areas adjacent to the border with Palestine and in the same vicinity as the lands to be annexed by Israel. However, Israel's Camp David proposal of a nine-to-one land swap (in Israel's favor) was viewed as so unfair as to seriously undermine belief in Israel's commitment to a fair territorial compromise.

4. How did Israel's proposal envision the territory of a Palestinian state?

    Israel's proposal divided Palestine into four separate cantons surrounded by Israel: the Northern West Bank, the Central West Bank, the Southern West Bank and Gaza. Going from any one area to another would require crossing Israeli sovereign territory and consequently subject movement of Palestinians within their own country to Israeli control. Not only would such restrictions apply to the movement of people, but also to the movement of goods, in effect subjecting the Palestinian economy to Israeli control. Lastly, the Camp David proposal would have left Israel in control over all Palestinian borders thereby allowing Israel to control not only internal movement of people and goods but international movement as well. Such a Palestinian state would have had less sovereignty and viability than the Bantustans created by the South African apartheid government.

5. How did Israel's proposal address Palestinian East Jerusalem?

    The Camp David Proposal required Palestinians to give up any claim to the occupied portion of Jerusalem. The proposal would have forced recognition of Israel's annexation of all of Arab East Jerusalem. Talks after Camp David suggested that Israel was prepared to allow Palestinians sovereignty over isolated Palestinian neighborhoods in the heart of East Jerusalem, however such neighborhoods would remain surrounded by illegal Israeli colonies and separated not only from each other but also from the rest of the Palestinian state. In effect, such a proposal would create Palestinian ghettos in the heart of Jerusalem.

6. Why didn't the Palestinians ever present a comprehensive permanent settlement proposal of their own in response to Barak's proposals?

    The comprehensive settlement to the conflict is embodied in United Nations Resolutions 242 and 338, which were accepted by both sides at the Madrid Summit in 1991 and later in the Oslo Accords of 1993. The purpose of the negotiations is to implement these UN resolutions (which call for an Israeli withdrawal from land occupied by force by Israel in 1967) and reach agreement on final status issues. On a number of occasions since Camp David especially at the Taba talks the Palestinian negotiating team presented its concept for the resolution of the key permanent status issues. It is important to keep in mind, however, that Israel and the Palestinians are differently situated. Israel seeks broad concessions from the Palestinians: it wants to annex Palestinian territory, including East Jerusalem; obtain rights to Palestinian water resources in the West Bank; maintain military locations on Palestinian soil; and deny the Palestinian refugees' their right of return. Israel has not offered a single concession involving its own territory and rights. The Palestinians, on the other hand, seek to establish a viable, sovereign State on their own territory, to provide for the withdrawal of Israeli military forces and colonies (which are universally recognized as illegal), and to secure the right of Palestinian refugees to return to the homes they were forced to flee in 1948. Although Palestinian negotiators have been willing to accommodate legitimate Israeli needs within that context, particularly with respect to security and refugees, it is up to Israel to define these needs and to suggest the narrowest possible means of addressing them.

7. Why did the peace process fall apart just as it was making real progress toward a permanent agreement?

Palestinians entered the peace process on the understanding that (1) it would deliver concrete improvements to their lives during the interim period, (2) that the interim period would be relatively short in duration i.e., five years, and (3) that a permanent agreement would implement United Nations Resolutions 242 and 338. But the peace process delivered none of these things. Instead, Palestinians suffered more burdensome restrictions movement and a serious decline in their economic situation.. Israeli colonies expanded at an unprecedented pace and the West Bank and Gaza Strip became more fragmented with the construction of settler "bypass" roads and the proliferation of Israeli military checkpoints. Deadlines were repeatedly missed in the implementation of agreements. In sum, Palestinians simply did not experience any "progress" in terms of their daily lives.

However, what decisively undermined Palestinian support for the peace process was the way Israel presented its proposal. Prior to entering into the first negotiations on permanent status issues, Prime Minister Barak publicly and repeatedly threatened Palestinians that his "offer" would be Israel's best and final offer and if not accepted, Israel would seriously consider "unilateral separation" (a euphemism for imposing a settlement rather than negotiating one). Palestinians felt that they had been betrayed by Israel who had committed itself at the beginning of the Oslo process to ending its occupation of Palestinian lands in accordance with UN Resolutions 242 and 338.

8. Doesn't the violence which erupted following Camp David prove that Palestinians do not really want to live in peace with Israel?

Palestinians recognized Israel's right to exist in 1988 and reiterated this recognition on several occasions including Madrid in 1991 and the Oslo Accords in September, 1993. Nevertheless, Israel has yet to explicitly and formally recognize Palestine's right to exist. The Palestinian people waited patiently since the Madrid Conference in 1991 for their freedom and independence despite Israel's incessant policy of creating facts on the ground by building colonies in occupied territory (Israeli housing units in Occupied Palestinian Territory not including East Jerusalem increased by 52% since the signing of the Oslo Accords and the settler population, including those in East Jerusalem, more than doubled). The Palestinians do indeed wish to live at peace with Israel but peace with Israel must be a fair peace not an unfair peace imposed by a stronger party over a weaker party.

9. Doesn't the failure of Camp David prove that the Palestinians are just not prepared to compromise?

The Palestinians have indeed compromised. In the Oslo Accords, the Palestinians recognized Israeli sovereignty over 78% of historic Palestine (23% more than Israel was granted pursuant to the 1947 UN partition plan) on the assumption that the Palestinians would be able to exercise sovereignty over the remaining 22%. The overwhelming majority of Palestinians accepted this compromise but this extremely generous compromise was ignored at Camp David and the Palestinians were asked to "compromise the compromise" and make further concessions in favor of Israel. Though the Palestinians can continue to make compromises, no people can be expected to compromise fundamental rights or the viability of their state.

10. Have the Palestinians abandoned the two-state solution and do they now insist on all of historic Palestine?

The current situation has undoubtedly hardened positions on both sides, with extremists in both Israel and the Occupied Palestinian Territories claiming all of historic Palestine. Nevertheless, there is no evidence that the PA or the majority of Palestinians have abandoned the two-state solution. The two-state solution however is most seriously threatened by the ongoing construction of Israeli colonies and bypass roads aimed at incorporating the Occupied Palestinian Territories into Israel. Without a halt to such construction, a two-state solution may simply be impossible to implement already prompting a number of Palestinian academics and intellectuals to argue that Israel will never allow the Palestinians to have a viable state and Palestinians should instead focus their efforts on obtaining equal rights as Israeli citizens.

11. Isn't it unreasonable for the Palestinians to demand the unlimited right of return to Israel of all Palestinian refugees?

The refugees were never seriously discussed at Camp David because Prime Minister Barak declared that Israel bore no responsibility for the refugee problem or its solution. Obviously, there can be no comprehensive solution to the Palestinian-Israeli conflict without resolving one of its key components: the plight of the Palestinian refugees. There is a clearly recognized right under international law that noncombatants who flee during a conflict have the right to return after the conflict is over. But an Israeli recognition of the Palestinian right of return does not mean that all refugees will exercise that right. What is needed in addition to such recognition is the concept of choice. Many refugees may opt for (i) resettlement in third countries, (ii) resettlement in a newly independent Palestine (though they originate from that part of Palestine which became Israel) or (iii) normalization of their legal status in the host country where they currently reside. In addition, the right of return may be implemented in phases so as to address Israel's demographic concerns.

Index

FUTURE
FASTFORWARD

The Zionist Anglo-American Empire Meltdown

Is the alliance between the United States, the British Empire, and Israel a paper tiger or a mighty empire?

Is global "Empire Capitalism" about to come crashing down?

Will there be a worldwide "people's war" against the super-capitalists and their Zionist allies?

Is nuclear war inevitable?

These are just some of the provocative questions addressed in *Future Fastforward*, a forthright, no-holds-barred new book by a prominent Asian political figure and globe-trotting diplomat.

In *Future Fastforward*, author Matthias Chang, former top-level political secretary for Malaysia's outspoken long-time Prime Minister, Dr. Mahathir Mohamad, takes a stark look at the realities of global power politics and the ultimate and inevitable consequences for the not-so-secret forces that are behind the push for a New World Order.

Now being published for the first time in the United States. this book is a remarkable "insider's" view of world power politics from a point of view that few Americans have ever had the opportunity of hearing.

The big question is how the American forces supporting Israeli hard-liner Benjamin "Bibi" Netanyahu got their hands on an internal White House video—made in November 1996—showing President Bill Clinton hugging his young friend, Monica Lewinsky, in a White House receiving line. A still image of Clinton, clearly taken from the video, was utilized in an advertising smear accusing Clinton of having "turned his back on Israel." The advertisements appeared in American Jewish newspapers in mid-January 1998, six days before the Lewinsky scandal was unveiled in the media. The advertisements were sponsored by a group allied with William Kristol, the neo-conservative intriguer who was a leading publicist for the Netanyahu forces in Israel. Kristol just happened to be the first to reveal (before the scandal "officially" broke) that there was an impending scandal involving the president and a White House intern.

Softcover, 400 pages, $25. No S&H.

The High Priests of War

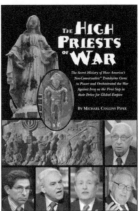

The Secret History of America's Neo-Cons

THE HIGH PRIESTS OF WAR: The Secret History of How America's Neo-Conservative Trotskyites Came to Power and How They Orhestrated the War Against Iraq as the First Step in Their Drive for Global Power—The secret history of how America's "neo-conservative" Trotskyites came to power and orchestrated the war against Iraq as the first step in their drive for Global Empire, the so-called New World Order. This is the only full-length book on the "neo-cons" that tells the entire story—no holds-barred. The book is now being circulated internationally and is being translated into a variety of languages, acclaimed as the one book that explains the "who, what, when, where, why and how" of the tragic involvement of the United States in the Iraq war. This fast-reading, carefully-documented 144-page volume has helped spread the word about the REAL reason for the Iraq war and how it is all part of a grand design that is being suppressed by the Controlled Media.

Softcover, 144 pages, $19.95. No S&H.

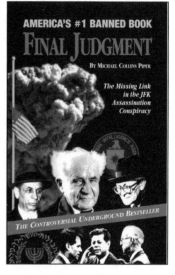

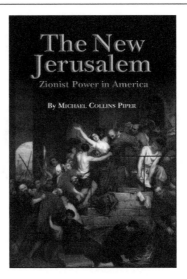

Dirty Secrets

Crime, Conspiracy & Cover-Up During the 20th Century

A Compendium of the Writings of Michael Collins Piper, Interviews with the Author & Reviews of His Works

Here's an amazing collection of the writings (many never before seen in print), transcripts of UNCENSORED interviews with Michael Collins Piper, reviews of his works and much more—all compiled in one "must-read" volume. Read where Piper's investigations have led him on such diverse and explosive topics as the Martin Luther King assassination, the JFK assassination, the Oklahoma City bombing, the attack on the *USS Liberty*, the suppression of freedom of speech in America today, the power of the Zionist lobby and much, much more. Compiled by Wing TV's Victor Thorn and Lisa Guliani, *Dirty Secrets* is possibly the most important compendium of thought produced in the last decade—the thoughts of one of America's hardest-hitting journalists and lecturers. Softcover, 256 pages, $22. No charge for S&H.

Once copy is $22. No S&H.

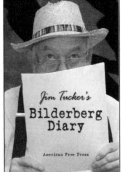

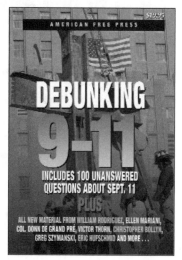